Technical and Risk Management Reference Series

# Security, Audit and Control Features

# SAP® ERP

## 3rd Edition

**ISACA®**

Serving IT Governance Professionals

## ISACA®

With more than 86,000 constituents in more than 160 countries, ISACA (*www.isaca.org*) is a leading global provider of knowledge, certifications, community, advocacy and education on information systems assurance and security, enterprise governance of IT, and IT-related risk and compliance. Founded in 1969, ISACA sponsors international conferences, publishes the *ISACA® Journal*, and develops international information systems auditing and control standards. It also administers the globally respected Certified Information Systems Auditor™ (CISA®), Certified Information Security Manager® (CISM®) and Certified in the Governance of Enterprise IT® (CGEIT®) designations.

ISACA developed and continually updates the CobiT®, Val IT™ and Risk IT frameworks, which help IT professionals and enterprise leaders fulfill their IT governance responsibilities and deliver value to the business.

## Disclaimer

ISACA has designed and created *Security, Audit and Control Features SAP® ERP, 3rd Edition* (*Technical and Risk Management Reference Series*) (the "Work"), primarily as an educational resource for control professionals. ISACA makes no claim that use of any of the Work will assure a successful outcome. The Work should not be considered inclusive of any proper information, procedures and tests or exclusive of other information, procedures and tests that are reasonably directed to obtaining the same results. In determining the propriety of any specific information, procedure or test, control professionals should apply their own professional judgment to the specific control circumstances presented by the particular systems or information technology environment.

While all care has been taken in researching and documenting the techniques described in this text, persons employing these techniques must use their own knowledge and judgment. ISACA and Deloitte, its partners and employees, shall not be liable for any losses and/or damages (whether direct or indirect), costs, expenses or claims whatsoever arising out of the use of the techniques described or reliance on the information in this reference guide.

SAP, SAP R/3, mySAP, SAP R/3 Enterprise, SAP Strategic Enterprise Management (SAP SEM), SAP NetWeaver, ABAP, mySAP Business Suite, mySAP Customer Relationship Management, mySAP Supply Chain Management, mySAP Product Lifecycle Management, mySAP Supplier Relationship Management and other SAP product/services referenced herein are the trademarks or registered trademarks of SAP AG in Germany and in several other countries. The publisher gratefully acknowledges SAP's kind permission to use these trademarks and reproduce selected diagrams and screen shots in this publication. SAP AG is not the publisher of this book and is not responsible for it under any aspect of press law.

## ISACA

3701 Algonquin Road, Suite 1010
Rolling Meadows, IL 60008 USA
Phone: +1.847.253.1545
Fax: +1.847.253.1443
E-mail: *info@isaca.org*
Web site: *www.isaca.org*

ISBN 978-1-60420-115-4
*Security, Audit and Control Features SAP® ERP, 3rd Edition* (*Technical and Risk Management Reference Series*)

Printed in the United States of America

CGEIT is a trademark/servicemark of ISACA. The mark has been applied for or registered in countries throughout the world.

# Acknowledgments

## ISACA wishes to recognize:

**Researcher**
Mark Sercombe, CISA, CA, CIA, Sponsoring Partner, Deloitte, Australia
Matthew Saines, CISA, CISSP, Deloitte, Australia
Maria Woodyatt, CISA, Deloitte, Australia
Bernadette Louat, CISA, Deloitte, Australia
Najeeba Hossain, Deloitte, Australia
Mark Hickabottom, Ph.D, CISA, Deloitte, UK
Neal J. Velayo, CISA, Deloitte, USA
Iain Muir, CISA, Deloitte, Australia

**Project Leaders**
Pippa G. Andrews, CISA, ACA, CIA, KPMG, Australia
Anthony P. Noble, CISA, CCP, Viacom Inc., USA

**Expert Reviewers**
Akin Akinbosoye, CISA, CISM, CGEIT, PMI-RMP, Healthcare Corporation of America (HCA), USA
Robin Basham, CISA, CGEIT, SOAProjects Inc., USA
Steve Biskie, CISA, CPA, CITP, ConnectINT Solutions, USA; ACL Services, Ltd., Canada
Michael Brinkloev, KPMG, Denmark
Adrienne C. Chung, CISA, CISM, CA, Chungs' Computer Assistance LLP, Canada
Chang Lu Miao, CISA, ACIB, CPA, MCSE, SAP T/C, Auditor-General's Office, Singapore
Mayank Garg, CISA, Atmel Corportation, USA
David T. Green, Ph.D., Governors State University, USA
Guhapriya Iyer, CISA, ACA, Grad CWA, Cerebrus Consulting, India
Babu Jayendran, CISA, FCA, Babu Jayendran Consulting, India
Emma Johari, CISA, KPMG, Australia
Pam Kammermeier, CISA, Altran Control Solutions, USA
Rajni Lalsinghani, CISA, CISM, TechnoSols Consulting Services, Australia
K. K. Mookhey, CISA, CISM, CISSP, Network Intelligence India (NII), India
Stane Moškon, CISA, CISM, VRIS d.o.o., Slovenia
Moonga Mumba, CISA, Zambia Revenue Authority, Zambia
Babu Shekhar Shetty, CISA, CISSP, Timken Pvt. Ltd., India
Surapong Surabotsopon, CISA, CISM, CGEIT, ITIL, Goodyear (Thailand) PCL, Thailand
William G. Teeter, CISA, CGEIT, PMP, USA
Jinu Varghese, CISA, OCA, PricewaterhouseCoopers LLP, Canada
Chakri Wicharn, CISA, CISM, Thailand
David Yeung, CISA, CIA, CFE, KPMG, China

**ISACA Board of Directors 2008-2009**
Lynn Lawton, CISA, FBCS CITP, FCA, FIIA, KPMG LLP, UK, International President
George Ataya, CISA, CISM, CGEIT, CISSP, ICT Control SA, Belgium, Vice President
Howard Nicholson, CISA, CGEIT, City of Salisbury, Australia, Vice President
Jose Angel Pena Ibarra, CGEIT, Consultoria en Comunicaciones e Info. SA & CV, Mexico,
    Vice President
Robert E. Stroud, CGEIT, CA Inc., USA, Vice President
Kenneth L. Vander Wal, CISA, CPA, Ernst & Young LLP (retired), USA, Vice President
Frank Yam, CISA, CCP, CFE, CFSA, CIA, FFA, FHKCS, FHKIoD, Focus Strategic Group Inc.,
    Hong Kong, Vice President
Marios Damianides, CISA, CISM, CA, CPA, Ernst & Young, USA, Past International President
Everett C. Johnson Jr., CPA, Deloitte & Touche LLP (retired), USA, Past International President
Gregory T. Grocholski, CISA, The Dow Chemical Company, USA, Director
Tony Hayes, CGEIT, Queensland Government, Australia, Director
Jo Stewart-Rattray, CISA, CISM, CGEIT, AFCHSE, CHE, FACS, FCPA, FIIA, CSEPS,
    RSM Bird Cameron, Australia, Director

# Acknowledgments *(cont.)*

**Assurance Committee 2008-2009**
Gregory T. Grocholski, CISA, The Dow Chemical Company, USA, Chair
Pippa G. Andrews, CISA, ACA, CIA, KPMG, Australia
Richard Brisebois, CISA, CGA, Office of the Auditor General of Canada, Canada
Sergio Fleginsky, CISA, ICI, Uruguay
Robert Johnson, CISA, CISM, CGEIT, CISSP, Executive Consultant, USA
Anthony P. Noble, CISA, CCP, Viacom Inc., USA
Robert G. Parker, CISA, CA, CMC, FCA, Deloittte & Touche LLP (retired), Canada
Erik Pols, CISA, CISM, Shell International—ITCI, Netherlands
Vatsaraman Venkatakrishnan, CISA, CISM, CGEIT, ACA, Emirates Airlines, UAE

# Table of Contents

1.  FOREWORD................................................................................................ 1

2.  INTRODUCTION TO ENTERPRISE RESOURCE PLANNING
    SYSTEMS AND SAP ERP ....................................................................... 2
    Major SAP Modules and Functionality...................................................... 5
    Navigating the SAP ERP System ............................................................. 11
    Fundamental Changes in Business Controls ............................................. 36

3.  STRATEGIC RISK MANAGEMENT IN AN SAP ENVIRONMENT ..... 38
    Strategic Business Risks and Key Management Controls ....................... 38
    Application Security and Technical Infrastructure................................... 44
    The Importance of Establishing a Control Framework............................ 48
    Summary .................................................................................................... 50

4.  ERP AUDIT APPROACH......................................................................... 51
    Audit Impacts Arising From the Implementation of ERP ...................... 51
    Recommended SAP ERP Audit Framework............................................. 56
    Case Study................................................................................................. 68
    Numbering Sequence for Risks, Controls and Testing Techniques ........ 79
    Summary .................................................................................................... 81

5.  SAP ERP REVENUE BUSINESS CYCLE ............................................. 82
    Master Data Maintenance ......................................................................... 82
    Sales Order Processing.............................................................................. 84
    Shipping, Invoicing, Returns and Adjustments........................................ 87
    Collecting and Processing Cash Receipts................................................. 91
    Summary .................................................................................................... 92

6.  AUDITING THE SAP ERP REVENUE BUSINESS CYCLE ................. 93
    Master Data Maintenance ......................................................................... 93
    Sales Order Processing.............................................................................. 98
    Shipping, Invoicing, Returns and Adjustments...................................... 101
    Collecting and Processing Cash Receipts............................................... 107
    Revenue Cycle Controls and Financial Statement Assertions............... 108
    Summary .................................................................................................. 110

7.  SAP ERP EXPENDITURE BUSINESS CYCLE ................................... 111
    Master Data Maintenance ....................................................................... 111
    Purchasing ............................................................................................... 112
    Invoice Processing .................................................................................. 117
    Processing Disbursements ...................................................................... 121
    Summary .................................................................................................. 122

8.  AUDITING THE SAP ERP EXPENDITURE BUSINESS CYCLE......... 123
    Master Data Maintenance ....................................................................... 123
    Purchasing ............................................................................................... 126
    Invoice Processing .................................................................................. 131
    Processing Disbursements ...................................................................... 134
    Expenditure Cycle Controls and Financial Statement Assertions ........ 136
    Summary .................................................................................................. 137

9. **SAP ERP INVENTORY BUSINESS CYCLE** .......................................... 138
   Master Data Maintenance ............................................................ 138
   Raw Materials Management .......................................................... 139
   Producing and Costing Inventory ................................................ 140
   Handling and Shipping Finished Goods......................................... 141
   Summary ................................................................................... 142

10. **AUDITING THE SAP ERP INVENTORY BUSINESS CYCLE** ............. 143
    Master Data Maintenance ............................................................ 143
    Raw Materials Management .......................................................... 146
    Producing and Costing Inventory ................................................ 149
    Handling and Shipping Finished Goods......................................... 150
    Inventory Cycle Controls and Financial Statement Assertions ....... 152
    Summary ................................................................................... 153

11. **SAP ERP BASIS APPLICATION INFRASTRUCTURE**....................... 154
    SAP ERP Architecture................................................................. 154
    SAP ERP Basis Application Infrastructure .................................... 156
    The Implementation Guide and Organization Management Model ............... 157
    The Profile Generator and Security Administration....................... 166
    Audit Implications...................................................................... 169
    Summary ................................................................................... 170

12. **AUDITING THE SAP ERP BASIS APPLICATION
    INFRASTRUCTURE**........................................................................ 171
    Implementation Guide................................................................ 172
    Organizational Management Model ............................................. 174
    Critical Number Ranges.............................................................. 175
    Modifying Critical Tables............................................................ 177
    Custom Transaction Codes ......................................................... 178
    ABAP/4 Workbench and Transport Management System ............................ 179
    Customizing and Executing ABAP/4 Programs ............................. 181
    ABAP/4 Development in Production ............................................ 182
    Data Dictionary Changes ............................................................ 183
    Queries...................................................................................... 184
    Company Code Settings............................................................... 185
    CCMS Configuration .................................................................. 186
    Batch Processing ....................................................................... 188
    Application Server Parameters ................................................... 190
    Locking Transaction Codes ......................................................... 192
    Restricted Passwords.................................................................. 193
    SAP Router................................................................................. 194
    External or Operating System Commands .................................... 195
    SAP Service Marketplace ............................................................ 196
    RFC and CPI-C Communications ................................................. 197
    Profile Generator and Security Administration Risk ..................... 198
    Authorization Documentation..................................................... 201
    Superuser SAP* ......................................................................... 202
    Default Users.............................................................................. 203
    SAP_ALL and SAP_NEW ............................................................ 204
    Maintenance of Powerful User Groups ........................................ 205
    Central User Administration ....................................................... 206
    Table Logging ............................................................................ 207

Data Dictionary Reports.................................................................. 208
Log and Trace Files........................................................................ 209
Outline of Case Study on SAP Access Security............................. 210
Summary ......................................................................................... 213

**13. GOVERNANCE, RISK AND COMPLIANCE IN AN SAP ERP
ENVIRONMENT**.............................................................................. 214
SAP BusinessObjects GRC ............................................................ 216
Risk Analysis and Remediation (RAR)........................................... 217
Superuser Privilege Management (SPM)......................................... 221
Compliant User Provisioning (CUP)............................................... 224
Enterprise Role Management (ERM)............................................... 225
SAP BusinessObjects Process Control ........................................... 225
Summary ......................................................................................... 233

**14. TRENDS AND DISCUSSIONS AROUND SAP ERP
AND ERP AUDIT**........................................................................... 234
SAP Product and Technology Changes............................................ 234
The Changing Compliance Landscape............................................. 237
Using SAP Tools to Support Corporate Governance....................... 240
Integrated ERP Audit ...................................................................... 242
Conclusion....................................................................................... 246

**APPENDIX A—FREQUENTLY ASKED QUESTIONS**...................................... 247

**APPENDIX B—RECOMMENDED READING** ...................................... 254

**APPENDIX C—SUGGESTED SAP ERP TABLES TO LOG
AND REVIEW**............................................................................................... 256

**APPENDIX D—SAP ERP REVENUE, EXPENDITURE,
INVENTORY, BASIS AUDIT/ASSURANCE PROGRAMS** ............................ 261

**APPENDIX E—SAP ERP AUDIT ICQS** ............................................................ 424

**APPENDIX F—CobiT CONTROL OBJECTIVES** ............................................ 451

**APPENDIX G—TRANSACTIONS RECOMMENDED
TO BE LOCKED** .............................................................................................. 452

**INDEX** ............................................................................................................... 456

**PROFESSIONAL GUIDANCE PUBLICATIONS**............................................. 458

# 1. Foreword

Enterprise resource planning (ERP) systems, such as SAP ERP, Oracle® E-Business Suite and PeopleSoft® Enterprise, are now pervasive in large enterprises worldwide. An ERP system is a packaged business software system that allows an enterprise to:
• Automate and integrate the majority of its business processes
• Share common data and practices across the entire enterprise
• Produce and access information in a real-time environment

ERP systems continue to transform enterprise business processes by automating manual tasks, such as authorizations, and empowering users to initiate transactions and monitor performance online. As a result, the integrity framework supporting these business processes has been transformed. The level of automated controls and the importance of logical access security and configuration controls have increased. The web enablement of ERP systems and the integration of back-end ERP systems with front-end web-enabled systems continue to transform business process and technical infrastructure risk/control frameworks.

SAP is one of the developers of enterprise applications. Its primary ERP product is SAP ERP Central Component (known as ECC but previously named SAP R/3). This third edition of the technical reference guide on the audit of SAP ERP is one in a series of three technical reference guides providing information relating to the world's three major ERP systems. The other guides in the series focus on Oracle E-Business Suite and PeopleSoft.

Some sections of the guides covering the introduction to ERP and strategic risk management in an ERP environment and directions in ERP audit are common to all three guides. The remaining sections covering ERP product-specific characteristics and auditing techniques are unique to each of the respective technical reference guides.

The purpose of the third edition of this research is to update the current best practices and identify future trends in ERP risk and control. The objective is to enable audit, assurance, risk and security professionals (IT and non-IT) to evaluate risks and controls in existing ERP implementations and to facilitate the design and building of better practice controls into system upgrades and enhancements. The publication is designed to be a practical how-to guide based on SAP ECC versions 5.0 and 6.0. However, most of the features and testing techniques described are also applicable to the earlier versions of SAP R/3, namely 4.6c and 4.7, which are also described in the first and second editions of this guide.

The popularity of the earlier editions of this guide confirmed the need for a series of audit guides for these products. Using a definitive approach, the authors sought to provide detail on testing techniques within the ERP products and their execution, rather than generic descriptions of the audit tests to be performed.

# 2. Introduction to Enterprise Resource Planning Systems and SAP ERP

Before ERP systems were developed, an enterprise's systems typically were set up around functions or departments (e.g., sales, purchasing, inventory, finance), as shown in **figure 2.1**, and not around the business processes (e.g., purchase-to-pay, order-to-cash). Functions evolved independently from each other. Each function may have had an individual application system or a number of systems to support it, with or without interfaces among the systems. This approach resulted in time delays, additional cost, the need for reconciliation, and data redundancy. Frequently, business controls had a significant manual component. Before the widespread use of ERPs, it was common for purchase orders (POs), for example, to be approved when generated. When the invoice arrived, the PO was either printed out again or retrieved from filing and then stapled to the invoice. The invoice was then approved for payment. The documents may have been scrutinized once again and approved during the check payment process.

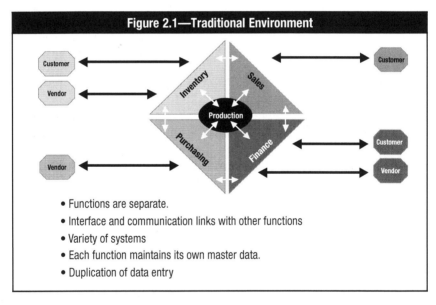

**Figure 2.1—Traditional Environment**

- Functions are separate.
- Interface and communication links with other functions
- Variety of systems
- Each function maintains its own master data.
- Duplication of data entry

Non-ERP systems also suffer from a design problem. Typically, they are designed around disparate and independent modules that transmit transaction data among themselves by means of interfaces, where the information is normally summarized (e.g., totals or balances only). In such cases, further details of individual transactions often are difficult to ascertain, unlike the ability to drill down provided by ERP systems.

ERP systems have a business process focus. They grew out of the need to integrate separate sales operations planning (SOP) systems, materials resource planning

(MRP) systems (used to integrate material requirements with production, demand and capacity) and financial accounting systems in manufacturing organizations. The integration of these functional capabilities into an online and real-time application system designed to support end-to-end business processes enables enterprises to plan and optimize their resources across the enterprise. Their relational database tables are designed around a complete set of the core functions for an enterprise rather than disparate modules that merely pass transaction data from one module to another. In particular, with the SAP ERP software the Financial Accounting and Controlling modules are tightly integrated into the logistical chain that begins with purchasing and ends in sales and distribution. Every business transaction is recorded in the Financial Accounting and Controlling (or Management Reporting) modules automatically, if configured correctly. For example, consider the purchase of inventory in the SAP ERP software:

- A purchase requisition in the Procurements and Logistics Execution (MM) module creates a commitment in the Financial and Management Accounting, Controlling (CO) module, as shown in **figure 2.2**. This purchase requisition also can be evaluated in the Controlling component.
- The placement of the purchase order (MM module) will then confirm the commitment in CO and in the Treasury Applications (CM) module simultaneously.
- Entering the receipt of the goods ordered in MM will generate an accounting document in Financial and Management Accounting (FI), General Ledger (GL) and CO. The receipt will also update the material masters (stock records) in MM.
- Receipt of the invoice will generate an accounting document in FI accounts payable and also updates CO and CM.

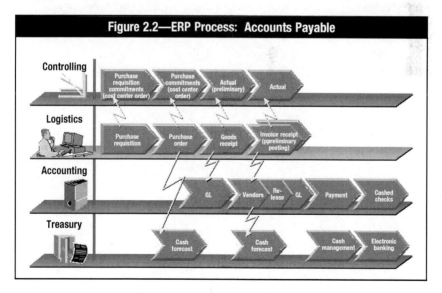

Figure 2.2—ERP Process:  Accounts Payable

An ERP environment operates in line with the business, online and in real time. Management has access to online and up-to-date information on how the business is performing. Common and consistent information is shared among application modules and among users from different departments simultaneously. It has been observed that following implementation of an ERP, enterprises typically report completion of period or year-end closes in one or two days, as opposed to two to three weeks under their legacy system environment. Another key change brought about by the implementation of ERP systems is that the systems are owned and driven by business process owners/end users, with the technical support of information technology, rather than being owned and driven by the IT function alone.

Enterprises implementing ERP systems can achieve significant benefits such as:
• Reductions in inventory
• Redeployment of personnel into more value-producing activities
• Productivity improvements
• Order management cycle improvements
• Financial close/cycle reduction
• IT cost reduction
• Procurement cost reductions
• Cash management improvement
• Transportation/logistics cost reductions
• Hardware and software maintenance reductions
• On-time delivery improvements

The intangible benefits of an ERP implementation—while difficult to quantify—can deliver significant business value through improved enterprise capabilities, including:
• Information/visibility (e.g., drill-down capability, consistent and reliable information across business areas)
• New/improved processes
• Improved customer responsiveness
• Integration and standardization
• Flexibility
• Globalization

Since launching its first product offering almost 30 years ago, SAP has grown globally. It has approximately 12 million users and 96,400 installations in more than 120 countries and is the third-largest independent software company in the world. The company name, SAP, is a German acronym that loosely translates in English to Systems, Applications and Products in data processing.

Before SAP ERP, SAP had two main products: the mainframe system SAP® R/2® and the client/server-based system SAP R/3. Both R/2 and R/3 are targeted to business application solutions and feature complexity, business and organizational experience, and integration. The R/2 and R/3 terminology is sometimes taken to mean release 2 and release 3, respectively; however, this is not the case. The R in R/2 and R/3 stands for "real time." Release levels are annotated separately to the R/2 or R/3 descriptors. For example, in SAP R/3 4.6B, the 4 is the major release number, the 6 is the minor release number following a major release, and the B is the version within a release.

R/3 was introduced in 1992 with a three-tier architecture paradigm. In recent years, SAP has introduced Service Oriented Architecture (SOA) as part of SAP ERP. This combines ERP with an open technology platform that can integrate SAP and non-SAP systems on the SAP NetWeaver® platform. Although SAP NetWeaver is not covered extensively in this book, it may be in future ISACA publications. The current core ERP solution offered by SAP is called SAP Enterprise Central Component (ECC 6.0), which is referred to in this book as SAP ERP, and will be the key focus of this book. **Figure 2.3** provides an overview of the SAP ERP architecture.

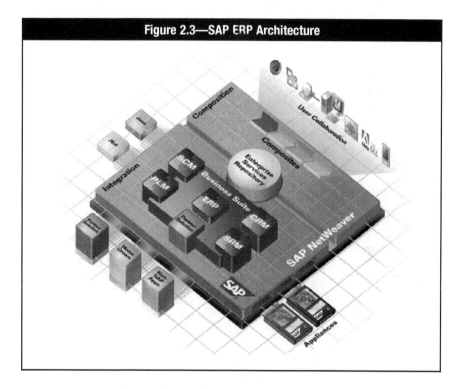

**Figure 2.3—SAP ERP Architecture**

## Major SAP Modules and Functionality

SAP has based the functionality of its SAP R/2, R/3 and ERP systems on the business process concept. For SAP, a business process is the complete functional chain involved in business practices for whatever software module has to work with it. This means that the chain might run across different modules. For instance, what travel expenses, sales orders, inventory, materials management and almost all types of functions have in common is that most of them finally link to the finance modules. SAP R/2, R/3 and ERP are particularly noted for this type of comprehensive business functionality that underpins the systems' reputation as being highly integrated. By the time SAP released R/3 4.6, it already had incorporated a library of more than 3,000 predefined business process maps across all functional modules so customers could select and adapt these maps as their own way of doing business.

SAP ERP software consists of different components, each of which handles particular functional aspects of the business processes. Each area of a business is handled by a separate module within the system; however, all modules feed into the central database server, as shown in **figure 2.4**. This database forms the heart of the SAP ERP system and is controlled by a series of tables that validate and process data.

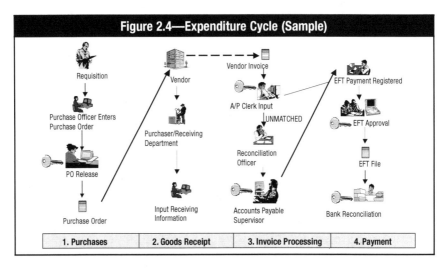

**Figure 2.4—Expenditure Cycle (Sample)**

SAP ERP components are usually categorized in terms of specific industry solutions or the following four core functional areas:
• SAP ERP Financials—Covers all the key financial and accounting functions:
  – Financial and management accounting
    · General ledger
    · Accounts receivable
    · Accounts payable
    · Contract accounting
  – Financial supply chain management
    · Credit management
    · Electronic invoicing and payments
    · Dispute management
    · Collections management
  – Treasury applications
    · Cash and liquidity management
    · In-house cash management
    · Treasury and risk management

- · Bank communication management
- · Integration package for SWIFT
- – Governance, risk and compliance
- • SAP ERP Human Capital Management (HCM)—Covers human resource management (hiring, termination, etc.):
  - – End-user service delivery
  - – Workforce analytics
    - · Workforce planning
    - · Workforce cost planning and simulation
    - · Workforce benchmarking
    - · Workforce process analytics and measurement
    - · Talent management analytics and measurement
    - · Strategic alignment
  - – Talent management
    - · Recruitment
    - · Succession management
    - · Enterprise learning management
    - · Employee performance management
    - · Compensation management
  - – Workforce process management
    - · Employee administration
    - · Organizational management
    - · Global employee management
    - · Benefits management
    - · Time and attendance
    - · Payroll and legal reporting
    - · HCM processes and forms
  - – Workforce development
    - · Project resource planning
    - · Resource and program management
    - · Retail scheduling
- • SAP ERP Operations—Covers the supply chain as well as sales and support:
  - – Procurement and logistics execution
    - · Procurement
    - · Inventory and warehouse management
    - · Inbound and outbound logistics
    - · Transportation management
  - – Product development and manufacturing
    - · Production planning
    - · Manufacturing execution
    - · Product development
    - · Life-cycle data management
  - – Sales and service
    - · Sales order management
    - · Aftermarket sales and service
    - · Professional-service delivery

- SAP ERP Corporate Services—Covers cross-application services not directly related to a specific business process:
  - Real estate management
  - Enterprise asset management
    - Investment planning and asset specification and design
    - Procurement and asset construction, installation and implementation
    - Maintenance and operations management
    - Decommissioning and disposal
  - Project and portfolio management
    - Strategic portfolio management
    - Project planning
    - Resource and time management
    - Project execution
    - Project accounting
  - Travel management
  - Environment, health and safety management
  - Quality management
    - Audit management
    - Quality engineering
    - Quality assurance and control
    - Continuous improvement
    - Global trade services

SAP also offers Industry Solutions, a set of programs developed for a specific industry, such as banking, that can be applied to the core SAP ERP modules. SAP Industry Solutions is available for:
- Aerospace and defense
- Automotive
- Banking
- Chemicals
- Consumer products
- Defense and security
- Engineering, construction and operations
- Healthcare
- High-tech
- Higher education and research
- Industrial machinery and components
- Insurance
- Life sciences
- Logistics services provider
- Media
- Mill products
- Mining
- Oil and gas
- Pharmaceuticals
- Postal services

• Professional services
• Public sector
• Railways
• Retail
• Telecommunications
• Utilities
• Wholesale distribution

The most commonly implemented components in SAP ERP include Financial and Management Accounting (FI/CO), Procurements and Logistics Execution (MM), Product Development and Manufacturing (PP), and Sales and Service (SD). The Basis System (BC) underlies all SAP ERP application components and is integrated within the SAP NetWeaver platform. It handles classification and document management and interfaces with the operating system, database, network and the user presentation interfaces. Each of the commonly implemented SAP ERP modules is described in more detail in the following paragraphs.

The SAP ERP Financial and Management Accounting module is integrated into the logistical chain that begins with procurement and ends in sales and distribution. The user can define the chart of accounts. The chart of accounts serves as the basis for all of the automatic integrated postings. Business transactions are entered and stored on the database in the form of documents. The Financial and Management Accounting system supports the real-time generation of the income statement and balance sheet. Financial and Management Accounting includes the following submodules:
• General Ledger
• Accounts Receivable
• Accounts Payable
• Contract Accounting

The Sales and Service component performs sales, distribution, transportation, pricing and invoicing functions. It automates the administrative work involved from the time a customer quote is created, to distribution and invoicing of goods. This improves the capability to deliver products on a timely basis. The key subcomponents in Sales and Service include:
• Sales support
• Sales order management
• Aftermarket sales and service
• Professional-service delivery

The Procurements and Logistics Execution component controls various functions related to inventory and purchasing, including the purchase and receipt of goods, inventory management and valuation, and warehouse management. The subcomponents in Procurements and Logistics Execution include:
• Procurement
• Inventory and warehouse management

- Inbound and outbound logistics
- Transportation management

The Product Development and Manufacturing component controls various functions related to production planning and processing. It tracks the purchase, storage and transfer of materials and intermediate products. The subcomponents in Product Development and Manufacturing include:
- Production planning
- Manufacturing execution
- Product development
- Life-cycle data management

Other SAP ERP modules, including SAP Human Capital Management and SAP Workflow, are not covered in this book but may be in future ISACA publications.

In 2004, SAP R/3 was replaced with SAP ERP. This included the combination of SAP Web Application Server (SAP Web AS) with other integration components to create SAP NetWeaver. Essentially, the SAP NetWeaver platform is a group of integrated components, both new and those provided as individual separate services. The various components and tools that make up SAP NetWeaver include:
- Components
  - SAP Web Application Server (SAP Web AS)
  - SAP NetWeaver Business Intelligence
  - SAP NetWeaver Business Process Management
  - SAP NetWeaver Master Data Management
  - SAP Auto-ID Infrastructure
  - SAP NetWeaver Portal
  - SAP NetWeaver Mobile
  - SAP NetWeaver Process Integration
  - SAP NetWeaver Identity Management
- Tools
  - Adaptive Computing Controller
  - SAP NetWeaver Composition Environment
  - SAP NetWeaver Developer Studio
  - SAP NetWeaver Visual Composer
  - SAP Solution Manager

The Basis Component (BC) or Basis System is integrated within the SAP Web AS and provides the underlying application architecture for SAP ERP. This consists of the system software and services that underpin the SAP ERP applications, including:
- The customization of functions via central table control, without program modification and using the SAP ERP Implementation Guide (IMG)
- Tools to create and modify tables, change screen design and enhance the system using Advanced Business Application Programming/4 (ABAP/4), a fourth-generation application development language

- ABAP/4 Workbench
- A tool (Profile Generator) to implement access security for the various modules, including the Basis System
- The maintenance of the database and the ABAP/4 dictionary
- Tools for system administration and monitoring, such as the Computing Center Management System (CCMS)
- Support for electronic data interchange (EDI)
- Online documentation of help information

A unique characteristic of SAP is the feature it provides for customization. While features such as Business Add In (BADI) (transaction code SE18), which has since replaced user exits, and Business Application Interface (BAPI) (transaction code BAPI) facilitate customization and linking of standard SAP functionality through the use of an object-oriented programming approach, need-based custom tables to take care of additional data requirements can also be defined. While these features provide an enhanced business process capability, they also lead to greater risks (e.g., incorrect table definition, authorization overrides and adverse impact on system performance). Therefore, an auditor should also consider the extent of customization during the course of an SAP security and control audit.

## Navigating the SAP ERP System

### Logging On
The sign-in page will appear after selecting a client on the SAP ERP logon pad. The sign-in page contains the following logon screen fields:
- Client—The highest organizational level; a unique company or possibly the testing or training system
- User—The unique identifier assigned to each user
- Password—Unique to each user and subject to several controls concerning length, change frequency and other factors
- Language—The user may override the default language for the application server

User and password are required fields and are not case-sensitive, as shown in **figure 2.5**. The screenshots in this guide have been taken from an SAP Release ECC 6.0 system. The SAP ERP online security validates the user ID and password against the database. If they do not match, then an error message is displayed, as shown in **figure 2.6**. The sign-in page also provides the facility to change the current password, as shown in **figure 2.7**. The user is required to enter the correct user ID and password, and can then select the button New Password to change the current password. Once logged onto the SAP ERP application, the user profile(s) associated with the user ID determines the menus, pages and action types to which the user has access. The SAP ERP security features are discussed in more detail in chapters 4 and 12.

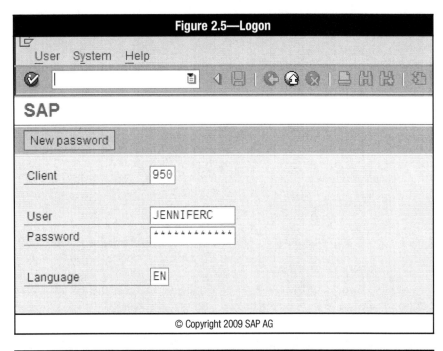

Figure 2.5—Logon

© Copyright 2009 SAP AG

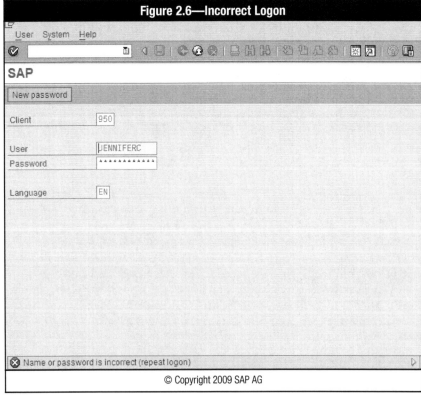

Figure 2.6—Incorrect Logon

© Copyright 2009 SAP AG

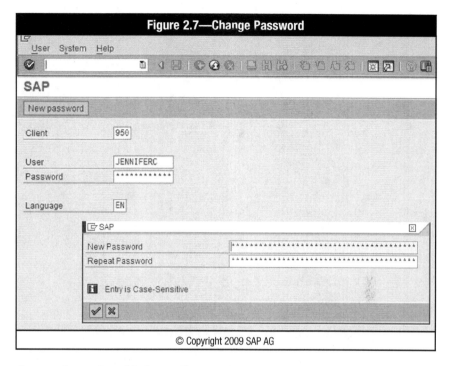

Figure 2.7—Change Password

© Copyright 2009 SAP AG

## Screen Layout and Information

The SAP ERP graphical user interface (SAP ERP GUI) provides technical features that enable users to exchange information with the SAP ERP system (by entering data, choosing functions and so on).

The SAP ERP GUI consists of three main screen areas (screen header, screen body and status bar), as shown in **figure 2.8**.

The screen header consists of:
- Menu bar—These are the choices listed in the toolbar at the top of the screen. Before the SAP ERP Easy Access menu was available, all the SAP ERP choices were included in this menu. Now only cross-modular/application functions— functions that are not specifically associated with a particular module, such as printing and saving—are listed in this menu. The menu bar also contains the Minimize, Maximize and Close buttons on the right side and the GUI interaction options on the left side.
- Standard toolbar—This is the area beneath the menu with buttons for the most common tasks, such as saving data or returning to previous screens. It is also within this toolbar that the command field, within which a transaction code or command can be entered, can be opened. By default, the command field is closed. To display it, choose the arrow to the left of the Save icon.

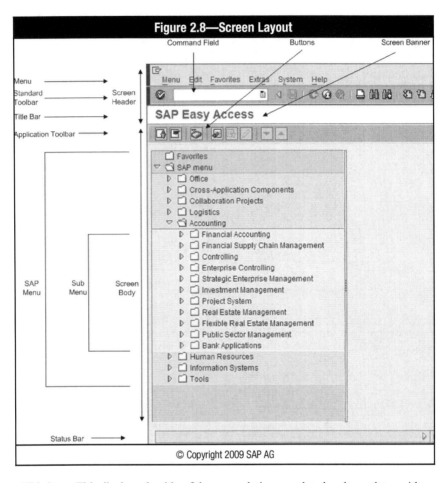

Figure 2.8—Screen Layout

© Copyright 2009 SAP AG

- Title bar—This displays the title of the screen being populated and correlates with the description of the transaction code that ran to access the particular screen.
- Application toolbar—It contains tabs and buttons that provide access to further information and functions relating to the screen being accessed.

The screen body is the area between the screen header and the status bar. This section differs between the SAP ERP Easy Access screen and the SAP ERP window screen. The SAP ERP Easy Access screen is the first screen appearing and serves as the user interface to the SAP ERP system. After the sign-on page has successfully been completed, all other screens within the SAP R/3 software are referred to as the SAP ERP windows.

The SAP ERP Easy Access screen body has a unique layout and contains specific information that will help the user navigate through the system:
- The SAP ERP menu—This is the list of choices down the left side of the screen. The SAP ERP menu provides the means to select functions or submenus. The choices listed in these menus are modular/application-specific. One can expand

and collapse these menus by choosing the drop-down arrows to the left of the menu items. If a user's SAP ERP menu has been defined by the system administrator, it will appear when the user logs onto the system. If a user menu has not been assigned or the user requires access to items that are not contained in the user menu, the SAP ERP standard menu can be selected by choosing Menu ▶ SAP Menu. This menu provides a complete overview of the SAP ERP system with which the user is currently working.

• Submenus are indicated by whether the SAP ERP Menu is opened up. The submenus differ depending on the applications that have been chosen, e.g., logistics or accounting within the SAP ERP Menu options.

The SAP ERP window contains additional features within the screen body that are not available on the SAP ERP Easy Access screen, as shown in **figure 2.9**:

• Data are the information on the screen or reports being displayed.
• Input fields are the rectangular areas next to a field name into which data are entered. A checkmark icon at the left end of the field indicates a required input field.

The status bar is the line at the bottom far right of the screen. It indicates:

• Warning and error messages
• System ID/instance, session number, client, host/node name (These fields can be hidden. To display them, choose the arrow pointing to the left.)
• Another field in the System/Status dialog box is component version, which tells users what system they are running, e.g., ECC for 6.0.

## Navigating Menus

A user can navigate through the system and perform tasks using the menu path in one of the following ways.

### Using Menus and the Mouse

By clicking with the mouse on the desired menu in the menu bar or the SAP ERP Easy Access workplace menu, it will open and its contents (functions, submenus or both) will appear. In the menu bar of the SAP ERP window, the drop-down arrows indicating submenu options are to the right of each menu item, as shown in **figure 2.10**. In the SAP ERP Easy Access workplace menu, the drop-down arrows indicating submenu choices are beneath each menu item, as shown in **figure 2.11**. After a submenu has been opened, the drop-down arrow of that submenu will point downward. If there is no arrow next to a menu item, the user will go directly to the transaction screen.

By clicking with the mouse on the desired submenu, users will open the submenu next to the original menu. The user can cancel or close any menu with its submenus by clicking on them. To choose a function from an open menu or submenu, the user clicks the desired function. This will result in the selected menu and any submenus closing, and the system will execute the chosen function.

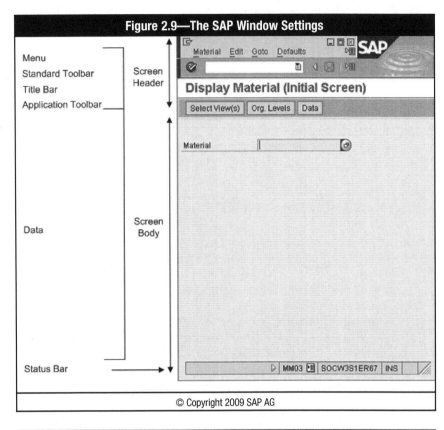

Figure 2.9—The SAP Window Settings

© Copyright 2009 SAP AG

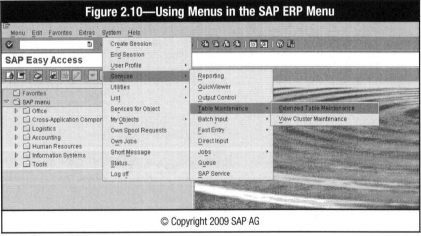

Figure 2.10—Using Menus in the SAP ERP Menu

© Copyright 2009 SAP AG

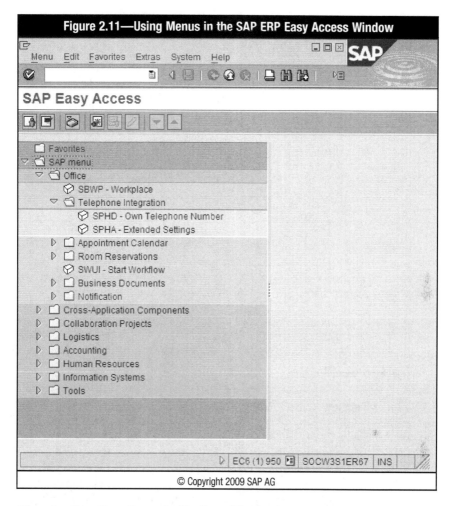

Figure 2.11—Using Menus in the SAP ERP Easy Access Window

© Copyright 2009 SAP AG

### Choosing Functions From the Toolbars (Shortcut)

Depending on the current task, various buttons are available on the standard toolbar and on the application toolbar. To choose a function with one of these buttons, the user needs to click the appropriate button. On the standard toolbar, these buttons can include Save, Display or Exit.

The buttons appear as tabs in the screen body. These tabs enable the user to enter, display and alternate among multiple screens. In transactions containing multiple screens, the tabs provide a clearer overview. In addition, tabs enable the user to proceed from one tab page to the next without having to complete all the data. To access a tab page, the user selects the corresponding tab header. In some cases, the user is required to complete certain input fields on a tab page before the user can move to the next tab page, as shown in **figure 2.12**. Tabs are arranged in order of importance or in the process order of the transaction. Tab headers can contain text, icons or both.

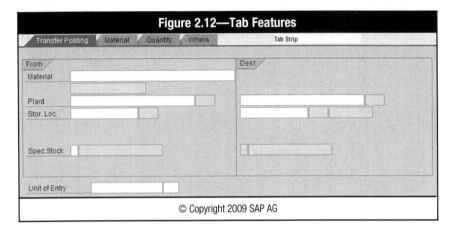

### Choosing Functions From the Context Menu (Shortcut)
The context menu can be displayed by clicking the right mouse button. Since the only other way to access some of these functions may be to navigate the menus, these context menus can be used as a shortcut.

To choose a function from the context menu on any screen:
• Place the cursor anywhere below the toolbars.
• Click the right mouse button.
• Choose the desired function.

### Choosing Menus and Functions With the Keyboard
To navigate in the SAP ERP Easy Access workplace menu, the user can use the up and down cursors as well as the Delete and Enter keys. To choose a menu from the menu bar, the user can use the F10 key, the cursors and the Enter key. To move up and down in the workplace menu, the user uses the up and down cursors. The user can also delete a favorite from the favorites list by choosing Delete, and open a folder or start a transaction by choosing Enter, which sends the information for validation.

At any time a user can choose to cancel or close any menu or submenu by pressing ESC or F10. The system will close the respective menu and submenus and deactivate the menu bar. The user can then choose another menu by pressing F10 again.

## Multiple Sessions

A session is an instance of the SAP ERP software on the screen of the user. Multiple sessions provide users with the ability to work on more than one task at a time. Not only can this save time, but it also reduces the need for the user to jump from screen to screen. The user can open up to six sessions and do a different task, or even the same task, in each one. The user can move around among the open sessions and can close a session without having to log off from the system. A new session can be created and closed from anywhere in the SAP ERP system.

To start a new session the user selects System ▷ Create Session from the menu bar. The system will open a new window with a new session, placing it in front of all the other windows. A user can start a task within a new session by entering the command /o (letter o) and the transaction code, e.g., /o fd01, and pressing Enter. The system will then open a new window for the new session. To move to a different session, the user clicks on any part of the window that contains the session to which the user wants to go. If the required session is hidden, the user moves the current session aside (by positioning the mouse on the title bar and holding the left button down while moving the mouse). Users can also use the operating system Alt-Tab key combination. To end the session, the user can choose System ▷ End Session, press the Exit button or log off the system completely (which will automatically end all open sessions). The user must save the data before closing a session, as he/she will not be prompted by the system.

## Executing Commands

Once logged onto the SAP ERP system, the user can choose any task on which he/she desires to work and can switch to different tasks at any time. Tasks can be chosen through the menu path or by typing a transaction code in the command field. Each function in the SAP ERP system has a transaction code associated with it. A transaction code can consist of up to 20 alphanumeric characters (letters, numbers or both), for example, ME21N, F-02 or SE06. Each of these transaction codes represents the menu path the user has to go through to process a function. For example, by typing in ME21N in the command field, the user does not have to go through the SAP ERP menu Logistics ▷ Purchasing ▷ Purchase Order ▷ Create ▷ Vendor/Supplying Plant Known, as shown in **figure 2. 13**.

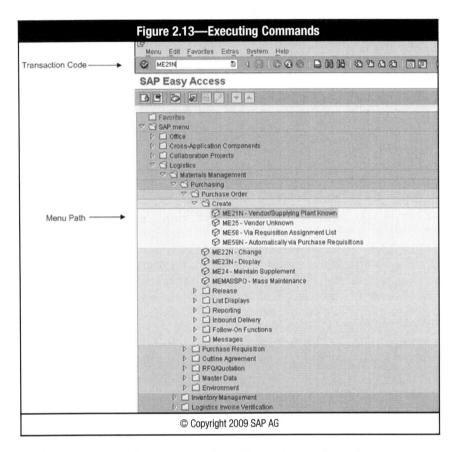

**Figure 2.13—Executing Commands**

Transaction Code ⟶

Menu Path ⟶

© Copyright 2009 SAP AG

It is important to note that the transaction codes can be typed into the command field from any screen but will not generate correctly unless the command field includes /n to the left of the transaction code. The /n ends the current task and allows the user to enter a task as if it were entered at the main menu. By using /n, data in the current task will not be saved before starting the new task. The code /n, typed into the command field and followed by Enter, will return the user to the main menu from anywhere in the SAP ERP system. Before users can use a transaction code, they have to find the right transaction code for the task they want to start. Thus, the transaction code of either new tasks or the current task on which the user is working may be required.

## *Identifying Transaction Codes*

To identify the transaction code of a new task, the user places the cursor on the appropriate menu item in the SAP ERP Easy Access menu, and chooses either Extras ▷ Technical Details, which will result in a dialog box displaying the details for the selected menu item, as shown in **figure 2.14**, or Extras ▷ Settings ▷ Display Technical Names, which will result in the menu closing. Once reopened, the system displays the transaction code (not only for the selected item, but throughout the menu), as shown in **figure 2.15**. The user can then start the task by double-clicking on it or by choosing Enter or Start This Task from any screen in the SAP ERP system.

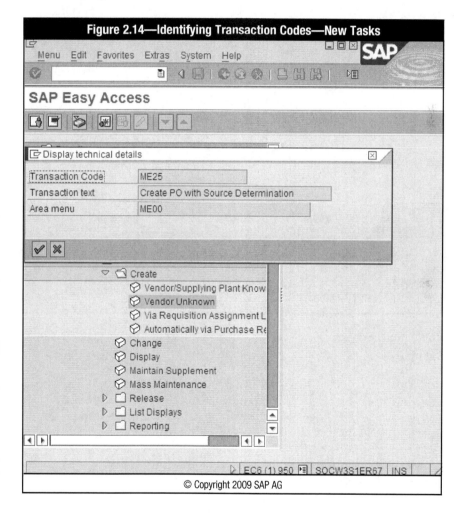

**Figure 2.14—Identifying Transaction Codes—New Tasks**

© Copyright 2009 SAP AG

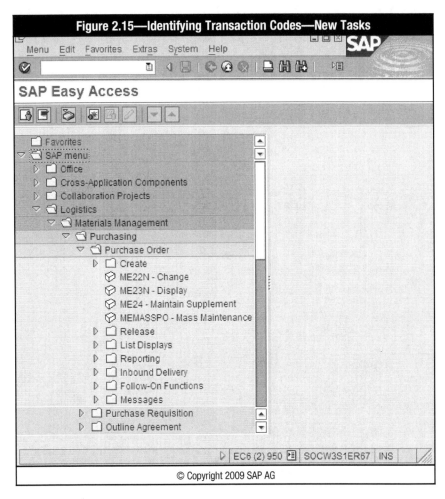

Figure 2.15—Identifying Transaction Codes—New Tasks

To identify the transaction code of the current task, the user chooses System ▷ Status from the menu bar. The code is displayed in the transaction field, as shown in **figure 2.16**. Another field in the System Status dialog box is component version, which tells users what system they are running, e.g., ECC 6.0. The user also can choose the arrow at the far right of the first status field, which will indicate the transaction code with other system information, as shown in **figure 2.17**. The user can also select the transaction code by clicking on the command field's Possible Entries arrow. This will show all transactions run since the user has logged on. The user then can select the desired transaction code and press the Enter key, as shown in **figure 2.18**.

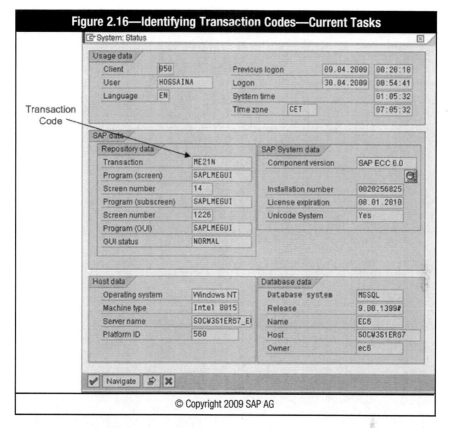

Figure 2.16—Identifying Transaction Codes—Current Tasks

© Copyright 2009 SAP AG

## Entering Data on the Screens

Once a task has been initiated through the menu bars or a transaction code, the user is required to enter data on the initial screen of the task. Each subsequent screen also contains input fields in which the user is required to enter data. Some fields are mandatory to complete, others are not. Once all mandatory fields have been completed, the user hits Enter to proceed to the next screen. If Enter is selected, the system checks the entries, proceeds to the next screen and temporarily stores the data just entered, if no errors were found. The user can still return to the previous screens to make changes, skip screens that are not required or go to related tasks. To cancel all the data just entered on a screen, the user chooses Edit ▷ Cancel. The system then removes the data on the current screen, closes the current screen and returns to the previous screen. Finally, the user is required to save data from all the completed screens. This is performed by pressing Ctrl and S or clicking on the Save icon (Disk icon). The system then processes the stored data and saves them in the appropriate database. The user can also end a task without completing it by pressing Shift and F3.

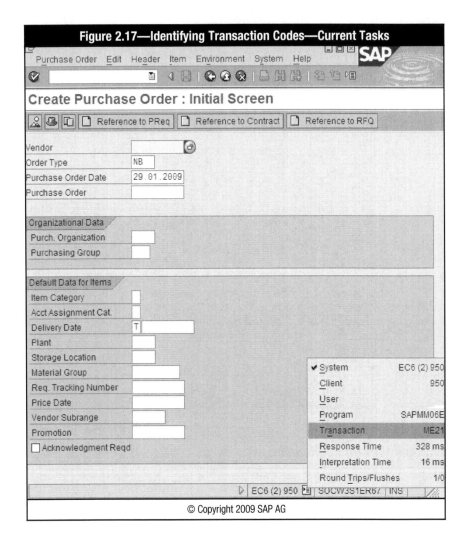

Figure 2.17—Identifying Transaction Codes—Current Tasks

© Copyright 2009 SAP AG

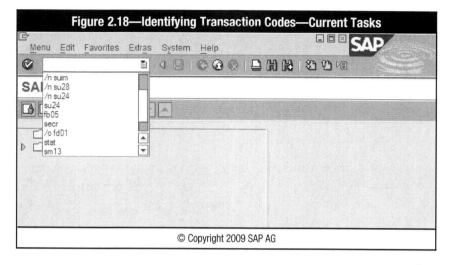

Figure 2.18—Identifying Transaction Codes—Current Tasks

© Copyright 2009 SAP AG

## Running Reports

A report is an executable program that allows users to read and evaluate data in the SAP ERP database. The output of a report can be displayed on the screen, sent to a printer or saved to a file. This is an important feature since reading large volumes of original data impair the performance of the system. ABAP reports, queries and drill-down reports are examples of reports that can be run.

ABAP reports may be run through transaction code SA38, by inserting the technical name of the report, e.g., RSUSR002, as shown in **figure 2.19**. If the technical name of the report is not known, the user can enter F4 in the program field and then, in the next screen, insert known fields or simply execute the generate button to retrieve a list of all reports with descriptions.

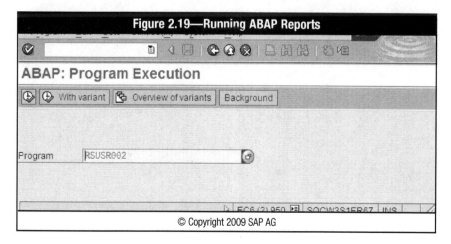

Figure 2.19—Running ABAP Reports

© Copyright 2009 SAP AG

Drill-down reports are run from the report tree. The SAP ERP software delivers a standard hierarchy of report trees containing reports across a range of applications, as shown in **figure 2.20**. Additional reports can be designed and added to this report tree. It is highly recommended, from a security point of view, that reports be generated through the report tree rather than through SA38 since SA38 provides wider access than that required for simply running reports. All standard reports now have a transaction code associated with them and should be made available to the user through a personal menu. Customized reports should be allocated a transaction code and included in the user's menu.

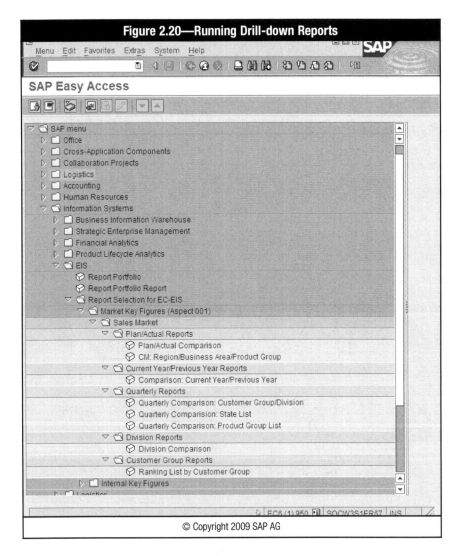

Figure 2.20—Running Drill-down Reports

Queries can be run in two ways. A user can start the InfoSet Query, which is a query allowing several data sources to be linked using a join, from either role menus or the SAP ERP menu. The InfoSet Query is made available as a menu entry for the role and as an option on the menu. If the query is called this way, the end user will not be confronted by the user groups of the query, only with the infosets that have been assigned to the particular role.

The InfoSet Query can also be started through the SAP ERP Easy Access menu by choosing Tools ▷ ABAP Workbench Utilities SAP Query ▷ Queries (transaction SQ01), and selecting the function InfoSet Query, as shown in **figure 2.21**. If the user is not assigned to a role and has started an InfoSet Query this way, the user will get

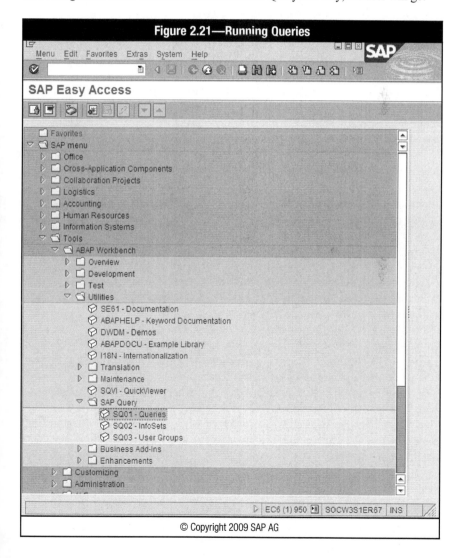

Figure 2.21—Running Queries

© Copyright 2009 SAP AG

a dialog box first, which will require the user to select the query area, a user group and an infoset. This also will be required when InfoSet Query is started for the first time since logging onto the system. If the user already has used InfoSet Query after logging on, the user group and the infoset that were used last will be displayed.

Note that access to InfoSet Query may be considered a high risk as users may have access to data to which they are not properly authorized. Executing infoset queries may also require large amounts of processing that may reduce system performance.

The user group serves as additional security as users can execute and maintain queries only in the user groups to which they have been assigned by their system administrator. It can be desirable to set up authorizations within a user group so that some end users can maintain and execute queries, while others can only execute existing queries. However, it must be noted that improperly or inaccurately created queries may also adversely affect system performance. Hence, the users entrusted with the task of creating and maintaining queries should be adequately trained in the technicalities of query maintenance. Duplicate and test queries are routinely noticed in many SAP installations and, as such, query maintenance should be subject to formal change management procedures.

Infosets provide special views of data sources, i.e., they determine which fields of a data source can be evaluated in queries. By assigning infosets to user groups, the system administrator determines the range of reports the individual application departments or end users can generate using the SAP ERP query. The system administrator is required to assign a minimum of one infoset to each user group, which will limit users within that user group to certain infosets.

By going through the menu path System ▷ Services ▷ Jobs ▷ Define Job (SM36), the user can define jobs that need to be run in batches. The user completes the following fields:
• Job name—A freely definable name that identifies the batch job
• Program name—The ABAP program to be run in the batch
• Variant—The name of the variant to which the batch job refers
• User name—The indicator for authorization check
• Repetition period—The time period (e.g., hour or day) after which the batch job is to be repeated automatically
• Start date—The specific time of the first batch job run. It is possible to restart batch jobs that already have been run by assigning new dates and print specifications to them.

Available within the SM36 screen is a tab key, called Job Wizard, which assists the user in completing the data. The output from the batch run can be displayed through transaction SM37. Job selection can be by job status, job start condition and/or job step, as shown in **figure 2.22**. For reports generated through the batch process, the results can be reviewed through transaction SP01, as shown in **figure 2.23**. Users can select their own name, the date and the display contents to review the actual results, as shown in **figure 2.24**.

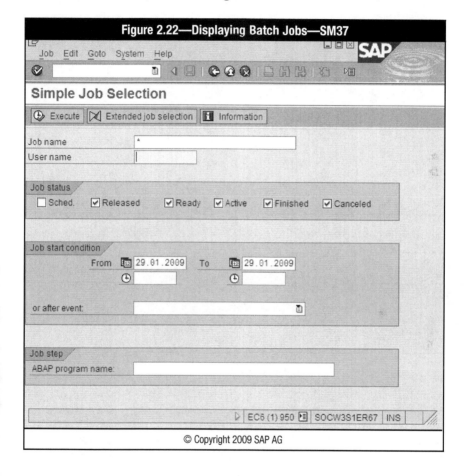

**Figure 2.22—Displaying Batch Jobs—SM37**

Job   Edit   Goto   System   Help

**Simple Job Selection**

⊕ Execute   ☒ Extended job selection   ℹ Information

Job name        *
User name

Job status
☐ Sched.   ☑ Released   ☑ Ready   ☑ Active   ☑ Finished   ☑ Canceled

Job start condition
From   29.01.2009   To   29.01.2009

or after event:

Job step
ABAP program name:

▷ EC6 (1) 950   SOCW3S1ER67   INS

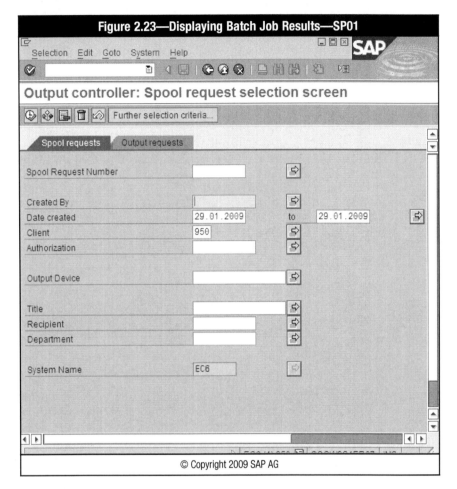

Figure 2.23—Displaying Batch Job Results—SP01

## Browsing Tables

Tables can be browsed within the SAP ERP software by using transaction code SE16 or SE16N. The technical name of the table needs to be specified/inserted, e.g., USOBT, as shown in **figure 2.25**. Within the next screen, the user has the ability to specify which fields need to be viewed by selecting Settings ▷ Format List ▷ Choose Fields. As noted in chapter 12, transaction codes SE16 and SE16N allow the user not only to view, but also to modify, tables and, therefore, represent a significant risk if access is not strictly controlled. See the Modifying Critical Tables Risk section in chapter 12.

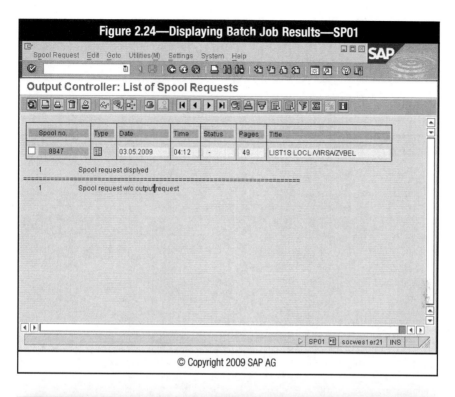

Figure 2.24—Displaying Batch Job Results—SP01

© Copyright 2009 SAP AG

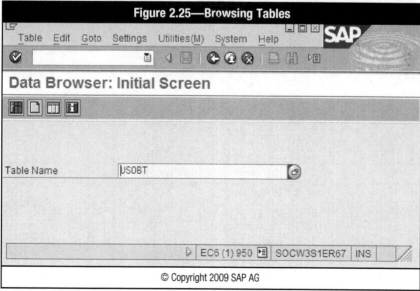

Figure 2.25—Browsing Tables

© Copyright 2009 SAP AG

If the name of the table is not known, the user can select F4 (fields for selection) and drill down until the required table name is found. Alternatively, the user can identify the table within any screen in the SAP ERP system by selecting F1 in that field and then selecting the Technical Details button. The table and field names will be displayed as shown in **figure 2.26**. To display the English titles of the fields, the user can select the menu path Settings ▷ List Format ▷ Choose Fields.

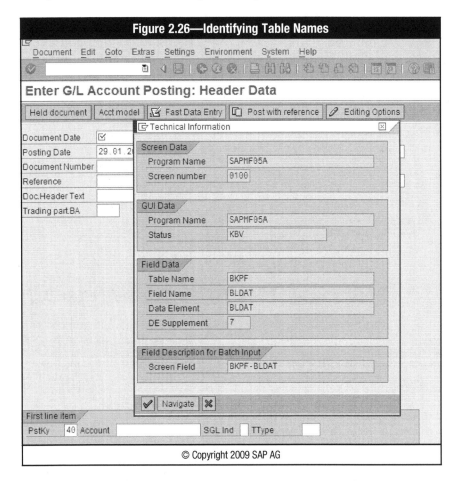

The following steps need to be followed to save the information:
• To save to an external file format such as a Microsoft Excel spreadsheet or an HTML page, the user chooses System ▷ List ▷ Save ▷ Local File and then specifies the external format type, as shown in **figure 2.27**.
• To save to a report tree, the user chooses System ▷ List ▷ Save ▷ Report Tree. The system saves this list to the node and report tree specified by the user.

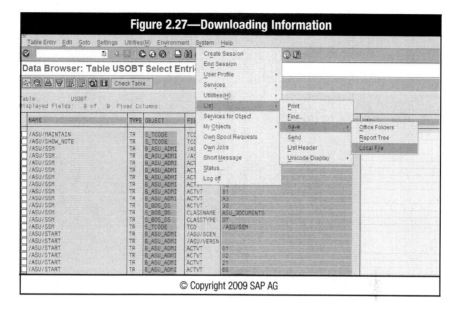

Figure 2.27—Downloading Information

© Copyright 2009 SAP AG

## Running a Trace

The USOBT_C table lists, by transaction code, the associated default authorization objects that can be maintained through the profile generator within the SAP ERP software. The configuration of how these objects can be maintained can be performed using transaction code SU24. It is possible that this table can become out of date so that not all transaction codes and their correct associated authorization objects will appear. This information can be obtained through a system trace. It is important that the user have multiple sessions open. Within session one, the user goes through the menu path Tools ▶ Administration ▶ Monitor ▶ Traces ▶ System Trace (ST01), selects Authorization Check and clicks the Trace On button. The user then goes to session two, and types /n and the transaction code for which authorization check needs to be determined. He/she then goes back to session one, and selects Trace Off. It is important to select Trace Off since this function influences table space and the performance of the system if not switched off. The user selects the Analyze button and deselects all switches except Trace for authorization checks and clicks on the Start Reporting button. The results will be displayed as shown in **figure 2.28**.

## Logging Off

A user can log off from the system in two ways. The user can deliberately log off the system or the system will automatically log the user off after a specified number of minutes. By using transaction RZ10 and selecting Extended Maintenance, the parameter setting rdisp/gui_auto_logout can be defined, indicating the number of seconds of no screen activity after which the system will automatically log off the user.

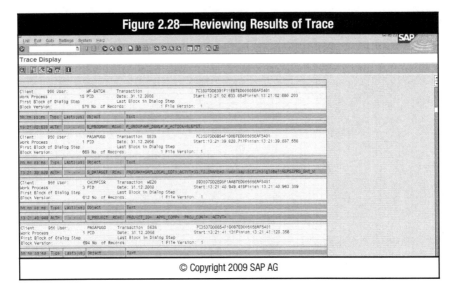

Figure 2.28—Reviewing Results of Trace

© Copyright 2009 SAP AG

This setting can also be reviewed through the transaction SA38 and running RSPARAM, or by going to transaction code TU02. It is important that this setting be defined since it ensures additional security. If the setting is defined as 0 it means it has not been specified, as shown in **figure 2.29**, and therefore the users will never be logged off for screen inactivity.

Figure 2.29—Logging Off Automatically

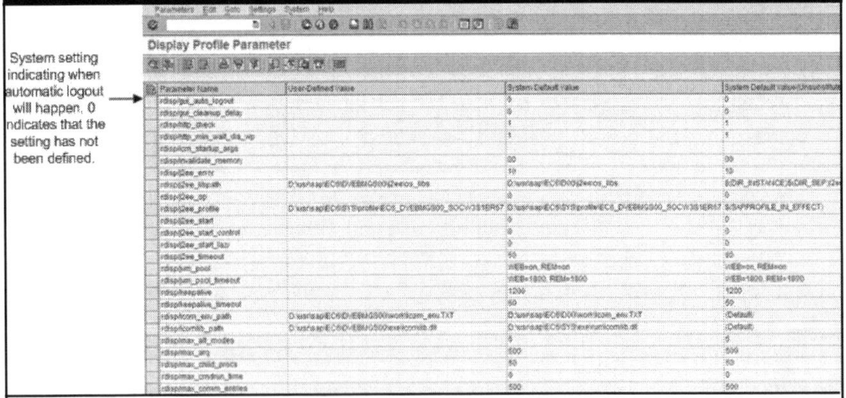

System setting indicating when automatic logout will happen. 0 indicates that the setting has not been defined.

Display Profile Parameter

© Copyright 2009 SAP AG

Users can log off the system by clicking on the Close button in the right top corner or selecting System Log Off from the menu. In both cases, a pop-up screen will appear asking the user to confirm whether he/she wants to log off, as shown in **figure 2.30**.

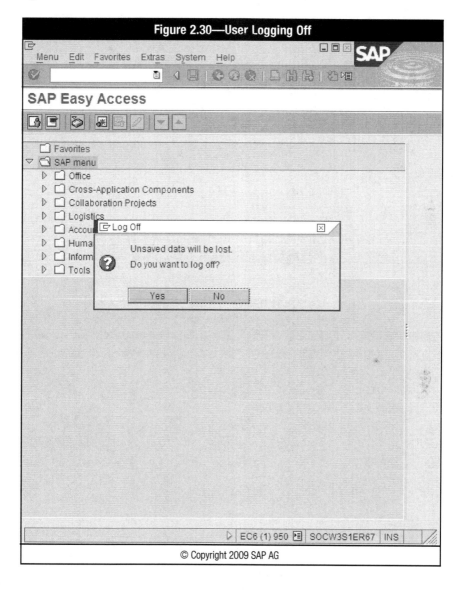

**Figure 2.30—User Logging Off**

## Fundamental Changes in Business Controls

An ERP implementation and its associated business process changes transform critical elements of the business, resulting in increased business, process, system and project risk. Some reasons for the increased risk include:
• Decisions taken on erroneous real-time information are often irreversible or costly to set right.
• Batch-oriented controls are not the focus in an online and real-time environment.
• Traditional (paper-based) audit trails are lost.
• Access requirements have expanded vastly to include field personnel and, increasingly, suppliers and customers.
• Master data changes can have a significant impact on transactional data across multiple business processes and business units due to the integrated nature of SAP.
• A single, significant point of failure exists.
• There is potential erosion of segregation of duties since end-to-end business processing now occurs in one system.

As a result, the integrity and control structure supporting ERP-enabled business processes must also be transformed. ERP systems can change internal controls in three fundamental ways:
• The methods of control—From rechecking and revalidating paper-based records to online monitoring and measurement
• The point of control—From multiple validations of transactions, often based on printed outputs and source documents, to a single validation at the point of creation, often an online approval
• The amount of control—From many redundant, process-impeding controls to fewer, automated and strategic controls

Consequently, it makes business sense to ensure that these enhanced controls are integrated into the reengineered and ERP-enabled processes. **Figure 2.4** shows the four main steps in the expenditure (noninventory) business cycle for an ERP-enabled enterprise. Some examples of fundamental changes in business controls are described in the following sections.

## Case 1—Three-way Match

An educational institution employs three-way matching on purchase orders, goods receipts and invoice processing. Purchase orders are entered and approved online under delegated authority. Goods receipt information entered online is matched to the purchase order quantity and tolerances set for over/under receipt. When the invoice arrives, a three-way matching process occurs whereby the quantity on the purchase order is matched to the quantity on the goods receipt, and the amount on the invoice is compared to the amount on the purchase order. If these fields match within preset tolerance levels, the transaction automatically passes for payment. This matching process effectively reduces the extensive manual and paper-based control activities, such as printing already approved purchase orders and stapling them to the back of invoices for reapproval at invoice receipt and then again at the payment stage. Controls have moved up to the front of the process and to an electronic form.

## Case 2—Evaluated Receipt Settlement

When a food company loads purchase orders into its system, orders are validated against vendor master data details already loaded into the ERP application system. Details of contractual arrangements and prices with vendors also have been loaded into the system. When the goods are received, there is a two-way match on quantity and, providing it matches within preset tolerance limits, the vendor is paid based on the set payment terms. There is no need to process a physical invoice. The SAP ERP system, for purposes of accounts payable processing, automatically generates an invoice within the system. The controls in this example reside at the beginning of the process cycle—at the approval of requisitions or orders and receipt of the goods/services.

These two cases demonstrate that controls are being shifted from detective to preventive and traditional matching reconciliation controls are automated in the SAP ERP software.

# 3. Strategic Risk Management in an SAP Environment

While the implementation of an ERP package may provide significant benefits for an enterprise, it also may introduce new risks and changes in the enterprise's risk profile. This chapter outlines:
• Strategic business risks and key management controls
• The importance of establishing a control framework

## Strategic Business Risks and Key Management Controls

The strategic business risks associated with the implementation of an ERP package are described in terms of the following four areas:
• Project management and program governance
• Business process/function
• Applications security and technical infrastructure
• Data conversion and program interfaces

Immediately following each strategic risk area is a summary of the key management controls that, when executed, may remove or mitigate the risk. The risks may apply to any ERP implementation and are not particular to an SAP ERP implementation. The benefits resulting from a well-executed ERP implementation may be significant. The purpose of this chapter is to assist enterprises in minimizing the risks of not obtaining those benefits.

### Project Management and Program Governance
The major concerns for ERP implementations involve organizational issues rather than technological issues.[1] This section discusses the risks of and key controls for an ERP project, including:
• Organizational change management and training
• Planning and problem management
• Lack of executive sponsorship
• Reliance on third parties
• Project cost blowout

#### Organizational Change Management and Training Risks
Organizational change management and training often rank as the primary areas of risk for enterprises implementing an ERP system. During the initial budgeting and business case phase for a project, these areas often are de-scoped or downscaled due to the need to reduce project costs. However, literature on enterprise systems confirms

---

[1] Manual, J.E.; *Definition and Analysis of Critical Success Factors for ERP Implementation Projects*, 2004

that failure to address the human and organizational aspects of change all too frequently contributes to rather poor outcomes in such investments.[2] Employees often defer their involvement in the ERP development, even though it may significantly affect the way they perform their roles in the new ERP-enabled enterprise. In addition, employees require considerable training on changed business processes and hands-on exposure to the system to adapt to the new processes and systems. An important aspect of the change management that is sometimes inadequately emphasized is the role of the users and the impact that their actions have on an integrated, enterprisewide application. Another key factor concerns the retention of employees once they are trained in new processes and systems.

### *Organizational Change Management and Training Key Controls*
The project sponsor must ensure that the enterprise has the same vision as the original motivations for implementing ERP-enabled processes: the targeted capabilities as well as the targeted benefits. Aligning on the true destination (as opposed to the initial go-live phase) is a hearts-and-minds issue, which requires special focus on people: communicating, managing expectations, offering education and providing senior management support. The change management and training program must reach affected people at all levels and provide them with the skills and knowledge required to participate appropriately in the development, understand the changes to their job role in the post-go-live environment, and contribute to the next milestone. Typically, this is not an area where the budget can be successfully trimmed. Enterprises need to establish business process owners and champions who own the business processes and understand the impact of the actions of one group on another. A key success factor for the business process owners often revolves around how early and to what extent they obtain hands-on experience on the new or redesigned processes and the new ERP system. These owners and champions should ensure that an understanding of the dependencies among processes and modules is effectively communicated.

### *Planning and Project Management Risks*
Key challenge areas for an enterprise implementing an ERP system include detailed planning and project management of the people, process and technology factors. Approximately 50 percent of the issues and obstacles facing an ERP implementation concern people factors.[3] These factors include prioritization, resource allocation, team/project structure, discipline, ownership and communication. Failure to place sufficient emphasis on these factors, as opposed to process and technology factors, often leads to disappointment with the implementation outcomes.

---

[2] Lau, K. Linda; *Managing Business With SAP: Planning, Implementation and Evaluation*, Idea Group Publishing, USA, 2005

[3] Deloitte Consulting, *ERP's Second Wave: Maximizing the Value of ERP-Enabled Processes*, USA, 1998

*Planning and Project Management Key Controls*

Enterprises need a strong business imperative to implement ERP so their projects do not stop in midstream and end in disillusionment. This imperative needs to be embodied in the business case and carried through to an effective implementation plan and design with appropriate user involvement. Successful projects are guided by detailed work, milestones and rollout plans. Key dates and deliverables are spelled out and dependencies synchronized while benefit scoreboards are created and results are tracked and communicated. There is a need for a professional project manager with the ability to:

• Integrate IT and business users into joint decision making
• Facilitate significant and difficult decisions, such as whether to implement existing processes enabled by the ERP package, or implement the ERP package for reengineered or redesigned processes

The bright star of going live—large as it looms at the time—is only a point in time. It is not the point where the full constellation of business benefits is realized. It is the beginning of a journey. Benefits such as improved cost structures, faster response to customers and more effective business processes are why the journey starts and they should be milestones on the way to the full power of the integrated enterprise. Successful enterprises may miss a scheduled milestone or sometimes a date to go live, but they never miss an expected benefit.

*Lack of Executive Sponsorship Risks*

Project management and users may become frustrated and effective change may not be achieved if there is no sponsorship by or active involvement of executive management. Project resources may be redirected to other priorities and the project may stall in the middle. Conflicts may arise between the business areas and IT (or between business areas) and effective resolution may not be achieved. The right level of investment may not be maintained and the project may lose its purpose.

*Lack of Executive Sponsorship Key Controls*

Senior executive buy-in and sponsorship are needed to achieve the right mix of business and IT involvement in the project and to resolve conflicts. Business process reengineering needs championing and systems architecture needs investment. Risks must be managed and business controls effectively designed and deployed. To succeed, these aspects need executive support. During implementation the responsibility for going live, on time and on budget, usually rests with the project leader. However, going live is only an interim destination. In successful enterprises, there is no mystery about the accountability for results. An unambiguous responsibility and accountability structure should be set up for the benefits of the project and this should be communicated to the entire enterprise.

*Reliance on Third Party Risks*

While consultants bring valuable experience and methodologies to a project, their presence alone does not guarantee success. The enterprise may overdelegate to consultants or third-party suppliers of ERP solutions, expecting them to intuitively know their business requirements and effectively test and implement the solution. A major pitfall may also involve the payment of large sums of money on the delivery of documents, such as designs and flowcharts, without any tangible delivery of the computer system solution. Often enterprises focus so much on going live as the end product, that the need for a postimplementation stabilization phase and benefits realization phase is ignored or not well understood. This results in the consultants or the project team being let go too early, skills and knowledge not being effectively transferred to the enterprise, and inadequate support being provided in the postimplementation environment. Another consequence of funding or remunerating consultants to go live (or on going live) may result in the enterprise being pushed to go live irrespective of its readiness.

### Reliance on Third Party Key Controls
Business process owners who understand the enterprise and its business requirements need to be appointed. These business process owners must gain hands-on experience with the solution and must champion the cause, ensuring effective testing and implementation of the solution. The enterprise needs to contract effectively with its suppliers to ensure the quality of deliverables and effective postimplementation support. This may take the form of warranties or retainers until the delivered product is proven in production. Effective transition planning and training are required to transfer skills from vendors or consultants to appropriate staff. Retention plans are required to ensure that employees, once trained and marketable, remain with the enterprise.[4] Each key member of the team should have a backup staff member with similar training and experience.

### Project Cost Blowout Risks
Some of the major causes of project cost blowout have already been discussed. These include change management, training and a lack of software functionality. In addition, the customization and integration of software packages can make up a considerable component of total implementation costs.[5] Changes to the vendor-supplied software or customizations usually build in upgrade costs since additional testing of the changes is required during the upgrade. Generally, it is better not to customize; however, the enterprise needs to be sure that the "vanilla" solution can handle the major parts of its business. Other areas that are often underestimated include program interfaces, data conversions, report changes, integration testing, process rework and consequent increases in consulting fees. Unexpected project costs may also be hidden in business area desktop computing budgets or in other IT infrastructure budgets.

### Project Cost Blowout Key Controls[6]
Change management and training challenges involve an understanding of the integration between business areas, the data flow through the enterprise and the impact of one area's actions in the system on another. The change management

---

[4] Herbert, L., et al., *Successfully Managing ERP Implementation Providers*, Forrester, 2008
[5] Wang, R., et al., Enhancement Packages Improve SAP Upgrade Value, Forrester, 2008, *www.forrester.com/Research/Document/0,7211,45741,00.html*
[6] *Ibid.*

and training program that accompanies an ERP implementation needs to be presented to (and understood by) executive management. The program needs to be targeted and funded appropriately. Project cost overruns need to be identified early through effective reporting to the appropriate governance mechanism.

The business case should not be a static, one-time exercise intended to secure funding. On the contrary, the business case needs to be a dynamic and evolving management tool—one that should live beyond the go-live phase through to the benefits realization phase. Successful enterprises use the business case tool in a variety of ways including:
• Justifying the program
• Validating the design
• Setting postimplementation targets and managing them
• Prioritizing postimplementation change initiatives

Too often, the business case for an ERP implementation consists of a high-level mission statement or description of intangible, unquantified business benefits. A proven business case template should be employed and tailored to the enterprise's environment. Factors that should be considered include:
• Total cost of ownership—factoring in, for example, the additional cost of upgrading as a result of making software customizations
• Appropriate due diligence in determining benefit and cost items involving the input of variables and formulas for determining inventory, people savings, and conversion and integration costs
• A discounted cash flow analysis, including appropriate risk factors and cost of capital

Measurements need to be initiated in the legacy systems environment to baseline costs and benefit streams so that the improvements in the postimplementation ERP environment can be measured effectively.

## Business Process/Functional
Users who are familiar with the functional orientation of a legacy system's environment can find it challenging to embrace the notion of an integrated ERP environment based on business processes. As with any integrated environment, errors in one part of the process may have effects throughout the processes. This section discusses the risks and key controls for business process reengineering and software functionality.

### Business Process Reengineering Risks
Reengineering of the business processes will most likely result in structural and job role changes within the enterprise. Staff who had worked within the legacy environment for an extended period of time may find it difficult to adapt to new roles, and, as a result, certain business functions may not be properly performed in the postimplementation environment. Also, there is a risk that the reengineered

business processes may not have been configured properly, resulting in incorrect processing (e.g., incorrect tax indicators) or inadequate business controls (e.g., three-way match on purchases being bypassed).

### *Business Process Reengineering Key Controls*
The change management and training program needs to provide users with an appropriate overview and understanding of the impact of their actions on the process, system and others. Users need to be trained sufficiently and the appropriate procedural controls need to be defined so that users are able to execute their new role in the new and integrated processes and system on the first day of going live.

Enterprises, even those successful at implementing ERP, usually experience a temporary dip in performance after going live. Going live with ERP is a significant change for any enterprise. The dip varies among enterprises, depending on how well they were prepared for the introduction of this new system. Most users need to walk before they run. After mastering the basics on the live environment, they may require refresher training on the more advanced topics. The enterprise needs to be prepared for contingencies and the considerable effort often involved in correcting errors made in an online, real-time environment. This may require additional trained data entry or programming resources to correct data errors.

Configurable options need to be thoroughly explained to users and appropriately documented in the business requirements, design or blueprint documentation. Changes in the system or business controls need to be considered early in the implementation process and included in the design in order to minimize the cost of retrofitting controls at a later time.

### *Software Functionality Risks*
Enterprises often find when they get down to the detail or, worse still, are in production that the ERP solution cannot handle the major parts of their business. While the enterprise perceived that the vendor or reseller represented that the solution could meet the business requirement, the requirement may not have been clearly specified or effectively detailed. Whatever the reason for the misunderstanding, if there is a fundamental mismatch between the system and the business need, the consequences may be costly.

### *Software Functionality Key Controls*
Management needs to take the time to effectively complete its due diligence on the new system. This includes translating business requirements into a high-level design specification for software acquisition, taking into account the enterprise's technological direction and information architecture. Management should review and approve the design specifications to ensure that the high-level design addresses the requirements. When significant technical or logical discrepancies occur during development or maintenance, the document will need to be reassessed.

Appropriate software selection guidelines should be used. Factors to consider include:
• Others in the industry using the solution
• Particular local requirements
• Legislative or compliance requirements (e.g., tax, statutory reporting, industrial awards/agreements)
• Foreign currency handling (e.g., financial vs. management accounting treatment and reporting through time on a transaction and across country borders)
• Particular reporting requirements (e.g., external reporting and reconciliation needs)
• The impact that the loss of specific legacy system functionality may have on customer service (However, caution needs to be exercised prior to replicating legacy functionality; only if it is the best, or at least the better, process should the enterprise consider replicating it. It should not be replicated only because the enterprise is used to it.)
• Stability of the current software release
• Specific operational needs (e.g., handling fresh produce or livestock)
• Marketing needs (e.g., bulk discounting across product lines)

Further along in the implementation, adequate user acceptance and system and integrated testing need to be performed to ensure that the system performs as anticipated. System performance is another critical area that must be tested to ensure that the application and the related infrastructure can handle the typical transaction loads processed by the enterprise.

## Application Security and Technical Infrastructure

### Single Point of Failure Risks
Within the legacy environment, the impact of a component failure within a system has limited, if any, impact on other systems. This is so even in the case of a total loss of a particular application system. For example, in most cases a purchasing system could be managed through manual work-arounds. In an ERP environment, where the entire enterprise may be reliant on the system, the loss of the system for any extended period of time is likely to have significant effects on the enterprise's operations and substantial financial implications. In the legacy systems environment, systems could typically be unavailable for a few days before offsite and contingency facilities had to be invoked. In an ERP environment, the period of time between the system becoming unavailable and the need to invoke the contingency plan is typically measured in hours, not days. Because the enterprise has moved to operating in an online, real-time mode, its business operations may be disrupted when the system is unavailable. For example, in one case, a distributor of perishable food went live with its ERP using a legacy front end that processed orders from field personnel using handheld devices. The process consisted of field personnel entering data into a legacy front end that, in turn,

updated the ERP's back end system. When the front-end legacy system failed—unable to handle the volume of data—the enterprise was forced to use manual data entry for orders completed by field personnel. The customer service personnel, with no experience in entering orders, made errors when entering the data. Orders were incorrect and out of sequence, which played havoc with the back-end warehousing operations of the business. The warehousing personnel, also new to the system, had considerable difficulty dealing with incorrect order details, returns and corrections. Incorrect deliveries were made, inventory-level information became inaccurate and the entire episode resulted in a significant write-off.

At the core of the SAP system is a single relational database. This database uses complex technology to ensure that it can feed the system the necessary information to complete all business processes. The complexity of the database and the amount of information that is fed into and extracted from the database require that careful controls be instituted.

Four characteristics of ERPs that may impact business continuity planning (BCP) are:
• The large number of modules that cover a broad range of the enterprise's business processes
• A large and integrated database
• The physical and logical intertwining of all modules and data and subsequent potential need to be recovered at the same time
• ERP's increasingly direct interface with suppliers and other third parties

## Single Point of Failure Key Controls

Business continuity management plans need to be revised, taking into consideration the ERP as a single point of failure.

Rapid recovery may necessitate a complete rethink and redesign of the enterprise's BCP arrangements. An online, real-time system also needs an online, real-time business environment that can effectively monitor and deal with exceptions before they turn into significant problems and impact other areas. System maintenance and version control are also important in terms of maximizing system availability and integrity.

ERP systems in general, and SAP in particular, have features to technically configure and appropriately monitor system performance and initiate corrective actions, as needed, in a real-time mode that can minimize the probability of a single-point failure. Typically, SAP is implemented as three separate instances (development, integration and production). By ensuring that the integration system is maintained as a near replica of the production system, adequate redundancy can be built in whereby the integration server can act as a backup.

## Distributed Computing Experience Risks

Although it is sometimes overlooked, the IT architecture may be totally overhauled with the implementation of ERP. The enterprise may move from a centralized mainframe environment to a distributed client-server environment. New skills are required to manage and maintain this environment, and the impact of this change is often underestimated.

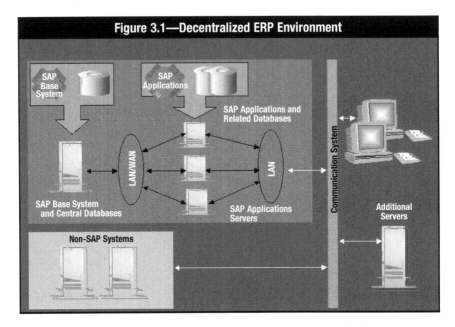

**Figure 3.1—Decentralized ERP Environment**

**Figure 3.1** illustrates how complex an ERP technical environment can become. This environment is indicative of the environment on which SAP ERP applications and legacy applications can be run (a client-server computer architecture). Depending upon the IT architecture used in the implementation, the audit may be centralized or decentralized. Extra care needs to be taken in scoping the first-year audit of enterprises that have implemented ERP systems. In this type of environment, there is often a combination of centralized accounting controls and decentralized operational controls.

## Distributed Computing Experience Key Controls

The IT infrastructure requires the same planning as the business processes. IT staff may require training and may also need to develop new skills. These areas are often underestimated in the initial planning for an ERP implementation. IT staff may become extremely marketable following training in the new environment, and for that reason, it is advisable to consider retention and succession plans.

## System Access Risks

By bringing a number of the enterprise's business processes together into one enterprisewide application, users potentially have access to additional information and processing functions. ERP systems are designed to allow wireless or remote access for field and sales staff and, if necessary, customers and suppliers. This level of access directly to the system from remote locations allows the system to be kept up to date and in real time. Yet, increased remote access may create an environment in which the system is far more susceptible to hacking or other malicious tampering. It may also increase the likelihood that incorrect data are introduced into the system.

### *System Access Key Controls*
SAP contains a number of security parameters covering passwords, intruder lockout, superuser access, etc., that, when set appropriately, serve to secure the system. Other ERP systems have varying degrees of security functionality and some require add-on packages to adequately secure them. User access to the system should be designed and built in accordance with the enterprise's security policy or needs. Some of the factors to be considered include:
• The segregation of access/duties
• The provision of access to only the transactions or objects required by users to perform their job or process role (the "least privilege" concept)
• The provision of access based on risk assessment of the consequences of providing the additional access vs. the cost of implementing tighter security (e.g., access to view all plants vs. maintaining separate security profiles for users in each plant)

Segregation of duties and security are covered in greater detail in chapter 4.

## *Data Conversion and Program Interfaces*
### *Data Quality Risks*
Since an ERP system may be reliant on a single, central database, the integrity of the data within the system is paramount. Data fed from legacy systems may be inaccurate, incomplete or duplicated, resulting in operational difficulties in a more automated and integrated environment. For example, a higher education institution converted its supplier master file complete with fax numbers for each supplier. In the new ERP environment, they moved to online faxing of purchase orders on approval by the appropriate delegated authority. Since some of the fax numbers were out of date, this resulted in a number of misdirected or lost faxes. Further, the enterprise had implemented the ERP solution with a third party's middleware and was unable to receive fax completion or OK messages without logging off its ERP system and logging on again. Data can be locked away in the complex data structures of ERP systems. As integrated e-business opportunities increase and prevail, it will become increasingly important to be able to unlock the data within the ERP systems. Data quality is becoming more important in the e-enabled ERP environment, as external parties access invoice and financial information via the World Wide Web.

*Data Quality Key Controls*

All data should be effectively cleansed prior to loading into the enterprise's ERP system. Cleansed information should be secured while awaiting conversion to the ERP environment. Control techniques such as control totals (often embodied in ERP conversion and load utilities) and data editing criteria should be employed as appropriate. Test conversions should be performed and financial reports reconciled between the two systems during the test and final conversions to confirm the completeness and accuracy of the data conversion. Data conversion is an area of key importance for an enterprise and its auditors.

*Program Interface Risks*

While ERPs enable many different types of functions to be completed, some enterprises have requirements that are not met by an enterprise application program or have requirements to transfer information to suppliers, customers and financial institutions. As a result, program interfaces are established to transfer transactional information between systems. If interfaces are not controlled effectively, there is a risk of inaccurate, incomplete, unauthorized or untimely information being fed into the ERP system or extracted from it. Further, the timing of the program interface can often be significant, particularly where there are a number of program interfaces that must be executed within a short processing window.

Service Oriented Architecture (SOA) provides methods for systems development and integration, where system functionality is grouped around business processes and these are packaged as interoperable services. Because SOA is often enterprise in nature, it encompasses dispersed and heterogenous systems. Thus, quality assurance risks are presented for SOA implementations since services are distributed and have many interfaces.[7]

*Program Interface Key Controls*

Controls over program interfaces are similar to those operating over data conversions (e.g., control totals, data editing criteria and periodic reconciliations), except that they may be performed in an interactive manner rather than in batch mode.

# The Importance of Establishing a Control Framework

A control framework for an ERP environment can create a robust management tool and methodology for ascertaining the risks associated with an ERP environment and a standard for defining the established controls. This can be achieved by:
• Establishing an organizational control framework
• Defining the control framework for an ERP environment

---

[7] *http://it.toolbox.com/blogs/the-soa-blog/soa-benefits-challenges-and-risk-mitigation-8075*

## *Establishing an Organizational Control Framework*

The Committee of Sponsoring Organizations of the Treadway Commission (COSO) developed a model for evaluating internal controls with the objective of assisting organizational management to improve its entity's internal control systems and to provide a common understanding of internal control among interested parties. This model has been adopted as the generally accepted framework for internal control and is widely recognized as the definitive standard against which enterprises measure the effectiveness of their systems of internal control. The framework defines internal control as:

> *...a process, effected by an entity's board of directors, management and other personnel, designed to provide reasonable assurance of the achievement of objectives in the following categories:*
> * *Effectiveness and efficiency of operations*
> * *Reliability of financial reporting*
> * *Compliance with applicable laws and regulations.*

The framework defines five interrelated components of internal control:
* Control environment
* Risk assessment
* Control activities
* Information and communication
* Monitoring[8]

The COSO framework is an effective starting ground for defining an enterprise's internal control framework and methodology with regard to an ERP environment. It can then be used for defining the elements of a control environment that are specific to an ERP implementation.

## *Defining the Control Framework for an ERP Environment*

The implementation of an ERP system can introduce new risks and alter an enterprise's risk profile. As a result, enterprises need to redefine their approach toward risk management and control assessment to cater to the differences in risk encountered in an ERP environment and to achieve complete coverage of the associated management controls. An ERP control framework is required to facilitate the assessment of risk and the completeness of controls. There are several frameworks that can be adopted to model the ERP control environment. One that is consistent with the ERP business process-driven approach and works well in practice is outlined in **figure 3.2**. The control framework consists of the following five areas:
* Business process controls—which include automated (e.g., online approval, three-way matching of purchase order amounts, goods receipt quantities and invoice particulars) and manual controls (e.g., reconciliations, manual approvals, review of exception reports) within the reengineered business processes.

---

[8] COSO, *Enterprise Risk Management—Integrated Framework*, USA, 2004

Business process controls are most cost-effective when incorporated from the beginning of the project and throughout the design and development phase. Retrofitting controls after the implementation is often costly.

- Application security—which includes maintenance of user profiles that provide access to application functionality and system services. It includes user, system and security administration procedures. It incorporates the setting of security parameters (e.g., password lengths) and the granting and removing of user access to the SAP application system.
- Program interface and conversion controls—which also need to be considered within the framework to address the risks associated with converting or interfacing data from legacy or external systems
- Technology infrastructure—which includes controls surrounding the technology platform on which the application resides. The technology infrastructure consists of the servers, operating system, database and network layers.
- Project management—specifically, the aspect of the control framework relating to change management and project disciplines discussed earlier

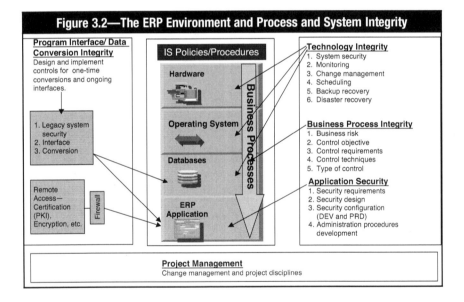

Figure 3.2—The ERP Environment and Process and System Integrity

## Summary

This chapter outlined key risks and controls associated with the implementation of ERP systems. Key risks include change management, cost blowout, single point of failure, and data conversions. Associated key controls include, for example, executive sponsorship, training, backup and recovery, and data cleansing and control totals. This led to a conclusion regarding the need for enterprises to redefine their approach to risk management in an ERP environment and the importance of establishing a control framework to facilitate the assessment of risks and the completeness of controls.

# 4. ERP Audit Approach

An audit approach should be developed to address the issues involved in implementing an ERP. This chapter recommends an audit framework for SAP ERP and discusses a risk-based audit approach. A case study is provided along with a numbering sequence for risks, controls and testing techniques used in the audit programs and internal control questionnaires (ICQs) provided in the appendices.

## Audit Impacts Arising From the Implementation of ERP

The nature and manner of auditing an enterprise that has implemented or is in the process of implementing an ERP system may need to change dramatically. An ERP implementation results in increased risk and potentially significant impacts on the internal control environment. Based on the enterprise embracing an ERP package solution, it is more important than ever for audit to address the new environment through or in the following ways:
• Managing the change
• Audit methodology
• Role of the auditor
• Audit involvement in the project
• Audit responsibilities

### Managing the Change
Audit needs to manage the change to an ERP environment by focusing on two key aspects:
• Staffing—The complexity of the environment usually requires a staffing model with a higher ratio of IT auditors. Traditional financial and operational auditors must transform to become integrated auditors understanding the nature of ERP and dependencies among different subprocesses. The audits of complex and technical areas may need to be supplemented by skilled and experienced resources.
• Training—A detailed knowledge of ERP is necessary to effectively understand and audit security, control and implementation issues over application areas and the technical environment. Extensive training is necessary to adequately understand the new environment. Auditors may need to learn security and controls implementation methodology, e.g., as part of the AcceleratedSAP™ methodology for SAP ERP. Auditors also may need to attend ERP training, join ERP user groups and learn new tools (e.g., ABAP/4 in SAP ERP software) to effectively audit the ERP.

### Audit Methodology
Significant reengineering of the audit approach needs to be undertaken to adjust to the new ERP environment. The enterprise's concept of the audit universe may need to change to effectively audit the new system. A risk assessment should be performed and the audit approach should be modified accordingly.

Integrated audits covering business process and security aspects are necessary in the ERP environment. Segregation of duties and security management come together in risk management of the new reengineered business process. Trade-offs in separation of duties are made and compensated by automated controls such as object-level security, release strategies, master data validation and tolerance levels. Further, effective audit practices in the ERP environment require new automated diagnostic tools. ERPs have powerful and complex security arrangements, and testing security is not just a matter of looking up the security matrix of users to functions. Composite security roles may be used and unraveling these to find out who has access to what often requires the use of automated diagnostic tools from third parties.

SAP ERP software is flexible yet complex and can be customized to fit each enterprise's environment. The configuration of business processes and degree of customization, the scope of the implementation, and the version of SAP ERP software all contribute to the uniqueness of the environment. Therefore, it is not possible to design one standard audit program that will work in every SAP ERP environment.

Although SAP-specific audit programs can be developed to assess a set of predetermined control objectives (in terms of transaction codes and menu path), the review approach may vary to some extent from version to version. Basis review, for instance, is hardly version-specific, while some business process transaction codes may differ slightly under different versions. Similarly, the IMG settings remain largely the same, although newer versions with additional functionality may have additional configuration settings to be reviewed. Depending upon the local regulatory reporting and compliance requirements, additional country-specific issues may have to be addressed as part of the overall SAP review. A case in point is the treatment of depreciation of a fixed asset that is not in operation. The Fixed Asset master data screen view (among others) includes an asset shutdown field, which, when activated for a specific asset, ensures that depreciation is not computed for that specific fixed asset as long as the indicator is active. By default, the asset shutdown indicator is configured as an optional field. In some countries (e.g., India) the local law stipulates that depreciation of a fixed asset should not be stopped, notwithstanding the fact that the fixed asset is not currently operational. It is best to configure the asset shutdown indicator as Not Required.

## Role of the Auditor

There are a number of opportunities whereby audit can and should contribute to the enterprise's ERP implementation. The role or roles chosen will depend on the circumstances and the enterprise's audit charter/strategy. The different levels of involvement that audit may have in the project may be characterized as follows:
• Integrated approach
• Preimplementation review
• Postimplementation review
• Quality assurance

The following paragraphs demonstrate that the IT auditor adopts the role of an IS risk management consultant when adopting the integrated approach or conducting a preimplementation review.

### *Integrated Approach*

Enterprises using the integrated method focus on the design and implementation of controls for the new systems. This approach requires audit to be involved from the earliest stage of the project, assisting the project team to design and build the controls. The approach considers project risks, technical risks and business process risk assessment and requires auditors to perform testing to ensure that controls have been properly implemented and benefits pursued.

Therefore, the IT auditor is responsible for non-audit roles associated with the ERP system and both the independence and the objectivity of the IT auditor may be impaired by non-audit involvement. Refer to the Audit Responsibilities section in this chapter for more information.

### *Preimplementation Review*

The preimplementation review approach allows the auditor to conduct a review of the controls, design and implementation plans at key stages in the project schedule and usually involves a review of:
• The business case
• Project risk
• Application security design
• Data conversion and program interface controls
• Business process risk assessment and controls design
• The adequacy of system testing
• Transition and system migration controls

The preimplementation review may also include project management aspects such as a review of:
• Performance measurement criteria
• User readiness to go live (e.g., adequacy of training provided, quality of user operating procedures)

A preimplementation review is obviously sensible since issues generally can be addressed before the system is put in place. This is usually far more cost-effective than reconfiguring the system after it is operational.

### *Postimplementation Review*

Another role that the auditor can undertake in the project is to conduct a postimplementation review that focuses on the implementation of controls for the new system and, as the name suggests, is conducted after the system has been implemented. This type of review considers:
• Control assessment of business processes
• Application security assessment

• Data conversion and program interface controls
• Achievement of project objectives and the business case
• User satisfaction and outstanding issues

Audits in the first year after implementation may be particularly complicated if the auditor has no prior involvement since the enterprise is in a state of significant change and is conducting business in a markedly new way. New systems and processes need to be documented. This step may be time-consuming, depending on the availability of existing documentation from the user team. Further, it may be challenging to get all the information needed to conduct an audit:
• Critical information may not be known.
• Resources may not be available.
• There may be processing problems, if not all things were considered during implementation.
• The system may have faults that could affect data integrity.

The process of auditing may be further complicated by the fact that little knowledge or experience of auditing this new environment exists within the enterprise. In particular, audit tools and methodologies may not be mature or robust enough for the new environment.

### Quality Assurance
The final and most complex role that an auditor may undertake is in the performance of a quality assurance audit. This approach requires the auditor's participation throughout the life of the project and, as such, is the most comprehensive approach. It focuses on the overall quality of the business process reengineering program and considers specific deliverables at each key project milestone.

## Audit Involvement in the Project
While the approach that is adopted will vary according to the enterprise implementing the ERP, the most effective approach usually involves audit having an extensive and active involvement during the project implementation. Involvement throughout the implementation allows audit to contribute to the establishment of the most effective control environment possible, as controls are built in during configuration, along with other changes. If this approach is adopted, an external or independent party may need to be called on to perform any postimplementation review.

New security, audit and control tools may need to be developed or acquired to facilitate the effective implementation, operation and review of the control environment. Whichever approach is adopted, it is worth reiterating that it is far more cost-effective to address issues during implementation than to reconfigure the system after implementation. It is also worth noting that audit's role remains ongoing after the implementation, during the stabilization phase and continuing into the review of future enhancements.

However, to participate actively and extensively during the implementation project, the auditor needs to have a good understanding of the ERP and its features and limitations in addition to knowledge of control design. The auditor runs a risk of being a party to incorrect configurations and weak control design if his/her knowledge levels are inadequate.

## Audit Responsibilities

Each environment needs to be evaluated on an individual basis from a risk perspective. A combined team needs to decide on the extent of involvement from the financial, operational and computer audit groups. In addition, subject matter specialists, such as tax personnel, may be needed to supplement the team. There are no hard and fast rules to split roles and responsibilities among the internal audit groups. An evaluation needs to be made as to how the roles and responsibilities should be defined. The important objectives are that users and management should have:
• A seamless and efficient audit
• A well-integrated and knowledgeable team

ISACA IT Audit and Assurance Guideline G21, Enterprise Resource Planning (ERP) System Review, states:
• The audit charter of the IT audit function may need to be modified as a result of an enterprise's decision to implement an ERP system. For example, business process reengineering (BPR) considerations associated with effective implementation of an ERP system could require the IT audit/assurance professional's scope of work or relationships with other audit functions (such as financial, operational) to be expanded and more closely integrated (such as a joint or collaborative audit initiative).
• The planned scope for audit by the IT audit/assurance professional should be defined in accordance with the IT audit charter.
• It is imperative that the enterprise's senior and system management fully understand and support the IT audit/assurance professional's role(s) as it relates to the ERP system or implementation project, as shown in **figure 4.1**. IT Audit and Assurance Guideline G5, Audit Charter, should be reviewed and considered within the context of the ERP system and related initiatives of the enterprise.
• If the IT audit/assurance professional is to perform or is responsible for nonaudit roles associated with the ERP system or an ERP system implementation project, IT Audit and Assurance Guideline G17, which outlines the effect of the nonaudit role on the IT audit/assurance professional's independence, should be reviewed and adhered to appropriately.
• If the IT audit/assurance professional is to have a nonaudit role in an ERP system or related initiatives, he/she should also review and adhere to ISACA's IS Control Professional Standards.

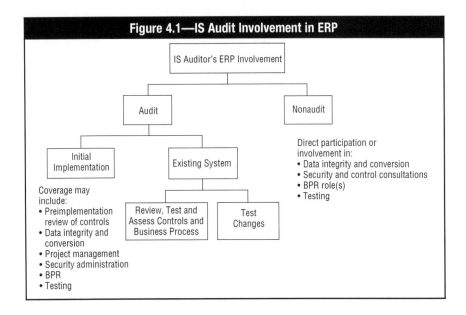

Figure 4.1—IS Audit Involvement in ERP

## Recommended SAP ERP Audit Framework

In chapter 3, the need for an overall control framework to facilitate the assessment of risk and the completeness of management controls was identified. The audit framework in **figure 4.2** shows the key components of an ERP environment from an audit perspective.

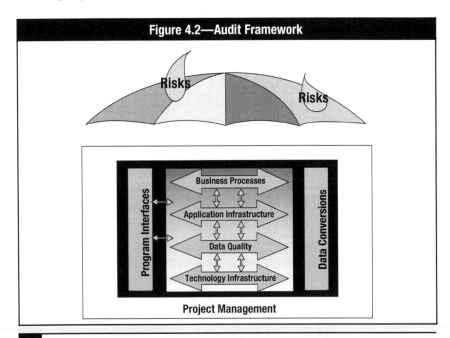

Figure 4.2—Audit Framework

The first component of this audit framework is the business processes or cycles. As described previously in this guide, the SAP ERP software is an integrated application system, and for that reason, it is important to assess the end-to-end business processes when performing risk and control assessments. The whole system of controls needs to be considered. A risk at the beginning of the process may be checked by a key control at another point in the process or a series of compensating controls throughout the process.

While the primary concern when auditing SAP ERP software should be with the business process, the auditor needs to know what system functionality needs to be audited. For that reason, it is important for the auditor to obtain an understanding of the relationships among audit business processes or cycles and the SAP ERP module groups. It is important to note that the definition of business cycles may differ among enterprises. An entity may combine the Expenditure and Inventory cycles into a larger cycle called purchase-to-pay. Note though that the Expenditure cycle links to other cycles such as Asset Management and, therefore, it may be preferable to assess it separately. The Revenue cycle is sometimes referred to as order-to-cash. Service organizations, such as educational institutions, may have a derivative of the Revenue cycle and may refer to it as enrollment-to-cash; instead of an Inventory cycle they may have a student education cycle involving admission-to-graduation. Enterprises dealing with large projects may have a project accounting cycle that combines the Revenue and Expenditure cycles and tracks the revenue and expenditure for particular projects to completion.

This presentation of linking audit cycles to the SAP ERP modules is shown in **figure 4.3**. The Financial Accounting cycle (involving setting up the chart of accounts, processing journal entries and preparing the financial statements) and the Treasury cycle (involving borrowing, managing cash and investments and managing derivative transactions) link directly into the SAP ERP Financial and Management Accounting module (FI/CO). The operational business cycles of Revenue, Expenditure and Inventory (discussed in more detail in later chapters) link to both the Financials (FI/CO) and the Operational (SD, MM, PP) modules. The Fixed Asset cycle (involving the maintenance of the fixed asset register, depreciating assets, managing fixed assets, and acquiring and disposing of fixed assets) links to both the Financials (FI/CO) and the Operational (MM and PM) modules. The Personnel/Payroll cycle links to both the Financials (FI/CO) and the Human Capital Management (HR) modules. The Industry Solutions module groups provide industry-specific business processing functionality that extends and enhances core SAP functions. The cross-applications and Basis component of SAP ERP cover all audit processes.

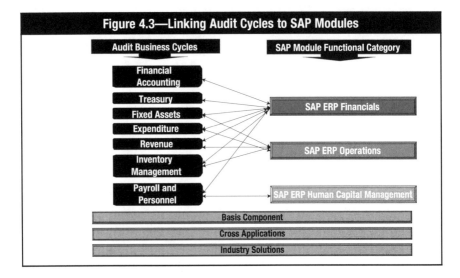

Figure 4.3—Linking Audit Cycles to SAP Modules

Figure 4.4 illustrates the relationships among the core business cycles. Sales are made in the Revenue cycle, generating a demand for the production of finished goods from the Inventory cycle. Production of goods necessitates the purchase of raw materials through the Expenditure cycle. All of this activity is recorded online and in real time in the Financial Accounting cycle and secured in connection with the Basis Application Infrastructure component. By way of example, the following sections in this technical reference guide describe how to audit the following core business cycles:

• Revenue
• Inventory
• Expenditure

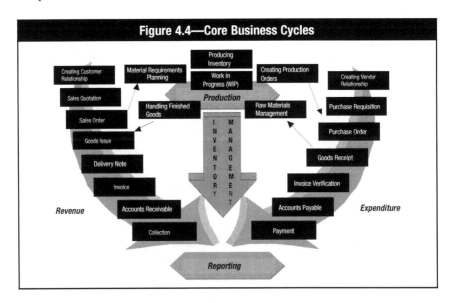

Figure 4.4—Core Business Cycles

The second overall component of the audit framework, as shown in **figure 4.2**, is called application infrastructure. It is referred to as Basis in an SAP ERP environment, and can be broken down into the major subcomponents identified in **figure 4.5**.

| Figure 4.5—Basis Subcomponents | |
|---|---|
| **Function** | **SAP ERP Tools and Utilities** |
| Installation | Implementation Guide and Organizational Model |
| Development | ABAP/4 Workbench and Transport System |
| Operation | Computer Center Management System |
| Security administration | Profile Generator |

Chapters 11 and 12 describe how to audit the SAP ERP Basis Application Infrastructure tools and utilities. The other major components of the control framework are discussed in chapters 2 and 3.

## Adopting a Risk-based Audit Approach

Having broken down the control framework into its components and subcomponents, a risk-based audit approach can be undertaken. (This guide assumes the adoption of a contemporary risk-based audit approach to the audit of the SAP ERP environment.) This may involve:
• Gaining an understanding
• Identifying the significant risks
• Determining key controls
• Testing those controls to confirm their adequacy

Techniques for gaining an understanding of the business process or function of the component or subcomponent under review include:
• Reviewing systems implementation or process documentation
• Interviewing implementers and others knowledgeable in the area
• Developing process flow diagrams and descriptions

Once an understanding of the area under review has been obtained, there are many techniques for identifying significant risks. Some techniques that may be employed include:
• Using a checklist approach (appendix E provides example checklists for risks and controls in the areas of core business cycles and Basis in chapters 6, 8, 9 and 12.)
• Using history or past experience (The risks included in this guide are based largely on past experience.)
• Determining objectives for the implementation and assessing potential or existing barriers
• Analyzing the requirements of legislation, policy or procedures
• Adopting and applying the COBIT framework
• Using a systems audit approach considering inputs, processing or calculations, and outputs

- Adopting a quality management perspective
- Performing a strategic analysis (e.g., strengths, weaknesses, opportunities and threats [SWOT] analysis or portfolio theory analysis)
- Questioning assumptions
- Assessing the needs of various stakeholders and the extent to which they are being met
- Evaluating hot spots (e.g., best and worst instances/stratified populations, key person dependencies, security issues, going concern or business continuity issues, integration or conversion difficulties, valuations, accountabilities and reconciliations)

Having identified the significant risks, key controls need to be determined. Determining the key controls involves:
- Understanding the controls culture of the enterprise (e.g., a just-enough-control philosophy consistent with the pursuit of an overall cost leadership position in the industry, or a belts-and-braces philosophy consistent with the pursuit of a position of differentiation based on image, product, distribution or service characteristics that need to be protected)
- Exercising judgment to determine the key controls in the process or function and whether the controls structure is adequate (Any weaknesses in the control structure need to be reported to executive management and resolved.)

There are four basic types of control in an ERP environment:
- Manual/procedural controls (such as report monitoring and manual reconciliations or approvals)
- Inherent controls (reliance on controls built into the operation of the system, e.g., edit and validation routines and certain password controls preventing the use of the last five passwords, passwords containing any three-character string contained in the user ID, and passwords beginning with three identical characters)
- Configuration controls (use of customizing options at installation or at a later time to control and direct processing operations in the system)
- Logical access controls (restriction of access to computer system functions based on the ERP and technical infrastructure security authorization techniques)

These key controls need to be tested to confirm they are operating effectively and as intended by management. The control testing techniques described in this guide focus on configurable controls and logical access security because:
- Manual controls are not unique to an ERP environment and testing techniques already have been covered in other forums and literature. However, remember that manual/procedural controls are necessary to complement the configurable and access controls in an ERP environment.
- Automated controls, such as inherent, configuration settings and logical access security, tend to be more pervasive in an ERP environment.
- Inherent controls are essentially built into the SAP ERP software and, therefore, do not require controls testing.

## Audit Information System

The Audit Information System (AIS) is a centrally organized location for the audit features and functions developed in SAP ERP. It can be used in all versions since 3.0D. Not all functions are available in each version since functionality is based on the release level. AIS does not provide any new SAP features; it merely consolidates and draws upon existing SAP information available within SAP standard transactions, tables and reports.

Until SAP Release 4.6C, AIS was invoked using a menu technique (transaction SECR). As of SAP Release 4.6, AIS is part of the SAP Standard System. As of SAP Release 4.6C (Support Package SAPKH46C27), the technical implementation of AIS in the program has been changed to a role-based maintenance environment (transaction PFCG). Additional development of AIS will be carried out only in this new environment. Furthermore, the transaction code SPRO may also be used to review business process configurations.

AIS is an auditing tool designed to improve the quality of an audit and rationalize the audit process.

AIS consists of an audit report tree structured around a range of auditing functions, including:
• Auditing procedures and documentation
• Auditing evaluations
• Downloading audit data

AIS is specifically targeted toward:
• External auditing
• Internal auditing/data protection
• Controlling
• System auditing

One of the primary objectives of AIS is to draw together all the tasks one would typically perform in an audit. These tasks have been assembled into an audit report tree. A user can drill down the tree structure to the specific task that needs to be performed. At the bottom level is a node that, when selected, usually runs a transaction code or report. These transaction codes/reports are mostly configurable to meet the user's needs. The tree is made up of two broad sections: system audit and business audit, as depicted in **figure 4.6**. The topics covered under each are:
• System audit
  − System configuration
  − Transport group
  − Repository/tables
  − Development/customizing
  − Background processing
  − System logs and status displays

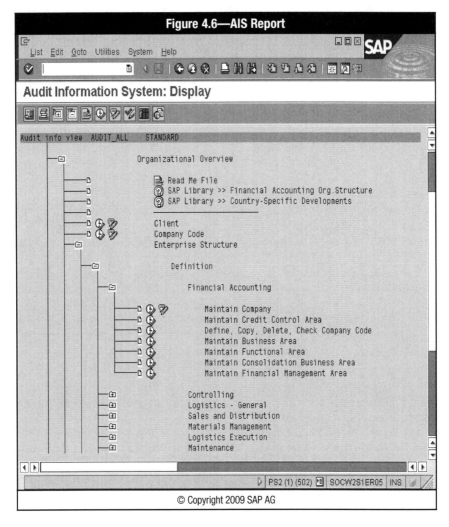

**Figure 4.6—AIS Report**

© Copyright 2009 SAP AG

- User administration
- Checklist according to security guidelines
- Checklist according to data protection guidelines
- Human resources audit/data protection audit
• Business audit
- Organizational overview
- Financial statement-oriented audit
- Process-oriented audit

Initially, the functionality of the FI/CO and Basis modules can be reviewed with the use of AIS. Many of the reports referenced previously in this guide for auditing security and other aspects of SAP ERP are available through the AIS tree structure. Auditors can define their own views with specific reports in the view.

Status analysis functionality and capabilities improve the ability of audit management to track tasks performed within SAP ERP by recording the:
• Percentage of completed audit steps for an audit objective, via traffic lights
• Percentage or actual number of steps completed for the audit
• Number of untested items
• Number of errors
• Number that passed the audit test

It also allows the creation of:
• Multiple views for a node
• Separate documentation for each node for each separate user review performed

To fully realize the value of AIS, enterprises may need to customize AIS to meet their needs. If so, documentation and standards should be developed and maintained. AIS maintains a central set of parameters or values (called variables). All AIS reports use these parameters when generating reports, e.g., company codes, number ranges and fiscal year. Parameter values can be manually overwritten. Enterprises must maintain these parameters in accordance with their audit needs. Custom variables may also be added. Variables, which may begin with AUDI*, are maintained in table TVARVC. Before using AIS, the auditor should review the TVARVC entries to ensure that report data will be relevant to the audit. This may also entail mapping those entries back to the enterprise's organizational model.

AIS can be configured and used to facilitate the audit of certain key areas on a continuing basis. However, users should be careful not to make the mistake of believing that once the standard reports in AIS are executed, that is all that is needed to review SAP ERP controls. A number of the controls outlined previously in this guide are not covered. There also may be an inherent assumption that the tables defined in SAP ERP to extract information for the reports are the correct tables and that all the correct information is being reported. This may not necessarily be the case, especially where reports have been customized. AIS does not eliminate the need for auditors to understand SAP ERP. Auditors should be aware that the security access that comes standard with AIS may be too lenient. They also should understand the implications of the reports they are running, both in terms of updates to data and performance overhead in the system. As part of the configuration and implementation of AIS, the access provided to users should be reviewed.

## SAP ERP Configuration Concept and Testing Configurable Controls
As with other application packages, configuration settings allow enterprises tremendous flexibility to customize and direct the operation and processing of SAP ERP software in their environment. The SAP ERP application programs read the configuration settings, and processing is directed accordingly. Configuration settings are stored in tables in the SAP ERP software. They may be field values

in a table (e.g., security parameters) or condition records (e.g., pricing condition records). Condition records are rows in a table arranged in a predefined logical sequence. In the case of pricing, each condition record is entered in the system using a condition type. This condition type determines whether the condition is a price, discount, tax or freight charge. The SAP ERP application programs interpret the condition records according to the predefined logical sequence to calculate the prices of goods or services.

Testing of configurable controls may be performed in three ways:
• Browsing table entries using transaction code SE16 or SE17 (e.g., table USR40 shows a list of passwords that are not allowed by the system)
• Executing transactions (e.g., transaction code SCC4 displays production client settings)
• Running reports using transaction SA38 (e.g., report RSPARAM for application security parameters)

## SAP ERP Security Authorization Concept
Within the SAP ERP software, the authorization concept provides for the protection of programs and data from unauthorized use. Access to the system is restricted through roles or authorization profiles. Roles are used to administer access using the Profile Generator, which is explained in chapter 11.

**Figure 4.7** shows how users are assigned roles (called activity groups in SAP ERP versions prior to 4.6C) or authorization profiles that determine the specific access a user is granted. With the exception of the default superuser ID SAP*, a user has no access to the SAP ERP software by default. Access must be explicitly granted by assignment to the user's master record. Only users with active user master records can log onto the system.

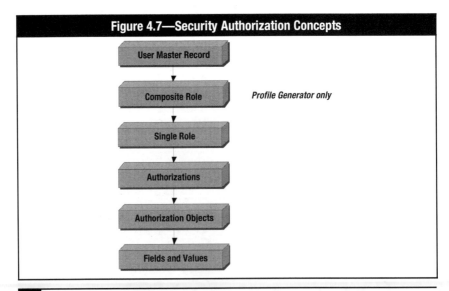

**Figure 4.7—Security Authorization Concepts**

User Master Record

Composite Role    *Profile Generator only*

Single Role

Authorizations

Authorization Objects

Fields and Values

A composite role generally equates to a job (e.g., accounts payable clerk, payroll manager, senior tax accountant, treasury analyst or distribution manager) or a role (e.g., journal entry creator, journal entry approver, payroll maintainer, invoice entry, recurring payment processor, personnel data reporter), or a single role may equate to a job task (e.g., create purchase order, release invoice, perform payment run).

Roles may be single (consisting of a number of authorizations) or composite (consisting of single roles and other composite roles). Each role is assigned a unique SAP ERP internal role number.

Authorization profiles are generated from the single role data maintained using the Profile Generator. The SAP ERP profiles are uniquely identified by a 10-character name.

Customized roles and profiles can begin with any letter; however, the roles delivered by SAP have the prefix SAP. Therefore, the SAP name space for customized user roles should not be used. SAP recommends that the names of custom-developed components start with a "Y" or a "Z" and has reserved those ranges for client customizations. The naming convention for customizations is consistent throughout SAP and therefore can be applied to programs, tables and transactions as well as to roles. When creating a customized role, the SAP standard role that most closely matches the required function should be copied (Z_*) as recommended by SAP, otherwise the standard role modified may be overwritten by a newly delivered standard role during a later upgrade or release change.[9] That way, the role name makes the source of the role immediately clear. For example, to create a customized role for clerks to post customer invoices and credit memos, the user copies the default role SAP_FI_AR_POST_ENTRIES to Z:FI_AR_POST_ENTRIES.

The SAP ERP software comes packaged with a number of predefined roles and profiles. These should be examined by enterprises to determine whether they are appropriate for use in their environment. Predefined roles, once populated with authorization values (e.g., create, change, display), may contain a greater level of system access than the enterprise desires its staff to possess.

Authorizations consist of authorization objects with specific fields and values, as shown in **figure 4.7**. Note that the description of security in this figure relates to role-based security. Users may also be assigned access using position-based security in the HR module.

Using position-based security, roles and authorization profiles are not normally assigned to user master records. Roles are assigned to positions, jobs or organizational units. Users are then assigned to positions, through the assignment of their user master record to the personnel ID and then to the position ID (using the authorization field infotype with value 0105 and field subtype with value 0001 in the HR master data with transaction PA30).

[9] http://help.sap.com/saphelp_nw70/helpdata/EN/52/6714b6439b11d1896f0000e8322d00/content.htm

Authorization objects are the basic building blocks of SAP ERP security, as shown in **figure 4.8**. An authorization object refers to one or more SAP ERP system elements to be protected. For example, a purchase order has an authorization object associated with it. Each authorization object consists of up to 10 authorization fields that represent a system element (e.g., company code, activity type). The SAP ERP software follows a naming convention for authorization objects, i.e., the first character denotes the module and the second character is an underscore. For example, the authorization object for company codes is F_BKPF_BUK. (A key field for this authorization object is BUKRS, which is an abbreviation of a German term that translates to "company codes.")

Authorization objects are grouped together in object classes. Object classes are organized in more or less the same way that modules are organized. To assign access to a specific program and data, an authorization value set is created for an authorization object. An authorization value set assigns permissible values to the fields of an authorization object and determines the authorized action for that object. For example, value 01 may be assigned for the create action, value 02 may be assigned for the change action, value 03 may be assigned for the display action, value 06 may be assigned for the delete action and value 05 for lock action.

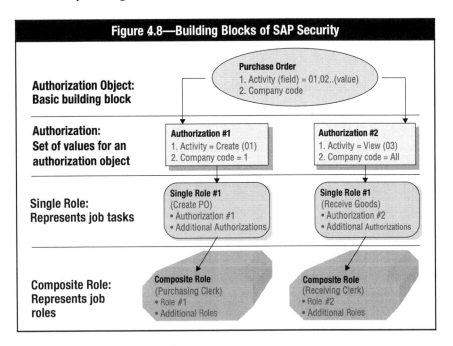

Figure 4.8—Building Blocks of SAP Security

**Figure 4.9** illustrates how purchase orders have an authorization object defined for them. The enterprise may then create authorization #1, which allows access to create purchase orders for company code #1. Authorization #2 may also be created.

Purchase orders can be viewed for all possible company codes (the ALL value is represented by an *, and auditors should consider this a signal that too much access may have been granted). Authorizations may continue to be created for all possible permutations of possible values for an authorization (note that an object may contain up to 10 fields, but usually contains between two and four). Users are allowed to perform a system function only if they have authorization access for every field in the authorization object. The validation against each field in the authorization object is performed with the logical AND operator. Enterprises may also use the logical OR operator to provide users with access to particular functions. This may be achieved by establishing several authorizations for the same authorization object (F_BKPF_BUK_1, F_BKPF_BUK_2 and so on), each with different values. Each of these authorizations (linked with the OR logic) may be assigned to a user master record. When the system checks the user's access privileges, it checks each authorization to determine whether the assigned values comply with the access condition. The system permits access with the first authorization that passes the check.

The SAP ERP software is shipped with a number of predefined authorizations. These may or may not be used in the enterprise's security framework, depending on its needs. Where the predefined authorizations are used, care should be taken because they may provide overly broad access. SAP ERP authorizations are identified uniquely by a 10-character name for authorizations generated using the profile generator and a 12-character name for manually generated authorizations.

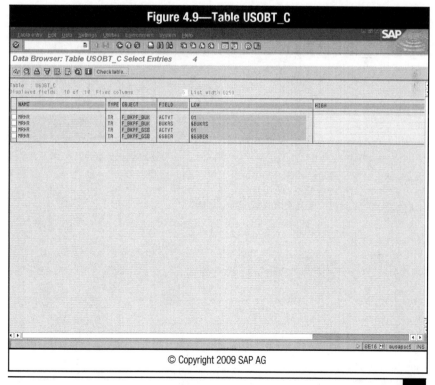

**Figure 4.9—Table USOBT_C**

SAP ERP default authorizations have an underscore in the second position. Authorization value sets by authorization object can be listed using table TACT using transaction code SE16.

## Testing SAP ERP Security

With SAP ERP software, it is important to test logical access to authorizations (i.e., authorization objects, fields and values), rather than simply preparing a matrix to which users have access to roles or authorization profiles. Although users may not have been explicitly granted access to a particular function through roles or authorization profiles, they may have been given access inadvertently through the combination of authorization objects, fields and values across the entire range of roles or authorization profiles assigned to them.

As described earlier with the SAP ERP authorization concept, the SAP ERP software checks the authorization requirements of the transaction being executed against all of the authorizations assigned to a user and permits execution to continue as soon as it finds a match.

It is not uncommon for roles and authorization profiles to be built initially with broad access (e.g., by using the value * or ALL as a field value in an authorization) to minimize disruption to operations during the initial implementation. For this reason, it is important to test access to the SAP ERP software at the authorization level, rather than at the level of role or authorization profile assignment.

Tools that can be used for automated security analysis of SAP ERP are discussed in chapter 13.

# Case Study

To more fully explain this concept and the steps necessary to test logical access security in the SAP ERP software, a case study involving testing access for a particular transaction is presented.

## Step 1: Identify High-risk Transactions

The auditor can identify transactions viewed as high risk through a combination of interviews with business management, questionnaires, a review of process flow and security documentation, and the auditor's knowledge of the business, the SAP ERP software and related risks.

Also, it may be useful to obtain an organization chart of employees within the department under review. Using this listing, the auditor can determine what transactions key users have executed within the past three months (using program RSSTAT10 or transactions ST03 and ST03N). This frequently provides insight as to the real transaction use by key business roles within the company. It may also uncover SAP ERP or customized transactions with which the auditor is not familiar, or which have not been uncovered through previous inquiries. For instance, there are two SAP ERP transactions that can be used to input an invoice into the SAP ERP software (F-43, FB10 and MIRO).

The comprehensive listing of all transactions generated by department is very useful if, for example, the F-43 Enter Invoice transaction code has been deemed to be high risk.

## *Step 2: Identify Relevant Authorizations*
A number of methods may be employed to identify the necessary authorizations, although the degrees of accuracy may vary:
1. Security documentation—If security has been sufficiently documented, the project team may have captured all the relevant authorizations in the course of the security implementation. When relying on security documentation, the auditor should consider corroborating with at least two members of IT and security management to ensure that the documentation has been maintained accurately and is up to date. Results should also be confirmed with management. Assessing access based on the roles created by the enterprise is unlikely to yield accurate results. Since the roles may have been created with authorizations that provide excessive access or through the combination of roles, users may have inadvertently been provided with access to functions contrary to management's intentions.
2. Direct extraction of the information from the SAP ERP system—Transaction code SU24 can be used to display the information or transaction code SE16 can be used to view the contents of table USOBT_C for the selected transactions. In the example in **figure 4.9**, this may yield the authorizations in **figure 4.10**.

| Figure 4.10—Example Transaction Authorizations | | |
|---|---|---|
| Object | Field | Value |
| F_BKPF_BUP | ACTVT | 01 |
| F_BKPF_BUP | BUKRS | $BUKRS |
| F_BKPF_GSB | ACTVT | 01 |
| F_BKPF_GSB | GSBER | $GSBER |

The previous authorizations are the standard SAP ERP authorizations from table USOBT. $BUKRS and $GSBER represent variables that must be tailored during profile generation or built to the enterprise's specific company codes and business areas. Table USOBT should be copied during the implementation to create the table USOBT_C (the C indicating customer), which should hold the authorizations created at implementation.

USOBT_C gives some guidance as to the minimum range of values required. Others may need to come from the scope of the audit and the relevant organization units (e.g., company codes, plants, sales organizations). The auditor needs to decide, for example, if access to all company codes, any company codes or particular company codes is of interest or concern and include the appropriate values during testing.

The authorization object for transaction code has been included as a mandatory authorization object in releases 3.0E and higher. It may not be required to access particular functions in releases before 3.0E. Assuming a more recent release, the following authorization must be added to the list for the transaction code:

| Object | Field | Value |
|--------|-------|-------|
| S_TCODE | TCODE | F-43 |

Auditors should be careful in situations where SAP ERP template transactions are used, e.g., a government template. In these situations, a customized transaction such as YE21 may be established to create a purchase order. The transaction performs particular functions, such as recording details of expenditure for the Government Gazette, and then calls the standard SAP transaction (ME21 or ME21N) to create a purchase order. In these circumstances, users may raise a purchase order if they have access to ME21 alone, irrespective of whether they also have access to YE21. Both transaction values need to be tested.

The standard SAP ERP authorizations contained in table USOBT_C are used by the Profile Generator when it generates authorizations; however, the generated profiles need to be tailored to add particular values relevant to the enterprise.

A general risk or concern is that the USOBT or USOBT_C tables may not be accurately maintained and may not reflect the actual authorizations in use and required to perform audit testing.

3. System trace—This approach involves executing transaction code ST01 to perform a system trace of the required authorizations. It requires access to perform the actual transactions in a nonproduction environment that is configured the same as in production, such as the test or quality assurance (QA) systems. The environment must have enough master and transactional data to permit the execution of transactions as they would occur in production. A significant amount of business process knowledge is required to successfully process all components within the transaction (i.e., valid combinations of G/L account, company code or business area). All of the relevant steps of the transaction must be executed, or key authority check statements in the underlying ABAP/4 code may not be properly identified.

Another approach involves generating a new user with no authorizations on the test or QA system, then adding the required transaction code for the function to be tested to the user's master record. The auditor should try to execute the transaction with particular combinations, and, when it fails, note the authorization objects, fields and values required. He/she can then update the user's master record to include the required authorizations, and cycle back through the test until the transaction can be completed. This approach may be used where trace facilities have not been set up and the auditor is proficient with the SAP ERP security tools. In the example given, this may yield the authorizations shown in **figure 4.11**.

| Figure 4.11—Example of Authorization Objects | | |
|---|---|---|
| **Object** | **Field** | **Value** |
| F_BKPF_BUK | ACTVT | 01 |
| F_BKPF_BUK | BUKRS | $BUKRS |
| F_BKPF_GSB | ACTVT | 01 |
| F_BKPF_GSB | GSBER | #GSBER |
| F_FICA_CTR | FM_AUTHACT | 10 |
| F_FICA_CTR | FM_FICTR | $FM_FICTR |
| F_FICA_CTR | FM_FICRS | $FM_FICRS |
| F_FICA_FKR | FM_AUTHACT | 10 |
| F_FICA_FKR | FM_FICTR | $FM_FICTR |
| F_FICA_FPS | FM_AUTHACT | 10 |
| F_FICA_FPS | FM_AUTHDAY | $FM_AUTHDAY |
| F_FICA_FPS | FM_FICRS | $FM_FICRS |
| F_FICA_FPS | FM_FIPOS | $FM_FIPOS |
| S_TCODE | TCODE | F-43 |

While this approach may be difficult to execute, it may yield the most accurate results. Several additional authorization objects relating to financial centers have been identified during the execution of the trace in this example. Without these objects, a user would not be able to execute the transaction under review. Testing and reporting based on the contents of table USOBT_C in this example may have yielded vastly incorrect results for this particular enterprise.

The auditor should exercise judgment in the situation under review to determine the appropriate authorizations for testing.

## *Step 3: Determine Which Users Have Access to the Relevant Authorizations*

To determine which users have access to the relevant authorizations, a number of methods with varying degrees of accuracy may be employed, including:

1. Execution of transaction code SUIM ▷ Users ▷ Users according to complex selection criteria (transaction code S_BCE_68001417), also accessible through the program RSUSR002 via the transaction SA38—This report, as shown in **figure 4.12**, allows the user to specify a transaction code, a "valid to" date for users and up to three other authorization objects (which also may be the authorization object for transaction codes S_TCODE) with associated values (two values under an AND relationship and three values under an OR relationship). The program can be executed in the live environment and online if needed. The provided example has one transaction and five authorization objects so the report would have to be executed twice and the results downloaded to a spreadsheet or database application, where a routine could be written to combine user IDs appearing on both lists (the correct outcome for the test). This report is generally sufficient for testing logical access security in relation to SAP ERP application infrastructure areas, but it is less suitable where large numbers of authorizations need to be reviewed, such as in segregation of duties analysis and in some of the more complex areas of business cycle controls.

2. As a more long-term solution, an enterprise may choose to configure its own rules to determine which users have access to the relevant authorizations and perform segregation of duties analysis, as opposed to the one-off tests described above.

   Execution of transaction code SUIM ▷ Users ▷ With Critical Authorizations (also accessible with program RSUSR008_009_NEW, which replaces programs RSUSR008, RSUSR009 and transaction codes SU98/SU99, for SAP Web AS 6.20 onwards). This transaction code offers improvements such as allowing differentiation between SAP defaults for critical data for different business areas, extended combination options for critical authorization data, improved performance, display of user filters, and more analysis options for users in the result list.[10] Furthermore, this program can be configured to provide segregation of duties risk management, also provided by the SAP Access Control tool, Risk Analysis and Remediation (RAR). For further information on the SAP Access Control tool, RAR, see chapter 13.
   – Critical Authorizations Report—Identifies the list of users with critical authorizations. As shown in **figure 4.13**, critical authorizations that are being reviewed (includes the associated transaction codes and objects) are loaded into a customizable table by a user-defined Authorization ID.

---

[10] *http://help.sap.com/erp2005_ehp_04/helpdata/EN/0e/4f8f40f3b19920e10000000a1550b0/frameset.htm*

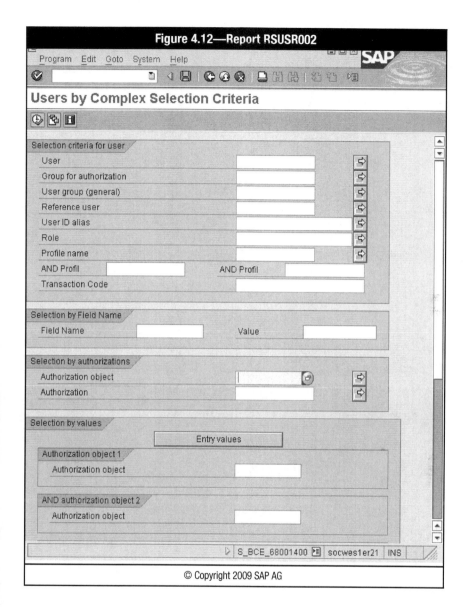

Figure 4.12—Report RSUSR002

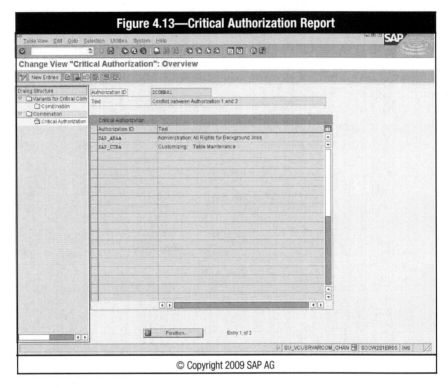

**Figure 4.13—Critical Authorization Report**

© Copyright 2009 SAP AG

– Critical Combinations Report—Identifies users with access to combinations of authorizations that may present a segregation of duties risk. As shown in **figure 4.14**, critical combinations that are being reviewed are loaded into a customizable table by a user-defined combination of two or more Authorization ID (which are required to be created as described in the previous section).

The tables populated by the user are defined as customizing tables, effectively requiring the user to populate the table in a development environment and promote the data to production in accordance with the company's change control methodologies.

3. Download of security tables and direct query of results—This approach involves downloading the required security data (using transaction SE16) and evaluating the result offline. As a guide, the following SAP ERP tables may contain the basic information required for this approach:
   • USR02—User details
   • AGR_1250 and AGR_1251—Authorization data for the roles
   • AGR_AGRS—Roles in composite roles
   • AGR_USERS—Assignment of roles to users

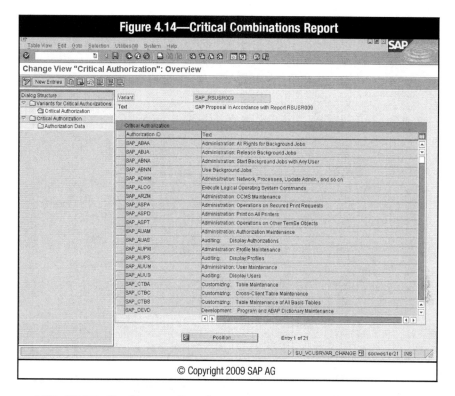

Figure 4.14—Critical Combinations Report

- AGR_PROF—Profile name for roles
- UST04—User names to profiles
- UST10C—Composite profiles
- UST10S—Single profiles
- UST12—Authorization values
- V_USERNAME—Affected users

The parent/child relationship that exists between the UST10C and UST10S tables may be difficult to interrogate. It may be possible to use one of the many widely available third-party reporting packages to prelink the required fields and extract the information from both tables at the same time. The auditor needs to confirm the feasibility of using these tools with the respective suppliers. Alternatively, ABAP/4 programs in the SAP ERP software, spreadsheet or database programs may be written to determine the interrelationships between the two tables and extract the required role, profile and authorization data. Once the information is extracted, it may be loaded into third-party reporting tools for analysis.

With a list of users who have the authorization objects and values necessary to execute the transaction, the auditor can use table USR02 to filter out users whose user IDs have been locked or whose "valid to" date is past. It may also be useful to filter out any nondialog users, depending on the scope of the audit.

Alternatively, the analysis can be subcontracted to a third party that has an in-house tool and is willing to contract for its use.

## Step 4: Evaluate the Business Impact of Findings

The auditor can download from the SAP ERP software the information for all invoice documents within the previous six months using table BKPF, which identifies the document number, the transaction code and the user ID that created it. The results can be summarized based on user ID and transaction code F-43, and compared to the list of users who can execute F-43 per the analysis in step 3. This allows the auditor to compare the percentage of users who can execute the transaction to those who have actually made use of the ability. This can be a powerful argument in illustrating the need for tighter security. A similar approach can be taken to most transactions under review.

## Testing Segregation of Duties/Excessive Access

Traditional systems of internal control have relied on assigning certain responsibilities to different individuals or segregating incompatible functions. Such segregation of duties is intended to prevent one person from having both access to assets and responsibility for maintaining the accountability for such assets. For instance, in an inventory management system, different individuals are typically responsible for duties such as:
• Initiating or requesting a purchase
• Placing and inputting purchase orders
• Receiving goods
• Ensuring custody of inventories
• Maintaining inventory records and/or authorizing adjustments to costs or quantities, including authorizing disposal or scrapping
• Making changes to inventory master files
• Performing independent inventory counts
• Following up on inventory count discrepancies
• Authorizing production requests and/or materials transfers
• Receiving/transferring goods into/from manufacturing
• Shipping goods

Physical counts of inventory should be performed by someone independent of custody of inventory and with no access to inventory records. An individual who is independent of the custody and recording of inventory should follow up on discrepancies noted in the comparison of the counts to inventory records. If one individual has responsibility for more than one of these functions, that individual could misappropriate assets and conceal the misappropriation. If one individual has the ability to process sales orders and access the inventory management master files, that person could modify product selling prices and process unauthorized sales. Legacy system environments necessitated and facilitated the segregation of duties because of the predominantly manual control framework surrounding them. The fragmentation of legacy systems also facilitated the segregation of duties since purchasing systems, warehousing systems and general ledger systems all were separate.

This traditional notion of segregation of duties needs to be refined in a fully automated SAP ERP environment. ERP systems have shifted the emphasis to user empowerment, enabling users to have access across business functions or, alternatively, to handle physical assets and record their movements directly into the computing and accounting system. As shown earlier in this guide, along with this transition, controls have moved up front in the process and have become increasingly more automated with online release, automated matching of transactions, increased integration, etc. The notion of the good business practice of the segregation of duties control needs to be developed to include a risk management perspective and a trade-off or balance between functional access and security in the new ERP environment. The ERP environment should be assessed from a risk and controls perspective. Key control steps should be modeled for each business process in the enterprise and appropriate trade-offs made between empowerment and the need to minimize the risk of fraud or unauthorized transactions. In the model of the Expenditure cycle, as shown in **figure 4.15**, a goods receipt is considered in the same way as an invoice approval, since it is the entry of a goods receipt that in many cases completes the matching process and gives rise to an authorized payment.

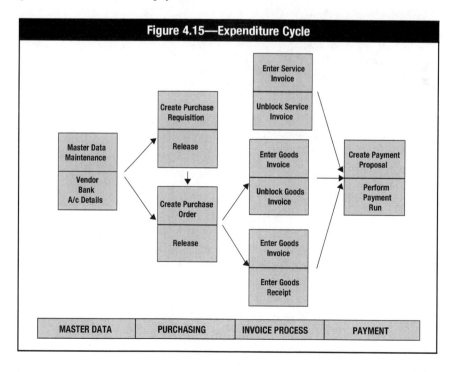

Figure 4.15—Expenditure Cycle

Any user who has access to a single step in the process may be considered to present a low risk from a segregation of duties perspective (i.e., the individual must collude to effect a fraudulent or unauthorized transaction). Any user who has access to two steps in the control model may be considered a medium risk from a segregation of duties perspective (i.e., the individual must influence at least one other to effect a fraudulent or unauthorized transaction). Any user who has access to three steps in the control model may be considered a high risk from a segregation of duties perspective (i.e., the individual can most likely effect a fraudulent or unauthorized transaction that may go undetected, at least for some time). Two examples of a high-risk situation are:

• Users with access to maintain master data and the ability to enter a service invoice and unblock it can make a payment to themselves.
• Users who can enter and release a purchase order and perform a goods receipt can misappropriate goods.

Specific techniques for testing automated controls (i.e., access security and configurable controls) in the SAP ERP software are described in chapters 6, 8, 10 and 12, which focus on testing the SAP ERP core business cycles and SAP ERP Basis Application Infrastructure while segregation of duties tools for SAP ERP are discussed in the above step 3 as well as in chapter 13. Depending on the level of risk and the amount of testing required, audit testing rotation plans may be established for each of the components or subcomponents of the audit framework.

In each of the business cycles, this guide:

• Describes the functionality of the SAP ERP business process and its subprocesses from a controls or operational audit perspective
• Identifies specific risks
• Outlines potential automated controls
• Suggests sample assurance techniques

Risks and controls vary among enterprises depending on external and internal factors, the configuration and the release in use for the SAP ERP system. In particular, this guide does not attempt to comprehensively address legal and regulatory compliance risks for any jurisdiction. The primary focus for controls is on automated controls that are unique to an ERP or the SAP ERP environment. Auditors should already be familiar with manual controls, such as reconciliations, manual approvals and dual signatories. Specific assurance techniques vary from enterprise to enterprise depending on the extent of customization, specific configuration options selected and whether automated diagnostics such as the SAP ERP Audit Information System are used. Therefore, the techniques do not necessarily include prescriptive lists of specific SAP ERP transaction codes, authorization objects, or fields and values, but rather provide a sample toolset for use or reference as appropriate in the reader's organizational environment.

Note that "customize" and "customization" in this guide are general terms that refer to the tailoring of an SAP ERP environment to suit the customer's specific needs by way of configuration, modification or additional development of tables or programs.

## Numbering Sequence for Risks, Controls and Testing Techniques

Because there may be more than one control per risk, a numbering sequence for risks, controls and testing techniques has been adopted throughout each of the chapters dealing with the auditing of core business cycles or the Basis Application Infrastructure, as shown in **figure 4.16**.

| Figure 4.16—Numbering Sequence for Risks, Controls and Testing Techniques ||
| Number | Description |
| --- | --- |
| **Risks** ||
| 1.1 | Risk number 1 for the first subprocess |
| 1.2 | Risk number 2 for the first subprocess |
| 2.1 | Risk number 1 for the second subprocess |
| **Controls** ||
| 1.1.1 | Control number 1 for risk number 1 of the first subprocess |
| 1.1.2 | Control number 2 for risk number 1 of the first subprocess |
| 1.2.1 | Control number 1 for risk number 2 of the first subprocess |
| 2.1.1 | Control number 1 for risk number 1 of the second subprocess |
| **Testing Techniques** ||
| 1.1.1 | Testing technique for control number 1 for risk number 1 of the first subprocess |
| 1.1.2 | Testing technique for control number 2 for risk number 1 of the first subprocess |
| 1.2.1 | Testing technique for control number 1 for risk number 2 of the first subprocess |
| 2.1.1 | Testing technique for control number 1 for risk number 1 of the second subprocess |

In this way, the relationship among risks, controls and testing techniques for subprocesses (such as master data maintenance, sales order processing and invoicing) should be evident as the reader progresses through each of the chapters dealing with auditing the core business cycles and Basis Application Infrastructure.

When control issues are identified, the auditor should attempt to uncover and report to management the causes of the problem, together with recommendations. In this respect, CoBiT 4.1 helps meet the multiple needs of management by bridging the gaps among business risks, control needs and technical issues. CoBiT provides good practices across a domain and process framework and presents activities in a manageable and logical structure. COBIT's good practices provide a measure to judge against when things do go wrong and can assist in identifying the causes of problems.

The COBIT framework consists of the following four domains illustrated in **figure 4.17**:

• Plan and Organize (PO)
• Acquire and Implement (AI)
• Deliver and Support (DS)
• Monitor and Evaluate (ME)

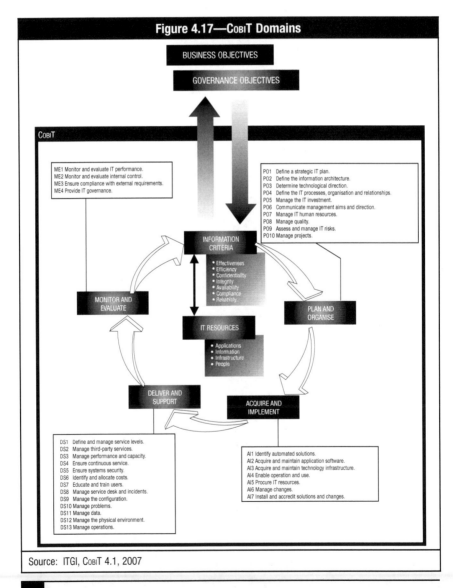

**Figure 4.17—CoBiT Domains**

Source: ITGI, COBIT 4.1, 2007

Some of the processes contained within these domains that are of particular relevance when assessing ERP systems include:
• AI6 *Manage changes*
• DS5 *Ensure systems security*
• DS9 *Manage the configuration*
• DS11 *Manage data*

## Summary

This chapter looked at the audit impacts arising from the implementation of an ERP system (e.g., changes to audit methodologies) and recommended an SAP ERP audit framework (including, for example, business processes and application security). The chapter detailed the steps involved in taking a risk-based audit approach to ERP, including a description of key concepts (e.g., authorization and configuration) and methods of testing configurable controls, access security and segregation of duties. Finally, the relationship between the recommended SAP ERP audit framework and CoBiT 4.1 methodology was discussed, including its usefulness in identifying the causes of control breakdowns.

# 5. SAP ERP Revenue Business Cycle

This chapter outlines the functionality of the SAP ERP Revenue business cycle to provide the reader with a high-level understanding of the process. From a risk and controls perspective, the Revenue cycle has four main subprocesses, shown in **figure 5.1**:
• Master data maintenance
• Sales order processing
• Shipping, invoicing, returns and adjustments
• Collecting and processing cash receipts

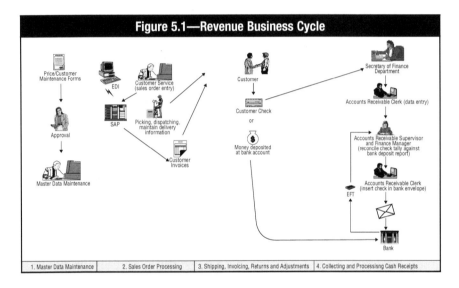

Figure 5.1—Revenue Business Cycle

| 1. Master Data Maintenance | 2. Sales Order Processing | 3. Shipping, Invoicing, Returns and Adjustments | 4. Collecting and Processisng Cash Receipts |

## Master Data Maintenance

There are three main types of master data employed in the Revenue cycle:
• Customer master data
• Material master data (shared with the Procurement, Inventory, Management and Expenditure cycles)
• Pricing master data

Customer master data are the general data (e.g., name, address), sales data (e.g., sales organization, distribution channel) and financial data (e.g., bank information, insurance, credit limit). Account numbers are assigned to customers to uniquely identify them in the system. Further, customers may be assigned account identifiers within a range to signify whether the customer is internal (e.g., may be used for promotions or intercompany accounts) or external (e.g., commercial customers paying wholesale or retail prices that are subject to credit checking).

Material master data are the general data (e.g., product units of measures), purchasing data (e.g., purchasing group, order unit relating to the Inventory Management and Expenditure cycles), accounting data (e.g., current price, pricing unit) and sales data (e.g., minimum quantities, sales status) of material. Customer and material master data can be created/maintained on either a centralized or a decentralized basis for the finance and logistics areas (e.g., credit limit information maintained in finance and general data maintained by customer service or sales). However, for data integrity and to avoid data duplication, having a centralized group maintaining the master records is a better option.

Pricing master data are used for pricing sales orders and can be extremely complex. For example, a unit may have a base price and a price for the duration of a promotion. The material may be a member of a price group, which also is subject to a surcharge or a discount. Some material may have to be priced to reflect exchange rates. A particular customer may get discounts or the quantity ordered may trigger more discounts. Payment in advance may generate a rebate.

The price a customer has to pay for a certain product is not only determined by the price of the specific product (i.e., current price of a material item) but, as indicated, also may contain discounts, surcharges, bonus elements, freight charges, value-added tax (VAT), etc. These elements that make up a price are called conditions and are defined during implementation. The way the price for a customer is determined is defined in a calculation schema. This schema consists of a number of condition records, each containing a condition type and a code consisting of four characters. As an example, a simple scheme has been outlined in **figure 5.2**.

| Figure 5.2—Example Price Conditions | | | | |
|---|---|---|---|---|
| **Condition** | **Description** | **Rate** | **Times** | **Value** |
| PR00 | Price | 100 per piece | 10 pieces | 1000 |
| | | | | — |
| Gross Price | | | | 1000 |
| DC00 | Discount | 10% | | 100 |
| SC00 | Surcharge | 20% | | 200 |
| | | | | — |
| Net Price | | | | 1100 |
| Services Federal Tax Administration | VAT | 20% | | 220 |
| | | | | — |
| Actual Price | | | | 1320 |

The calculation schema is basically an elaborate spreadsheet. Conditions in the sheet can be summarized or kept in subtotals. In this example, the PR00 condition multiplies the standard price of the product by the quantity of material to derive the first subtotal, the gross price. Other conditions then can use this subtotal as the basis for their calculation. The DC00 (discount) and SC00 (surcharge) conditions were not based on the value of the previous calculation but on the gross price to get the net price. Similarly, the service federal tax administration (VAT) condition was based on the net price. The last row is the actual price to be invoiced after applying the four conditions.

In the sheet, it also is possible to enter numbers representing programs that calculate either the basis for a condition or the actual value. Normally, however, the value of a condition is not determined by a user program but rather by the use of a condition technique. This technique defines the sequence in which the SAP ERP system searches the database for a valid record containing the value for the condition. As an example, the standard SAP ERP system configuration for the determination of the gross price is as follows:
• First, try to find a price for the combination of the sold-to party and the material entered. This is a customer-specific price.
• If not found, try to find the price using the price list type of the sold-to party, the material entered, and try to find this in the currency that belongs to the document. This is the currency specified at the sold-to party.
• If not found, use the same search but now use the currency of the company selling the product.
• If not found, try to find the price using only the material as a search term. This would be the most general price available.

If this sequence of searching the database still does not provide the gross price, the standard SAP ERP settings will generate a message, stating that the mandatory condition PR00 has not been found. This is called the access sequence.

For each condition in the calculation schema the database is searched in the way described in the access sequence attached to the condition. If no access sequence has been assigned to the condition, this indicates that the user may manually enter the condition value.

## Sales Order Processing

Sales-related business transactions are recorded in the system as sales documents. There are four broad groupings of sales documents, as shown in **figure 5.3**:
• Sales queries (inquiries and quotes)
• Sales orders (cash sale, credit sale, promotional goods order)
• Outline agreements (contracts and scheduling agreements)
• Customer problems (complaints and returns)

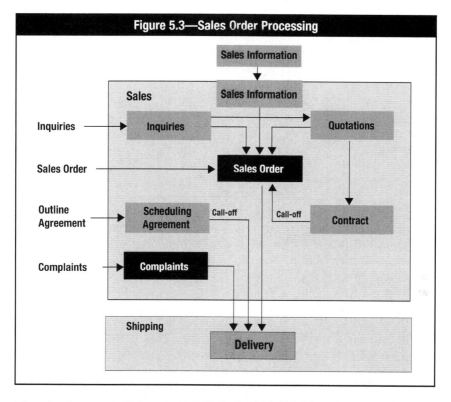

Figure 5.3—Sales Order Processing

The sales documents that are created are individual documents; however, they form part of a chain of interrelated documents. The data flow from one document into another, reducing manual activity and making problem resolution easier. Sales document types can be configured to distinguish among the different types of sales (e.g., cash sale, credit sale, rush order, promotional order). For each sales document type, copying controls can be configured to designate the type of sales document that can be copied into another sales document, delivery document or billing document. For instance, a sales quotation can be copied into a sales order. Additionally, the document type can be configured to require reference to a preceding document (mandatory referencing).

Sales document types can be configured to search for duplicate customer orders and existing contracts for customer or material (this check works only if all fields are identical). Depending on the configuration, the system will issue either a warning message or an error message when duplicates are detected. A sales order is a contract with the customer to supply products at an agreed-upon price, quantity, time and location. The primary input consists of the customer master number, customer account, product identification, quantity, delivery due date and delivery address. Sales orders are generated in the SD module and use information from the material master data (shared with the MM, PP, and FI/CO modules) and the customer master data (shared with FI/CO modules).

Sales orders provide the data used for the preparation of production orders, picking lists, delivery documents, etc., and thereby minimize the keying effort. Sales orders may be generated from:
• Sales queries, a customer inquiry or quotation (The system copies captured details to the sales order.)
• Processing a customer's purchase order
• Releasing orders against a contract or scheduling agreement
• Selected items from a product proposal (i.e., a list of products used frequently by the customer that serves as a reference)
• Copying an existing sales order
• Customer problems and complaints

When an order is created, a number of functions can occur, including:
• Determining or copying the price from a prior quotation or agreement
• Checking the customer's credit
• Checking the material for availability
• Updating sales forecasting data

The first two points are described in more detail in the following paragraphs.

The SD module can automatically carry out pricing, using predefined prices, surcharges and discounts. Depending on the configuration of the system, the price proposed by the system can be overridden or price tolerance limits may be set. Pricing is applied to quotations, sales orders and billing documents via condition records (as described previously in the section on master data) which make up a predefined logical sequence of criteria used by the system to determine the price. The system follows these conditions and calculates a price. The user and the customer can get details regarding how the price was generated. Once the price has been determined, it will flow through to the other sales documents, such as the billing document.

Credit checks can be performed at most stages throughout the sales process depending on the enterprise's needs. They can be performed at the sales order, delivery note or picking slip stage. Using the credit status, the creation of material reservations, purchase requisitions, production/planned orders, delivery due indices and deliveries can be blocked. Picking, packing, posting goods issue and printing delivery notes can also be blocked.

A number of credit checks can be defined, including, for example, maximum document value, static credit limit check and user-defined checks. The scope of a credit check can be defined for any valid combination of a credit control area (CCA), risk category or document credit group.

CCAs are used to manage credit and can be adapted for centralized or decentralized credit management, depending on the enterprise's requirements. One CCA can be defined for the entire enterprise, for each company code or for groups of company codes. For example, the enterprise sells to company A in the western region (WR) and the eastern region (ER). Company A has US $1 million in credit in both the WR and the ER. However, the enterprise wants to limit national exposure to company A to US $1.5 million. The enterprise could set up a CCA for the WR and the ER and limit company A's credit in that CCA to US $1.5 million. A CCA cannot span two SAP ERP clients. Credit master data are stored at the CCA level and can be maintained for one customer in multiple CCAs, if necessary.

Risk categories can be defined and assigned to individual customers along with specific credit limits in accordance with an enterprise's credit policy. In addition, credit groups for document types, known as document credit groups, can be defined. Document credit groups combine order types and delivery types for credit control purposes. Whether the system reacts with an error (processing stops) or a warning (the user can override it) can be defined for each checking rule. In the case of a warning, the system automatically enters a credit status in the document and saves the document.

The result of a credit check is described in the status text. It will say, for example, if the document was blocked because the customer's credit limit was exceeded. Depending on the requirements specified, the document can be blocked from further processing or released by persons with the appropriate access authority.

Credit holds can be cleared by a credit representative. A representative is assigned to a credit representative group and can be authorized to process credit holds for a customer up to a certain level within the customer's credit limit, e.g., junior staff can process a credit hold arising from a maximum value for an individual order where the amount of the order is up to 80 percent of a customer's credit limit, senior staff can process up to 100 percent and credit management approval is required where the individual order exceeds the customer's credit limit.

Document value classes enable the enterprise to authorize credit representatives to process documents up to a certain value. Different classes are defined to reflect the ranges of document value that occur in the enterprise's business. Particular credit representatives can then be assigned to particular document value classes, e.g., up to US $1,000.

## Shipping, Invoicing, Returns and Adjustments

SAP monitors dates of orders that are due for delivery. Material is due for shipping when the material availability date is reached or when the transportation scheduling date is reached. Once material is due for shipping, the delivery is prepared and processed, and the delivery is sent for picking.

The picking function is based on the delivery note created by the system from an order and is linked to the warehouse management system (WMS). The delivery note is the primary shipping document. Copying controls can be configured to designate the type of sales document that can or must be copied into a delivery document. A delivery can refer to a sales order or a stock transfer, or it can have no reference. A delivery uses data from the sales order and adds further information needed for the picking list. The delivery note can be created automatically or manually. After the goods have been picked, they are packed for shipping.

Delivery documents are assigned to sales areas to allow for different controls to be put in place for different organizational units within an enterprise. Under-delivery and over-delivery tolerances can be configured in the system. Minimum delivery quantities are specified in either the material master record or the customer material information record and are copied into the sales order. Under-delivery tolerances are specified as a percentage of the delivery quantity. If the quantity to be delivered is below the tolerance, a warning message is displayed. Over-delivery tolerances are input in the sales order directly, or copied from the customer material information record. These are copied to the item details screen in the delivery document. Delivery document types can be configured to verify tolerance limits, perform availability checks or require referencing to an existing sales document. Depending on configuration, the system will issue a warning message, error message or no message.

Goods issue occurs when the picked goods are loaded onto the transport vehicle and leave the company. Effective transportation planning ensures that shipments are dispatched without delay, shipments arrive on schedule and transport costs are minimized. Data required for the goods issue document and posting are copied from the delivery note. The goods issue document cannot be changed. This helps ensure that the actual quantity delivered is invoiced. After goods issue posting, only very limited changes can be made to the delivery. Goods issue can be posted for a delivery only if the following prerequisites are fulfilled:
- The data in the delivery must be complete. For example, the storage location, batch and valuation type are specified in the delivery.
- Picking must have been completed for all items in the delivery. This means that goods issue can be posted only for the picked quantity. Posting can occur on a line-item basis.
- If a delivery item was picked in warehouse management system MM-WM, the item must have the status set at Completed in MM-WM. For this status to be assigned, all transfer orders for the delivery must have been confirmed.

Goods issue posting creates a material document and an accounting document. It does not impact sales or revenue accounts. This is an audit consideration because it suggests that goods could be issued but sales may not be realized, thereby understating sales. As part of an audit, goods issued but not billed should be reviewed; a goods issue posting credits inventory and debits cost of goods sold. Revenues are not posted until a bill is created.

Should goods be returned or complaints received, the following sales documents are available for recording and processing such occurrences:

- Returns—Used for processing the return of damaged goods delivered to a customer or goods sent to a customer on a trial basis
- Free of charge deliveries—Used when the customer wants the goods to be replaced. In this case, reference is made to the return if the customer returns the goods, or to a sales order if the goods are not returned.
- Credit memo request—Used when the customer wants the corresponding amount to be refunded. In this case, reference is made to the return if the customer returns the goods, or to a sales order if the goods are not returned.
- Debit memo requests—May be used if the customer advises that additional goods were received

The billing functions include:
- Issuing invoices, credit and debit memos
- Canceling billing transactions
- Issuing rebates
- Transferring billing data to the Financial Accounting (FI) module

Invoices and other billing documents can be created selectively or based on a schedule. They can refer to a sales order or a delivery or combine several deliveries into one invoice.

If no errors occur in the billing run, the billing documents are created. When a billing document is created, the system transfers billing data to FI and updates:
- Accounting entries for sales, revenue and tax accounts
- The billing document status in all related sales, deliveries and billing documents
- The credit account of the customer
- Sales statistics in the sales information system
- Controlling elements, such as profitability analysis and profit center invoices

Billing documents may be created in the following ways:
- Explicitly specifying documents
- Processing a billing due list
- Specifying a billing schedule

There are two special numbers in the billing document header:
- The reference number in the accounting document header
- The allocation number in the customer line item

The reference number can be the customer's business transaction number or the purchase order (PO) number. This number can be used as a search criterion for changing or displaying the accounting document. The reference number can be printed in all business correspondence instead of the accounting document number.

The allocation number provides additional information in the customer line item of the accounting document. The account line items are sorted and displayed according to the allocation number.

The billing function (specifically, the creation of billing documents such as invoices and credit memos) can be performed directly within the FI module as a journal entry. Creating billing documents through the FI module bypasses the controls inherent in the sales and distribution cycle; therefore, access to this function should be restricted appropriately.

Any subsequent documents that relate to the invoice, such as a cancellation document or credit/debit memo, will have the same reference and/or allocation number. In this way, the system can view these documents as belonging to a single business transaction. When customizing for sales, the following can be used as reference or allocation numbers: the customer's PO number, sales order number, delivery number, external delivery number or billing document number of the invoice. Billing and allocation numbers can be entered manually or by the system. Costs and revenues associated with billing may be posted to:
• Customer accounts receivable
• A cash clearing account
• Revenue
• Sales deduction
• Accrual accounts (for rebate agreements)

The system posts these costs and revenues according to the business area. The business area can be equivalent to the sales area (if the accounts are to be posted according to sales) or the plant/division (if the accounts are to be posted according to products).

The system can automatically post entries to accounts via account assignment. Account assignment is used to find the revenue accounts to which sales are posted and the sales deduction accounts to which surcharges and discounts are posted. Using this approach, billing documents may be assigned to account assignment groups. The condition technique is then used to carry out account assignment based on assignment groups. Assignment groups are needed for the customer data and the material data. These groups must be defined and maintained appropriately to ensure proper posting.

In the standard version of SAP, all billing types are defined in such a way that the offsetting entry is made to the customer account. If the offsetting entry is to be made to the GL account (for example, a cash clearing account), it must be configured using a special cash-clearing key (e.g., EVV).

Billing documents are blocked if:
• The billing type automatically blocks the billing document when it is created (e.g., credit notes)
• Errors occur in account assignment (i.e., the system could not determine the account number to use for accounting)

• The billing document is incomplete
• Errors occur in pricing

If a bill is blocked, revenue is not recognized. Blocked billing documents must be explicitly released. Billing documents not passed to accounting can be listed.

A rebate is a special discount paid retroactively to a customer. This discount may be based on the customer's sales volume over a specified time period, early payments, etc. The details of the rebate are defined in a rebate agreement. The agreement specifies, for example:
• Who receives the rebate payment
• Upon what criteria the rebate is based (e.g., customer or customer and material)
• How long the rebate agreement is valid

Within the rebate agreement, separate condition records can be created for each product the customer buys. These records specify the rebate amount or percentage for each product. A pricing scale can be specified so the customer can earn an increased rebate by ordering more. Because rebates are always paid retroactively, the system keeps track of all billing documents (invoices, credit and debit memos) that are relevant for rebate processing. The system can automatically post accruals so that the accumulated value of a rebate is recorded for accounting purposes. A rebate agreement is finally settled when a credit memo is issued to the customer for the accumulated rebate total.

## Collecting and Processing Cash Receipts

Processing cash receipts consists of:
• Receiving payments (e.g., cash, checks, direct bank transfers and intercompany transfers)
• Recording the amounts in the cashbook
• Matching receipts to sales invoices in the sales ledger
• Following up and collecting outstanding amounts

During the recording of cash receipts, open invoices are selected, open customer items within those invoices are cleared, correspondence (an advice) may be sent to the sales function or the customer, and the bank account is posted.

Payment advices can be classified at the line-item level with reason codes (e.g., reason for payment differences, discount rate or calculation error) to determine how the advice will be recorded.

Reason codes may be configured to determine:
• The GL account and posting rules for each payment difference
• The type of correspondence sent to the customer
• The manner in which the customer's credit limit should be handled

When the reason codes are configured, a separate indicator is used to post any charge-off difference to a separate GL account. If this indicator is not checked, a new item is generated in the form of an outstanding receivable in the customer's account. This could potentially distort the accounts receivable aging.

## Summary

In terms of the recommended SAP ERP audit framework, this chapter provided an overall understanding of the Revenue business cycle and its subprocesses from a controls perspective prior to identifying risks, key controls and testing techniques in the next chapter.

# 6. Auditing the SAP ERP Revenue Business Cycle

Chapter 5 outlined the four main subprocesses of the Revenue business cycle. This chapter looks at the significant risks, key controls and techniques to test the controls for each of the four main subprocesses:
• Master data maintenance
• Sales order processing
• Shipping, invoicing, returns and adjustments
• Collecting and processing cash receipts

The authorization objects and associated activity values contained in the Testing Techniques sections of this chapter are indicative only. An understanding of the enterprise's implementation of processes in SAP is required to ensure that testing is complete and includes all necessary authorization objects and values.

Refer to the numbering system outlined in chapter 4, page 79.

## Master Data Maintenance

### Master Data Maintenance Risks
Master data affect the efficient flow of documents and transactions through the system. The inaccurate, incomplete, invalid or untimely creation or maintenance of master data can affect multiple areas within the enterprise as a transaction progresses through the Revenue cycle. Significant risks associated with the maintenance of customer, material and pricing master data include:
1.1     Changes to master data are invalid, incomplete, inaccurate or untimely. For example:
   • An invalid shipping name and address could cause shipment of goods to the wrong address, potentially resulting in misappropriation of such goods.
   • An invalid billing name and address could result in invoices sent to the wrong address, resulting in slow collections, uncollectible accounts and/or inappropriate assessment of late fees.
   • If persistent demands are made of customers as a result of invoices sent to the wrong address, it reflects poorly on the company and could result in customer dissatisfaction.
   • An invalid credit limit could result in processing of orders in excess of the approved credit limit, potentially resulting in uncollectible accounts.
   • Invalid terms of sale could result in the processing of orders using unauthorized terms, potentially resulting in delayed collections, or, if terms require earlier payment than agreed with the customer, customer dissatisfaction.

• An invalid customer discount level could result in the inaccurate pricing of orders, resulting in either lost revenue if customer discounts are raised inappropriately or customer dissatisfaction and collection difficulties if discounts are not applied appropriately.
• An invalid price could result in under- or overcharging customers and consequent customer disputes or loss of revenue.

1.2    Master data do not remain current and accurate. For example, a duplicate customer record could result in billing and collection confusion and could potentially lead to debt exposure. For an enterprise that processes orders for one-time customers, master data may have a high risk of inaccuracy.

## Master Data Maintenance Key Controls

Key controls over the maintenance of customer, material and pricing master data include:

1.1.1  The comparison of reports detailing changes to customer master data to authorized source documents and/or a manual log of requested changes, to ensure that they were input accurately and on a timely basis. For example, a person other than the initiator should reconcile online reports of master data changes to source documentation. Alternatively, details of non-credit/financial-related customer data changes could be returned to the customer for confirmation.

1.1.2  The restriction of access to create and change customer master data to authorized users. For example:
• The creation and maintenance of master data are often assigned and restricted to dedicated areas within the enterprise that understand how these activities may impact organizational processes and the importance of timely changes.
• Enterprises should consider segregating the creation and maintenance of credit limit information and payment details (e.g., direct debit) to the credit and the accounts receivable sections, respectively.

1.1.3  Configurable controls, designed to maintain the integrity of master data, including:
• The use of customer account groups for the customer master record, which determine the number range assignment, field status, pricing information and business partner determination (defines the role the customer plays in the system, i.e., sold-to party and ship-to party). This also determines the output that can be received by the customer (e.g., a delivery address cannot receive an invoice).
• The use of material types for the material master record, which define how quantities and values are updated for that material
• The use of industry sectors, which can be configured so products may be sold and packaged in different ways (e.g., single units for the retail industry sector and pallets for the wholesale industry sector) and so each sector has a different costing and billing structure
• The specification of upper and lower limits for pricing condition types. This would preclude a user from entering a rebate less than 1 percent or higher than 30 percent during condition maintenance, for example.

1.2.1 The periodic review by management of master data to check accuracy and appropriateness

## Master Data Maintenance Testing Techniques

Testing techniques for customer, material and pricing master data controls include:

1.1.1 Use standard reports and transactions to assess the accuracy and timeliness of change maintenance applied to master data records against authorized source documents on a sample basis. For example:

- For customer master data, use transaction code OV51 (also accessible using transaction code SA38 and program RFDABL00) to generate a list denoting the date and time of change, old and new values for fields, and details of the user who input the change.
- Use transaction code S_ALR_87009993 (also accessible using transaction code SA38 and program RFDKLIAB) to display changes to credit management and credit information change details for comparison to authorized source documents.
- Use transaction MM04 to display master data changes for individual material records.
- Generate a list of pricing changes using transaction VK12 and subsequently selecting the following path from menu options: Environment ▷ Changes ▷ Change Report. Check the accuracy of changes made to the pricing master records and also the time at which these changes have been applied (which is essential to the effective processing of pricing changes) against authorized source documentation.

1.1.2 Review organizational policy and process design specifications regarding access to maintain master data. Test user access to create and maintain customer, material and pricing master data as follows:

- Customer master data (note that data can be maintained from finance, sales or central view):

| Transaction(s) | Authorization Objects | Fields | Values |
|---|---|---|---|
| FD01 (Finance) | B_BUPA_RLT | ACTVT | 01 |
| | F_KNA1_AEN | ACTVT | 01 |
| | F_KNA1_APP | ACTVT | 01 |
| | F_KNA1_BED | ACTVT | 01 |
| | F_KNA1_BUK | ACTVT | 01 |
| | F_KNA1_GEN | ACTVT | 01 |
| | F_KNA1_GRP | ACTVT | 01 |

Also test user access to transactions FD02/FD05/FD06 with the authorization objects used for FD01 above, but with ACTVT field values of 02, 05 and 06, respectively. As described in chapter 4, the meaning of the values in the field ACTVT are: 01: Create, 02: Change, 05: Lock, 06: Delete.

| Transaction(s) | Authorization Objects | Fields | Values |
|---|---|---|---|
| VD01(Sales) | B_BUPA_RLT | ACTVT | 01 |
| | B_BUPR_BZT | ACTVT | 01 |
| | F_KNA1_AEN | ACTVT | 01 |
| | F_KNA1_APP | ACTVT | 01 |
| | F_KNA1_BED | ACTVT | 01 |
| | F_KNA1_GEN | ACTVT | 01 |
| | F_KNA1_GRP | ACTVT | 01 |
| | V_KNA1_BRG | ACTVT | 01 |
| | V_KNA1_VKO | ACTVT | 01 |
| Also test user access to transactions VD02/VD05/VD06 with the authorization objects used for VD01 above, but with ACTVT field values of 02, 05 and 06, respectively. | | | |
| XD01(Central) | B_BUPA_RLT | ACTVT | 01 |
| | B_BUPR_BZT | ACTVT | 01 |
| | F_KNA1_AEN | ACTVT | 01 |
| | F_KNA1_APP | ACTVT | 01 |
| | F_KNA1_BED | ACTVT | 01 |
| | F_KNA1_BUK | ACTVT | 01 |
| | F_KNA1_GEN | ACTVT | 01 |
| | F_KNA1_GRP | ACTVT | 01 |
| | V_KNA1_BRG | ACTVT | 01 |
| | V_KNA1_VKO | ACTVT | 01 |
| Also test user access to transactions XD02/XD05/XD06/XD07 with the authorization objects used for XD01 above, but with ACTVT field values of 02, 05 and 06, respectively. Test user access to transaction XD99 (Customer Master Mass Maintenance). | | | |
| Test for access to create/amend customer master data by company code by including the following authorization object/value combination in search criteria. | | | |
| | F_KNA1_BUK | BUKRS | Insert company code |
| Material master data: | | | |
| MM01 | C_AENR_RV1 | ACTVT | 01 |
| | C_DRAD_OBJ | ACTVT | 01 |
| | C_KLAH_BKL | ACTVT | 01 |
| | M_MATE_BUK | ACTVT | 01 |
| | M_MATE_LGN | ACTVT | 01 |
| | M_MATE_MAT | ACTVT | 01 |
| | M_MATE_MEX | ACTVT | 01 |

| Transaction(s) | Authorization Objects | Fields | Values |
|---|---|---|---|
| | M_MATE_MZP | ACTVT | 01 |
| | M_MATE_STA | ACTVT | 01 |
| | M_MATE_VKO | ACTVT | 01 |
| | M_MATE_WGR | ACTVT | 01 |
| | M_MATE_WRK | ACTVT | 01 |
| Also test user access to transactions MM02/MM06 with the authorization objects used for MM01 above, but with ACTVT field values of 02 and 06, respectively. | | | |
| Pricing master data: | | | |
| VK11 | V_KONH_VKS | ACTVT | 01 |
| | V_KONH_VKO | ACTVT | 01 |
| Also test user access to transactions VK12 with the authorization objects used for VK11 above, but with ACTVT field value of 02. | | | |

1.1.3 Determine whether the configurable control settings address the risks
pertaining to the validity, completeness and accuracy of master data, and
whether they have been set in accordance with management intentions.
View the settings online using the IMG as follows:
• Customer account groups—Transaction SPRO menu path: Financial
Accounting ▷ Accounts Receivable and Accounts Payable ▷ Customer
Accounts ▷ Master Data ▷ Preparation for Creating Customer Master
Data ▷ Define Account Groups With Screen Layout (Customers)
• Material types—Transaction SPRO menu path: Logistics—General ▷
Material Master ▷ Basic Settings ▷ Material Types ▷ Define Attributes
of Material Types
• Industry sector—Transaction SPRO menu path: Logistics—General ▷
Material Master ▷ Field Selection ▷ Define Industry Sectors and
Industry-Sector-Specific Field Selection
• Pricing—When reviewing pricing, be aware of three main configuration scenarios:
– Pricing may be coded into condition records in the system and manual
override may not be possible.
– Pricing may be coded into the system; however, the system may be
configured to allow the user to override the price at the time of order entry.
– The system may be configured to allow the user to enter the price at the time
of order entry with price listings or schedules being maintained manually.

Review pricing condition types and records against the organization's
pricing policy using the following menu path and transaction codes:
– Transaction SPRO menu path—Sales and Distribution ▷ Basic
Functions ▷ Pricing
– V-44 for material price condition record
– V-48 price list type condition records
– V-52 customer-specific condition type

Review manual (e.g., spot-checking, review of customer pricing complaints) or automated (e.g., release approval) supervisor controls over user price overrides. However, due to the complexity of pricing configuration, it is often most effective to take a sample of sales orders (e.g., using transaction VA05) and reperform the pricing calculation outside the system using the organization's pricing policy as the basis for the calculation. Any anomalies can then be followed up with the users in the case of manual override or against the pricing configuration.

1.2.1 Determine whether management runs the following reports, or equivalent, by master data type and confirm evidence of review of the data for completeness and accuracy:
- Customer master data—Run transaction code F.20.
- Material master data—Run transaction code MMS3.
- Pricing master data—Run transaction code VK13.

Determine whether the customer regularly reviews master data for duplicate customers or materials via manual or automated methods. Consider obtaining an extract of key customer or materials master data tables (KNA1, MARA) and search for duplicates based on likely unique fields (post/zip code, material name, weight/dimensions, etc.)

Use transaction F.32 to provide an overview of customers for whom no credit information has been entered. Understand the number ranges used for customers and which customers should have a credit limit assigned. Check the output from transaction F.32 to confirm that a credit limit has been set for customers in the range requiring a limit.

# Sales Order Processing

## Sales Order Processing Risks
Significant risks associated with sales order processing include:
2.1    Sales orders are processed with invalid prices and terms or processing is incomplete, inaccurate or untimely. For example:
- If orders are processed at unauthorized prices or terms, profitability may be reduced or cash flow may be slowed, as customers may withhold or delay payment when querying invoices.
- If orders are entered inaccurately, shipping and/or pricing errors may result. For instance, goods may be shipped without a valid customer order or to the wrong customer address, or pricing errors may result from inaccurate entry of the customer's discount or quantity ordered. Such errors may result in inaccurate income recognition, an increase in returned goods, uncollectible accounts receivable, late collection of receipts or reduced profitability.

- If orders are not entered into the system, they may not be completed and potential revenue may be lost. Further lost revenue may result from customer dissatisfaction if orders go unfilled. Finally, orders may be filled but never recorded, resulting in customers not being invoiced and inventory shrinkage.
- If invalid or duplicate orders are entered, goods may be shipped but not accepted by the customers or shipped to fictitious customers. This could result in customer dissatisfaction, the loss of goods, or fraud. If the shipments are invoiced, this may result in the overstatement of revenue and accounts receivable in the financial statements since the resulting accounts receivable may not represent valid sales.

2.2    Orders are processed outside of approved customer credit limits. For example, if orders are accepted in excess of customer credit limits, collection of the resulting accounts receivable may be difficult.

2.3    Order entry data are not completely and accurately transferred to the shipping and invoicing activities. If order entry data are not transferred to the shipping subsystem, the order may not be filled, resulting in lost business. In addition, if order entry data are not transferred to the invoicing subsystem, the order may be filled, but not invoiced, possibly resulting in loss of revenue and cash.

## Sales Order Processing Key Controls

Key controls over the processing of sales orders include:

2.1.1  Restriction to authorized personnel of the ability to create, change, delete, block and unblock sales orders, contracts and delivery schedules

2.1.2  Restriction to authorized personnel of the ability to modify the SAP ERP sales pricing information

2.1.3  Configuration of the system such that a sales order is blocked for further processing when the customer either gets too low a price or indicates the price that the sales person gives is not satisfactory. The minimum price ensures that the sales order cannot be processed at all. The customer-expected price blocks the order and a list containing all these orders should be reviewed by management on a regular basis. The system should also be configured to specify maximums for a certain conditions. A customer, for example, receives a certain discount in the system, up to a defined amount only. The amount is cumulated each time the customer places an order. When the maximum is reached, the discount is automatically deactivated. A maximum number of sales orders that benefit from this discount also can be specified (for example, when introducing new products).

2.1.4  Periodic reconciliation of fax orders between the system and fax printouts to reduce the risk of duplicate orders. A confirmation should be sent to the customer for telephone or e-mail orders. Orders received via postal mail should be reconciled periodically with the system.

2.2 Configuration of the SAP ERP software to disallow the processing of sales orders that exceed customer credit limits

2.3 Preparation of reports of open sales documents and monitoring of same to check for timely shipment

## Sales Order Processing Testing Techniques

Testing techniques for sales order processing include:

2.1.1 Gain an understanding of the organization's policies, procedures, standards and guidance related to the ability to create, change, delete, block and unblock sales orders, contracts and delivery schedules. Test user access to create, maintain, block and unblock sales orders, contracts and delivery schedules, and compare the results against the understanding of the business process and controls obtained earlier. The following are some examples of transactions to include in testing (note that data can be maintained through finance or sales views):

| Transaction(s) | Authorization Objects | Fields | Values |
|---|---|---|---|
| VA01 (Sales) | V_VBAK_AAT | ACTVT | 01, 02, 05, 06, 43 (Release) |
| | V_VBAK_VKO | ACTVT | 01, 02, 05, 06, 43 (Release) |
| Also test user access to transaction VA02 with the same authorization objects and field values shown above. | | | |
| FB75 (Finance) | F_BKPF_BLA | ACTVT | 01 |
| | F_BKPF_BUK | ACTVT | 01 |
| | F_BKPF_GSB | ACTVT | 01 |
| | F_BKPF_KOA | ACTVT | 01 |

Also review blocked orders to ensure that they have been resolved in a timely manner. Depending on the volume of sales input manually it may also be necessary to verify a sample of sales input for accuracy.

2.1.2 Test user access to create and maintain sales pricing information. Refer to 1.1.2.

2.1.3 Review configuration options for pricing in the IMG as per 1.1.3.

2.1.4 Gain an understanding of the policies and procedures regarding reconciliation of sales orders. Review operations activity at selected times and check for evidence that reconciliations are being performed.

2.2.1 Determine whether the configurable control settings address the risks pertaining to the processing of orders outside customer credit limits and whether they have been set in accordance with management intentions. View the settings online using the IMG as follows:
   • Transaction SPRO menu path—Financial Accounting ▷ Accounts Receivable and Accounts Payable ▷ Credit Management ▷ Credit Control Account

- Execute transaction OVAK to show the type of credit check performed for the corresponding transaction types in order processing.
- Execute transaction OVA7 to determine whether a credit check is performed for appropriate document types being used.
- Execute transaction OVAD to show the credit groups that have been assigned to the delivery types being used.
- Execute transaction OVA8 to show an overview of defined credit checks for credit control areas.

2.3.1 Obtain a full list of incomplete sales documents from the system using transaction V.00 (also accessible using transaction code SA38 and program RVAUFERR). Review items on the list with the appropriate operational management and ascertain whether there are legitimate reasons for the sales documents that remain incomplete.

# Shipping, Invoicing, Returns and Adjustments

## Shipping, Invoicing, Returns and Adjustments Risks

Significant risks associated with shipping, invoicing, returns and adjustments include:

3.1 Shipments of goods to customers may be duplicated or delayed. This may lead to, for example, additional processing costs associated with processing returns or customer queries and customer dissatisfaction arising from errors or delays in processing the order.

3.2 Invoices are not generated using authorized terms and prices or are inaccurately calculated and recorded. For example:
- If invoices are generated with unauthorized terms and/or prices, accounts receivable may be misstated. Customers may withhold or delay payment of inaccurate invoices, resulting in reduced or delayed cash flow. Also, use of unauthorized terms and/or prices may result in customer disputes.
- Errors in invoices can lead to a misstatement of accounts receivable and revenue, uncollectible accounts and customer dissatisfaction.
- If invoices are issued but not recorded, revenue and accounts receivable in the financial statements may be understated. The related cash receipts may not be recorded and may be misappropriated. Alternatively, if the invoice has not been recorded, the organization is unlikely to notice or follow up on delinquent payments.

3.3 Not all goods shipped are invoiced or goods are not invoiced in a timely manner. For example:
- Shipments not invoiced or not invoiced in a timely manner result in understated revenue and accounts receivable and lost inventory and cash flow.
- If invoices that do not relate to valid shipments are issued and processed, revenue and accounts receivable will be overstated.

3.4   Credit notes and adjustments to accounts receivable are inaccurately calculated and recorded. For example:
- Inaccurately recorded credit notes can lead to a misstatement of accounts receivable and revenue and may result in uncollectible accounts and/or customer dissatisfaction.
- Credit notes issued but not recorded can result in misstated accounts receivable and revenue and in customer dissatisfaction. The notes may have a negative impact on cash flow because customers may refuse to pay invoices for which they are awaiting credits, even if the credits are for only a small portion of the invoices.

3.5   Credit notes for all goods returned and adjustments to accounts receivable are not issued in accordance with organizational policy or are not issued in a timely manner. For example:
- If credit notes are not properly issued or are not issued in a timely manner for returned goods, accounts receivable and revenue will be overstated and customers may be dissatisfied.
- Valid credit notes typically relate to an authorized return of goods, resolution of invoicing discrepancies or other customer disputes. Invalid credit notes may result in the understatement of accounts receivable and lost revenue. Invalid credit notes may arise from the following circumstances:
  - Credits in excess of the original invoice amount
  - Credits without receipt of returned goods
  - Credits for return of goods used or damaged by the purchaser

### Shipping, Invoicing, Returns and Adjustments Key Controls

Key controls over the processing of invoices, shipping, returns and adjustments include:

3.1.1  SAP ERP's matching of goods shipped to open line items on an open sales order and closing of each line item as the goods are shipped, thereby preventing further shipments for those line items

3.1.2  Use of some of the following shipping reports to assist in controlling the shipping process:
- Backlog reports
- Delivery due list
- Picking list
- Picking confirmation
- Loading list
- Transportation list
- Goods issue list

3.2.1  SAP ERP's automatic calculation of invoice amounts and posting of invoices based on system configuration data

3.3.1  Preparation and prompt investigation of reports of goods shipped but not invoiced and uninvoiced debit and credit note requests

3.3.2  Restriction of the ability to create, change or delete picking lists, delivery notes and goods issues to authorized personnel

3.3.3  Preparation and prompt investigation of reports of invoices issued but not posted in FI

3.4.1  Restriction of the ability to create, change or delete sales order return and credit requests and subsequent credit note transactions to authorized personnel

3.5.1  Match of sales order return and credit request transactions to invoices

3.5.2  Configuration of processing controls, including a delivery block and a billing block, to block the processing of documents that do not comply with the organization's policy on credits or returns. A credit memo or a free-of-charge subsequent delivery can be blocked until the returns are unblocked.

## *Shipping, Invoicing, Returns and Adjustments Testing Techniques*

Testing techniques for shipping, invoicing, returns and adjustments include:

3.1.1  Generate the list of current system configuration settings relating to copy control between sales and shipping documents using transaction VTLA— Display Copying Control: Sales Document to Delivery Document. Select each combination of delivery type and sales document type, and click the Item button. Double-click on each item category, and verify that the entry for the indicator quantity/value pos/neg has been set to + (automatic update occurs between documents as deliveries are made for line items specified in the sales document). Depending on the volume of shipping and sales input manually it may also be necessary to verify a sample of shipping and sales input for accuracy.

3.1.2  Interview management and determine whether any of the following reports are used to check the complete and timely shipment of goods to customers:
- Backorders Reports—V.15
- Sales Orders/Purchase Orders Worklist—VL04
- Outbound Deliveries for Picking—VL06
- Outbound Deliveries for Confirmation—VL06C
- Outbound Deliveries for Loading—VL06L
- Outbound Deliveries for Transportation Planning—VL06T
- Outbound Deliveries for Goods Issue—VL06G

Review a sample of any hard copy reports used for evidence of action taken and a sample of the reports online, and check the aging of items to determine whether entries have been cleared in a timely manner.

3.2.1  Display current system settings relating to invoice preparation online using the IMG. Transaction SPRO menu path: Sales and Distribution ▷ Billing ▷ Billing Documents. Determine whether the connection between source and target documents supports the accurate flow of billing details through the sales process and supports the accurate calculation and posting of invoice data.

3.3.1 Execute transaction VF04—Maintain Billing Due List. All documents that have not been invoiced, or that have been only partially invoiced, will appear on the list, sorted by invoice due date. Review the aging of items in the list. For items outstanding for more than one billing period, seek an explanation from management as to why the items have not been billed. Documents may not be invoiced fully for reasons that include:
• An invoice block set in either the document or the customer master record
• Incomplete delivery

Although both of these reasons are valid, documents that have not been invoiced fully should be investigated promptly to ensure that revenue is matched with costs and the delay is resolved.

3.3.2 Assess user access to picking lists, delivery notes and goods issues. Deliveries can be created in the SAP ERP system using two transactions, which allow the user to create:
• VL01 for a single delivery
• VL04 for multiple deliveries

Deliveries can be changed using transaction code VL02. The authorization object for the general handling of the delivery is V_LIKP_VST, and the authorization object for the posting of the goods issue is M_MSEG_BWE. Any individual who is authorized to post the goods issue for a delivery must also be authorized to change a delivery. Movement types 601 and 651 are required to post goods issues for outgoing sales orders and incoming returns. Movement types 621 through 624 are required to handle deliveries for returnable packaging. Movement types 631 through 634 are required to handle deliveries for customer consignment. The typical values used in carrying out this test are as follows:
• Create—01
• Change—02
• Display—03
• Print—04

3.3.3 Invoices in the SAP ERP system can be entered via the SD module or the FI module. When invoices are posted via the SD module, these invoices are transferred to the FI module, where they become open items. During the transfer of invoices from SD to FI, errors can occur or invoices may be deliberately blocked for approval. Execute transaction VF03 Display Billing Document, click on the expansion button next to the billing document field and select Billing Documents Still To Be Passed Onto Accounting. Obtain an explanation for any invoices that appear in this list. Test user access to enter invoices and confirm this is consistent with staff job roles and management's intentions. Test user access to create and maintain invoices as follows:

Sales accounts receivable entry:

| Transaction(s) | Authorization Objects | Fields | Values |
|---|---|---|---|
| VF01, VF04 | V_VBRK_FKA | ACTVT | 01,02 |
| | V_VBRK_VKO | ACTVT | 01,02 |
| | V_KONH_VKO | ACTVT | 03 |
| | V_KONH_VKS | ACTVT | 03 |

Finance entry:

| Transaction(s) | Authorization Objects | Fields | Values |
|---|---|---|---|
| FB70 | F_BKPF_BLA | ACTVT | 01,02 |
| | F_BKPF_BUK | ACTVT | 01,02 |
| | F_BKPF_GSB | ACTVT | 01,02 |
| | F_BKPF_KOA | ACTVT | 01,02 |

3.4.1 Assess user access to sales order returns and credit notes. Typical transactions and authorization objects involved in this test include the following.
Sales entry:

| Transaction(s) | Authorization Objects | Fields | Values |
|---|---|---|---|
| VA01, VA02 | V_VBAK_AAT | ACTVT | 01, 02, 05, 06, 43 |
| | V_VBAK_VKO | ACTVT | 01, 02, 05, 06, 43 |

Finance entry:

| Transaction(s) | Authorization Objects | Fields | Values |
|---|---|---|---|
| FB75 | F_BKPF_BLA | ACTVT | 01, 02 |
| | F_BKPF_BUK | ACTVT | 01, 02 |
| | F_BKPF_GSB | ACTVT | 01, 02 |
| | F_BKPF_KOA | ACTVT | 01, 02 |

3.5.1 In the SAP ERP system, it is possible to configure the system so that when a document is entered, a reference document is required. A reference to a source document ensures accurate copying of details, including the customer number, material numbers, pricing date, quantities, payment and shipping terms. It is common for the mandatory reference field for document types not to be defined when the system is implemented. Often a document that has been created needs to reference a document that was created in another system, for example, a credit note raised in the SAP ERP system that relates to an invoice created in the previous system. When there are no more of these documents in the system, the mandatory reference field should be created. However, this often is overlooked. View the sales document types configured by using transaction VOV8. Look for all the sales document types that relate to sales order returns and credit requests. Double-click on one of these document types. In the General Control section of the screen, there is a field—reference mandatory—with the following possible options:

| Value | Reference |
|---|---|
| Blank | No reference required |
| A | With reference to an inquiry |
| B | With reference to a quotation |
| C | With reference to a sales order |
| E | Scheduling agreement reference |
| G | With reference to a quantity contract |
| M | With reference to a billing document |

Verify that the setting has been set to M. Repeat this for all of the other relevant document types. Discuss with management the reference field settings in place for the selected document types. Determine whether the configuration in place is set as management intended.

3.5.2 In the SAP ERP system, it is possible to block all sales documents from further processing by assigning shipping and/or billing blocks. It is also possible to customize the system so specific types of sales documents are blocked for specific customers. This ensures that credit notes and/or debit notes are processed only with correct authorizations and allows workflow triggers at this stage, if needed. Using configuration, make this setting at the sales document type level. Note: a delivery block at header level is effective only if it has been assigned to the corresponding delivery type in customizing (table TVLSP). Regardless of this assignment, the delivery block is still effective at the schedule line level.

Review the configuration settings for delivery and billing blocks online using the IMG as follows:
- Shipping—Transaction SPRO menu path: Logistics Execution ▷ Shipping ▷ Deliveries ▷ Define Reasons for Blocking in Shipping
- Billing—Transaction SPRO menu path: Sales and Distribution ▷ Billing ▷ Billing Documents ▷ Define Blocking Reason for Billing

Determine whether the settings support the processing of credits in line with the organization's credit management policy and are consistent with management's intention.

Assess user access to sales order and delivery release. SD documents can be released in the SAP ERP system using the following transactions:
- VKM3 for sales documents release
- VKM5 for delivery release
- VKM1, VKM2 and VKM4 for SD documents release

# Collecting and Processing Cash Receipts

## *Collecting and Processing Cash Receipts Risks*
Significant risks associated with collecting and processing cash receipts include:
4.1 Cash receipts may not be entered accurately, completely and in a timely manner. For example:
- Inaccurately entered cash receipts can lead to receipts being allocated to the incorrect customer account. Alternatively, posting of the wrong amount may result in an out-of-balance condition between the general ledger and the bank statement.
- Incomplete or untimely entry of cash receipts can lead to an overstatement of accounts receivable.
4.2 Duplicate or invalid cash receipts may be issued, which may result in an overstatement of cash and understatement of accounts receivable.
4.3 Cash discounts may not be calculated and recorded accurately. If cash discounts are inaccurately calculated, revenue may be misstated. If they are allowed beyond the period for which they are offered, revenue may be lost and the discounts may no longer provide customers with an incentive for paying promptly. However, to maintain customer goodwill, an organization may establish policies for allowing discounts beyond the specified terms.
4.4 The timely collection of cash receipts may not be monitored. Monitoring collection of accounts receivable helps maximize the amount collected on such accounts. Through timely follow-up, collection problems may be identified earlier, thereby allowing the organization to restrict future sales and avoid incurring additional losses due to collection problems.

## *Collecting and Processing Cash Receipts Key Controls*
Key controls over the collection and processing of cash receipts include:
4.1.1 Regular reconciliation of bank statements to the general ledger
4.1.2 Configuration of the system to not allow processing of cash receipts outside of approved bank accounts
4.1.3 Preparation and regular analysis of customer open items and accounts receivable aging reports
4.2.1 Receipts allocated to a customer's account supported by a remittance advice that cross-references to an invoice number. Any unallocated cash or amounts received that are not cross-referenced to an invoice number are immediately followed up with the customer. The SAP ERP software will not allow a duplicate receipt to be allocated to the same customer line item.
4.3.1 Definition of tolerance levels for allowable cash discounts and cash payment differences in the SAP ERP system. Amounts in excess of such levels cannot be entered into the SAP ERP system.
4.4.1 As for 4.1.3, preparation and regular analysis of customer open items and accounts receivable aging reports

### *Collecting and Processing Cash Receipts Testing Techniques*

Testing techniques for collecting and processing cash receipts include:

4.1.1 Take a sample of bank reconciliations and test for adequate clearance of reconciling items and approval by finance management.

4.1.2 Execute transaction FI12 and ascertain to which bank accounts a cash receipt can be posted. Determine whether this is consistent with management's intentions.

4.1.3 Use the transaction code F.21—Customer Open Items (also accessible using transaction code SA38 and program RFDEPL00) to review customer open items. The report lists each item and the amount owed. At the end of the listing, the total amount still to be collected is calculated. Transaction code S_ALR_87009956—Customer Open Item Analysis (days overdue analysis, also accessible through transaction code SA38 and program RFDOPR10) can be used to review accounts receivable overdue items. For each balance overdue, the report shows the days in arrears and amount overdue. A number of selection criteria can be specified when running the report, such as open items at a key date, customer account, company code, balance and overdue items balance. Determine whether these reports are reviewed and actioned regularly by locating evidence of their review or through corroborative inquiry with management.

4.2.1 Review the accounts receivable reconciliation and determine whether there are any amounts unallocated or any reconciling items. Determine the aging of these items and ask management the reasons for these items remaining unallocated or unreconciled.

4.3.1 Review the settings in place for tolerance levels for allowable cash discounts and cash payment differences by using the following transactions:
• Transaction OBA4 to determine the tolerance groups that have been set up for users, and the tolerance limits that have been set for those groups
• Transaction OB57 to determine the users who have been allocated to the groups identified previously

Discuss with management the settings in place for tolerance levels for allowable cash discounts and cash payment differences. Determine whether the configuration in place agrees with management's intentions.

4.4.1 As for 4.1.3, review the accounts receivable aging reports regularly to ensure that the collection of payments is performed in a timely manner.

# Revenue Cycle Controls and Financial Statement Assertions

The Revenue cycle risk numbers from this chapter have been mapped to controls listed in figure 23—Application Control Objectives for the Sales Cycle from the IT Governance Institute's publication, *IT Control Objectives for Sarbanes-Oxley, 2ⁿᵈ Edition*,[11] as shown in **figure 6.1**. The risk number mapping should be looked

---

[11] IT Governance Institute, *IT Control Objectives for Sarbanes-Oxley, 2ⁿᵈ Edition*, ISACA, USA, 2006

at in conjunction with the associated control and testing technique numbers to
help gain an understanding of the impact of the risks and controls on the financial
reporting process in terms of completeness, occurrence, valuation and validity.

| Figure 6.1—Revenue Risk Cycle Controls | | |
|---|---|---|
| Illustrative Control Objectives | Financial Statement Assertions | Revenue Cycle Risk Number |
| Orders are processed only within approved customer credit limits. | Valuation | 2.2 |
| Orders are approved by management as to prices and terms of sale. | Existence | 2.1 |
| Orders and cancellations of orders are input accurately. | Valuation | 2.1 |
| Order entry data are transferred completely and accurately to the shipping and invoicing activities. | Valuation Completeness | 2.3 |
| All orders received from customers are input and processed. | Completeness | 2.1 |
| Only valid orders are input and processed. | Existence | 2.1 |
| Invoices are generated using authorized terms and prices. | Valuation | 3.2 |
| Invoices are accurately calculated and recorded. | Valuation | 3.2 |
| Credit notes and adjustments to accounts receivable are accurately calculated and recorded. | Valuation | 3.4 |
| All goods shipped are invoiced. | Completeness | 3.3 |
| Credit notes for all goods returned and adjustments to accounts receivable are issued in accordance with organizational policy. | Existence | 3.5 |
| Invoices relate to valid shipments. | Existence | 3.3 |
| All credit notes relate to a return of goods or other valid adjustments. | Completeness | 3.5 |
| All invoices issued are recorded. | Completeness | 3.2 |
| All credit notes issued are recorded. | Existence | 3.4 |
| Invoices are recorded in the appropriate period. | Valuation | 3.4 |

| Figure 6.1—Revenue Risk Cycle Controls *(cont.)* | | |
|---|---|---|
| **Illustrative Control Objectives** | **Financial Statement Assertions** | **Revenue Cycle Risk Number** |
| Credit notes issued are recorded in the appropriate period. | Valuation | 3.4 |
| Cash receipts are recorded in the period in which they are received. | Valuation | 4.1 |
| Cash receipts data are entered for processing accurately. | Valuation | 4.1 |
| All cash receipts data are entered for processing. | Existence | 4.1 |
| Cash receipts data are valid and are entered for processing only once. | Completeness | 4.2 |
| Cash discounts are accurately calculated and recorded. | Valuation | 4.3 |
| Timely collection of accounts receivable is monitored. | Valuation | 4.4 |
| The customer master file is maintained. | Completeness Existence | 1.1 |
| Only valid changes are made to the customer master file. | Completeness Existence | 1.1 |
| All valid changes to the customer master file are input and processed. | Completeness Existence | 1.1 |
| Changes to the customer master file are accurate. | Valuation | 1.1 |
| Changes to the customer master file are processed in a timely manner. | Completeness Existence | 1.1 |
| Customer master file data remain up to date. | Completeness Existence | 1.2 |

## Summary

This chapter outlined the risks, key controls and testing techniques surrounding the SAP ERP Revenue business cycle. Among the key risks are invalid master data such as billing addresses and credit limits, duplicate customer records, invalid entry and processing of sales orders, and inaccurate entry and processing of invoices and cash receipts.

# 7. SAP ERP Expenditure Business Cycle

This chapter outlines the functionality of the SAP ERP Expenditure business cycle to provide the reader with a high-level understanding of the process. From a risk and controls perspective, the Expenditure cycle has four main subprocesses:
• Master data maintenance
• Purchasing
• Invoice processing
• Processing disbursements

## Master Data Maintenance

Data in vendor master records control how transaction data are posted and processed for a vendor. The master record is used not only in the Accounting, but also in the Materials Management, module. By storing vendor master data centrally and sharing them throughout the enterprise, they need to be entered only once. As described earlier, in relation to the Revenue cycle, inconsistencies in master data may be minimized by maintaining them centrally. If one of the vendors changes its address, the data have to be changed only once, and the accounting and purchasing departments will always have up-to-date information. A vendor master record contains information such as:
• Vendor's name, address, language and phone numbers
• Tax numbers
• Bank details
• Account control data such as the number of the general ledger reconciliation account for the vendor account
• Payment methods and terms of payment set up with the vendor
• Purchasing data

Vendor master records are stored in one database. The information is split into three parts:
• General information, such as name and address, which is maintained only once by vendor
• Financial information, such as reconciliation account, which is maintained by the company code with which a vendor is associated
• Logistical information, such as purchasing group, which is maintained by the purchasing organization with which a vendor works

The maintenance transactions are split into three groups, which enable both centralized and decentralized maintenance of vendor master records. Using the authorization object F_LFA1_APP, a user can be granted maintenance authorization for all information (*), financial information (F) or logistical information (M). Vendor master records can be further secured in the SAP ERP system in two different ways:

- A field in the vendor master record containing an authorization group code. The end user must be authorized for that code to be able to perform any changes on that specific vendor. If, however, no value is present in that field, no authorization is required. This technique can be used to secure sensitive vendor accounts and accounts for the enterprise's own personnel.
- The grouping of fields in the vendor master record. When a field is grouped (a group contains one or more fields), the end user must be authorized for that specific group to be able to change the content of that field. If a field does not belong to a group, no authorization is required. This technique can be used to secure sensitive fields such as bank account details.

By definition, sensitive fields require "dual control." Sensitive vendor master data fields such as bank details can be configured to require approval from a second user prior to being accepted and updated in vendor master data tables. This technique can be used to prevent inappropriate changes to sensitive fields.

Vendor pricing information resides in condition records, which can be maintained via purchasing information record maintenance (purchasing information records are records containing additional information on vendors and specific material master records) or general condition record maintenance. Pricing information that is specific to an individual vendor is maintained via the purchasing information record, while pricing information that is common to a group of vendors is maintained via general condition record maintenance. For example, cash discounts and other payment terms offered by a vendor are typically maintained via purchasing information record maintenance, whereas value-added tax (VAT) rates for vendors in a specific country are maintained via general condition record maintenance. The purchasing department typically performs maintenance of pricing information, while the accounts payable department typically performs maintenance of vendor master records.

## Purchasing

The SAP ERP software provides comprehensive functionality for purchasing to optimize relevant work processes, ranging from the generation of purchase requisitions to the printing of purchase orders and longer-term purchase agreements. Purchasing decides whether orders can be placed on the basis of existing quotations or it is first necessary to issue additional requests for quotation. To a large extent, purchase orders can be created automatically on the basis of data already available, as in the case where items are allocated to outline purchase agreements. An outline agreement is an agreement to purchase goods or services repeatedly from the same supplier over a period of time. Under an outline

agreement, individual releases of goods are requested periodically. In addition, the system makes information available for:
• Vendor evaluation purposes
• Vendor selection
• Volume tracking (with regard to a material or a vendor)
• Ordering activity monitoring

When a purchasing document is created, the relevant document type appears as a default. Each enterprise can define its document structure. Standard document types are defined by the SAP ERP software as:
• Purchase requisition—Defines a requirement for a material or service
• Request for quotation (RFQ)—Transmits a requirement defined in a requisition for a material or service to potential vendors
• Quotation—Contains a vendor's pricing and terms of delivery provided in response to an RFQ and is the basis for selecting the vendor to supply the required material or service
• Purchase order (PO)—The buying entity's request to a vendor (external supplier) to supply certain materials or perform certain services containing specific details of dates and prices
• Contract—A type of outline agreement or long-term buying arrangement
• Scheduling agreement—Another type of outline agreement providing for the subsequent issue of a delivery schedule and specifying purchase quantities, delivery dates and possibly delivery times
• Service entry sheet—Records services as they are performed by the vendor or subcontractor
• Goods receipt (GR)—The posting of the receipt of goods from a vendor or from production

Purchase requisitions normally are used only if an independent purchasing function has been established. A purchasing function procures goods and services to fulfill the enterprise's requirements, as approved by management. The purchasing function should not acquire goods or services for which purchase requisitions have not been approved by management. Purchase requisitions may be paper-based or entered online, or they may originate from an inventory management system. Purchase requisitions are often rolled into purchase orders for particular vendors covering a number of purchase requisitions.

Where purchase requisitions are not used, purchasing decides whether orders can be placed on the basis of existing quotations or whether it is first necessary to issue additional requests for quotation. Purchase orders can be created automatically on the basis of data already available, as when items are allocated to outline purchase agreements.

A source list is used to restrict the purchase of specific materials to specific vendors. Examples of business reasons for using a source list include an established relationship with a vendor, the proven reliability of a vendor, or the existence of a special deal with a vendor. For reasons such as these, the enterprise will want to prohibit people from buying materials from different vendors. For specified materials, it is possible to restrict the allowable vendors. Allowable vendors are maintained in the source list for the specified material. When a purchase order or outline agreement is created for materials with a source list, only vendors on the list can be entered. Management in an enterprise may want source lists to be maintained for specific (types of) materials. On the other hand, for materials for which free, competitive bidding should occur, no source lists should be available in the system. Controls for access to source lists should exist, along with a process to review such access on a regular basis.

The SAP ERP system can automatically block purchase requisitions, purchase orders and calls on outline agreements. This functionality helps enforce management's approval of unusual purchases. Accordingly, the ability to release such blocked orders should be restricted to authorized purchasing management personnel.

The SAP ERP functionality allows the systematic approval of purchase requisitions and other purchasing documents. This is known as the release strategy. Within purchasing, two alternative procedures are available for release of purchase requisitions:
• Release procedure 1 allows for correction and approval of purchase requisitions. It is used to check the accuracy of the values for material, quantity and dates and to ensure the correctness of the specified account assignment and source of supply. Purchase requisitions are released item by item. This procedure is available only for purchase requisition documents.
• Release procedure 2 is used to replace manual authorization procedures for documents with electronic signatures. The person responsible processes the relevant document in the system, thereby marking it with an electronic signature. This procedure involves the approval or release of the entire document, as opposed to the release of individual line items. Release procedure 2 is used for all types of purchasing documents, including RFQs, contracts, scheduling agreements and outline agreements (standing purchase orders).

In release procedure 1, three control aspects determine whether a purchase requisition requires approval or release before it becomes an order:
• Release conditions
• Release strategy
• Release prerequisites

The release conditions of a requisition item can be based on one or a combination of the following items (these items can be defined and changed only with customizing functionality):
• Account assignment category
• Material group
• Plant
• Total value of the requisition

If the purchase requisition meets one of the specified release conditions (for example, total value exceeds a certain monetary amount and/or the material belongs to a specified material group), the system automatically assigns a release strategy to the requisition and the requisition has to undergo an approval process. If none of the conditions is applicable to the purchase requisition, it is released automatically.

The release strategy defines the approval process for the release of the requisition. It defines the people who should approve the requisition and the order of approval. The release strategy is assigned to the requisition based on the release conditions for each line item; that is, individual items on the requisition may have different release strategies. Each person or department authorized to approve a requisition within a given strategy represents a release point in the sequence of authorization. Up to eight release points may exist for each release strategy.

The release prerequisites determine the order in which the release points must approve a requisition. Release prerequisites are defined in the release strategy. For example, the accounts payable manager may need to approve a requisition before the inventory manager finally approves it. Thus, approval by the accounts payable manager is a prerequisite for approval by the inventory manager.

Release procedure 2 uses the following release conditions:
• Value
• Material group
• Account assignment
• Plant and MM classification

In the case of release procedure 2 (with classification), release strategies can be determined for all purchasing documents, with the aid of characteristics. For this purpose, class types for the release procedures are defined containing a separate class for each purchasing document (for example, one for requisitions and one for outline agreements). Each purchasing document is then checked for relevant characteristic values within the class, after which it is automatically assigned to a release strategy. With release procedure 2, a link may be made with SAP ERP Workflow. With Workflow, release points—that is, people responsible for authorization—are automatically sent the documents for purchase requisitions requiring approval by electronic SAP ERP mail. Release points that participate in the workflow are defined during the customization process.

In addition, the system makes information available for:
• Vendor evaluation purposes
• Vendor selection
• Volume tracking (with regard to a material or a vendor)
• Order activity monitoring

Once goods are delivered by the vendor, the goods are receipted into the SAP ERP system. The GR increases warehouse inventory on hand for stock transactions. GRs should be planned because:
• The system tracks ordered materials.
• The receipts are used to regulate the level of inventory in the warehouse.
• GRs are used to determine whether promised materials have been received from vendors or in-house production.
• The goods receiving point verifies the materials received and routes them for consumption or to a warehouse.
• Transactions that lead to changes in inventory levels, such as goods receipts, return deliveries, planned and unplanned stock withdrawals, stock transfers and stock adjustments, are handled within this component. Through real-time entry, checking and correction of goods movements, data are kept as up to date as possible and error levels are reduced to a minimum. This is an essential prerequisite for accurate and efficient materials planning and control.
• At the time of goods receipt, all relevant data are defaulted from the purchase order. The system keeps track of under- and over-deliveries. Each material movement causes the quantities of stock on hand to be updated. Stock values are updated via the automatic account determination facility.

The PO number should be used for the receipt of goods when a PO initiated the delivery, because:
• The delivery can be verified against the order.
• Data from the PO can be transferred to the GR, which reduces data entry and simplifies checking for over- and under-deliveries.
• The PO history is updated with delivery data, which makes the monitoring of late deliveries possible.
• The vendor invoice is checked against the ordered and the delivered quantities.

Goods receipt transactions influence the availability of materials necessary for production and sales. The SAP ERP software authorizes these transactions based on the type of source document. Source documents can be POs, production orders or sales delivery notes. Especially of interest are goods receipt transactions for which there are no source documents. For such goods receipt transactions, the inventory is changed without hard copy documentation. GRs of this kind are entered into the database using the other goods receipt transaction. Goods movement in the SAP ERP system is entered using a movement type. Movement types in the 500 range are movements that have no source documents attached. Movement types 561 through 566 are special movement types that reflect the initial stock entry in the SAP ERP system at the time of conversion to the SAP ERP system.

The ability to enter goods receipt transactions should be restricted from individuals who have access to enter purchase orders, which will lead to goods receipt transactions, or to enter invoices, which will eventually lead to disbursements. Individuals who have access to more than one of these transaction types could order, receive and pay for goods that may not be needed and may never be received by the enterprise. Within the SAP ERP system, goods receipt transactions can be reversed to correct errors. However, the ability to cancel (or reverse) a material document (i.e., ability to use transaction MBST) should be restricted to high-level inventory managers.

## Invoice Processing

The Invoice Verification component provides the link between the Materials Management component and the Financial Accounting, Controlling and Asset Accounting components. Specifically, it serves the following purposes:
• It completes the materials procurement process, which starts with the purchase requisition, continues with purchasing and goods receipt, and ends with the invoice receipt.
• It allows invoices that do not originate in materials procurement (for example, services and expenses) to be processed.
• It allows credit memos to be processed, either as invoice cancellations or discounts. Invoice Verification does not handle the payment or the analysis of invoices.

Invoice Verification tasks include:
• Entering invoices and credit memos that have been received
• Checking the accuracy of invoices with respect to content, prices and arithmetic
• Executing the account postings resulting from an invoice
• Updating certain data in the SAP ERP system, for example, open items and material prices
• Checking invoices that were blocked because the variance from the purchase order was too great

Invoices must be verified and cleared for payment. Tolerance levels can be configured within the SAP ERP software to automatically allow small differences to be posted. User access to set/configure tolerance setting must be strictly controlled and management must ensure that a robust change/authorization process exists.

Each invoice contains various items of information. To post an invoice, this information must be entered into the system. If an invoice refers to an existing transaction, certain items of information already are available in the system. The system proposes this information as default data so that the user needs only to compare it and, if necessary, correct any variances. For example, if an invoice refers to a purchase order, only the number of the purchase order needs to be entered. The system selects the right transaction and proposes data from the purchase order, including the vendor, material, quantity ordered, terms of delivery and terms of payment. The user can overwrite this default data if there are any variances. The purchase order history can also be displayed to check, for example, which quantities have been delivered and how much has been invoiced. When invoices are received from infrequently used vendors that have not been set up in the SAP ERP master data, a one-time vendor account may be used, which allows the user to enter the necessary vendor details and, subject to appropriate approvals/authorizations, process the invoice for payment.

When a vendor invoice is entered in the system, it can be blocked. Blocking can be enforced manually (the user enters a blocking code) or automatically. Automatic blocking of an invoice occurs if the vendor master record contains a blocking code, or the invoice contains information inconsistent with the information in the PO or GR. In the SAP ERP system, tolerance levels are set to verify the price charged for the product, the invoice due date and the quantity invoiced.

The invoice verification (invoice matching or invoice clearance) functionality clearly demonstrates the degree of integration operating in an SAP ERP environment. Information is available from the material master record, the PO and GRs. On data entry, three items are automatically checked by the SAP ERP system:
• The price charged for the product is compared to the price in the PO.
• The invoice due date is compared to the date at which the goods should have been received.
• The quantity invoiced is compared to the quantity received.

The invoice verification transaction initiates this three-way match process. If there are variances between the PO or GR and the invoice, the system will issue a warning on the screen. If the variances are within the preset tolerance limits, the system will allow the invoice to be posted. If the variances are outside of the preset tolerance limits, then, depending on the way the system has been configured, it will:
• Require the user to conduct an investigation and make the required corrections before processing can continue
• Allow the invoice to be posted but automatically block it for payment and require that the invoice be approved and released in a separate step
• Allow the warning message to be overridden and processing to continue

Granting staff authority to override match exceptions must be considered carefully. The organizational policies concerning the override of match exceptions must be robust and adhered to carefully with specific consideration given to the tolerance configurations.

The actual postings to the GR/IR account are as follows: on goods receipt, debit inventory or expenses (at #1 in **figure 7.1**) and credit GR/IR a/c (#1) for the quantity received $\times$ price in the PO (e.g., 10 units $\times$ 10 = 100 in **figure 7.1**).

### Figure 7.1—GR/IR "T" Accounts Example

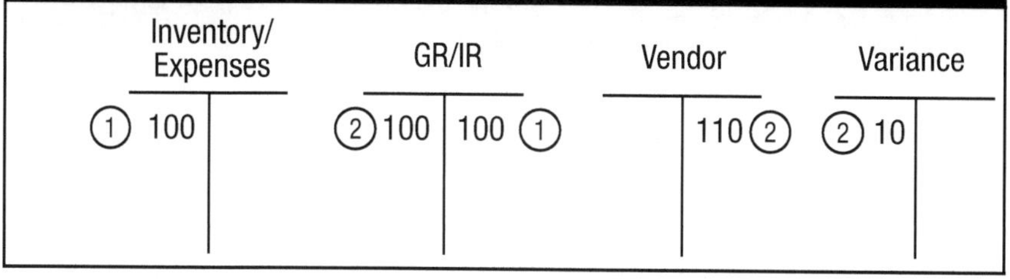

| Inventory/<br>Expenses | GR/IR | Vendor | Variance |
|---|---|---|---|
| ① 100 | ② 100 \| 100 ① | 110 ② | ② 10 |

Later when the invoice is received, the SAP ERP software may perform a three-way match (#2 in **figure 7.1**) and generate the following accounting entries: debit GR/IR account for quantity per the invoice × price per the PO. If there is a difference between the PO price and the vendor invoice price (e.g., the vendor invoice price is 110 in **figure 7.1**), an entry to a price variance account is made (e.g., 10 in **figure 7.1**). If the goods receipt is posted to inventory, there may also be a standard cost variance posting if the PO price differs from the standard cost. Automatic postings for sales tax, cash discount clearing and price variances are also generated and the posting records displayed. Quantity variances are handled in the same way.

The GR/IR account normally has tolerances set (through transaction OMR6) such that a variance of up to 5 percent between the PO price and the invoice price will be automatically accepted and the automatic posting will occur. Variances can be set for:

• Incoming and outgoing payments
• Under- and over-receipt of material
• Quantity and price differences
• Weight and volume for shipping material

If the variance is greater than the tolerance level, the posting to GR/IR and to the vendor account will still occur, but the calculation of the variance and the clearing of the PO transaction out of GR/IR will **not** take place. The invoice will be blocked in the Accounts Payable module and cannot be paid until a manual override is entered (transaction MR02). If the tolerance level is exceeded, a user will have to use transaction MR11—Maintain GR/IR Clearing Account and manually link the two transactions, then authorize the clearance and generation of a variance, either in price or quantity.

In the ideal case, the user need enter only the invoice sum total for the items in the PO. In the event of agreement with the preplanned values, all postings are affected and the invoice is released, or cleared, for payment. In practice, though, there sometimes are differences around items such as freight. These differences can cause items to be held in the GR/IR account as the three-way match process will fail. Manual intervention is required to clear the mismatched items and post the additional costs to the relevant accounts, be they inventory, expenses or price variance accounts. As far as possible, freight and other delivery costs should be included in the PO under the planned delivery costs.

Evaluated receipt settlement (ERS) allows an enterprise to settle on goods receipt without receiving an invoice. Based on the order price specified in the PO and the quantity entered in the goods receipts, the system can determine the correct invoice amount. ERS functionality is available via transaction MRRS. ERS is used for long-term vendors with proven records of quality and reliability. The ERS function has the following advantages:
• Reduction of steps involved in the purchasing/receipt/invoice/payment cycle and associated clerical errors
• Elimination of price and quantity variances in the invoice verification process

The system will not set the ERS indicator on an item if the purchasing information recorded for that item has been flagged as non-ERS. Otherwise, if the vendor is subject to ERS, the system will automatically set all line items as being ERS-relevant. Note that the ERS indicator can be removed for a particular purchase order line item, if required. User access to turn on the ERS indicator should be reviewed and audited due to the risk of a PO being entered and payment being made without validation of the invoice. The risk exists that a staff member could fraudulently collude with a vendor—specifically, a one-time vendor—and process a payment that is not consistent with the agreed price. From a segregation of duties perspective, it is important to ensure that the same employee does not have access to the transaction codes pertaining to creating/changing a vendor master record in order to change the purchase information record and ERS.

The contents of the SAP ERP exchange rate table have great impact on any transaction in the system performed in a foreign currency. Accuracy of the contents is, therefore, essential to the enterprise. Maintenance of the exchange rates should be restricted to only a few people in the accounting department.

Accounting for a company code is carried out in the local country currency of the company code. Therefore, the local currency for each company code must be specified. All other currencies are indicated as "foreign" from the point of view of the company code.

When posting in foreign currency, the currency key for the foreign currency and the posting amount in foreign currency must be entered. The SAP ERP software verifies whether this currency is defined and therefore permitted and calculated automatically. The rate at which the automatic conversion of the currency is calculated is taken from the central currency conversion table (TCURR) in the SAP ERP system. Accordingly, the reliability and effectiveness of this control depends largely on the controls over the access to maintenance of the currency conversion table.

The exchange rate can also be entered manually, either in the document header or for the individual line item. In both cases, an exchange rate must be defined in the system. Percentage tolerances can be defined to verify that the difference between the currency entered and the currency defined in the system is acceptable. Exceeding the percentage tolerance results in the system providing a warning.

A document must have a zero balance in local and foreign currency before it can be posted. Rounding differences that may occur when translating foreign currency amounts are processed automatically. Each foreign currency must be entered into the system, together with the currency into which it is being translated. Before the exchange rate can be defined, the relation among foreign currencies must be defined. For example, a ratio of 1,000:1 is given for Italy/Germany (ITL/DEM) transactions.

# Processing Disbursements

Vendor invoices for transactions such as payment of utilities and service fees are processed through the Finance module (transaction F-43). The configuration can allow for one-, two- and three-level payment release steps, dependent on whether a GR can be raised for the services, among other factors. The release procedure can be dependent on variables such as the document type or the amount.

## Payment Processing

Vendor payments (FI—Accounts Payable) are an integral part of the purchasing system. The user can monitor open items (e.g., due date forecasts and vendor discount maximization). Open items usually are paid as late as possible without losing the vendor's cash discount. The payment program settles outstanding accounts payables. It supports:
• Standard payment methods (checks and transfers) in printed form
• Electronic form (diskette, data transmission)
• Country-specific payment

The user specifies the date of the new payment run, which is used to determine whether an item should be paid now or later. The payment run in the SAP ERP system is split into the following steps:
• The parameters containing company, payment methods and vendors to be paid are entered.
• The payment proposal is generated (the payment program identifies open items to be paid).
• The payment proposal is manually edited by management (management may block payments, cancel payment blocks or change payment methods or banks).
• The actual payments are executed (the program makes the payments, posts documents and produces the appropriate output, e.g., remittance advice, payment summary and transmission files).

The payment run can be done for vendors and customers. Payments can be initiated only from an invoice; they cannot be added at the time of the payment run. The SAP ERP software does not require any formal approval to execute the actual payment. Also, the editing step is not mandatory, so the ability to edit and/or execute the payment proposal should be restricted to only the cash disbursements manager.

Note that although controls in SAP may be effective, the weakest link may be the final payment processing. EFT payments and controls surrounding the encryption and processing of the EFT file to the bank for payment should be considered. The key risk is unauthorized or accidental alterations of the final pay file, resulting in financial loss to the enterprise.

## Summary

This chapter provided an overall understanding of the operation of the Expenditure business cycle in an SAP ERP environment. It summarized important functionality from an audit perspective, including PO release strategies, three-way matching of POs, goods receipts and invoices, and the creation of payment proposals.

# 8. Auditing the SAP ERP Expenditure Business Cycle

Chapter 7 outlined the four main subprocesses of the Expenditure business cycle. This chapter looks at the significant risks, key controls and techniques to test the controls for each of the four main subprocesses:
• Master data maintenance
• Purchasing
• Invoice processing
• Processing disbursements

The authorization objects and associated activity values contained in the Testing Techniques sections of this chapter are indicative only. An understanding of the enterprise's implementation of processes in SAP is required to ensure that testing is complete and includes all necessary authorization objects and values.

Refer to the numbering system in chapter 4, page 79.

## Master Data Maintenance

### Master Data Maintenance Risks
Significant risks associated with vendor master data maintenance include:
1.1
Expenditure cycle, entry and changes to the vendor master data are invalid, incomplete, inaccurate and/or untimely. For example, these errors could result in:
   • Ordering goods from unapproved suppliers, sending payments to incorrect addresses, valuing foreign currency payables inaccurately, or making unauthorized payment and discount terms
   • Duplicate vendor records being established or inappropriate use of the one-time vendor account and subsequent duplicate or misdirected payment
   • Unauthorized payments processed
   • With the use of one-time vendor accounts, removal of the automatic segregation of duties arising from the processing of purchasing transactions and the maintenance of a vendor master record due to master data being entered manually during the creation of the purchasing and invoice documents
1.2 Master data do not remain current and accurate.
   • If supplier data are not up to date, payments could be made to the wrong bank account.
   • Obsolete vendor records may be maintained in the system.

## Master Data Maintenance Key Controls

Key controls over the maintenance of vendor master data include:

1.1.1  Relevant management, other than the initiators, checking online reports of master data changes back to source documentation on a sample basis. Changes to vendor master records, such as bank accounts, should either require second approval within SAP or be logged and reviewed regularly for unauthorized changes.

1.1.2  Assignment of the creation and maintenance of master data and their restriction to dedicated people within the enterprise who understand how they may impact organizational processes and the importance of timely changes. Segregation of duties increases control surrounding master data maintenance.

1.1.3  Configurable controls designed to maintain the integrity of master data. These configurable controls for vendor master data include the setup of vendor account groups, which allow different controls to be applied to different types of vendors and the use of additional authorization field requirements. For example, one-time vendors can be set up as a separate account group (this will require users to have the authorization object F_LFA1_BEK, with the appropriate value for the one-time vendor account group). Access to create a one-time vendor should be restricted to key persons. Access to enter an invoice for a one-time vendor should also be restricted by marking authorization as a required field during the creation of the one-time vendor account group (this will require users to have the authorization object F_BKPF_BEK, with the appropriate value for the one-time vendor account group).

1.1.4  Use of a naming convention for vendor names (e.g., as per letterhead) to minimize the risk of establishing duplicated vendor master records

1.2.1  Periodic review of master data by relevant management to check currency and ongoing pertinence

## Master Data Maintenance Testing Techniques

Testing techniques for vendor master data controls include:

1.1.1  On a sample basis, review standard reports and transactions against authorized source documents to assess the accuracy and timeliness of change maintenance applied to master data records. The transaction code S_ALR_87010039 (also accessible through transaction code SA38 and program RFKABL00) can be used to produce a list of the changes made to selected vendor master records. Review a sample of vendor master records to ensure that all audit logs cannot be modified.

Determine whether any sensitive fields are defined to require approval by a user ID other than the one initiating the change. To review fields configured for dual control, access the IMG and navigate to IMG ▷ Financial Accounting (New) ▷ Accounts Receivables & Accounts Payables ▷ Vendor Accounts ▷ Master Data ▷ Preparation for creating Master Data ▷ Define Sensitive Fields for Dual Control (Vendors).

1.1.2 Review organization policy and process design specifications regarding access to maintain master data, as shown in **figure 8.1**. Test user access to transactions to create and maintain vendor master data (note that data can be maintained from finance, purchasing or centrally).

| Figure 8.1—Access to Maintain Master Data | | | |
|---|---|---|---|
| **Task** | **Finance** | **Purchasing** | **Centrally** |
| Create | FK01 | MK01 | XK01 |
| Change | FK02 | MK02 | XK02 |
| Block/unblock | FK05 | MK05 | XK05 |
| Delete | FK06 | MK06 | XK06 |

The respective authorization objects, fields and values can be determined using the techniques outlined in chapter 4.

Proper enforcement of a segregation of duties strategy improves controls surrounding master data maintenance. Test user access to transactions to maintain vendor pricing information:
• Create Purchase Info Record—ME11
• Change Purchase Info Record—ME12
• Flag Info Record for Deletion—ME15
• Create Condition—MEK1
• Change Condition—MEK2
• Create Condition With Reference—MEK4

| Transaction(s) | Authorization Objects | Fields | Values |
|---|---|---|---|
| ME11 | M_EINF_EKG | ACTVT | 01 |
| | M_EINF_EKO | ACTVT | 01 |
| | M_EINF_WRK | ACTVT | 01 |
| | V_KOND_VEA | ACTVT | 01 |
| | V_KONH_EKO | ACTVT | 01 |
| | V_KONH_VKS | ACTVT | 01 |
| Also test user access to transactions ME12 with the same authorization objects as above but with ACTVT field value of 02. | | | |
| ME15 | M_EINF_EKG | ACTVT | 06 |
| | M_EINF_EKO | ACTVT | 06 |
| | M_EINF_WRK | ACTVT | 06 |

| Transaction(s) | Authorization Objects | Fields | Values |
|---|---|---|---|
| MEK1 | V_KOND_VEA | ACTVT | 01 |
| | V_KONH_EKO | ACTVT | 01 |
| | V_KONH_VKS | ACTVT | 01 |
| Also test user access to transactions MEK2 with the same authorization objects as above but with ACTVT field value of 02. | | | |
| MEK4 | V_KONH_EKO | ACTVT | 01, 02 |
| | V_KONH_VKS | ACTVT | 01, 02 |

1.1.3 Determine whether the configurable control settings address the risks pertaining to the validity, completeness and accuracy of master data and whether the settings have been set in accordance with management intentions. View the settings online using the IMG as follows: Execute transaction code OBD3 and ascertain whether account groups have been set up covering one-time vendor or other vendor accounts. For high-risk account groups such as one-time vendors, check whether authorization has been marked as a required field. Determine whether these settings are consistent with management's intentions.

1.1.4 Extract a list of vendor account names from table LFA1 (fields: NAME1 for the name, LIFNR for the vendor number). Review a sample for compliance with the organization's naming convention. View or search the list (using scan search software tools, if available) for potential duplicates.

1.2.1 Using transaction code F.40 (also accessible using transaction code SA38 and program RFKKVZ00) determine whether the appropriate management report displays or produces a list of vendors. Confirm evidence of management's review of the data on a rotating basis for currency and ongoing pertinence.

# Purchasing

## *Purchasing Risks*

Significant risks associated with purchasing include:

2.1 Purchase order entry and changes are invalid, incomplete, inaccurate and/or untimely. For example:
- Inaccurate input of POs could lead to financial losses due to incorrect goods or services being purchased.
- A PO raised but not subject to a release strategy could result in an unauthorized purchase.

2.2 Goods (or materials or equipment) are received for which there are no valid POs, or goods receipts are recorded incompletely, inaccurately or on an untimely basis. For example:
- If goods are received for which no valid PO exists, goods may be received for which the organization has no need.

- If raw materials received are not recorded, there may be delays in production as well as subsequent delays in supplying customers with finished goods.
- Incomplete recording of raw material receipts may result in a misstatement of inventory.
- Failure to record raw materials received may also lead to supplier disputes and/or inventory obsolescence.

2.3 If defective goods are not returned in a timely manner to suppliers, credits may be lost and disputes may arise.

## Purchasing Key Controls
Key controls over purchasing include:

2.1.1 Restriction to authorized personnel of the ability to create, change or cancel purchase requisitions, POs and outline agreements (standing purchase orders)

2.1.2 The SAP ERP source list functionality that allows only specified materials to be purchased from vendors that are included in the source list for the specified material

2.1.3 Use of the SAP ERP release strategy to authorize POs, purchase requisitions, outline agreements and unusual purchases (for example, capital outlays)

2.2.1 Matching of goods received to open POs and investigation of receipts with no PO or those that exceed the PO quantity by more than an established amount. Management reviews exception reports of goods not received on time for recorded purchases.

2.2.2 Restriction of the ability to input, change or cancel goods received transactions to authorized inbound logistics—raw materials personnel

2.3.1 Adequate segregation of rejected or defective goods (or materials or equipment) from other goods in a quality assurance bonding area and regular monitoring (assigned a specific movement type, e.g., 122) to ensure the timely return to suppliers and receipt of credit

## Purchasing Testing Techniques
Testing techniques for purchasing controls include:

2.1.1 Review organization policy and process design specifications regarding testing user access to transactions for purchase requisitions and POs:
- Create Purchase Requisition—ME51 or ME51N
- Change Purchase Requisition—ME52 or ME52N
- Release Purchase Requisition—ME54 or ME54N
- Collective Release of Purchase Requisition—ME55

| Transaction(s) | Authorization Objects | Fields | Values |
|---|---|---|---|
| ME51/ME51N | M_BANF_BSA | ACTVT | 01 |
| | M_BANF_EKG | ACTVT | 01 |
| | M_BANF_EKO | ACTVT | 01 |
| | M_BANF_WRK | ACTVT | 01 |
| Also test user access to transactions ME52/ME52N, ME54/ME54N and ME55/ME55N with the same authorization objects as above but with ACTVT field values of 02, 03 and 08, respectively. | | | |

• Create Purchase Order, Vendor Known—ME21 or ME21N
• Change Purchase Order—ME22 or ME22N

| Transaction(s) | Authorization Objects | Fields | Values |
|---|---|---|---|
| ME21/ME21N | M_BEST_BSA | ACTVT | 01 |
| | M_BEST_EKG | ACTVT | 01 |
| | M_BEST_EKO | ACTVT | 01 |
| | M_BANF_WRK | ACTVT | 01 |
| Also test user access to transactions ME22/ME22N with the same authorization objects as above but with ACTVT field value of 02. | | | |

• Maintain Purchase Order Supplement—ME24
• Create Purchase Order, Vendor Unknown—ME25
• Create Stock Transport Order —ME27

| Transaction(s) | Authorization Objects | Fields | Values |
|---|---|---|---|
| ME24/ME24N | M_RAHM_BSA | ACTVT | 01 |
| | M_RAHM_EKO | ACTVT | 01 |
| Also test user access to transactions ME25/ME25N and ME27 with the same authorization objects as above but with ACTVT field values of 01 and 09, respectively. | | | |

• Create Outline Agreement—ME31

| Transaction(s) | Authorization Objects | Fields | Values |
|---|---|---|---|
| ME31 | M_RAHM_BSA | ACTVT | 02 |
| | M_RAHM_EKG | ACTVT | 02 |
| | M_RAHM_EKO | ACTVT | 02 |

- Change Outline Agreement—ME32
- Maintain Outline Agreement Supplement—ME34

| Transaction(s) | Authorization Objects | Fields | Values |
|---|---|---|---|
| ME32, ME34 | M_RAHM_BSA | ACTVT | 02 |
| | M_RAHM_EKO | ACTVT | 02 |

2.1.2   Through discussions with management, determine the (types of) materials for which source lists should be available in the system. Also, determine materials for which a source list should not be present. Examine a selection of materials and ask to see the corresponding source list to corroborate the performance of the control activity in the appropriate accounting period. ME06 reports on all material items and whether they belong to a source list. ME0M indicates all material items and any associated vendors (including historic data). To run ME0M, a material or a range of materials must be specified. Select the Material By Material Group tab to get a list of materials. Select the aforementioned sample of orders and check against source list reports to determine whether specific materials have been procured with unlisted vendors.

2.1.3   Obtain a sufficient understanding of the system configuration to assess the adequacy of the release strategy as defined and implemented by the enterprise as well as the functioning and effectiveness of established policies, procedures, standards and guidance. View the settings online using the IMG as follows:

- Release Procedure Purchase Orders—Transaction SPRO menu path:  Materials Management ▷ Purchasing ▷ Purchase Order ▷ Release Procedure for Purchase Orders ▷ Define Release Procedure for Purchase Orders
- Release Procedure for Purchase Requisitions (with classification)— Transaction SPRO menu path:  Material Management ▷ Purchasing ▷ Purchase Requisitions ▷ Release Procedure ▷ Procedure with Classification ▷ Set Up Procedure with Classification
  - Select the Release Strategy option. Select the strategies one by one, by double-clicking on the strategy. Note the release codes that are shown; authorization (authorization objects M_BANF_FRG and M_EINK_FRG) for these release codes should be checked.
  - Click on the Classification button. This will show the conditions under which the purchase document will be blocked. Ascertain whether these conditions comply with management's intentions.
- Release Procedure Purchase Requisitions (without classification)— Transaction SPRO menu path:  Material Management ▷ Purchasing ▷ Purchase Requisitions ▷ Release Procedure ▷ Set Up Procedure Without Classification
  - Select the Release Points Prerequisites option. Note the release codes that are shown; authorization for these release codes should be checked. Go back to the previous screen and select the Determination of Release

Strategy option. This will show the conditions under which the purchase document will be blocked. Ascertain whether these conditions comply with management's intentions.
- Test user access to transactions for release strategies:
  - Release (Approve) Purchasing Order —ME28 or ME29N
  - Release (Approve) Outline Agreement—ME35
  - Release (Approve) Scheduling Agreement—ME35L
  - Release (Approve) Contract—ME35K
  - Release Purchase Requisition—ME54/ME54N
  - Collective Release of Purchase Requisitions—ME55
2.2.1 Run the transaction code VL10B (also accessible using transaction code SA38 and program RM06EM00) to produce a listing of outstanding POs. Ascertain from management whether there are reasons for any long-outstanding items on the report.
2.2.2 Test user access to transactions for goods receipt:
- Goods Receipt for Purchase Order—MB01
- Goods Receipts, Purchase Order Unknown—MB0A

| Transaction(s) | Authorization Objects | Fields | Values |
|---|---|---|---|
| MB01, MB0A | M_MSEG_BWE | ACTVT | 01 |
| | M_MSEG_WWE | ACTVT | 01 |

- Goods Receipt for Production Order—MB31

| Transaction(s) | Authorization Objects | Fields | Values |
|---|---|---|---|
| MB31 | M_RAHM_BSA | ACTVT | 01 |
| | M_RAHM_EKO | ACTVT | 01 |

- Enter Other Goods Receipts—MB1C

| Transaction(s) | Authorization Objects | Fields | Values |
|---|---|---|---|
| MB1C | M_MSEG_BWA | ACTVT | 01 |
| | M_MSEG_BWE | ACTVT | 01 |
| | M_MSEG_WWA | ACTVT | 01 |

- Cancel Material Document—MBST

| Transaction(s) | Authorization Objects | Fields | Values |
|---|---|---|---|
| MBST | M_MSEG_BMB | ACTVT | 01 |
| | M_MSEG_WMB | ACTVT | 01 |

Test user access to high-risk movement types 561 through 566. These special movement types reflect the initial stock entry in the SAP ERP system at the time of conversion to the SAP ERP system.

2.3.1 Ascertain from management the movement type used to block processing and for returning rejected goods to suppliers (e.g., movement type 122). Execute transaction MB51 with the appropriate movement type. Determine if there are any long-outstanding materials pending return to suppliers/ receipt of appropriate credits.

# Invoice Processing

## Invoice Processing Risks

Significant risks associated with invoice processing include:

3.1 If amounts posted to accounts payable do not represent goods or services received, then unauthorized payments may be made and the organization may incur a financial loss. In addition, accounts payable may be misstated, as will the relevant expense, inventory or asset accounts.

3.2 Accounts payable amounts are not completely and accurately calculated or not recorded in a timely manner.
   • If accounts payable amounts are not recorded completely and accurately, suppliers may not be paid in full, possibly damaging supplier relations.
   • If invoice verification and three-way matching are not performed effectively, large balances may build up in the GR/IR account that ultimately cannot be reconciled and must be written off.

3.3 Credit notes and other adjustments are not completely and accurately calculated or not recorded in a timely manner.

## Invoice Processing Key Controls

Key controls over invoice processing include:

3.1.1 Restriction of the ability to input, change, cancel or release vendor invoices for payment to authorized personnel. The ability to input vendor invoices that do not have a purchase order and/or goods receipt as support is further restricted to authorized personnel.

3.2.1 Configuration of the SAP ERP software to perform a three-way match

3.2.2 Configuration of the SAP ERP software with quantity and price tolerance limits

3.2.3 Configuration of the GR/IR account

3.2.4 Regular review of reports of outstanding purchase orders

3.2.5 The SAP ERP software's restriction of the ability to modify the exchange rate table to authorized personnel. Management approves values in the centrally maintained exchange rate table. The SAP ERP software automatically calculates foreign currency exchanges based on values in the centrally maintained exchange rate table.

3.2.6 Scrutiny of supplier invoices and credit notes received at, before or after the end of a statutory accounting period and/or their reconciliation to ensure complete and consistent recording in the appropriate period

3.3.1 Restriction to authorized personnel of the ability to input, change, cancel or release credit notes

## Invoice Processing Testing Techniques

Testing techniques for invoice processing controls include:

3.1.1 Test user access to transactions for invoice processing:
- Functionality: Create/change invoice
  - Enter Invoice—MRHR, MIRO, MR01

| Transaction(s) | Authorization Objects | Fields | Values |
|---|---|---|---|
| MRHR | F_BKPF_BUK | ACTVT | 01 |
|  | F_BKPF_GSB | ACTVT | 01 |
| MIRO | M_RECH_AKZ | ACTVT | 01 |
|  | M_RECH_WRK | ACTVT | 01 |
| MR01 | F_BKPF_KOA | ACTVT | 01 |

  - Change Invoice—FB02

| Transaction(s) | Authorization Objects | Fields | Values |
|---|---|---|---|
| FB02 | F_BKPF_BLA | ACTVT | 02 |
|  | F_BKPF_KOA | ACTVT | 02 |

  - Process Blocked Invoices—MR02

| Transaction(s) | Authorization Objects | Fields | Values |
|---|---|---|---|
| MR02 | M_RECH_SPG | ACTVT | 02 |

  - Cancel Invoice—MR08
  - Enter Credit Memo—MRHG

| Transaction(s) | Authorization Objects | Fields | Values |
|---|---|---|---|
| MR08, MRHG | F_BKPF_KOA | ACTVT | 01 |

3.2.1 View the settings online using the IMG as follows:
Define Screen Layout at Document Level—Transaction SPRO menu path: Materials Management ▷ Purchasing ▷ Purchase Order ▷ Define Screen Layout at Document. Select ME21 (create purchase order) and then select GR/IR control. Determine whether GR/IR control has been set globally to required entry. If the GR/IR control indicator has not been set globally for all vendors, determine whether it has been set for particular vendors by displaying table LFM1, field name WEBRE, using transaction SE16. Where GR/IR control has not been set, ascertain from management whether there are any reasons.

3.2.2 Check tolerance limits for price variances and message settings for invoice verification (online matching) as follows:
- Variance settings—Execute transaction OMR6. The system will show an overview of the defined tolerance limits. Double-click on the entries that relate to the company being audited. Two entries need to be checked: one for tolerance key PE (price) and one for tolerance key SE (discount). Note the values shown. Lower and upper limits may be specified as a percentage value. (PE allows setting an absolute value.) Ascertain whether the values noted comply with management's intentions.
- Message settings—View the settings online using the IMG as follows: Transaction SPRO menu path: Materials Management ▷ Purchasing ▷ Environment Data ▷ Define Attributes of System Messages. Click on the Position button. Enter values 00, 06 and 207 (message for price variance) and press Enter. Note the value in the cat field. Possible values are W, for warning, and E, for error. Ascertain whether the values noted comply with management's intentions.

3.2.3 Using transaction code S_P6B_12000135 (also accessible using transaction code SA38 and program RM07MSAL), determine whether GR/IR account balances are executed and reviewed periodically. Check that there are appropriate procedures in place to investigate unmatched POs. In particular, long-outstanding items should be followed up and cleared.

3.2.4 As for 2.2.1, run the transaction code SA38 and program RM06EM00 to produce a listing of outstanding POs.

3.2.5 Determine whether management reviews a sample of changes to exchange rates above a certain percentage in regard to the volume and value of foreign currency transactions for the organization. Test user access to the exchange rates and the related authorization objects:
- Functionality: Exchange rate via standard transaction. First execute transaction SUCU. Click on the Position button. Enter value V_TCURR and press Enter. Note the value in the authorization group field.

| Transaction(s) | Authorization Objects | Fields | Values |
|---|---|---|---|
| 0B08 | S_TABU_DIS | ACTVT | 02 |

• Functionality: Exchange rate via view maintenance

| Transaction(s) | Authorization Objects | Fields | Values |
|---|---|---|---|
| SM30 | S_TABU_DIS | ACTVT | 02 |

• Functionality: Maintenance rounding units/foreign currency ratios

First execute transaction SUCU. Click on the Position button. Enter table name value V_T001R, and click on the Choose button. Note the value in the authorization group field. Do the same for table V_TCURF.
– Field transaction code: Select values from the following:
  · Maintain Table Rounding Units—OB90
  · Maintain Table Foreign Currency Ratios—OBBS
  · Table View Maintenance—SM30

| Transaction(s) | Authorization Objects | Fields | Values |
|---|---|---|---|
| OB90, OBBS, SM30 | S_TABU_DIS | ACTVT | 02 |

3.3.1 Test user access to post invoices directly to vendor accounts:
• Enter Credit Note—MRHG

| Transaction(s) | Authorization Objects | Fields | Values |
|---|---|---|---|
| MRHG | F_BKPF_KOA | ACTVT | 01 |

• Enter Invoice— MRHR, MIRO, MR01

| Transaction(s) | Authorization Objects | Fields | Values |
|---|---|---|---|
| MRHR, MR01 | F_BKPF_KOA | ACTVT | 01 |
| MIRO | M_RECH_AKZ | ACTVT | 01 |
| | M_RECH_WRK | ACTVT | 01 |

# Processing Disbursements

## Processing Disbursements Risks
Significant risks associated with processing disbursements include:
4.1 Disbursements should be made only for goods and services received, and should be accurately calculated, recorded and distributed to the appropriate suppliers in a timely manner. For example:
• Unauthorized payments could be made to fictitious parties if disbursements are not made to the appropriate suppliers. Such errors may go undetected.

• Incorrect disbursements could result in suppliers being paid incorrect amounts, not being paid, being paid before or after due dates, or being paid for goods or services that have not been received. Accurate calculation of disbursements includes accurate calculation of any available discounts. Cash flow decisions could also be affected if data on which these decisions are made are incorrect.

• Disbursements that are not recorded can affect cash flow decisions and cause reconciliation difficulties. Failure to record disbursements may also result in duplicate payments.

## Processing Disbursements Key Controls

Key controls over invoice processing include:

4.1.1 Management approval of the SAP ERP payment run parameter specification. The SAP ERP software restricts to authorized personnel the ability to modify the payment run parameter specification or to initiate a payment run.

4.1.2 The SAP ERP software's restriction to authorized personnel of the ability to release invoices that have been blocked for payment, either for an individual invoice or for a specified vendor

## Processing Disbursements Testing Techniques

Testing techniques for processing disbursements controls include:

4.1.1 Test user access to transactions to process disbursements:
• Automatic Scheduling of Payment Transactions—F110S
• Parameters for Automatic Payment—F110

| Transaction(s) | Authorization Objects | Fields | Values |
|---|---|---|---|
| F110, F110S | F_REGU _KOA | ACTVT | 01, 02, 03, 11, 12, 13, 14, 15, 21, 23, 24, 25, 31 |

• Payment With Printout—F-58

| Transaction(s) | Authorization Objects | Fields | Values |
|---|---|---|---|
| F-58 | F_BKPF_KOA | ACTVT | 01 |

4.1.2 Test user access to release invoices that have been blocked:
• Change Document—FB02

| Transaction(s) | Authorization Objects | Fields | Values |
|---|---|---|---|
| FB02 | F_BKPF_BLA | ACTVT | 02 |
| | F_BKPF_KOA | ACTVT | 02 |

- Change Line Items—FB09

| Transaction(s) | Authorization Objects | Fields | Values |
|---|---|---|---|
| FB09 | F_BKPF_KOA | ACTVT | 02 |

- Block/unblock Vendor (centrally)—XK05

| Transaction(s) | Authorization Objects | Fields | Values |
|---|---|---|---|
| XK05 | F_LFA1_BUK | ACTVT | 05 |
| | F_LFA1_GEN | ACTVT | 05 |

- Block/Unblock Vendor—FK05

| Transaction(s) | Authorization Objects | Fields | Values |
|---|---|---|---|
| FK05 | F_LFA1_BUK | ACTVT | 05 |
| | F_LFA1_GEN | ACTVT | 05 |

## Expenditure Cycle Controls and Financial Statement Assertions

The Expenditure cycle risk numbers from this chapter have been mapped to controls listed in **figure 24**—Application Control Objectives for the Purchasing Cycle of *IT Control Objectives for Sarbanes-Oxley, 2nd Edition*, IT Governance Institute,[12] as shown in **figure 8.2**. The risk number mapping should be looked at in conjunction with the associated control and testing technique numbers to help gain an understanding of the impact of the risks and controls on the financial reporting process in terms of completeness, occurrence, valuation and validity.

| Figure 8.2—Expenditure Risk Cycle Controls | | |
|---|---|---|
| Illustrative Control Objectives | Financial Statement Assertions | Expenditure Cycle Risk Number |
| Purchase orders are placed only for approved requisitions. | Existence | 2.1 |
| Purchase orders are accurately entered. | Valuation | 2.1 |
| All purchase orders issued are input and processed. | Completeness | 2.1 |
| Amounts posted to accounts payable represent goods or services received. | Existence | 3.1 |
| Accounts payable amounts are accurately calculated and recorded. | Valuation | 3.2 |

[12] *Ibid.*

| Figure 8.2—Expenditure Risk Cycle Controls *(cont.)* | | |
|---|---|---|
| **Illustrative Control Objectives** | **Financial Statement Assertions** | **Expenditure Cycle Risk Number** |
| All amounts for goods or services received are input and processed to accounts payable. | Completeness | 3.2 |
| Amounts for goods or services received are recorded in the appropriate period. | Valuation | 2.2 |
| Accounts payable are adjusted only for valid reasons. | Completeness Existence | 3.1 |
| Credit notes and other adjustments are accurately calculated and recorded. | Valuation | 3.3 |
| All valid credit notes and other adjustments related to accounts payable are input and processed. | Completeness Existence | 3.3 |
| Credit notes and other adjustments are recorded in the appropriate period. | Valuation | 3.3 |
| Disbursements are made only for goods and services received. | Existence | 4.1 |
| Disbursements are distributed to the appropriate suppliers. | Existence | 4.1 |
| Disbursements are accurately calculated and recorded. | Valuation | 4.1 |
| All disbursements are recorded. | Completeness | 4.1 |
| Disbursements are recorded in the period in which they are issued. | Valuation | 4.1 |
| Only valid changes are made to the supplier master file. | Completeness Existence | 1.1 |
| All valid changes to the supplier master file are input and processed. | Completeness Existence | 1.1 |
| Changes to the supplier master file are accurate. | Valuation | 1.1 |
| Changes to the supplier master file are processed in a timely manner. | Completeness Existence | 1.1 |
| Supplier master file data remain up to date. | Completeness Existence | 1.2 |

## Summary

This chapter outlined the risks, key controls and testing techniques surrounding the SAP ERP Expenditure business cycle. Among the key risks are duplicate payments, overuse of the one-time vendor account, failure to reconcile the goods received/invoice received account on a regular basis, and inappropriate access to release purchase orders, blocked invoices or payment runs.

# 9. SAP ERP Inventory Business Cycle

This chapter outlines the functionality of the SAP ERP inventory business cycle to provide a high-level understanding of the process. From a risk and controls perspective, the inventory cycle has four main subprocesses, as depicted in **figure 9.1**:
• Master data maintenance
• Raw materials management
• Producing and costing inventory
• Handling and shipping finished goods

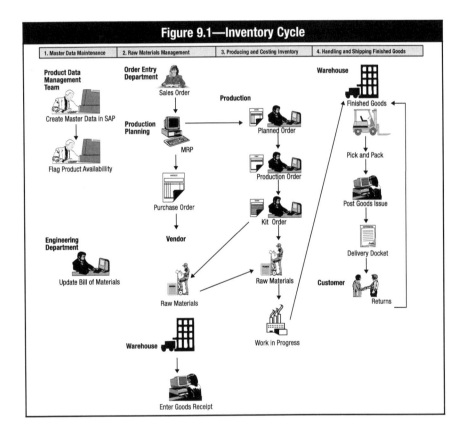

### Figure 9.1—Inventory Cycle

| 1. Master Data Maintenance | 2. Raw Materials Management | 3. Producing and Costing Inventory | 4. Handling and Shipping Finished Goods |
|---|---|---|---|

## Master Data Maintenance

The material master is the enterprise's central source for retrieving material-specific data. It is used by all the components in the SAP ERP logistics system. The integration of all material data in a single database object eliminates redundant data storage. Areas such as purchasing, inventory management, material requirements planning (MRP), warehouse management and invoice verification can all use the same data.

In the SAP logistics system, the data contained in the material master are required in the following functions, among others:
• Purchasing for ordering
• Inventory management for goods movement postings and physical inventory
• MRP
• Warehouse management
• Invoice verification for posting invoices
• Sales and distribution for sales order processing
• Production planning and control for MRP, scheduling and work scheduling
• Financial and management accounting for reporting, valuing and cost control purposes

As mentioned in the description of master data relating to the Revenue cycle, material master data are stored as general data (e.g., material number, description, unit of measure, technical data) that relate to every company code as well as a variety of other data including accounting data, purchasing data, production data, storage information and quality management information (e.g., "use by" date).

Another important component of Inventory master data is a bill of materials (BOM). It is a list of the resources needed to build a product or part. These resources can include other products/parts, man-hours and equipment-hours needed. These lists can have an effect on the valuation of inventory as the parts are constructed. A BOM can have multiple levels. For example, separate BOMs may exist for raw materials, work in progress and finished goods. As materials move through the production process their value from an accounting perspective can be estimated based on the multilayered BOM. Once production has been completed, the actual costs of production can be transferred to general ledger accounts for finished goods or general ledger accounts for variances based on production or process order settlement rules specified in the SAP ERP system.

# Raw Materials Management

Distribution requirements planning (DRP) refers to the process of determining which finished goods warehouses need to satisfy customer demand in that location. DRP may be linked to MRP, so raw material requirements and the production of finished goods keep pace with demand in a cost-effective manner. The MRP procurement type defined in the material master determines the requirements for procuring materials from external or internal sources. It refers to the management, tracking, ordering and recording of movements of inventory/materials. Through the use of the purchasing and warehouse/inventory systems, the MM module is able to provide the basis for MRP, which is the process of determining the raw materials a plant needs to satisfy the needs of production and minimize the enterprise's investment in inventory. Consumption-based MRP depends on consumption (usage) data to generate procurement proposals, either on the reorder point principle (inventories are automatically replenished once they have been depleted to a certain level) or based on forecasts (e.g., from sales orders in the system or forecasts from sales and marketing). Additional requirements are recorded in the form of requisitions and are allocated to the responsible buyers in purchasing. In the process, appropriate order quantities are determined and an adequate service level ensured.

## Producing and Costing Inventory

Raw materials received from suppliers are administered by the Inventory Management module until they are delivered to customers (sale or distribution of raw materials) or used for internal purposes (such as production). The user can:
- Manage inventory on a quantity and value basis. When managing inventories on a quantity basis, physical inventory reflects all transactions resulting in a change in quantities held and thus in updated inventory levels. The user can easily obtain an overview of the current availability of any given material. When managing inventories by value, inventories are managed not only on a quantity basis but also by value—a prerequisite for effective management and financial accounting. Both the quantity and the value are updated automatically when entering a goods movement. With every goods movement, the following values are updated:
  - The stock value for inventory management
  - The account assignment for cost accounting
  - The corresponding general ledger accounts for financial accounting, via automatic account assignment
- Carry out physical inventory counts. The adjustment between the physical and book inventories can be carried out independently of the physical inventory method selected. The SAP ERP system supports the following physical inventory methods: periodic inventory, inventory sampling and cycle counting.
- Plan, enter and check any goods movements, which include external movements (goods receipts from external procurement, goods issues for sales orders) and internal movements (goods receipts from production, withdrawals of material for internal purposes, stock transfers and transfer postings). For each goods movement, a material document is created that is used by the system to update quantities and values and serves as proof of goods movements. Goods receipts/ issue slips are printed to facilitate physical movements and the monitoring of the individual materials in the warehouse.

Raw materials are often formed into kits that consist of the appropriate materials for a particular production function. These kits are then transferred to production as needed to satisfy particular production orders.

The production process is organized into a series of work centers consisting of people and manufacturing equipment grouped together to carry out particular production functions (e.g., in automobile manufacturing, there may be work centers for assembly, painting and inspection). Materials and costs flow through these work centers and are reflected in the appropriate inventory accounts for valuation purposes.

# Handling and Shipping Finished Goods

Once goods are produced, they are transferred to the warehouse as finished goods. Management of warehouses is important for efficient and effective processing of logistical requirements within a company for finished goods and raw materials. The Warehouse Management (WM) module manages complex warehouse structures and several different types of warehousing facilities, including automatic warehouses, custom-designed storage areas, high-rack storage, block storage, fixed-bin storage and all other commonly used storage areas.

WM has the ability to define and adapt a variety of storage bins for use in a specific warehousing complex. It can process all warehousing activities and movement tasks, e.g., goods receipts, goods issues, internal and external stock transfers, automatic replenishment of fixed bins, material staging to production areas and stock difference handling.

The Warehouse Management system also can:
- Use random slotting for multiple owners of goods
- Display summary evaluations of all goods movements in the warehouse
- Implement a variety of put-away and picking strategies, including self-designed strategies
- Support the storage and retrieval of hazardous materials and all other goods that require special handling
- Maintain up-to-the-minute inventory records at the storage bin level, using real-time continuous inventory techniques
- Support the use of automated barcode scanners and radio frequency technology for all stock movements
- Interface to external non-SAP ERP warehousing systems
- Integrate the Warehouse Management system for instantaneous interaction with other SAP ERP components MM, MM-IM), PM, PP, QM and SD
- Perform analysis of requirements and automatic assignment of goods to optimum locations in the warehouse, using put-away strategies that can be easily defined to match the characteristics of each storage area
- Configure areas for back-order staging and cross-docking of received goods
- Set up forward pick areas and production supply areas with automatic continuous replenishment from case or reserve storage when the threshold is reached

WM is fully integrated into SAP as a whole. Availability checks are performed whenever transactions are initiated. Book inventories in Inventory Management always match inventory in the warehouse—no separate interface programs are required.

# Summary

This chapter provided an overall understanding of the operation of the Inventory business cycle in an SAP ERP environment. It summarized important functionality from an audit perspective, including material and distribution requirements planning, bills of material, work centers, process order settlement rules, stock transfers and goods issue.

# 10. Auditing the SAP ERP Inventory Business Cycle

Chapter 9 outlined the four main subprocesses of the Inventory business cycle. This chapter looks at the significant risks, key controls and techniques to test the controls for each of the four main subprocesses as follows:
• Master data maintenance
• Raw materials management
• Producing and costing inventory
• Handling and shipping finished goods

The authorization objects and associated activity values contained in the Testing Techniques sections of this chapter are only a selection of key authorization objects for the transaction. An understanding of the enterprise's implementation of processes in SAP is required to ensure that testing is complete and includes all necessary authorization objects and values.

Refer to the numbering system in chapter 4, page 79.

## Master Data Maintenance

### Master Data Maintenance Risks
Significant risks associated with material master data include:
1.1   In the inventory cycle, changes to the material management master data are invalid, incomplete, inaccurate and/or untimely. Because the material management master file is used by a number of applications, errors in input have more impact than errors relating to transactions (i.e., such errors tend to cascade). For example, inaccurate changes to the inventory management master file may result in errors as follows:
• Invalid product information may result in incorrect inventory items being produced and shipped to customers.
• Invalid product numbers may cause shipment of the wrong products, resulting in returned goods and customer dissatisfaction.
• An invalid product location may cause inventory to be misplaced and, potentially, become obsolete.
• Invalid unit costs may result in incorrect valuation of inventory and recording of inventory and cost of goods sold.
• Invalid quantities on hand may cause unnecessary production or delays in production, which may lead to excess inventory or delays in supplying customers.

1.2    Inventory master data do not remain current and pertinent. For example, a duplicate product record could result in confusion as to the availability of inventory.

1.3    Settings or changes to the bill of materials or process order settlement rules may be invalid, incomplete, inaccurate and/or untimely. This could result in incorrect valuation of finished goods for financial and management accounting purposes.

## *Master Data Maintenance Key Controls*

Key controls over the maintenance of inventory master data include:

1.1.1  Checking by relevant management, other than the initiators, of online reports of master data additions, changes and deletions to source documentation on a sample basis

1.1.2  The creation and maintenance of master data being assigned and restricted to dedicated people within the organization who understand how they may impact on organizational processes and the importance of timely changes

1.1.3  Configurable controls designed to maintain the integrity of master data. These configurable controls for material master data include:
  • The material type, which defines if the material can be configured and how quantities and values are updated for that material
  • Industry sector, which can be configured so products may be sold and packaged in different ways (e.g., single units for the retail industry sector and pallets for the wholesale industry sector) and each sector has a different costing and billing structure
  • Default price type settings for material types
  • Definition of tolerances for physical inventory differences to restrict the value of physical inventory differences users can post. If the difference between physical and theoretical inventory exceeds the tolerance, the user may not post the difference.
  • Periodic review by management of material master data (purchasing materials only) to verify if the over-delivery tolerance is different from 0.0% or the unlimited delivery is set.

1.2.1  The relevant management's periodic review of master data to ensure currency and ongoing pertinence. In addition, negative stock settings are allowed only for those material records that require it.

1.3.1  As for control 1.1.2, restriction of the ability to create, change or delete the bill of material to authorized personnel

1.3.2  As for control 1.1.1, comparison by relevant management, other than the initiators, of online reports of bill of material or settlement rule additions and changes to source documentation on a sample basis

## Master Data Maintenance Testing Techniques

Testing techniques for inventory master data controls include:

1.1.1 Take a sample of source documents for evidence of comparison to inventory file updates. Confirm that management executes transaction MM04 and compares against source documents for a sample of changes that have been effected.

1.1.2 Review organization policy and process design specifications regarding access to maintain master data. Test user access to create (transaction MM01), maintain (transaction MM02) and delete (transaction MM06) material master data. Use transaction code SUIM to examine user access to the transactions and authorization objects.

| Transaction(s) | Authorization Objects | Fields | Values |
|---|---|---|---|
| MM01 | M_MATE_MAR | ACTVT | 01 |
| | M_MATE_STA | ACTVT | 01 |
| Also test user access to transactions MM02/MM06 with the same authorization objects as above but with ACTVT field values of 02 and 06, respectively. | | | |

1.1.3 Determine whether the configurable control settings address the risks pertaining to the validity, completeness and accuracy of master data and whether they have been set in accordance with management's intentions. View the settings online using the IMG as follows:
  • Material types: Transaction SPRO menu path Logistics—General ▷ Material Master ▷ Basic Settings ▷ Material Types ▷ Define Attributes of Material Types
  • Industry sector: Transaction SPRO menu path Logistics—General ▷ Material Master ▷ Field Selection ▷ Define Industry Sectors and Industry-Sector-Specific Field Selection
  • Default price types: Execute transaction OMW1, and determine whether default settings have been set for the price type for material records.
  • Tolerances for physical inventory differences: Execute transaction OMJ2, compare defined tolerances to organizational policy and judge for reasonableness. If OMJ2 is executed, the screen will provide two options for maintenance of inventory tolerance settings, either by physical inventory tolerance groups or by user name. If the company has adopted inventory tolerance control at the group level, execute transaction OMJ2 and click Physical Inventory Tolerance Groups. If the tolerance has been set by specific users, select User Name.

1.2.1 Determine whether appropriate management is running the MM60 Materials List, or equivalent, by material type and confirm evidence of management's review of the data on a rotating basis for currency and ongoing pertinence.

1.3.1 Review organization policy and process design specifications regarding access to maintain bill of material and process order settlement rules. Test user access to create (transaction code CS01), change (transaction code

CS02), make mass changes to (transaction code CS20), change single-layered work breakdown structure bill of materials (transaction code CS72) and change multilayered work breakdown structure bill of materials (transaction code CS75).

| Transaction(s) | Authorization Objects | Fields | Values |
|---|---|---|---|
| CS01 | C_AENR_RV1 | ACTVT | 01 |
| | C_STUE_BER | ACTVT | 01 |
| CS02 | C_STUE_BER | ACTVT | 02 |
| | C_STUE_WRK | ACTVT | 02 |
| CS20 | C_STUE_BER | ACTVT | 02 |
| CS72 | C_STUE_BER | ACTVT | 02 |
| | C_STUE_WRK | ACTVT | 02 |
| | C_AENR_BGR | ACTVT | 22 |
| CS75 | C_STUE_BER | ACTVT | 02 |
| | C_STUE_WRK | ACTVT | 02 |
| | C_AENR_BGR | ACTVT | 22 |

Test user access to change settlement rules (transaction code COR2: Menu path: Logistics ▷ Production—Process ▷ Process Order ▷ Process Order ▷ COR2—Change, then enter the process order number and press Enter. Finally, go to Header ▷ Settlement Rule).

1.3.2 Take a sample of BOM updates using transaction CS80 and compare to authorized source documentation.

# Raw Materials Management

## Raw Materials Management Risks

Significant risks associated with raw materials processing include:

2.1 Inventory is not salable, usable or adequately safeguarded. For example, the organization may have produced inventory that is no longer in demand and, therefore, is not salable. In certain industries, e.g., the chemical industry, the cost of disposing of obsolete inventory can be high. In addition, certain types of inventory (e.g., food products and other perishables), have a limited life span. Adequate coordination of sales, inventory management and production, adequate storage facilities, and ongoing monitoring are key to maintaining the salability of inventory and maximizing its life span.

2.2 Raw materials are received and accepted without valid purchase orders and/or are recorded inaccurately or untimely.

2.3 Defective raw materials are not returned in a timely manner to suppliers.

## *Raw Materials Management Key Controls*

Key controls over raw materials processing include:

2.1.1 Planning of raw material requirements based on forecasts, orders and production plans. The forecasts and production plans form the input to a distribution requirements planning run to determine raw material requirements by location. Each plant location then runs MRP to produce purchase orders for vendors. The system functionality monitors and maintains inventory levels in accordance with organization policies. The salability of finished goods and the usability of raw materials (including shelf life dates) are assessed regularly during continuous inventory counts, and any scrapped goods or raw materials are approved appropriately. The quality department tests a sample of raw materials and rejected raw materials are segregated from other raw materials into a separate quality assurance bonding area and regularly monitored by the quality department personnel to ensure the timely return to suppliers. Management reviews reports of slow-turnover inventory to ensure that it is still salable or usable. Goods inward/outward personnel monitor all incoming and outgoing vehicles and ensure that all goods leaving the premises are accompanied by duly completed documentation (e.g., intercompany stock transfer orders, delivery dockets or goods-returned notes). Goods are delivered only to designated, physically secure loading bays within the warehouses and are accepted only by authorized inbound logistic/raw materials personnel. Inventory is stored in properly secured (gates locked at night and premises alarmed), environmentally conditioned warehouse locations where access is restricted to authorized personnel.

2.2.1 Online match of goods received with PO details and/or invoices. Long-outstanding goods receipt notes, POs and/or invoices are investigated in a timely manner and accrued as appropriate. Documents are marked as matched or paid, once matched or upon payment of the invoice, to prevent reuse. Management reviews exception reports of goods not received on time for recorded purchases.

2.2.2 When goods received are matched to open POs, investigation of receipts with no PO or those that exceed the PO quantity by more than an established amount

2.2.3 Restriction to authorized inbound logistics/raw materials personnel of the ability to input, change or cancel goods-received transactions

2.2.4 Count of physical inventory on a continuous inventory basis by persons independent of day-to-day custody or recording of inventory. Physical inventory counts are reconciled to inventory records, and inventory records are reconciled to the general ledger (through transfer documents in the SAP ERP system). Monthly stock takes are also performed to record movements in the appropriate period. Where inventory adjustment forms are used, they should be sequentially prenumbered and the sequence accounted for. Physical inventory counting methods include continuous inventory basis, monthly stock takes and cycle counting.

2.2.5 For raw materials/finished goods that are batch managed, matching and accounting with an appropriate batch management strategy, including a periodic investigation on date expired, short expiry and defective batches, which are correctly matched with returned stock transactions

2.3.1 Adequate segregation of rejected raw materials from other raw materials in a quality assurance bonding area and regular monitoring (assigned a movement type of 122) to ensure timely return to suppliers. Defective raw materials received from suppliers are logged and recorded in the quality management system; the log is monitored to ensure that the defective goods are returned promptly and credit is received in a timely manner.

## Raw Materials Management Testing Techniques

Testing techniques for raw materials management controls include:

2.1.1 Confirm that the DRP process takes into account stock on hand, forecast requirements, economic order quantities and back orders. Execute transaction code MB5M and ascertain the reason for any old stock being held (shelf life list). Use transaction MC46 to identify slow-moving items and MC50 for dead stock (i.e., stock that has not been used for a certain period of time). Test to ensure that managers are reviewing this information on a regular basis.

2.2.1 As for the Expenditure cycle 2.2.1, test that management executes the report of outstanding POs using transaction ME2L, and follow up on any long-outstanding items.

2.2.2 Review the reconciliation of the goods received/invoice received account (transaction code MB5S, refer to Expenditure cycle 3.2.3) and confirm that unmatched items have been investigated on a timely basis.

2.2.3 Test user access to transactions for goods receipt (refer to Expenditure cycle 2.2.2).

2.2.4 Ensure that changes to the quantities of the inventory take place when they are moved (for sale to customer, rework, transfer, etc.). A movement type dictates these moves. Movement types explain the reason for the quantity change in inventory. Review materials quantity changes/movements and corresponding movement types via transaction MB51, which allows for the review of changes to several materials at the same time. The SAP ERP transaction MB59 allows for the performance of a search on multiple materials by a particular range of dates. Take a further sample of inventory file updates using transaction MB59 and compare the results to authorized source documentation. Review the process for physical stock-takes to confirm the complete, accurate, valid and timely recording of stock differences.

2.3.1 As for the Expenditure cycle 2.3.1, ascertain from management the movement type used to block processing and to return rejected goods to suppliers (e.g., movement type 122). Execute transaction MB51 with the appropriate movement type. Determine whether there are any long-outstanding materials pending return to suppliers/receipt of appropriate credits.

# Producing and Costing Inventory

## Producing and Costing Inventory Risks
Significant risks associated with producing and costing inventory include:

3.1 Transfers of raw materials to production may not be recorded accurately, completely and in the appropriate period. Recorded production costs may not be consistent with actual direct and indirect expenses associated with production or are not recorded accurately and in a timely manner. Transfers of completed units of production to finished goods inventory may not be recorded completely and accurately in the appropriate period. Defective products and scrap resulting from the production process may not be valid and recorded completely and accurately in the appropriate period.

## Producing and Costing Inventory Key Controls
Key controls over producing and costing inventory include:

3.1.1 Count of inventories received, including transfers, and their comparison to the pick list (used to record movements of inventory in the financial records) by personnel in the area, assuming responsibility for the inventory (e.g., production, finished goods storage) and their recording in the appropriate period. The goods-in-transit accounts should always reconcile against other plants' outgoing goods-in-transit accounts. Management should reconcile these accounts regularly. An appropriate costing method is used for raw materials at purchase order price. The raw materials costs are rolled into finished goods that are valued on a monthly basis using the appropriate costing method. The quality department, based on its knowledge of day-to-day activities, reviews records of scrapped and reworked items and checks whether such items have been correctly identified and properly recorded in the appropriate accounting period.

3.1.2 Restriction—to authorized personnel—of the ability to create or change bills of material

3.1.3 Restriction—to authorized personnel—of access to the material transfers and adjustments transactions

3.1.4 Restriction—to authorized personnel—of the ability to create or change work centers

## Producing and Costing Inventory Testing Techniques
Testing techniques for producing and costing inventory controls include:

3.1.1 Review the policy and procedures concerning the transfer of materials and confirm that the previously described controls are in place and operating. Test that inventory-in-transit accounts are regularly reviewed to ensure that the accounts are cleared and reconciled. Confirm that default price types have been established for all materials (refer to 1.1.3).

3.1.2 Test user access to bills of materials (refer to 1.3.1).

3.1.3  Test user access to issue goods (transaction code MB1A) and to posting of transfers among plants (transaction code MB1B).

| Transaction(s) | Authorization Objects | Fields | Values |
|---|---|---|---|
| MB1A, MB1B | M_MSEG_BWA | ACTVT | 01 |
| | M_MSEG_WWA | ACTVT | 01 |

3.1.4  Test user access to create (transaction code CR01) or change (transaction code CR02) work centers.

| Transaction(s) | Authorization Objects | Fields | Values |
|---|---|---|---|
| CR01 | C_ARPL_WRK | ACTVT | 01 |
| Also test user access to transactions CR02 with the same authorization object as above, but with ACTVT field value of 02. | | | |

# Handling and Shipping Finished Goods

## Handling and Shipping Finished Goods Risks

Significant risks associated with handling and shipping finished goods include:

4.1  Finished goods received from production may not be recorded completely and accurately in the appropriate period.

4.2  Goods returned by customers may be accepted, contrary to the organization's policies.

4.3  Shipments may not be recorded accurately, in a timely manner and in the appropriate period. For example, shipments not recorded in a timely manner may result in overstatement of finished goods inventory, which, in turn, may result in production schedules being set too low. Shipments not recorded in the appropriate period may result in the misstatement of inventory and accounts receivable. Unrecorded shipments are unlikely to be invoiced, resulting in a loss.

## Handling and Shipping Finished Goods Key Controls

Key controls over handling and shipping finished goods include:

4.1.1  Count of physical inventory on a continuous inventory basis by persons independent of day-to-day custody or recording of inventory (refer to 2.2.4)

4.1.2  Restriction—to authorized users—of the changing of the settlement rules (refer to 1.3.1)

4.2.1  Performance of quality control inspections for finished goods returned by customers and/or received from production to assess whether such goods should be returned to inventory, reworked or scrapped. The QA team inspects the goods before a credit note can be issued.

4.3.1 Restriction of access to or transfer of stock among plants or the ability to execute the post goods issue that creates the intercompany stock transfer advice and/or generates an EDI or manual invoice. Outbound logistics/ finished goods personnel monitor all incoming and outgoing vehicles and ensure that all goods leaving the premises are accompanied by duly completed documentation (e.g., delivery docket or goods returned note). Before goods are shipped, the details of the approved order are compared to actual goods prepared for shipment by an individual independent of the order-picking process. The shipping area performs this task when executing the post goods issue in the SAP ERP system.

4.3.2 Preparation of the SAP ERP reports (delivery-due list and owed-to-customer report) of open sales documents and their monitoring to ensure timely shipment. The SAP ERP account assignment configuration ensures that amounts for shipped goods are posted to the appropriate cost-of-goods-sold account. This is based on the material master data, which determine the valuation category to credit and debit cost of goods sold.

## Handling and Shipping Finished Goods Testing Techniques

Testing techniques for handling and shipping finished goods controls include:

4.1.1 Test inventory stock-take procedures (refer to 1.1.1—Testing Techniques).

4.1.2 Test user access to change settlement rules (refer to 1.3.1—Testing Techniques).

4.2.1 Review the policies and procedures for receiving inventory back into the warehouse. Review some returns of inventory and ensure that they are supported with adequate documentation from the quality inspector. Ascertain from management the movement type used for goods returned from customers. Execute transaction MB51 with the appropriate movement type. Determine whether there are any long-outstanding materials pending the return to inventory/provision of appropriate credits.

4.3.1 Test user access to transfer stock among plants (transaction code LT04) or change outbound delivery (transaction code VL02N).

| Transaction(s) | Authorization Objects | Fields | Values |
|---|---|---|---|
| LT04 | L_TCODE | TCD | LT04 |
| VL02N | V_LIKP_VST | ACTVT | 02 |

4.3.2 Take a sample of the delivery-due list and owed-to-customer report and test for evidence of management action. Review settings using transaction code OMWB, and confirm that accounts assignments are set to valid COGS accounts.

# Inventory Cycle Controls and Financial Statement Assertions

The Inventory Cycle risk numbers from this chapter have been mapped to controls listed in **figure 25**—Application Control Objectives for the Inventory Cycle of *IT Control Objectives for Sarbanes-Oxley, 2nd Edition*, from the IT Governance Institute,[13] as shown in **figure 10.1**. The risk number mapping should be looked at in conjunction with the associated control and testing technique numbers to help gain an understanding of the impact of the risks and controls on the financial reporting process in terms of completeness, valuation and existence.

| Figure 10.1—Inventory Risk Cycle Controls | | |
|---|---|---|
| **Illustrative Control Objectives** | **Financial Statement Assertions** | **Inventory Cycle Risk Number** |
| Adjustments to inventory prices or quantities are recorded promptly and in the appropriate period. | Existence Completeness Valuation | 1.1 |
| Adjustments to inventory prices or quantities are recorded accurately. | Valuation | 1.1 |
| Raw materials are received and accepted only if they have valid purchase orders. | Existence | 2.2 |
| Raw materials received are recorded accurately. | Valuation | 2.2 |
| All raw materials received are recorded. | Completeness | 2.2 |
| Receipts of raw materials are recorded promptly and in the appropriate period. | Valuation Completeness | 2.2 |
| Defective raw materials are returned promptly to suppliers. | Existence | 2.3 |
| All transfers of raw materials to production are recorded accurately and in the appropriate period. | Valuation Completeness | 3.1 |
| All direct and indirect expenses associated with production are recorded accurately and in the appropriate period. | Valuation | 3.1 |
| All transfers of completed units of production to finished goods inventory are recorded completely and accurately in the appropriate period. | Valuation Completeness | 3.1 |
| Finished goods returned by customers are recorded completely and accurately in the appropriate period. | Valuation Completeness | 4.1 4.2 |

---

[13] *Ibid.*

| Figure 10.1—Inventory Risk Cycle Controls *(cont.)* | | |
|---|---|---|
| **Illustrative Control Objectives** | **Financial Statement Assertions** | **Inventory Cycle Risk Number** |
| Finished goods received from production are recorded completely and accurately in the appropriate period. | Valuation Completeness | 4.1 |
| All shipments are recorded. | Existence | 4.3 |
| Shipments are recorded accurately. | Valuation | 4.3 |
| Shipments are recorded promptly and in the appropriate period. | Valuation | 4.3 |
| Inventory is reduced only when goods are shipped with approved customer orders. | Completeness Existence | 4.3 |
| Costs of shipped inventory are transferred from inventory to cost of sales. | Existence Valuation | 4.3 |
| Costs of shipped inventory are accurately recorded. | Valuation | 4.3 |
| Amounts posted to cost of sales represent those associated with shipped inventory. | Completeness Existence | 4.3 |
| Costs of shipped inventory are transferred from inventory to cost of sales promptly and in the appropriate period. | Valuation | 4.3 |
| Only valid changes are made to the inventory management master file. | Existence Completeness | 1.1 |
| All valid changes to the inventory management master file are input and processed. | Existence Completeness | 1.1 |
| Changes to the inventory management master file are accurate. | Valuation | 1.1 |
| Changes to the inventory management master file are promptly processed. | Existence Completeness | 1.1 |
| Inventory management master file data remain up to date. | Existence Completeness | 1.2 |

## Summary

This chapter outlined the risks, key controls and testing techniques applicable to the SAP ERP Inventory business cycle. Among the key risks are invalid, incomplete, inaccurate and/or untimely changes to material master data; inventory that is not salable or usable; and shipments and returns from customers that are not recorded accurately, in a timely manner and in the appropriate period.

# 11. SAP ERP Basis Application Infrastructure

This chapter provides an overview of the SAP ERP Basis technical infrastructure, introducing important SAP ERP utilities and functionality. Note that the terms "customize" or "customization" in this guide are general and refer to the tailoring of an SAP ERP environment to suit the customer's specific needs by way of configuration, modification or additional development of tables or programs.

## SAP ERP Architecture

As outlined previously, when the SAP R/3 software was introduced in 1992, it was based on a three-tier, client-server architecture. The client-server architecture continued to apply to the renamed SAP R/3 product known as SAP ERP when it was introduced. Client-server is a style of computing that distributes the workload of a computer application across several cooperating computer processing units within a computer network. The architecture is a design model that describes how the various components of a computer application will be deployed in a given processing environment. Client and server are roles in which processes communicate: the client requests services and the server provides them. This type of computing, as depicted in **figure 11.1**, separates user-oriented tasks (presentation layer), application tasks (application layer) and data management tasks (database layer).

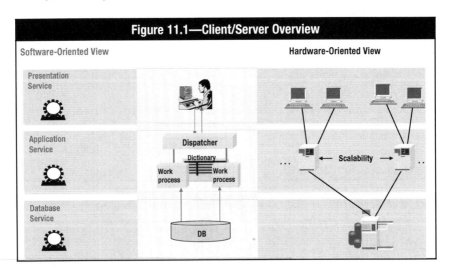

**Figure 11.1—Client/Server Overview**

The presentation layer is the portion of the SAP ERP software with which users interact directly. It displays information to users through a graphical user interface (SAP ERP—GUI or web interface) and transfers data entered by users to the application server layer.

The application layer consists of one or more application servers. An application server is an SAP ERP system kernel that runs ABAP/4 programs and, therefore, can run the SAP ERP application programs that manipulate data obtained from the user and the database. The application layer contains the business rules/logic and consists of:
- A dispatcher process managing the processing queues, balancing the transaction load and other processes while performing memory management functions
- One or more work processes carrying out the processing requests

The dispatcher receives user inputs from the presentation layer and requests services from other application servers and from work processes themselves. The dispatcher then allocates these requests for services to its work processes, which carry out the requests.

Support services provided by the application server include dialog management, background processing, updates, queue management and spooling services.

Multiple application servers can run in a single host, each server being distinguished by its SAP ERP system number. Alternatively, each application server may run on a separate host. Thus, the number of application servers may not equal the number of physical servers since multiple application servers can run on a single physical server. Each logical application server, as opposed to physical server, is known as a separate SAP ERP instance.

In the SAP ERP software, there are two types of instances: central instances and dialog instances. Each SAP ERP system has just one central instance. At the time of installation, it contains all the basic services, such as gateway, message server, update, enqueue, spool, dialog and background. An SAP ERP system may have multiple dialog instances. At the time of installation, these contain a subset of the basic services, such as background and dialog work processes. Following installation, Basis administrators can customize the services provided in all the application servers using SAP ERP instance profiles.

Note, though, that where there is only one physical server and one application server, the computer server equals the application server, which equals one SAP ERP instance. The configuration of the application servers is important from an audit perspective because the security parameters may or may not be synchronized across application servers. Audit testing may need to be carried out on all the application servers or on a sample thereof.

The database layer consists of the relational database system (e.g. Oracle®, Informix®, Microsoft SQL Server®) used by all application servers. The database is the heart of the SAP ERP system. It is the central source of information for an enterprise's business data and also the container of user information, software components, documentation and administrative statistical data to be used when

managing or monitoring the system. One of the most important logical parts of the database is the ABAP/4 object repository, which contains:
- The ABAP/4 dictionary, which is the central source for the definition of objects, such as type and length of fields, indexes and table relationships
- The ABAP/4 source code and executable programs

An SAP ERP system is usually implemented with a single database server. In each SAP ERP system, there is a central instance application server. It is common for the database server to be combined with the central instance application server (often called the database server instance or central instance). Where the presentation, application and database services are run on separate computers, a three-tier client-server architecture is established.

There are a number of advantages of the client-server approach:
- Flexible configuration—There are many possibilities for configuring a client-server installation, from a centralized configuration to a distributed system, using communication interfaces.
- Workload distribution—Application servers can be configured to operate in parallel and communicate with the database server. They can be located in business areas to improve response times for users.
- High scalability—The client-server approach permits users to adapt the capacity of their hardware according to the performance needs of their businesses, such as by adding application servers for additional users or modules.

SAP ERP is also based on an open systems philosophy, allowing the application to run on multiple operating systems (e.g., various forms of UNIX or Windows NT®), databases (e.g., Oracle, Microsoft SQL Server) and user interfaces (e.g., personal computer, Macintosh®).

## SAP ERP Basis Application Infrastructure

As mentioned, the SAP Basis component provides the means for administering the SAP architecture. Each SAP instance has its own single Basis component, as depicted in **figure 11.2**. The SAP Basis component is the processing core for SAP ERP, as it also was for previous versions of the SAP application (e.g., SAP R/3). However, as depicted in **figure 11.2**, SAP Basis has evolved as an integrated component of SAP Web Application Server, which itself has become a component of the SAP Netweaver platform.

Key Basis tools and significant utilities from an audit perspective include:
- The Implementation Guide (IMG) and Organization Management Model (OMM)
- ABAP/4 Workbench and Transport Management System (TMS)
- Computer Center Management System (CCMS)
- The Profile Generator (PFCG) and Security Administration (SA)

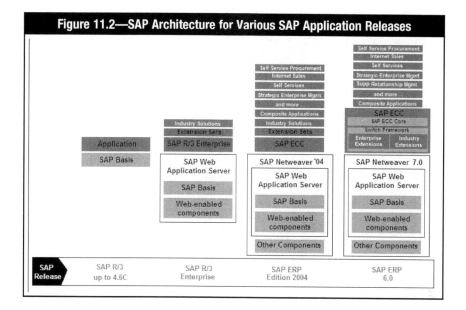

Figure 11.2—SAP Architecture for Various SAP Application Releases

# The Implementation Guide and Organization Management Model

The Implementation Guide (IMG) is an online manual used to facilitate the configuration of the SAP ERP software. It can be accessed using transaction SPRO, as depicted in **figure 11.3**, and includes:
• Global settings
• OMM
• Implementation activities specific to each SAP module (e.g., defining business processing options, master data and screen layouts)
• Features to document and monitor the implementation

The definition of the OMM (also known as the Enterprise Structure, the SAP ERP Hierarchy or the Corporate Structure) is a key aspect of the configuration of an SAP ERP system. It maps the structure of the enterprise onto the SAP ERP system organizational units and is central to the operation and control of the SAP ERP software. The OMM is defined during implementation and is not easy to change once implemented. OMM defines and influences:
• How business processes are carried out
• How reporting and consolidation are accomplished
• What business objects are used (e.g., sales orders, purchase orders)
• How SAP ERP functionality will meet the business requirements
• How data are defined in the system (e.g., the complexity of data input, the size of master data files)
• How cross-company processing will take place

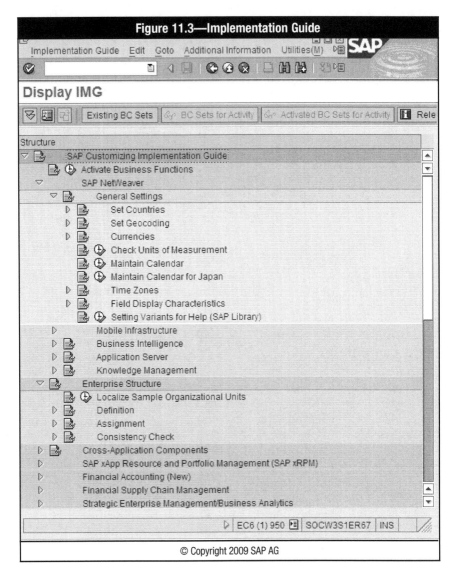

Figure 11.3—Implementation Guide

© Copyright 2009 SAP AG

The goal of modeling the enterprise is to create a structure that is an accurate reflection of the enterprise being modeled and is consistent with the business processes and reporting facilities provided by the SAP ERP software. The OMM is flexible yet complex, and this sometimes means that it is difficult to design and configure the OMM appropriately. Failure to do so, though, may have a significant and extended impact on the enterprise's information management, as reporting and processes will be configured based on or around the OMM. The OMM may also require the enterprise to make certain trade-off decisions (e.g., between alignment with geographic reporting requirements or cost center reporting and consolidation).

The minimum required elements for the OMM include:
• A client—This is the highest organizational level within each central SAP ERP instance. It represents an entity within a system that is discrete commercially, organizationally and technically. There is usually one client for an entire organization. Separate clients may be used for different organizations using the same SAP ERP system (e.g., by an application service provider or for organizations involved in a joint venture or strategic alliance). A client has its own master data and its own full set of tables. It represents a logical grouping of multiple SAP ERP companies. Some data are defined at the client level and apply to all company codes. Full functional and data integration occurs within a client. Minimal integration is available between clients (although financial consolidations across clients may be possible). Objects (such as screens or transactions) may be either client-dependent (relate only to a particular client) or cross-client (relate to all clients on the SAP ERP system). Note that the risk of cross-client configuration and system elements (e.g., ABAPs) should be considered. SAP is delivered with three standard clients already defined:
  1. Client 000, the SAP reference or technical client—All SAP tables are in the SAP reference client. Sample entries, which can be changed, exist for the tables in which the organizational structure is stored. The SAP reference client contains the following:
     – Tables with default values, independent of the organization units
     – Examples of the organization units
     – A default customizing setting

     It contains no application data, i.e., no master data and no transaction data. This client is used for implementing system updates and other technical changes, and should not be used in production processing.
  2. Client 001, the production preparation client—The production preparation client is identical to the SAP reference client, i.e., this client cannot be used in production processing. The customizing settings are made in this client to create the test environment.
  3. Client 066, the Earlywatch client—Earlywatch is a diagnostic service available from SAP, under which SAP specialist staff can log onto a copy of the production client and perform tests to identify processing bottlenecks and potential problems. The production system (PRD) client is copied into client 066, which the SAP staff can log onto using the specialized user Earlywatch and perform their tests.
• The company code—A legally and organizationally independent entity with its own financial statements (i.e., set of books, balance sheet, and profit and loss statement). Assignments at the company level include fiscal year, chart of accounts and accounting currency. The financial statements for multiple companies can be consolidated. All financial documents are posted at this level. Some master data are defined at the company level and multiple companies may be defined per client.

Within a client, each functional area can define its own structure. Once the organizational structures are defined, views (e.g., on master data) can be created. The SAP ERP software modules allow multiple views, including:
• Financial
• Controlling
• Consolidation
• Sales
• Purchasing

## ABAP/4 Workbench and Transport Management System

ABAP/4 stands for Advanced Business Application Programming/4. ABAP/4 is a fourth-generation programming language and is the main programming language used for SAP ERP systems. The ABAP/4 Workbench (SAP ERP transaction code S001) constitutes the development environment for an SAP ERP system, providing tools for programming, navigating, debugging and controlling development, as depicted in **figure 11.4**. These tools include:
• ABAP/4 dictionary
• ABAP/4 editor
• Function library
• Screen painter
• Menu painter
• Object browser
• ABAP/4 repository
• Data browser
• SQL trace
• Runtime analysis
• Online debugger
• System log
• Workbench organizer
• TMS

The TMS utility is of particular significance to auditors. TMS performs and manages the transport of development objects across different SAP ERP clients, i.e., from development through test to production.

The SAP ERP software defines several different types of systems to provide a structure (often referred to as the system landscape) for controlling custom development and transporting changes to objects across the systems. These system types include:
• Integration system—Carries out development work; the application configuration master
• Consolidation system—For quality assurance and configuration testing; may be used for training
• Recipient system—Receives finished corrections or releases; usually part of the production environment
• SAP special system—Exists at SAP and contains SAP-created objects

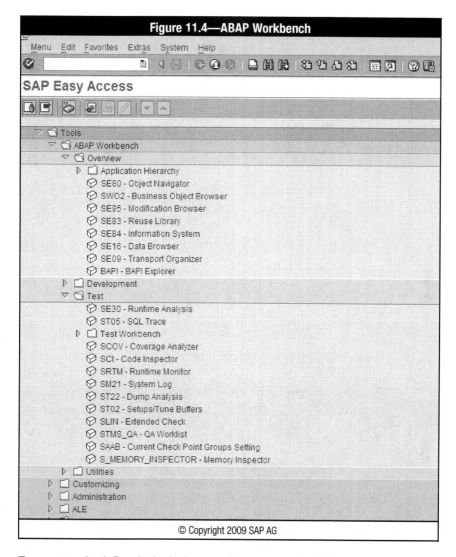

Figure 11.4—ABAP Workbench

© Copyright 2009 SAP AG

Transport paths define the logical connections among the different systems in an environment. System changes must be moved among systems along a predefined transport path. Transport paths indicate what role each system plays in the environment, e.g., development, consolidation and recipient. Transport paths are defined during initial landscape design and implementation. **Figure 11.5** shows an example of a multisystem landscape where changes are migrated from development to multiple production systems in different countries. This example depicts a landscape where it makes sense to have multiple systems based on culture, performance, etc. The country's development systems play a dual role (delivery and integration). The entry point is a central integration system, which is used for international software development. Independent system landscapes are then connected for country-specific software development.

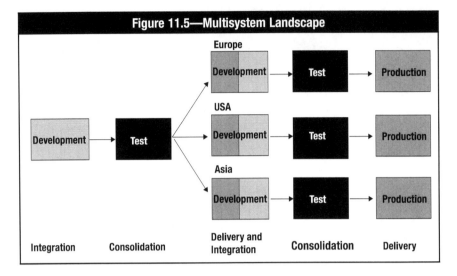

Figure 11.5—Multisystem Landscape

A transport layer is always created from all systems to the SAP special system, allowing changes made by SAP to objects to be delivered into the system for maintenance or emergency change purposes.

Change options can be defined for each SAP ERP system receiving changes using transaction codes SCC4 or SE06. The system change option determines whether cross-client and repository objects can be changed directly in the production system. It is a global setting consisting of the following options:
• Modifiable—Repository and cross-client objects can be changed.
• Not modifiable—Repository and cross-client objects cannot be changed.

If the global setting is set to modifiable, the objects can be specified as modifiable. Additional settings can be maintained at the client level. At the client level, there are four settings to control changes to development objects:
• Objects cannot be changed.
• Only original objects can be changed.
• All customer objects can be changed.
• All objects can be changed.

A modification to an original object is called a correction. A modification to an object in a system in which the object was not created is called a repair, e.g., modifications to SAP objects are always repairs. Corrections and repairs to SAP original objects are submitted to SAP for resolution. When SAP corrects the problem, a patch will be provided for download and installation.

A developer must request a key in the SAP Service Marketplace front end to become registered. A request that a valid developer's key be entered is triggered when a repository object is created or changed for the first time. Developers' keys entered in a client are stored in the table DEVACCESS. No SAP objects should be changed. If organizations need to alter the SAP standard objects, they must obtain an object key. The key is a 20-digit number that uniquely identifies and controls that object. Object keys can be requested as needed from the SAP Service Marketplace front end. However, developers must document why they need one. If changes are made to the standard SAP objects, they can affect the SAP warranty and support.

All SAP objects are grouped in several development classes. A development class contains all the development objects that must be developed, maintained and transported together. Typically, the objects that make up a transaction belong to one development class. If an organization wishes to develop programs, screens, tables, etc., of its own, special development classes have to be created (e.g., Y and Z classes for custom objects). The development class also determines the system to which objects may be transported.

The classes are assigned to transport layers and application areas. The class values are:
• A-S, U-X for the SAP standard objects. These are owned by SAP, and will be overwritten by new objects when an upgrade takes place.
• Y, Z for customer-developed objects. These are owned by the organization and will not be changed during an upgrade. The organization will have to test that these objects still function as intended following an upgrade since the elements of SAP with which they interact may have changed.
• T for test classes not assigned to a transport layer. These cannot be transported between systems.
• $ for non-transportable local classes outside the control of the workbench organizer
• $TMP for a predefined local development class

Solution Manager is the SAP change request workflow. Whether Solution Manager or another method is used, change requests should be used to record all changes made to development objects or to customize settings. All Solution Manager requests are automatically assigned a unique identifying number. Change request information should include:
• A list of transports included in the request
• A list of the objects included for transport in the request
• Purpose of the transport
• Transport type (assigned automatically)
• Target system (assigned automatically)
• One or more change tasks that are part of the project (Tasks are lists of objects that are created or modified by individual users. They are not transportable by themselves; rather, they are transportable only as part of a change request. The change request can only be released and exported after all the tasks underneath it have been released.)

Note that for medium to large projects, one Solution Manager Request may exist. When this is the case, a list of changes including transports, changed objects, dates, responsible, etc., should be maintained in another form (e.g., an Excel spreadsheet).

Whether the changes will be recorded is set for each client in table T000 or using transaction code SCC4, depending on the role of the client (development, test, sandbox, production) and the class of object being transported.

Third-party products are sometimes used to manage transports in an SAP ERP environment. In this case, the standard SAP ERP transport functionality should be disabled to prevent changes from bypassing the third-party change control software.

## Computing Center Management System

The Computing Center Management System (CCMS) consists of a toolset and utilities to monitor, control and configure the SAP ERP system. CCMS can be accessed using transaction SRZL, as depicted in **figure 11.6**. It has built-in functionality to actively and centrally monitor all SAP ERP hardware, i.e., the application and database servers. The CCMS system log (transaction code SM21) is the most important log for SAP ERP operations and is written locally for each application server. CCMS is useful for monitoring SAP ERP systems only. More complex environments may require additional third-party software.

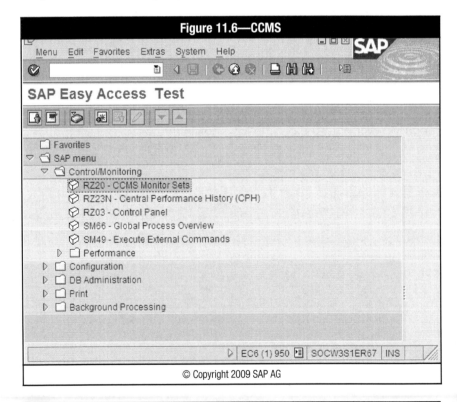

**Figure 11.6—CCMS**

CCMS's primary functions include:
• System start-up and shutdown
• Unattended 24-hour operation support
• System monitoring and analysis
• Network monitoring and analysis
• Automatic trouble reporting (alerts)
• Troubleshooting
• Dynamic logon load balancing and control
• System configuration
• System profile management
• Processing and controlling background jobs
• Database administration
• Profile security

System and start-up profiles (not to be confused with authorization profiles) are stored in the shared central profiles directory. They are ASCII files that can be accessed from any application server. The SAPSTART program uses a start-up profile. SAPSTART is the program used by the STARTSAP and STOPSAP scripts to start and shut down the system. Start profiles list the commands that SAPSTART performs. With profiles, the start-up and shutdown of SAP ERP system processes can be automated networkwide.

CCMS helps system administrators:
• Monitor, control and configure the operations of an ERP system
• Distribute processing workloads
• Check system status and operation modes
• Report on resource consumption for system components
• Locate and eliminate malfunctions promptly
• Diagnose problems early, such as resource problems in the database system
• Analyze and tune the ERP system and its environment using:
  – Graphical monitors for continuous viewing, with red, yellow and green displays to indicate system conditions
  – List-oriented monitors for analysis of statistics for tuning

CCMS is shipped with SAP ERP, but it is not ready for immediate use. The consistency and accuracy of the CCMS function depend on its configuration. Key CCMS configuration items include:
• Defining instance profiles—This sets the values for the resources needed by the SAP ERP instances, e.g., main memory size, number and type of work processes, message and database servers.
• Defining at least one operation mode—This defines how the SAP ERP services are to be allocated and started in the configured SAP ERP instances, e.g., an operation mode can be defined to have a number of dialog work processes during the day and then automatically switch to background work processes for processing batch jobs at night.

• Assigning operation modes to instances—An instance can incorporate one or several operation modes.
• Defining and maintaining the operation mode timetables—A normal operation timetable can be assigned, accounting for each timetable in a 24-hour period or an exception operation timetable for a specified date and defined time interval.

## The Profile Generator and Security Administration

SAP ERP Application Security is one of several security components that need to be considered in an audit of an SAP ERP environment, as depicted in **figure 11.7**. Other components that need to be secured and subject to independent review include:
• Operating Environment Security
• Technology Infrastructure Security

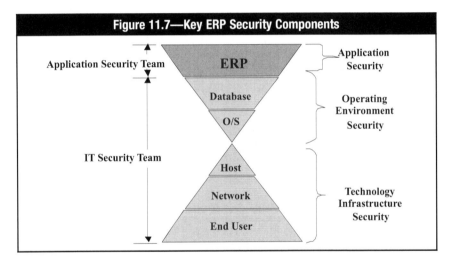

Figure 11.7—Key ERP Security Components

The Profile Generator (SAP ERP transaction code PFCG) is a tool, as depicted in **figure 11.8**, used for security design and configuration. It was first made available in SAP R/3 release 3.1G, and it can be installed retroactively in releases 3.0F and above. PFCG replaces the manual creation and maintenance of authorizations (transaction code SU03) and simple profiles (transaction code SU02). The security administrator selects the functions required, and the PFCG automatically determines the authorization objects, fields and values and places them into roles.

Note that not all values are entered automatically. Use of PFCG involves manual intervention during the role generation process for the fine-tuning of specific values. Some values are entered manually before generation (e.g., organizational structure information) and others may need to be entered manually after profile generation.

PFCG is driven by transaction codes (activities performed by users) that are assigned to each role. Authorization (simple) profiles are created and updated when roles are generated. Profiles generated using PFCG cannot be maintained manually using SU02 (maintain profile).

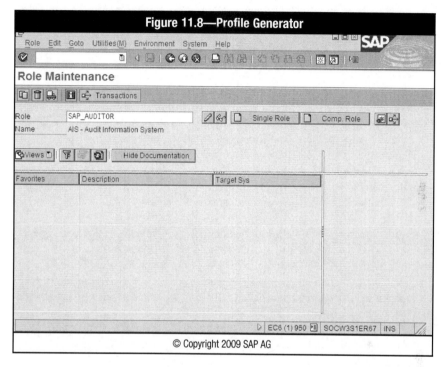

Figure 11.8—Profile Generator

© Copyright 2009 SAP AG

PFCG automates authorization assignment for transaction codes via the relationship delivered in the SAP ERP table USOBT. This table contains a list of standard SAP transactions and the authorization objects that may be required to execute them. Depending on how the system has been configured, the actual authorization objects that are required to execute the transactions may differ from those listed in the table. Running transaction SU25 creates the modifiable customer version of this table USOBT_C. PFCG references USOBT_C, once it is created. USOBT_C is modifiable via transaction SU24. It allows for the customization of whichever objects are added automatically for each transaction to PFCG and the limited ability to select the authorization objects that are checked by a transaction.

Prior to the use of PFCG, the SAP ERP transactions used in the administration of SAP ERP role-based security were:
• SUIM—User information system (Report tree: SAP ERP security reports have the prefix RSUSRxxx and can be accessed using transaction SA38 or SE38.)
• SU02—Maintain profiles (used to allocate authorizations to profiles)
• SU03—Maintain authorizations (used to maintain authorizations)

Note that users may be assigned to user groups or authorization groups to restrict security administrator access to maintain particular groups of users only (e.g., the user group SUPER to restrict access to maintain superusers, such as SAP*).

In addition to maintaining user master records, profiles and authorizations, the SAP ERP security administrators may perform a number of other important tasks, such as:
• Reset passwords and lock/unlock users
• Perform acceptance testing of new profiles and authorizations
• Administer system security parameters
• Research and create an SAP ERP access strategy as well as users/profiles/authorizations for future phases of project development
• Create and update documentation concerning security
• Perform security monitoring and analysis according to security policies and procedures
• Analyze the effects of system upgrades on the access security strategy and implement changes
• Provide online support system administration

The system administrator's effort to maintain users in the SAP ERP environment can be reduced through the use of the Central User Administration (CUA) function. With CUA, one central client is used to maintain the user master data for all clients in the system landscape. The organization can decide which part of the user master data can be maintained centrally only or which can also be maintained locally. A systems tab is available in transaction SU01 to allow the user to specify the logical names of the central system and all the component systems in the systems table. Communication between the central server and the component systems is performed using RFC.

**Figure 11.9** illustrates the CUA concept. Communication between systems is achieved using SAP Application Linked Enabling (ALE). ALE enables the exchange of data between SAP systems.

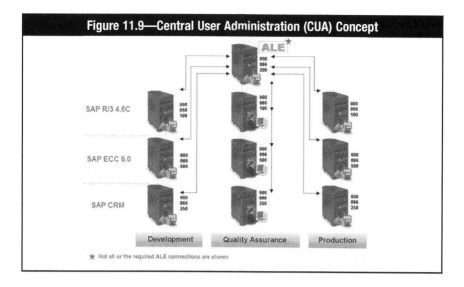

Figure 11.9—Central User Administration (CUA) Concept

## Audit Implications

As mentioned previously, in an ERP environment it is common for a large number of controls to be automated using access security or configuration settings. An understanding of the SAP ERP Security Authorization concept and the SAP ERP Basis Application Infrastructure tools and utilities (e.g., Profile Generator, Implementation Guide and Transport Management System) is essential in identifying the risks and understanding the controls and the techniques for testing them. An understanding of the SAP ERP architecture and an organization's particular systems landscape is essential in determining an effective audit approach.

Some of the audit aspects that the previously described factors may impact include:

- Testing of security parameters—How many SAP ERP servers are there and have security parameters been synchronized across all servers? If not, security parameters may need to be tested on each server or a sample of servers.
- Infrastructure testing requirements—How many systems are there? Which systems are running production?
- Testing under rotation plan—Is an audit rotation plan operating and, if so, what systems are relevant? Is the rotation plan operating at the Basis level or the business cycles level or both? If at the Basis level, what Basis areas are due for testing under rotation? If at the business cycle level, what business cycles are due for testing under rotation and on what systems or platforms are they running? What countries are they supporting?
- Specific identified risks—Have systems been upgraded? Have there been any country-specific changes?

# Summary

This chapter provided an overview and general understanding of the SAP ERP Basis technical infrastructure describing the client-server architecture and key SAP ERP utilities and functionality including:
- The Implementation Guide (IMG) and Organizational Management Model (OMM)
- ABAP/4 Workbench and Transport Management System (TMS)
- Computing Center Management System (CCMS)
- The Profile Generator (PFCG) and Security Administration

# 12. Auditing the SAP ERP Basis Application Infrastructure

This chapter provides a sample toolset for use in auditing the SAP ERP Basis Application Infrastructure, as shown in **figure 12.1**, including:
• Specific risks in the SAP ERP Basis Application Infrastructure
• Automated control activities to manage these risks
• Sample assurance techniques

The authorization objects and associated activity values contained in the Testing Techniques sections of this chapter are indicative only. An understanding of the enterprise's implementation of processes in SAP is required to ensure that testing is complete and includes all necessary authorization objects and values.

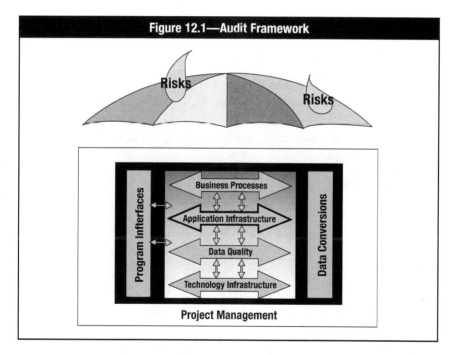

Figure 12.1—Audit Framework

The testing techniques employed may vary in each organization, depending on the extent of customization/specific configuration options selected, release in use, and whether automated diagnostics such as the SAP ERP Audit Information System are used. Consideration should also be given to the use of other tools such as SAP GRC and SAP NetWeaver, which are covered later in this guide. As noted previously, the terms "customize" or "customization" in this guide are general terms that refer to the tailoring of an SAP ERP environment to suit the customer's specific needs by way of configuration, modification or additional development of tables or programs. The assurance techniques provided, therefore, should not be regarded as prescriptive lists of specific transaction codes, authorization objects or values to test, but rather as a sample toolset for use or reference as appropriate in the reader's organizational environment. The assurance techniques outlined in this chapter were tested on an SAP ECC 6.0 system. Techniques for testing using the SAP ERP Audit Information System, as well as security considerations when using SAP GRC, are overviewed later in this guide.

**Figure 12.2** shows the major SAP ERP Basis Application Infrastructure functions as follows:
• Implementation Guide (IMG) and the Organizational Management Model (OMM)
• ABAP/4 Workbench and Transport Management System
• Computing Center Management System
• The Profile Generator and Security Administration

# Implementation Guide

## Implementation Guide Risk
A standard SAP system is made up of a minimum of three clients and three systems. One client is used by the SAP company itself (066), while the remaining two clients and three systems are used by the enterprise. The technical client (000) is used for installing patches and upgrades. The application client (commonly 010, but varies per installation) is made up of the development, quality and production systems. SAP allows each enterprise to administer its SAP systems in various manners, one of which controls where changes to system configuration and programs are allowed. Because system users enter business data and run processes in the production system, it is imperative that configuration and program changes be restricted in the production system. The SAP Basis Application Infrastructure (**figure 12.2**.) is used to manage SAP's key configuration elements:
• The Organizational Management Model
• Critical number ranges
• Critical tables (automated controls)

These are explored in more detail in the sections that follow.

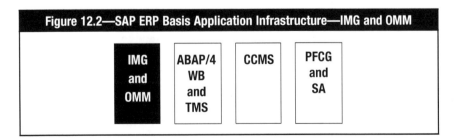

Figure 12.2—SAP ERP Basis Application Infrastructure—IMG and OMM

| IMG and OMM | ABAP/4 WB and TMS | CCMS | PFCG and SA |

## Implementation Guide Control
Access to the IMG in production should be restricted. The production client settings should be flagged to prevent changes to programs and configuration.

## Implementation Guide Testing Technique
Access to the transaction code (SPRO) and the authorization object (S_IMG_ACTV) for the IMG should be restricted in the production environment.

Transaction code SCC4, as shown in **figure 12.3**, allows direct control of the production client settings. Access to this transaction code should be severely restricted and changes should be logged. Execute this transaction code, and double-click on each client being tested. Review each of the settings for appropriateness, including the "last changed by" and "last changed" date fields. It is important to note that the No Changes setting should be used for cross-client tables. Protection for the Client Copier and Comparison Tool should be set to No Overwriting. Also ensure that eCAAT and CAAT are set to Not Allowed.

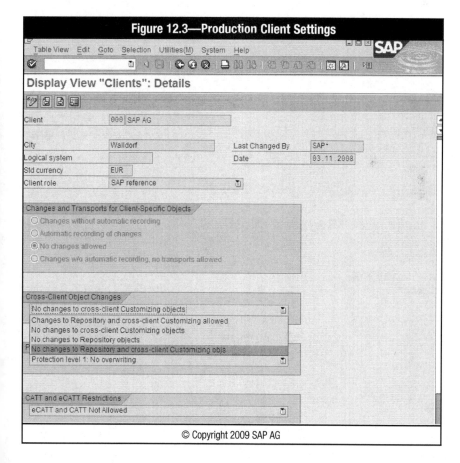

Figure 12.3—Production Client Settings

© Copyright 2009 SAP AG

Validate who has access to make changes directly to production client via transaction SUIM ▶ Authorizations ▶ Authorizations by Complex Selection Criteria. Review the following authorization objects:

| Transaction(s) | Authorization Objects | Fields | Values |
|---|---|---|---|
| SCC4 | S_TABU_DIS | ACTVT<br>Authorization group | 02<br>SS |
| | S_TABU_CLI | Cross-client Maintenance | X |
| | S_CTS_ADMI | Administration Task | TABL |

There may be a few occasions when there will be a need to make a change directly to the production client without going through the transport path. Any such changes should be investigated thoroughly for business need, management approval, etc.

If changes have been made to production client settings in the period under review, a log of changes to table T000 should be obtained to determine the nature of such changes obtained via transaction SCU3. All changes to these critical settings should be authorized, documented and verified. This critical setting should be reviewed by IT management at least annually.

Another alternative to identify changes made directly into production (bypassing the usual transport route) is to use transaction code SCC4, go to Utilities Menu ▶ Change Logs ▶ Input Data in Evaluation Period (the period for which one needs the direct production change log).

# Organizational Management Model

## Organizational Management Model Risk

A major risk associated with the OMM is that it is difficult to change the structure once it has been implemented. An incorrect or suboptimal implementation may result in significant issues such as:
• Inadequate reporting, incorrect consolidation or noncompliance with legal requirements
• Incorrect management information
• Inefficient reporting or manual workarounds
• Loss of information when the OMM is changed

Where the functionality in the OMM does not meet the needs of the organization, a costly re-implementation may need to be carefully considered.

### Organizational Management Model Control

The organizational model must be well thought out and agreed upon early in the implementation. The relevant organization groups should assist with key design decisions, and checkpoints should be included during the global design for review purposes. Any changes to the OMM should be controlled and should:
- Be performed by authorized configuration specialists
- Comply with change control procedures (i.e., the change should be authorized by senior management and thoroughly tested)

Access to the organization configuration functionality should be restricted.

### Organizational Management Model Testing Technique

Access to the transaction code (SPRO) and the authorization object (S_IMG_ACTV) for the IMG should be restricted in the production environment. Obtain information on the organizational model from the system by going through SPRO ▷ IMG ▷ Enterprise Structure or by utilizing the SAP ERP Audit Information System that depicts the OMM graphically, as shown in **figure 12.4**. Compare the model to the real organization structure and interview management in relation to differences or difficulties that may have emerged during or after the implementation.

# Critical Number Ranges

### Critical Number Ranges Risk

Number ranges are used to assign numbers to individual database records that belong to a business object. For example, numbers can be assigned to orders, operations or material master records. The numbers are part of a key that identifies a database record in the system and do not have any built-in significance. A number range contains a set of characters or numbers, which could be either:
- External—Numbers are assigned manually by the user and/or external, interfaced systems.
- Internal—Numbers are assigned automatically by the system.

The set of characters in the number range is identified by an interval. The number range interval consists of numbers or alphanumeric characters and is limited by the "from number" and "to number" fields.

Unauthorized changes to number ranges can to compromise the integrity of data in the system.

### Critical Number Ranges Control

The SAP ERP software security should be appropriately configured to restrict the ability to change critical number ranges (i.e., master data number ranges, document type number ranges). In addition, the production environment should be set to Not Modifiable at the client level (transaction code SCC4).

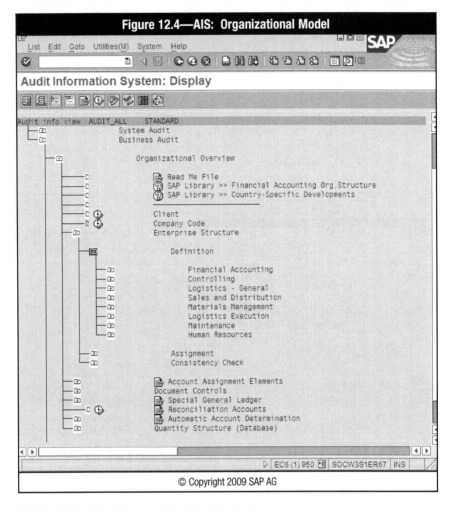

Figure 12.4—AIS: Organizational Model

*Critical Number Ranges Testing Technique*

Via transaction SUIM ▷ Authorizations ▷ Authorizations by Complex Selection
Criteria. Review the following authorization object:

| Transaction(s) | Authorization Objects | Fields | Values |
|---|---|---|---|
| SPRO | S_NUMBER | ACTVT | 02, 11, 13, 17 |

# Modifying Critical Tables

## Modifying Critical Tables Risk

Tables are the central and critical component of the SAP ERP system since they contain controlling information for the system as well as business information entered by users. Many of the tables control how programs function, and changing them is equivalent to changing a program. The customizing capabilities in SAP ERP software enable users to set cross-application and application-specific parameters in the tables without knowing the technical aspects involved, such as table name and transaction codes. The general rule for accessing objects in groups in SAP is: a user can access objects in groups for which he/she has authorization, plus all objects that are not assigned to a group. This rule does not seem to apply to table authorization groups. For example, in transactions SE16, SE16N, SM30 and SM31, if a user tries to access a table that is not assigned to an authorization group (there are thousands of them), the program automatically assigns it temporarily to the authorization group &NC&. If the user does not have access to this authorization group, then he/she cannot even display the table contents.

Changes to tables that are cross-client, which contain global definition data, could have unexpected side effects since the changes affect all clients in an SAP ERP system. Therefore, if test and production clients exist on the same instance, a global change in the test client may cause an undesirable result in the production client. Access to system control and customizing tables should be narrowly restricted to users who understand the possible impact of changes to these tables.

## Modifying Critical Tables Control

All of the customized SAP ERP tables should be assigned to the appropriate authorization group.

The ability to modify critical tables should be appropriately restricted in the production system. Changes to tables should be made in the development and test environments and migrated to production following appropriate testing. However, there are some table changes that can be affected only through the production system (e.g., opening and closing financial reporting periods).

Changes to critical tables may be logged for subsequent monitoring and review (refer to the Profile Generator and Security Administration section later in this chapter).

## Modifying Critical Tables Testing Technique

Use transaction codes SE16, Z* and Y* in the table name field, to browse table TDDAT for customized tables. The authorization field DICBERCLS will specify the tables' authorization groups necessary for user access. To maintain a table, the DICBERCLS (authorization field) value in a user's authorization must match the

DICBERCLS value for the table in the TDDAT file. The table must also be set in the data dictionary as "maintenance-allowed." The risk concerning customized tables may be mitigated by restricting access to modify critical tables.

Use transaction code SUIM ▷ Users ▷ Users by Complex Selection Criteria (also accessible using transaction code SA38 and program RSUSR002) to check restrictions on modifying critical tables via the following authorization objects:

| Transaction(s) | Authorization Objects | Fields | Values |
|---|---|---|---|
| SM31, SM30 | S_TABU_DIS | ACTVT | 02 |
| If the table is cross-client, the user master record must contain a third object: S_TABU_CLI (value X). | | | |

Critical systems tables, as well as security tables, are assigned to authorization group SS. Both view and update access to group SS should be tightly controlled. In the SUIM report tree, run a query of roles that have either update (activity 02) or view (activity 03) access to table authorization group SS. Update access Activity 02 is required for S_TABU_DIS. Nonsupport personnel should not have update access to the system tables. View access should be also appropriately restricted.

# Custom Transaction Codes

### Custom Transaction Codes Risk
In a production system, test/unauthorized customized transaction codes should not be available since users may have access to unauthorized activities in the production environment.

### Custom Transaction Codes Control
Only authorized customized transactions should be available for use in the production environment. A correct change management process should prevent the creation of unauthorized customized transaction codes in the production environment. Also, adequate user access management should prevent the user from executing the transaction, even if the transaction codes are available in the system.

### Custom Transaction Codes Testing Techniques
By using transaction code SE16, browse table TSTCT. In the table name field, enter Z* and then Y* to identify all of the custom T-codes. Determine transaction codes that appear to be test/backup codes and follow up with the SAP administrator regarding requirements.

# ABAP/4 Workbench and Transport Management System

### Transport Management System Risk

The ABAP/4 Workbench and Transport Management System (TMS) is depicted in **figure 12.5**. Regular maintenance, fixes, upgrades or enhancements to existing application systems should be scheduled and performed using a procedure including authorization, evaluation/testing, acceptance, and approval prior to implementation to ensure that they have the intended effect and minimize user disruption. Without sufficient testing and evaluation, modifications not performing as expected may cause disruption to service or loss of data.

A phased approach to performing changes should be used in complex system environments to ensure that, if there are difficulties, the cause is easily identified and corrected. For example, changes might be rolled out to the smaller and less critical processing locations first. Where possible, plans should be made to provide the ability to back out changes if the modification does not perform as anticipated.

Emergency changes to resolve processing errors may require modifications to be made using special procedures, providing for review and testing following implementation to ensure that they function in a manner that is consistent with management's intentions. Insufficient evaluation, planning and testing of any modifications may cause unexpected disruptions to the business and may negatively impact the completeness and accuracy of data.

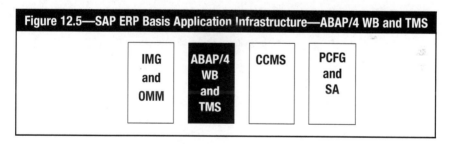

**Figure 12.5—SAP ERP Basis Application Infrastructure—ABAP/4 WB and TMS**

### Transport Management System Control

Appropriate change control procedures should be followed for all transports.

The production system change option should be set to No Changes Allowed, as shown in **figure 12.3**.

Repairs and modifications to original SAP objects should not be attempted without first seeking SAP Support via the SAP Service Marketplace. If not found, a ticket should be created with Send to SAP status. SAP Support will perform an initial analysis and determine whether a pre-existing solution exists. If the problem does not have a known solution, SAP Support will develop, test and provide a solution.

Where the error is not associated with SAP source code, SAP Support will update the ticket and provide a cost estimate. At this point, it is confirmed that the error is not an SAP source error, so the true origin of the error can be identified.

Development classes should be appropriately assigned to control changes. The abilities to create and release change requests should be segregated.

## *Transport Management System Testing Technique*

Gain an understanding of the system landscape and client strategy by reviewing:

- Transport procedures between clients and instances
- The change control policies and procedures for transporting objects between environments, including the enforcement of the procedures and available documentation
- Transports and transport paths to check that appropriate change controls are followed. To view transport routes in the SAP environment, use transaction code STMS and click on Transport Routes for a general view of the current transport route.
- A list of object types and procedures for objects that cannot be transported to production (e.g., some configuration, number ranges and master data changes) to ensure that they are documented and reviewed by management
- The emergency change procedures
- The SCC4 system change option
- STMS transport logs. A table E070 can also be used for the transport information that followed the transport path.
- Transaction SE16 and table TADIR if repairs have been made directly to the production system
- Development standards, including naming conventions and development class assignment (using transaction SE16 and table TDEVC) for:
  - Security
  - Programs
  - Transactions
  - Screens
- The access policies over transports through transaction code STMS and access to critical authorization objects (i.e., objects S_TRANSPRT and ACTVT except 03 and any transport type TTYPE). (Note that transaction code STMS now controls the movement of objects from one SAP system to another. This was previously performed using transaction code SE06.)

There are specific risks associated with ABAP/4 programming and the production environment that should be controlled:

- Customizing and executing ABAP/4 programs
- ABAP/4 development in production
- Data dictionary changes
- Queries
- Company code settings

These aspects are discussed in more detail in the sections that follow.

# Customizing and Executing ABAP/4 Programs

### Customizing and Executing ABAP/4 Programs Risk

In the absence of controls, any user who has the authorization object S_PROGRAM and access to transaction codes SA38 or SE38 or the transaction code for a particular program can execute that program. (Appendix G provides a list of transactions which are recommended to be locked. This list should be used to ensure that backdoor transactions to execute programs are not accessed, if enabled.) Authorization groups can be established to control access to customized programs. The customized ABAP/4 programs are assigned to authorization groups, and users can execute a program based on the authorization group specified by their profile.

Any user with the authorization to execute the program can start it and have access to all data accessed by the program. Therefore, it is the responsibility of the programming team and/or security to check whether the user who will be executing the program is duly authorized for the data.

### Customizing and Executing ABAP/4 Programs Control

Customized ABAP/4 programs should be assigned to authorization groups.

An authority-check statement should be included within customized ABAP/4 programs so that the user's authority to access objects is checked at run time. **Figure 12.6** depicts how program authorization checks operate.

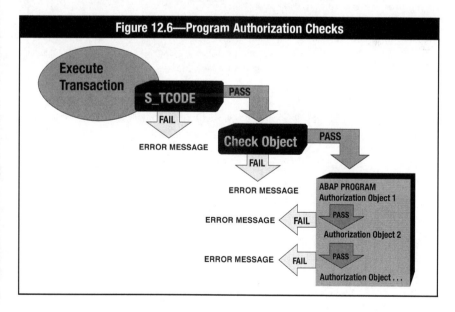

Figure 12.6—Program Authorization Checks

### Customizing and Executing ABAP/4 Programs Testing Technique

Use transaction code SE16 to identify customized programs that have not been assigned to an authorization group. Browse the table TRDIR with program name values Z* and then Y* to produce a list of all customized programs. (Note that Z and Y are the standard naming conventions used when creating customized programs.) Filter the list for programs without a value in the authorization group field (SECU).

Select a representative sample of customized programs from the list, and check the source code to ensure that an authority-check statement is in place. Use transaction code SA38 to run program RSABAPSC with the selected program name and "authority-check" in the ABAP/4 language commands selection field to display the authority-check statements for each sampled program. The results will include any other programs called by the selected program with authority-check statements. Confirm the results of the test with management.

Use transaction code SUIM ▷ Authorizations ▷ Authorizations by Complex Selection Criteria to test the number of users who have access to execute all programs, independent of the authorization group assigned.

| Transaction(s) | Authorization Objects | Fields | Values |
|---|---|---|---|
| SA38, SE37, SE38, SE80 | S_PROGRAM | ACTVT | SUBMIT, BTCSUBMIT |

SA38 allows program edit and execution. SE37 allows access to the function builder. SE80 allows object editing. SE38 allows users to edit the program as well as run it, creating an additional risk that the program may return inaccurate or incomplete information. Furthermore, allowing a user to run SE38 may lead to unauthorized changes to programs, potentially affecting system integrity.

Review the policy, procedures and criteria for establishing program authorization groups, assigning the programs to groups, and requiring authority-check statements in programs. Compare the results from testing to established policies, procedures, standards and guidance. (Note that organizations may use additional transactions, tables, authorization objects, programs and reports to control their systems.)

## ABAP/4 Development in Production

### Development in Production Risk

The creation or modification of programs should be performed in the development system and migrated through to the test or quality system for user acceptance testing (UAT). When UAT is complete and the change is accepted, the change transport may be imported into production. Sufficient UAT helps reduce the risk of disruption to business operations or unauthorized changes to production programs and data.

## Development in Production Control

Access to directly change production source code within the production environment should not be allowed. If an organization provides this option as an emergency change procedure, only the superuser/emergency fix ID or authority should have access to the authorization object S_DEVELOP with critical activity values in the production system. If this restriction is relaxed for a short period following the emergency change development, user activities in production must be carefully monitored. Development access to the production system should be removed as soon as possible. It is recommended that changes not be allowed directly into the production system. The update in production should be locked and no changes implemented without at least minimal testing in the quality system. (There are exceptions regarding testing. Single and composite roles/profiles and other configuration changes do not always conform to test scenarios.)

## Development in Production Testing Technique

Execute transaction SUIM ▶ Authorizations ▶ Authorizations by Complex Selection Criteria with the following authorization objects to obtain a list of users with authority to perform changes in the production system:

| Transaction(s) | Authorization Objects | Fields | Values |
|---|---|---|---|
| SE38, SE37, SE80 | S_DEVELOP | ACTVT | 01, 02, 06 |

The ABAP/4 programs that are not assigned to an authorization group may be changed by any user assigned a developer's key and the correct object keys. Use transaction codes SE16 with table DEVACCESS to identify the developer keys allowed in a client.

# Data Dictionary Changes

## Data Dictionary Changes Risk

Changes to the SAP ERP ABAP/4 data dictionary can have a fundamental impact on the system and may affect more than one client. Authority to change the dictionary must be restricted to authorized individuals who maintain the data dictionary as part of their job duties.

## Data Dictionary Changes Control

The ability to make changes to the SAP ERP data dictionary should be restricted and access privileges appropriately assigned based on job responsibilities. (Note: in addition to the appropriate authorizations, a developer's key and, in the case of changes to objects, an object key are required.) Aside from being assigned a developer's key and the correct object keys, settings in transaction code SCC4 should be set to allow for changes (see Implementation Guide Testing Techniques section for further details on how to allow for changes using transaction code SCC4). Users, including system administrators, should not be permitted to have access to the dictionary in a production system (the production system must also be set to not allow changes to objects, as described previously in this guide). Changes to the data dictionary should be performed in the development environment and transferred to the production environment using the Transport Management System (TMS).

## Data Dictionary Changes Testing Technique

To test this control, execute transaction SUIM ▷ Authorizations ▷ Authorizations by Complex Selection Criteria. Review users with the following authorization:

| Transaction(s) | Authorization Objects | Fields | Values |
|---|---|---|---|
| SE11, SE12, SE15, SE16, SE38, SE80 | S_DEVELOP | ACTVT | 01, 02, 06, 07 |

Note: there may be other authorization objects required, depending on how the system has been configured.

# Queries

## Queries Risk

Queries produce information and reports from the SAP ERP software that may be relied upon for management decision-making purposes. If access to modify and develop queries is not restricted, queries may be modified and may produce incorrect or unintended results, or queries may be developed that lack integrity.

## Queries Control

Authorization groups for creating and running the ABAP/4 queries should be established in the SAP ERP software in such a way that some end users can maintain and execute queries, while others can only execute existing queries.

## Queries Testing Technique

To be able to create new queries or modify existing ones in the Maintain Queries component, users must have an authorization for the authorization object S_QUERY with the value Change (02) in the roles assigned to their user master records. Without this authorization object, they can only execute existing queries. The components Maintain Functional Areas and Maintain User Groups can be accessed only by users authorized with the authorization object S_QUERY with the value Maintain (23).

Using transaction code SUIM ▷ Authorizations ▷ Authorizations by Complex Selection Criteria, enter the following authorization object to identify all users who can create and maintain queries:

| Transaction(s) | Authorization Objects | Fields | Values |
|---|---|---|---|
| SQ01 | S_QUERY | ACTVT | 02 |

In addition, use the following authorization object to identify all users who can maintain functional areas and user groups:

| Transaction(s) | Authorization Objects | Fields | Values |
|---|---|---|---|
| SQ02, SQ03 | S_QUERY | ACTVT | 23 |

This access should be restricted to limited users only (power users, Basis administrators) since they can expose confidential company information (human resources, financials, pricing and security) to an unauthorized user. End-user specific queries should be converted into custom transaction codes and users should be given access to these custom transaction codes. The same rule applies for the users with transaction codes SE16/SE16N and SE17 access.

# Company Code Settings

## Company Code Settings Risk

During implementation, company codes in the production system are normally not set to Productive. A company code that is used in production should be indicated by an X. Not setting company codes to Productive increases the risk that deletion programs can be executed (i.e., SAPF020 deletes all financial transaction data in the general ledger) and data reset in the company code by mistake. When the production client is created, it should be set to Productive.

During the development stage, the Productive indicator may be removed to facilitate the clean-up of inaccurate data during conversion or data load. This allows conversion or test data from external systems to be deleted from the SAP ERP system using standard deletion programs. Once testing has been completed and errors in the converted data are minimal, the Productive indicator should be activated for applicable company codes.

## Company Code Settings Control

Company codes that are used by the organization in the SAP ERP system should be set to Productive.

### Company Code Settings Testing Technique

Transaction code OBR3 contains a list of company codes and indicates whether they have been set to Productive. Review the XProd field in table T001 using transaction code SE16. Where the XProd field is set to X, the company code has been set to Productive. If company codes have not been set to Productive, investigate the reasons with management.

# CCMS Configuration

### CCMS Configuration Risk

CCMS is shown in **figure 12.7** as the third part of Basis Application Infrastructure. If operation modes, instances or the timetable are defined incorrectly, the CCMS display will not be meaningful. Changes to the profile parameters can have a profound impact on system functions. If system activities are not proactively monitored, processing problems may go undetected, impacting the SAP ERP operations and the integrity of the data.

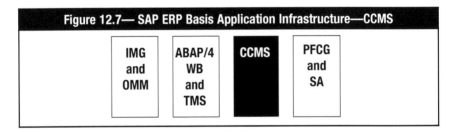

Figure 12.7— SAP ERP Basis Application Infrastructure—CCMS

| IMG and OMM | ABAP/4 WB and TMS | CCMS | PFCG and SA |

The CCMS does not provide virus protection or scanning. The SAP ERP GUI has marginal built-in virus protections; however, the application servers do not. Virus scanning must occur at the server level using an external package, which automatically polls the Internet for updates.

### CCMS Configuration Control

The SAP ERP CCMS should be set up in an appropriate manner and appropriate backups should be maintained.

The authorization object that allows access to the CCMS should be assigned properly.

Access to the system and start-up profiles must be tightly controlled. Change procedures must be followed strictly and changes to the profiles must be well documented. Access to the CCMS Alert Monitor should be properly secured.

Control panel alerts provide details relating to the operating system, lock management, activity in the system log and abends in ABAP/4 programs. Management should ensure that the log and abend messages are reviewed in a timely manner and appropriate follow-up actions are taken.

## CCMS Configuration Testing Technique

Determine via inquiry whether transaction RZ04 was used to set up operation's modes, instances and timetables to ensure that the CCMS displays meaningful data.

Generate a list of users with the ability to access the Alert Monitor by performing online access authorization testing using transaction code SUIM ▷ Authorizations ▷ Authorizations by Complex Selection Criteria for the following authorization object:

| Transaction(s) | Authorization Objects | Fields | Values |
|---|---|---|---|
| RZ20 | S_RZL_ADM | ACTVT | 01, 03 |

Determine how the organization is monitoring its SAP ERP system. Understand the policies, procedures, standards and guidance regarding the execution of SAPSTART and STOPSAP programs or their equivalent in the organization's environment. Ensure that only authorized personnel may execute these programs. Interview the individuals responsible for the control activity. Ask them to describe:
- The steps involved, including the procedures for defining system and start-up profiles and ensuring access is restricted to authorized users
- Reports and other information, including how they are used
- The procedures performed when exceptions or unusual items are encountered
- Procedures relating to the clearance of alerts
- How the control activity is performed in their absence
- Any changes to the control activity during the period of intended reliance, including changes in the individuals who perform the activity

Obtain evidence that corroborates the responses to those inquiries by examining documentation such as lists of users who can execute or modify the system and start-up profiles.

In addition to configuring the CCMS, the following aspects need to be configured or secured to adequately control the operational production system:
- Batch processing
- Application security parameters
- Locking transaction codes
- Restricted passwords
- SAP Router
- Online support system
- Remote function call and CPI-C communications

These are discussed in more detail in the sections that follow.

# Batch Processing

## Batch Processing Risk

There are two areas of risk relating to batch processing and powerful access:
• Batch input—Batch data communication (BDC) user types are primarily used by batch programs. Large data sets, such as interface programs, are transferred to an SAP ERP environment using batch input. A user dialog process, which is a user type defined for end users, is simulated for a batch input procedure. Effectively, batch input is an automatic procedure for transferring data to the SAP ERP system without a user dialog. The user dialog is simulated for this procedure, so the same checks and updates can be performed. The BDC user cannot log on interactively using the SAP ERP GUI or browser. There is a risk that BDC user types will be provided with excessive access and the authorization object batch input required to perform batch input will be provided to unauthorized users.
• Batch administration—Batch administrators can access all background jobs and perform any operation on any job in an SAP ERP system including releasing and deleting jobs, and running jobs against any user ID (which could circumvent segregation of duties controls). Batch operations may be disrupted if this access is assigned inappropriately.

## Batch Processing Control

The ability to administer, process and input batch jobs should be restricted through the SAP ERP security system to authorized users.

Upload programs created to load initial master data and take-on balances should be deleted from the production environment following go-live.

## Batch Processing Testing Technique

The capability to administer and release background jobs must be restricted through the use of the standard SAP ERP authorization objects. To test this control, obtain a list of users by executing transaction code SUIM ▷ Authorizations ▷ Authorizations by Complex Selection Criteria with the following authorizations:
• Batch input:

| Transaction(s) | Authorization Objects | Fields | Values |
|---|---|---|---|
| SM35 | S_BDC_MONI | BDCAKTI | DELE FREE, LOCK, REOG |
| | S_BDC_MONI | BDCGROUP | * |

• Batch administration:

| Transaction(s) | Authorization Objects | Fields | Values |
|---|---|---|---|
| SM36, SM37 | S_BTCH_ADM | BTCADMIN | Y |

• Batch scheduling:

| Transaction(s) | Authorization Objects | Fields | Values |
|---|---|---|---|
| SM36 | S_BTCH_JOB | JOBACTION | DELE, RELE |
| | S_BTCH_NAM | | * |

• Batch processing:

| Transaction(s) | Authorization Objects | Fields | Values |
|---|---|---|---|
| SM37 | S_BTCH_JOB | JOBACTION | DELE, RELE, PLAN |
| | S_BTCH_NAM | JOBACTION | * |

• Event triggering:

| Transaction(s) | Authorization Objects | Fields | Values |
|---|---|---|---|
| SM64 | S_BTCH_ADM | BTCADMIN | Y |

Determine by corroborative inquiry whether upload programs have been removed from the production environment as appropriate.

Check that access to schedule batch job (transaction code SM36) is appropriately assigned. Of particular importance is that batch jobs are able to be scheduled only by system (non-dialog) users. The level to which this is implemented is dependent on the organization's policies and procedures around batch job scheduling. The organization's policies and procedures around monitoring of batch jobs and handling of batch job exceptions should also be determined through corroborative inquiry. Note that users with S_BTCH_JOB object access can manage their own batch jobs. The object S_BTCH_JOB does not provide privileges to manage other jobs. The objects S_BTCH_ADM and S_BTCH_NAM determine the user's ability to manage all jobs, including the jobs created by others. Hence, it is quite possible for a few power users to create and manage their own jobs. However, the access to manage overall SAP jobs should be restricted to the people with SAP job-handling responsibility.

# Application Server Parameters

## Application Server Parameters Risk
As delivered, the SAP ERP software supplies default settings for system parameters, which often do not provide an adequate level of control over the system. Settings that have not been configured to the organization's environment may result in the system security being compromised and unauthorized access to the system.

## Application Server Parameters Control
During implementation, the organization should set the SAP ERP system profile parameters to appropriate values.

## Application Server Parameters Testing Technique
Configure system parameters for each instance using transaction codes RZ10 and RZ11. Ideally, these settings should be synchronized across servers and consistent with IT security policy for the SAP ERP application. It is important, where more than one instance is used and the parameters have not been synchronized, that this test be performed for each instance.

Run report RSPARAM via transaction code SA38 and review the key parameter settings for appropriateness. Alternatively, execute transaction code TU02 to obtain the current setting for all hosts and the history of changes to parameters. Set RSPARAM settings for key system parameters to match the organization's specifications and provide sufficient control to mitigate the risk of unauthorized access. Some of the more critical system parameters and their suggested values are summarized in **figure 12.8**. The suggested values should take into consideration the criticality of the SAP environment and the level of security appropriate for the enterprise.

The capability to configure application server parameters must be restricted through the use of the standard SAP ERP authorization objects. To test this control, obtain a list of users by executing transaction code SUIM ▷ Users ▷ Users by Complex Selection Criteria with the following authorizations:

| Transaction(s) | Authorization Objects | Fields | Values |
|---|---|---|---|
| RZ10, RZ11 | S_RZL_ADM | ACTVT | 01, 02 |

## Figure 12.8—Critical System Parameters

| System Parameter (Description) | Default Value | Suggested Value | Permitted Value |
|---|---|---|---|
| Login/password_expiration_time (The number of days after which a password must be changed. The parameter is deactivated when set to a value of 0.) | 0 | 30 days | 0-999 |
| Login/min _password_lowercase (the number of lower-case characters a password must contain) | 0 | 1 | 0-40 |
| Login/min _password_uppercase (the number of upper-case characters a password must contain) | 0 | 1 | 0-40 |
| Login/min _password_lng (the minimum password length) | 3 | 6 | 3-8 |
| Login/min_password_specials (The minimum number of special characters in the password. Permissible special characters are $%&/()=?'"*+~#-_.,;:{[]}\<>\| and space.) | 0 | > 0 | 0-8 |
| Login/fails_to_session_end (the number of times a user can enter an incorrect password before the system terminates the logon attempt) | 3 | 3 | 1-99 |
| Login/fails_to_user_lock (the number of times per day a user can enter an incorrect password before the system locks the user master records against further logon attempts) | 12 | 3 | 1-99 |
| Login/failed_user_auto_unlock (used to specify whether a user who has been locked as a result of invalid password attempts must have the login reset manually [value 0] or automatically at midnight) | 1 | 0 | 0 or 1 |
| Login/password_change_waittime (Determines the time period, measured in days, after which a user can change his/her password again. Only password changes requested by the user are taken into account.) | 1 | 1 | 1-1000 |
| Login/password_charset (defines the characters a password can consist of) | 1 | 0 | 0,1,2 |
| Login/password_compliance_to_current_policy (controls whether the system is to check during password-based logons whether the password used complies with the current password rules, and whether the user is to be prompted to change his or her password, if necessary) | 0 | 1 | 0 or 1 |

| Figure 12.8—Critical System Parameters *(cont.)* | | | |
|---|---|---|---|
| System Parameter (Description) | Default Value | Suggested Value | Permitted Value |
| Login/password_downwards_compatibility (defines backward compatibility of passwords) | 1 | 0 | 0-5 |
| Rdisp/gui_auto_logout (Specifies the number of seconds a user session can be idle before the user is automatically logged off. The parameter is deactivated when set to a value of 0.) | 0 | 901 - 1800 | Any numeric value |

# Locking Transaction Codes

## Locking Transaction Codes Risk

Some critical and sensitive transaction codes are used only in a development environment or sparingly in production. The development-related transaction codes should be locked permanently in the production environment. The production-sensitive transaction codes, including the archiving transaction codes, should be closely monitored and locked when not in use. Most organizations choose to secure transaction codes through the use of the S_TCODE authorization object. However, power users still may have access to sensitive transaction codes, and the following control provides another mechanism to prevent the inadvertent execution of these transactions in production.

## Locking Transaction Codes Control

Sensitive transaction codes should be locked in the production environment. The organization should have procedures for locking and unlocking these transaction codes, and access to perform such functionality should be appropriately restricted.

## Locking Transaction Codes Testing Technique

Use transaction code SUIM to provide a list of all users who have access to locked or unlocked transaction codes in the system (users with the transaction code SM01). Review and confirm the list with management to ensure that only authorized users have access. Enter transaction code SA38 and program RSAUDITC to display a list of transaction codes which are locked or unlocked. Review sensitive transaction codes to ensure that they have been locked from user access. Such transaction codes include, but are not limited to:
• SCC5—Client delete
• SCC1—Client copy (may overwrite the production client)
• SM49—Execute logical commands (may allow pass-through to the operating system)
• SM69—Execute logical commands (may allow pass-through to the operating system)

# Restricted Passwords

## Restricted Passwords Risk

SAP ERP software provides a facility to prevent users logging on with trivial passwords or passwords that can be guessed easily, e.g., passwords that describe the organization. By preventing the use of these passwords, plus restricted or illegal passwords, the risk that unauthorized users could access the system decreases.

## Restricted Passwords Control

During implementation, management should set up a list of illegal passwords that users are not allowed to use. There are also a number of inherent password controls in SAP ERP software:
• Requirement for first-time dialog users to change their initial passwords when logging on for the first time
• Minimum password length
• Disallowed use of SAP* or PASS as a password
• Definition of the number of digits, letters and special characters that must be contained in new passwords (using the profile parameters login/min_password_letters, login/min_password_digits and login/min_password_specials)
• Disallowed use of any three-character string that is contained in the user ID
• Disallowed use of ! or ? as the first character
• Disallowed use of space characters in the first three spaces
• Restriction on users reusing their last five passwords
• Restriction on passwords beginning with three identical characters
• Requirement that passwords differ from the last password by x characters (using the profile parameter Login/min_password_diff)
• Restriction on users changing their passwords more than once per day
• Number of failed password attempts to user lockout

## Restricted Passwords Testing Technique

All illegal passwords are maintained within table USR40, which can be accessed via transaction code SE16. Review this table to ensure that the illegal passwords contained in it appear reasonable and are consistent with management's intentions.

View configured password parameters via report RSPARAM (accessed via transaction SA38). Key parameters to review, and their default values, are highlighted in **figure 12.8**.

Obtain the last update of these values (to determine whether they have been in place for the entirety of the audit review period) by accessing transaction TU02 and selecting "history of file."

# SAP Router

## *SAP Router Risk*
SAP ERP software provides an application-level gateway program called SAP Router for SAP ERP communications with other systems. SAP Router acts as a secure gateway into and out of the SAP ERP environment. It is configured with a routing table that defines the permitted and denied IP addresses that have access to the network. If the route permission table is not defined, then the system will allow all connections, increasing the risk of unauthorized users connecting to the SAP ERP system.

## *SAP Router Control*
The SAP Router permission table should be configured with valid IP addresses. In addition, appropriate change management procedures for any modifications to the permission table should be in place and operating. The SAP Router log file may also be used to monitor remote communications activity.

## *SAP Router Testing Technique*
Request an extract of the SAP router permissions table (for example, by executing the UNIX command SAP router –L <path>) from the operating system administrator. This list contains the host names and port numbers of the predecessor and successor points on the route, as well as the passwords required to set up the connection.

Review this table to ensure that all entries have been authorized by management. This usually can be achieved by obtaining the relevant change control documentation for the last date on which the file was modified. In addition, determine from the listing if passwords have been established for all entries in the route permission table.

Obtain the file permissions set on the SAP Router table and review them to ensure that only authorized users have access to modify the entries within this table.

The SAP Router log file can be activated when SAP Router is started. The log will identify instances such as:
• Connection from (client name/address)
• Connection to (partner name/address)
• Partner service
• Start time
• End time
• Connection requests rejected after checking the route permission table

Activate this function by entering the operating system command SAP router –r –G <logfile>.

<logfile> is the relative path name specified for the log file.

Monitor the remote connections by checking the SAP Router log file and using the Monitoring Users Overview function from the administration menu.

# External or Operating System Commands

## External Commands Risk

External or operating system commands can be executed within the SAP system. These commands can be used to perform special functions, such as managing SAP interfaces with other systems and running critical maintenance activities, such as troubleshooting when the system malfunctions. However, there is a possibility of abuse of external commands or accidentally running external commands that may lead to deleting critical SAP system tables and shutting down SAP instances, which may result in system downtime.

## External Commands Control

Maintaining external commands requires additional authorization based on the authorization object S_RZL_ADM with Activity 01. Executing external commands is checked by the authorization object S_LOG_COM. This object has three fields: command, operating system and host, where specifications of which command can be executed for which operating system on a particular host are defined.

There must be control on which user has authorization, based on the authorization object S_LOG_COM, because programs can be accessed at the operating system level.

Secinfo file (a file that can be defined at the operating system level with parameters set) can be used to prevent executing any external command; however, by default this restriction is not configured. If the Secinfo file is missing, no restrictions apply to the start of external RFC programs.

## External Commands Testing Technique

Using transaction code SUIM ▷ Users ▷ Users by Complex Selection Criteria, review the system for users with the following authorizations:

| Transaction(s) | Authorization Objects | Fields | Values |
|---|---|---|---|
| SM69 | S_RZL_ADM | ACTVT | 01 |
| SM49 | S_RZL_ADM<br>S_LOG_COM | ACTVT<br>COMMAND<br>HOST<br>OPSYSTEM | 01<br>Check values |

Use transaction code SM69 (maintain external commands) and SM49 (execute external commands) to provide the list of commands that have been defined and those that can be executed, respectively. Review for appropriateness.

# SAP Service Marketplace

## SAP Service Marketplace Risk

Remote access by software vendors to assist with resolution of problems and for software maintenance is quite common. If it is controlled adequately, it assists in the timely implementation of corrections and ensures a better level of service to users. SAP provides online support by means of a system called SAP Service Marketplace. It is generally considered that the advantages provided by connection to SAP Service Marketplace outweigh the risks involved with allowing remote access to the system, provided adequate controls are in place. SAP Service Marketplace is used by SAP to supply bug fixes and to assist in tracing the cause of problems that may occur in a particular installation. EarlyWatch is one of the SAP Service Marketplace services that uses the SAP Service Marketplace remote connection. This service includes regular checkups of the SAP ERP system, the database and the operating system to facilitate system availability and data throughput.

In some sites, SAP may provide all technical support through SAP Service Marketplace, connected full-time to the production system. In these cases, management may have made a conscious decision that the cost/benefits outweigh the risks involved, but it is still important to raise the potential risks involved with management.

As a general rule, SAP or the support provider's access should be restricted to a test/development environment, ideally on a separate file server from the production environment and activated only on request. Additionally, all activity should be logged and reviewed by an individual with the ability to understand the actions that have been taken. Changes should be subject to normal testing and migration controls before being implemented on the production system. Restricting access to a development client on the production system may not be sufficient in terms of providing adequate controls over remote access by vendors.

Basis or superusers with administrative access are able to download hot patches, create SAP Service Marketplace IDs, grant developer keys, and open and close connections with SAP Service Marketplace. Having a large number of users with administrative access to the production client may affect the integrity of the configuration in the system.

## SAP Service Marketplace Control

Where practical, facilities with valid network connection addresses specified, such as dial-back, should be in place to ensure the authenticity of the remote access user. Multiple user ID/password access can also be implemented to reduce the potential for unauthorized access. Routing all remote access connections through a firewall may also be practical in some installations. Access to open a service connection through SAP Service Marketplace and access to the developers' keys should be restricted to a limited number of authorized users. Accounts with access to SAP Service Marketplace should be locked when not in use, and use of these accounts should be formally reviewed and approved. Hot packages should be tested in the development system and the normal change management procedures followed to apply them to production.

### SAP Service Marketplace Testing Technique

Because of the wide variation in remote access facilities available, it is difficult to specify what is acceptable for a particular site. However, management should be aware of the risks involved with remote access and have a specific policy to cover this. The policy should be consistent with good practice as outlined previously, and it should be possible to test compliance.

To obtain a list of SAP Service Marketplace users on the production client, enter transaction code OSS1 using the client's administrator ID. Click on the SAPNET icon followed by the Administration icon. Perform an authorization analysis by authorization object view. This will provide a list of all users assigned to SAP Service Marketplace by authorization object. In particular, ensure that management reviews for reasonableness the users who are assigned to administration authorization and open service connections.

# RFC and CPI-C Communications

### RFC and CPI-C Communications Risk

The SAP ERP program interfaces simplify and standardize communication among different systems and/or programs. The SAP ERP communication interfaces operate at various levels. The two main interfaces are Remote Function Call (RFC) and Common Programming Interface-Communications (CPI-C). All the SAP ERP connections contain an option to specify the system, client, user ID and password. If a dialog user ID and password are specified within the SAP ERP connections, then it is possible to automatically use RFC and CPI-C.

RFC is used for communication between the SAP ERP systems and other systems and is a standard programming interface for remotely calling functions that exist or operate on another system. RFC can be used to send and retrieve data processed or manipulated by another system or to balance the load between systems where the same functions exist on each. CPI-C is used for program-to-program communication such as for online interface programs and data conversion programs. CPI-C is a standardized communication interface originally defined and developed by IBM. CPI-C communication uses the SAP ERP gateway between systems to convert CPI-C calls to external communication protocols such as TCP/IP. The table RFCDES, which controls the communication, can be accessed by transaction code SM59. The table includes:
• RFC destinations
• R/2 connections

• R/3 connections
• SAP ERP connections
• TCP/IP

The SAP ERP connection contains an option to specify the system, client, user ID and password. RFC can directly log onto another SAP ERP system from table RFCDES if the password field is blank or *.

There is a risk that dialog or service users would be able to log on and perform unauthorized tasks if they are also defined as RFC users.

### RFC and CPI-C Communications Control
The SAP ERP RFC and CPI-C communications are secured so any user who makes use of a connection is prompted to enter a username and password. Furthermore, user IDs in RFC destinations should be set up as communication or system users. This will ensure that individuals cannot log on with the user ID and passwords do not expire.

### RFC and CPI-C Communications Testing Technique
Execute transaction code SM59 in all SAP systems in the landscape. This will display the table RFCDES, which controls the communication between systems. The table lists the RFC destinations, which includes all SAP ERP connections on the system. Expand each of the SAP ERP connections, and double-click on each connection to verify that no dialog user ID is listed with its password.

## Profile Generator and Security Administration Risk

Auditing security in an SAP ERP environment requires expert knowledge of SAP ERP and the organization's approach to security. There are a number of risks surrounding the use of the Profile Generator and Security Administration, as depicted in **figure 12.9**, including:
• Security Administration profiles
• Security authorization documentation
• Superuser SAP*
• Default users
• SAP_ALL and SAP_NEW
• Maintenance of powerful user groups
• Table logging
• Data dictionary reports
• Log and trace files

| 12.9—SAP ERP Basis Application Infrastructure—PFCG and SA | | | |
|---|---|---|---|
| IMG and OMM | ABAP/4 WB and TMS | CCMS | **PFCG and SA** |

Segregation of duties in the Security Administration environment is important to prevent any one individual from having excessive access within the system. Depending on the size of the organization, it is usually desirable to segregate the following four functions:
• Creation and maintenance of roles/profiles
• Assignment of roles/profiles to users
• Creation and maintenance of user master records
• Transportation of roles/profiles

Appropriate segregation among these functions will mitigate the risk of one security administrator creating roles/profiles, activating roles/profiles and maintaining roles/profiles.

### The Profile Generator and Security Administration Control

Security Administration profiles should be segregated and appropriately assigned to system management staff (refer to testing techniques in the following paragraphs). Where segregation of duties is not practical due to resource issues, compensating controls may be achieved through the independent management review of the SAP ERP change documents for users, profiles and authorizations through SUIM ▷ Change Documents ▷ For Users/For Profiles/For Authorizations (also accessible through transaction code SA38 and programs RSUSR100/101/102).

### The Profile Generator and Security Administration Testing Technique

Determine whether the system administrator tasks are segregated into the following administrator functions by generating user lists for the following authorizations using transaction code SUIM ▷ Authorizations ▷ Authorizations by Complex Selection Criteria.

For the Profile Generator:
• Create and change roles—Used to define and update roles

| Transaction(s) | Authorization Objects | Fields | Values |
|---|---|---|---|
| PFCG | S_USER_AGR | ACTVT | 01, 02 |

• Transport roles—Used to transport or activate roles to/in production

| Transaction(s) | Authorization Objects | Fields | Values |
|---|---|---|---|
| PFCG | S_USER_AGR | ACTVT | 21 |

• Assign roles/profiles to user master records—Used to assign or transfer roles/profiles into the user master records for the relevant users

| Transaction(s) | Authorization Objects | Fields | Values |
|---|---|---|---|
| PFCG, SU01 | S_USER_AGR | ACTVT | 02 |
| | S_USER_GRP | ACTVT | 22 |

For user master maintenance:
• Create/change/lock/delete changes:

| Transaction(s) | Authorization Objects | Fields | Values |
|---|---|---|---|
| SU01 | S_USER_GRP | ACTVT | 01, 02, 05, 06 |

If full segregation is not possible among the four functions listed above, management should at minimum consider segregating the creation of roles/profiles and assignment of roles/profiles. If the segregation of duties option is practical, assess hard copies of change documents for users, profiles and authorizations through SUIM ▶ Change Documents ▶ For Users/For Profiles/For Authorizations (also accessible through transaction code SA38 and programs RSUSR100/101/102) for evidence of review and action by management.

Consider identifying which user IDs have created, deleted, locked or unlocked user IDs during the period under review and determine whether such actions were appropriate. Obtain this information through SUIM ▶ Change Documents ▶ For Users (also accessible through transaction code SA38 and program RSUSR100), entering relevant date parameters and selection criteria.

Review access to effect mass changes to user master records (UMRs) as follows:

| Transaction(s) | Authorization Objects | Fields | Values |
|---|---|---|---|
| SU10, SU12 | S_USER_GRP | ACTVT | 01, 02, 05, 06 |
| | S_USER_PRO | ACTVT | 01, 02, 05, 06 |

Manual maintenance was used prior to the introduction of the Profile Generator for the purpose of role maintenance.

• Authorization maintenance

| Transaction(s) | Authorization Objects | Fields | Values |
|---|---|---|---|
| SU03 | S_USER_AUT | ACTVT | 01, 02, 07, 22 |

• User maintenance

| Transaction(s) | Authorization Objects | Fields | Values |
|---|---|---|---|
| SU02 | S_USER_PRO | ACTVT | 01, 02, 07, 22 |

Although the transaction codes SU02 and SU03 are still able to be used, SAP recommends the use of PFCG for role/profile maintenance.

# Authorization Documentation

## Authorization Documentation Risk
During the implementation of the SAP ERP software, organizations should develop adequate documentation that describes how authorizations and profiles are designed and establish a procedure for the maintenance of this documentation. Without detailed documentation of the development and implementation of the authorization and profiles, it may be difficult to adequately test security since irregularities may not be traceable back to their root causes. In addition, without documentation it is difficult to determine whether security has been implemented in accordance with management's intentions.

## Authorization Documentation Control
Original documentation of the SAP ERP authorizations and their use should be developed and approved by management during the implementation. Documentation that identifies changes made to the original authorizations should be maintained. It may be prudent to keep an offsite copy of the authorization documentation to be used in the event of a disaster. A profile and user owner, typically the business process or data owners, should be designated to approve the assignment of specific profiles or changes to certain users.

## Authorization Documentation Testing Technique
Review the system design documentation relating to authorizations and profiles; any established policies, procedures, standards and guidance related to the maintenance of profiles/authorizations; and the list of profiles/authorizations defined in the system.

Perform the following tests to ensure the appropriateness of the documentation:
• Review the process in place when new access is granted, such as who is authorized to approve the access and how the issues concerning segregation of

duties are addressed (use of automated tools such as SAP GRC Risk Analysis Remediation [RAR] or manual tracking of segregation of duties activities).

• Identify users created during the period of review and validate that the new users' access has been appropriately approved. The user creation date information is available in the USR02 table. The relevant fields from the USR02 table are:
  – BNAME—User ID
  – ERDAT—Date of user master record creation

• Validate that there is a periodic process to review users' access with the appropriate authority, e.g., module owners. This will identify users who have access to the system without a valid business need.

• Take a representative sample of profiles and authorizations from the system and confirm them against the original documentation. Resolve any discrepancies with management.

• Test changes to authorization and profiles since the implementation of the system, using the SAP ERP change documents for users, profiles and authorizations through SUIM ▷ Change Documents ▷ For Users/For Profiles/For Authorizations (also accessible through transaction code SA38 and programs RSUSR100/101/102). This involves taking a sample of changes from the system and tracing them back to current documentation. Management should be able to provide source documentation for the authorization of these changes.

# Superuser SAP*

## Superuser SAP* Risk

SAP* is the default superuser ID supplied with the SAP ERP software. If improperly protected, it could be used to access the system and perform unauthorized processing of transactions that may circumvent established controls in the system. This account may be used without individual accountability. The standard SAP ERP superuser, SAP*, does not require a user master record. However, when installing the SAP ERP software, a user master record for the SAP* user is automatically created in clients 000 and 001 with the initial password 06071992. The presence of an SAP* user master record will deactivate the special properties of the standard SAP ERP SAP* superuser. This SAP* UMR is then subject to authorization checks like all users. However, since the standard SAP* user is hard-coded into the system and does not require association with a UMR, deleting the SAP* user master record results in the possibility to authenticate directly to the kernel with a user ID of SAP* and default password of PASS. Any use of this user after the regeneration is not subject to authorization checks. The SAP* user is often where hackers make their first attempt to gain entry into an SAP ERP system.

Because SAP* is hard-coded in the system and used to communicate between the SAP ERP application and Basis, every new client creation exposes SAP* and its defaulted password PASS.

## Superuser SAP* Control

The SAP* user account should be secured by:

- Assigning SAP* to the security administration's authorization group (e.g., SUPER) to help prevent the SAP* UMR from being inadvertently deleted
- Changing the default password
- Segregating SAP* capabilities across newly created superusers with less functionality
- Deleting all profiles/roles and authorizations from the SAP* user
- Locking the user
- Monitoring audit logs for the user

Some practitioners recommend storing the new SAP* password in a safe, for emergency access only. However, in the event of an emergency, it needs to be accessible. Note that the use of the SAP* user can be further controlled by means of a system parameter (login/no_automatic_user_sapstar), which by default is not set (value 0). Setting this parameter to 1 will prevent SAP* from being regenerated when the UMR is deleted. However, if the parameter is set and the user master record table in the system becomes corrupted, then the system administration team may not be able to access the system using the hard-coded superuser SAP* with password PASS.

## Superuser SAP* Testing Technique

To determine whether the SAP* user has been locked, execute transaction SUIM ▶ Authorizations ▶ Authorizations by Complex Selection Criteria. Enter SAP* in the user field and press F8. Verify that the SAP* user group field is Super. Click on the Other View button twice. The user status field for SAP* should say Locked.

To test whether the default password has been changed for the account SAP*, execute transaction code SA38 and program RSUSR003. This report details all clients that have been installed in the SAP ERP instance subject to review. For each client, the report details whether the password used for SAP* is trivial, i.e., set at default.

Confirm that SAP* is not created in client 066 (EarlyWatch client).

# Default Users

## Default Users Risk

The SAP ERP software is delivered with a set of standard users (including SAP*, as mentioned previously) and passwords that should be secured appropriately. Their passwords should be changed as part of the implementation process. If these passwords are left unchanged, unauthorized users may gain access to the system.

The original (default) passwords for these are:
- SAP*=06071992 (In the standard installation, the SAP* user has this password in clients 000 and 001.)
- SAP*=PASS (When a new client is created, the SAP* user is created by default in the new client with password PASS. Once a user master record is created for SAP* and then deleted, it defaults back to this password.)
- DDIC=19920706 (User DDIC is the maintenance user for the ABAP/4 data dictionary. Like the SAP* user, DDIC is a user with powerful privileges. Unlike the SAP* user, it has its own user master record. It is required to perform certain installation and setup tasks in the system and special functions during upgrades. It should not be deleted.)
- SAPCPIC=ADMIN
- EarlyWatch=SUPPORT

### Default Users Control

The default SAP ERP passwords for SAP*, DDIC, SAPCPIC and EarlyWatch should be changed in all clients and access restricted to the superuser.

### Default Users Testing Technique

To test whether the default password has been changed for these users, execute the SAP ERP report RSUSR003 and determine whether the default passwords have been changed in all clients.

# SAP_ALL and SAP_NEW

### SAP_ALL and SAP_NEW Risk

The SAP ERP software provides certain powerful profiles that provide the equivalent of superuser access to the system. These profiles include:
- SAP_ALL (all authorizations for the SAP ERP system)
- SAP_NEW (all authorizations for newly created objects)

The SAP_ALL profile grants unlimited access to the system, including all functional areas and Basis security administration. The SAP_NEW profile may provide users with additional unauthorized access during an upgrade.

### SAP_ALL and SAP_NEW Control

Access to these powerful profiles should be restricted. Sometimes organizations may grant access to the SAP_NEW profile to users to minimize disruption to operations following an upgrade. However, in general, this access should not be required. A superuser account with the SAP_ALL and SAP_NEW profiles may be created with a confidential ID and secret password for emergency use. Their usage should be restricted and monitored closely, using transaction codes SM19 and SM20. Again, some practitioners recommend storing the superuser ID password in a safe, for emergency access only. However, in the event of an emergency, it needs to be accessible.

## SAP_ALL and SAP_NEW Testing Technique

Review users assigned the privileged profiles of SAP_ALL and SAP_NEW for appropriateness. Assign users who have been assigned these superuser profiles to user group Super or an equivalent, which should be maintained by a limited number of Basis personnel only.

To perform this test, execute transaction code SUIM ▷ Users ▷ Users by Complex Selection Criteria. In the Selection Criteria for User section, enter SAP_ALL into the profile field. Click on the button to the right of the text box. Enter SAP_NEW in the first empty text box. Click on the Copy button. This lists all users with superuser functionality. Other powerful profiles to check for user access include, S_A.SYSTEM (system administration authorizations), S_RZL_ADMIN (CCMS administration authorizations), S_USER_ALL (all user administration authorizations), S_A.USER (Basis authorizations for Basis end users), S_ABAP_ALL (all ABAP/4 authorizations) and S_A.ADMIN (system operation authorizations). These profiles provide SAP ERP administration and development authorizations.

Check the user list identified by this test to ascertain whether individuals who have access to privileged functionality require this access, based on their job responsibilities and established policies, procedures, standards and guidance.

# Maintenance of Powerful User Groups

## Maintenance of Powerful User Groups Risk

Administrators should not be able to modify their own authorizations, because it would allow administrators to give themselves powerful access and the potential to perform unauthorized transactions in the system. Their user IDs should be assigned to the user group containing potentially powerful predefined user IDs such as SAP* and DDIC. A senior person and a backup person without day-to-day job responsibilities for security administration should maintain this group.

## Maintenance of Powerful User Groups Control

The authorization group that contains powerful users should be restricted to the new superuser and a backup. This is typically the group Super.

## Maintenance of Powerful User Groups Testing Technique

Identify the system administrators within the organization and determine to what user groups their user IDs belong.

Using transaction code SUIM ▷ Users ▷ Users by Complex Selection Criteria, review the system for users with the following authorizations:

| Transaction(s) | Authorization Objects | Fields | Values |
|---|---|---|---|
| SU01 | S_USER_GRP | ACTVT | 01, 02, 06 |

The authorization field user group in user master maintenance should be similar to one of the values identified earlier. This is usually the group Super.

Conduct an independent review of SAP ERP change documents for users, profiles and authorizations through SUIM ▷ Change Documents ▷ For Users/For Profiles/For Authorizations (also accessible through transaction code SA38 and reports RSUSR100/101/102).

# Central User Administration

## *Central User Administration Risk*
Access to Central User Administration (CUA) may not be adequately secured, resulting in unauthorized changes to the access rights of users. The following data can be distributed with the CUA:
• User master record data (address, logon data, user defaults and user parameters)
• The assignment of users to roles or profiles for each child system
• The initial password, which is distributed to the child systems by default
• The lock status of a user. The new "global lock" is available using CUA and applies to all of the child systems in which the user is defined. It can be cancelled in the central system or locally, if required.

CUA configuration and ALE landscape may not be configured correctly, resulting in failure of systems to interface effectively. Furthermore, there is a risk that access to ALE configuration may not be adequately secured.

## *Central User Administration Control*
In CUA, the central system and every child system can be defined by name, using the transaction code SALE. In the central system, all child systems and the central system can be defined. In the child system, the child system itself and the central system can be defined. CUA can be activated centrally using transaction SCUA.

A field attribute can be defined for each input field of user maintenance transaction SU01, using the transaction code SCUM. The following field attributes are available:
• Global—Data can be maintained only by the central system.
• Default—A default value is automatically distributed to the child system when it is saved, and can be maintained when a user is created in the central system.

- Redistribution—The data can be maintained in both the central system and the child system. If a change is made to the child system, the data are returned to the central system and passed on to other existing child systems.
- Local—Data for the corresponding field can be administered only locally in the child systems.
- Everywhere—Data can be changed locally and globally. However, for local maintenance, no redistribution takes place.

### Central User Administration Testing Technique

Because all enterprises are structured differently and have different requirements, conduct an initial discussion with the enterprise to obtain an understanding of the its structure and the configuration requirements for CUA. To test whether CUA has been configured appropriately, execute the transaction codes SALE, SCUA and SCUM and review the appropriateness of the configured settings for the organization. Also, if CUA is configured to run in a separate client outside of production, then it should be determined who has administrator access through the CUA master client.

# Table Logging

## Table Logging Risk

The system uses change document objects to specify which tables are logged and the level of logging performed on each table. While there ideally should be no direct changes to tables in the production client, a list of the tables whose changes can affect the structure of the system should be developed to mitigate the risk that unauthorized or inaccurate changes are not identified.

## Table Logging Control

All changes to the critical SAP ERP tables should be logged by the system and the periodic review of these logs should form part of the security procedures for the organization.

## Table Logging Testing Technique

Review security procedures created by management that identify what tables are being logged and how often these logs are reviewed by management. For changes to be logged, the system profile parameter rec/client needs to be activated. Check this by reviewing the report RSPARAM and ensuring that the value for this parameter is set to All or to the client numbers that have table logging enabled.

Tables that require changes to be logged need to be specified within the table DD09L. In addition to being listed here, critical tables must have the LOG field activated within the technical settings of each individual table. To test this, enter transaction code SE16 and enter table DD09L as the object name, along with an X in the LOG field. This identifies tables that have their changes logged. To test each table, enter the specific table as the object name in transaction SE11 and press Display. Switch the view to show the technical settings for the table and review whether the checkbox Log Data Changes is set. Examples of tables that should be logged include:

• Clients (T000)
• Company codes (T001)
• Fiscal periods for company codes (T001B)
• Foreign currency exchange rates (TCURR)

To test whether this control has been effective, run transaction code SA38 and program RSTBHIST (table change analysis), which list all changes to tables that log data changes activated in their technical settings for the period specified. Take a representative sample of changes to this table and compare these to the original supporting information/documentation. Obtain explanations for any changes for which supporting information or documentation is not available. Logging all table changes is likely to have a severe, adverse impact on system performance. Therefore, management should identify a refined list of critical tables to log and review. Refer to appendix C—Suggested SAP ERP Tables to Log and Review.

# Data Dictionary Reports

## Data Dictionary Reports Risk

The data dictionary is a central catalog that contains the descriptions of an enterprise's data and provides information about the relationships among the data and their use in programs and screens. The data descriptions in a data dictionary are also called metadata, i.e., data that describe other data. It is important that changes made to the data dictionary be regularly reviewed since an unauthorized or inaccurate change to the data dictionary can affect the integrity of the data in the system.

The data dictionary information system consists of a number of reports (called DD reports), each of which implements a certain view of the data dictionary. Each report has a selection screen and an output list to display the objects found, along with their attributes. The modification analysis DD report generates a list of all objects that have been modified. The data dictionary information system can be started with transaction code SE15.

## Data Dictionary Reports Control

Security administrators need to identify areas that will be monitored and audited in the production environment. Details of modifications to the data dictionary should be maintained and should follow change control procedures. The SAP ERP data dictionary information system reports should be regularly generated and reviewed by management.

### Data Dictionary Reports Testing Technique

Understand management's policies and procedures regarding the review of data dictionary reports. Assess the adequacy of such policies, procedures, standards and guidance, taking into account the frequency with which the review is performed, the level of detail in the reports, other independent data to which management compares the reports, the likelihood that the people performing the review will be able to identify exception items and the nature of exception items that they can be expected to identify.

## Log and Trace Files

### Log and Trace Files Risk

The security audit log was introduced in SAP R/3 release 4.0. It can record the following security-related information:

• Successful and unsuccessful dialog logon attempts
• Successful and unsuccessful RFC logon attempts
• RFC calls to function modules
• Changes to user master records
• Successful and unsuccessful transaction starts
• Changes to the audit configuration

The user selects which information will be audited (SM19). The security audit log must be enabled specifically. Users can select the information to be reviewed/displayed (SM20). Due to the amount of information accumulated, it may be necessary to periodically archive and purge files (using SM18). The SAP ERP system log (accessed through transaction SM21) provides graphic and list-oriented monitors as well as logs and trace facilities for investigation and rectification of exceptions. The size of each local and central log must be large enough to hold enough messages for problem analysis. Inadequate specification of log sizes in the system profile will cause the system to automatically overwrite the historical data once the logs become full. The system provides trace functions for database access, ABAP/4 programs, internal system activity and developer traces. If these files are not secured at the operating system level, the integrity of the data contained within these files may be compromised.

### Log and Trace Files Control

Log and trace files should be secured at the operating system level at the location specified within the system profile. They should be regularly reviewed by management.

Logging should be appropriately configured.

## Log and Trace Files Testing Techniques

Generate the report RSPARAM and review the following parameter settings to obtain the locations of the log and trace files:

- Rslg/central/file (the active central log file name: default filename is SLOGJ)
- Rslg/central/old_file (the old central log file name: default filename is SLOGJO)
- Rslg/local/file (the local log file name: default filename is SLOG < SAPSYSTEM number >)
- Rstr/file (the absolute path name of the trace file: the trace file name is TRACE < SAP ERP System number >)

Obtain a copy of the permissions set on these files at the operating system level, and review it for adequacy.

Execute transaction SM21 and review the logging configuration settings for reasonableness, including the size of each local and central log file.

# Outline of Case Study on SAP Access Security

## Step 1: Identify High-risk Transactions

This can be achieved through a combination of interviews/questionnaires with business management, a review of process flow documentation and the auditor's knowledge of the business and related risks.

It may also be useful to obtain an organization chart of employees within the department under review. Using this listing, determine what transactions key users have executed within the past three months (using the transaction codes STAD or ST03N). Note that STAD reports only on 24-hour periods. This frequently provides insight as to the real transaction usage of key business roles within the company. Collate the lists of high-risk transactions to generate a segregation of duties matrix.

To continue this example, assume the following transaction code has been found to be significant: FB01—Create G/L Document.

## Step 2: Identify Relevant Authorization Objects

Outline the three primary methods of gathering this information while providing some of the respective strengths and weaknesses of each approach. This includes:

- System trace—Requires access to perform the actual transactions in a nonproduction environment that is configured the same as production. The environment must have enough master and transactional data to permit the execution of transactions as would occur in production. It also requires a significant amount of business process knowledge to successfully process all components within the transaction (i.e., valid combinations of G/L account, company code, business area). Finally, all the relevant pieces of the transaction must be executed or key authority check statements in the underlying ABAP code may never be identified properly. These limitations make this approach difficult to execute.

- Security documentation—If security has been documented sufficiently, the project team may have captured all the relevant authorization objects in the course of the security implementation.
- Extraction of the information directly from SAP—Use transaction code SU24 and enter FB01 or use transaction code SE16 and view the contents of table USOBT_C for the selected transactions. Add to this list the S_TCODE object checked at transaction start. In the example, this will yield the following authorization objects associated with the transaction code selected:

F_BKPF_BED
F_BKPF_BUP
F_BKPF_BEK
F_BKPF_GSB
F_BKPF_BES
F_BKPF_KOA
F_BKPF_BLA
S_TCODE
F_BKPF_BUK

## Step 3: Identify Values to Be Tested

Use USOBT_C to give guidance as to the minimum range of values required. Others must come from an understanding of the scope of the audit and the relevant organization units (e.g., company codes, plants, sales organizations). Finally, use the knowledge of the manner in which SAP has been implemented to filter out noncritical authorization objects (if, for example, authorization groups with the G/L are not used, then a number of objects listed previously are no longer necessary). For example, this might result in the need to test the items in **figure 12.10.**

| Figure 12.10—Values to be Tested | |
| --- | --- |
| Item | Value |
| F_BKPF_BUK | |
| ACTVT | 01, 02, 03 |
| BUKRS | 0023 (if company code 23 is the primary legal entity under audit) |
| S_TCODE | FB01 or F-02 |
| F_BKPF_KOAACTVT | 01, 02, 03 |
| KOART | All values |
| F_BKPF_GSB | |
| ACTVT | 01, 02, 03 |
| GSBER | Retail |

## Step 4:  Determine Ability to Execute Transactions

### Phase 1:  High-level Review

Based solely on the S_TCODE authorization object, identify users with the ability to execute transactions, in the following ways:

- Execute transaction code SUIM ▷ Users ▷ Users by Complex Selection Criteria (list of users according to complex selection criteria).
- Execute transaction code SUIM ▷ Users with Complex Selection Criteria ▷ With Critical Authorizations (also accessible with program RSUSR008_009_ NEW, which replaces programs RSUSR008 and RSUSR009 for SAP Web AS 6.20 onward). Note that this transaction allows the user to specify user-defined transactions that, if executable by the same user, present a segregation of duties risk. Its use presents a number of challenges, however, in that:
  - The table used to drive the report is a customizing table and most likely will not be editable in production.
  - Table maintenance access must be granted to audit (although this may be restricted to this table through the use of authorization groups).

Both of these approaches suffer the significant limitation that only the S_TCODE authorization object is checked and offers no indication of the user's ability to effect transactions over multiple organization units. In this example, the auditor will have no information on the business areas or company codes to which a user has access.

### Phase 2:  Detailed Review

A detailed review can be performed in a number of ways, including:

- Execute transaction code SUIM ▷ Users ▷ Users by Complex Selection Criteria. The user must be aware, however, that this can provide results based on only three authorization objects at a time. As the example has four, the transaction will have to be executed twice and the results downloaded to an application such as Microsoft Excel or Access where user IDs appearing on both lists can be identified (the true result of the test).
- Execute transaction code SUIM ▷ Users ▷ With Critical Authorizations (also accessible with program RSUSR008_009_NEW, which replaces programs RSUSR008 and RSUSR009 for SAP Web AS 6.20 onward). For further information, see chapter 4. This program can be configured to provide critical access and segregation of duties risk management, also provided by the SAP Access Control tool, Risk Analysis and Remediation (RAR). For further information on the SAP Access Control tool, RAR, see chapter 13. Download the contents of tables User Masters (UST04), Profiles (UST10C and UST10S) and Detailed Authorization Description (UST12) and directly query the results. Standard SE16 downloads do not work well in this instance since UST10C and UST10S are parent-child tables that may be difficult to interrogate with tools such as Access or ACL. Note also that the tables may be very large. The advent of ACL's tool, Direct Link, offers some hope in this regard by allowing multiple tables to be downloaded at once with all the fields prelinked.

• Use external SAP security tools (discussed further in chapter 14) or subcontract the analysis to one of the audit firms that has its own in-house tool and is willing to contract for its use.

### Step 5: Filter Out False Positives

With a list of users who have the authorization objects and values necessary to execute the transaction, use table USR02 to filter out users whose user IDs have been locked or whose "valid to" date is in the past. It may also be useful to filter out any nondialog users depending on the scope of the audit.

### Step 6: Evaluate the Business Impact of Findings

For all accounting documents generated within the previous six months, use the report S_ALR_87012293 (Display Changed Document) to download from SAP information that identifies the document number and the user ID that created it. Summarize the results based on user ID and compare the results to the list of users who can execute financial accounting transactions (e.g., FB01/F-02, FB05, FB08). Determine the percentage of users who can execute the transaction compared to those who have actually made use of the ability. This can be a powerful argument in illustrating the need to tighten security. A similar approach can be taken to most transactions under review.

## Summary

In this chapter, the reader was provided with an approach to identifying the risks, key controls and various testing techniques that are part of the Basis Application Infrastructure. The chapter provided a sample toolset that could be used in auditing the SAP ERP Basis Application Infrastructure. It included:
• Specific risks that are a part of the Basis Application Infrastructure
• Automated control activities
• Sample assurance techniques

# 13. Governance, Risk and Compliance in an SAP ERP Environment

The concept of continuous monitoring is becoming increasingly attractive as an approach to reviewing systems. This is partly attributable to the recent introduction of sophisticated toolsets that automate the generation and management of real-time information used in assessing system and business risks.

ERPs have powerful and complex security configurations. Testing security is not just a matter of reviewing the security matrix of users to functions. Using SAP roles and profiles to find out who has access to what often requires automated diagnostic tools to complete the task effectively. Security exposures can arise from the combination of security profiles assigned to a user. For example, a transaction code in one profile combined with the authorization object from another may inadvertently provide a user with excessive access, contrary to management's intentions. To effectively identify and assess this type of exposure, automated security diagnostic tools are required.

Benefits of automated security diagnostic tools are that they:
• Provide an historic view, e.g., identifying when security parameters were changed
• Provide evidence of continuous improvement of security controls
• Unravel complex security profiles
• Provide dynamic documentation of user access
• Produce plain-language output
• Promote independence (i.e., they are developed independently to access the required data)
• Perform noninvasively (i.e., there is minimal disruption to the operation of the production system, usually through extracting and downloading the required information offline for subsequent evaluation)

Over the last 10 years, the tools for auditing SAP security configuration and user access have evolved. The complex SAP security concept and built-in tools for querying access rights have discouraged the involvement of business users and management in SAP security. To facilitate analyzing security information, there first was a move from using simple query functions and reports (directly from within SAP) to third-party tools that download SAP data for local offline analysis. These third-party tools create documents that are easy to read and use nontechnical language. They highlight control weaknesses in the SAP ERP environment under analysis and offer recommendations for improvement. The third parties involved in creating these tools include the big four audit firms, who require quick, reliable mechanisms to evaluate and provide credible audit evidence.

Despite the deployment of business process and application security controls, transactions (such as duplicate payments) may continue to be processed that are inconsistent with management's intentions. Therefore, data assurance techniques are needed to control and test specific identified risks associated with ERP data. Knowledge of SAP tables, data structures, reports, programming and data extraction techniques is needed so that data can be extracted in the most cost-effective manner for analysis. Tools in this area have been evolving. For example, ACL® Direct Link® is a product certified for integration with SAP that extracts information from SAP ERP modules for offline analysis. Similar tools produced by some consulting firms are also available.

The next phase in analyzing security information involved the introduction of tools for continuous compliance. These tools are permanently installed on a client PC or integrated with the SAP environment and allow for continuous monitoring of security access, as well as business and IT process controls. Tools from SAP and Approva (*www.approva.net*) provide real-time preventive controls so that, as access is granted to a new or existing user, an automated check is made against his/her segregation of duties (SoD) table and (depending on the configuration of tools) helps prevent granting inappropriate access rights. These toolsets also offer solutions for managing the assignment of privileged access as well as workflow approval solutions and a full suite of reporting capabilities. This includes the ability to monitor execution of transactions in addition to static analysis on the controls and configuration in place. For example, an IT auditor may require review of the user IDs associated with transactions recorded in SAP to identify where potential SoD issues or critical activities have been executed. Forrester[14] and Gartner[15] have researched the automated control solutions available in 2007 for managing SoD risks and identified SAP, Approva and Logical Apps as vendors who have the strongest products.

Now, governance, risk and compliance (GRC) tools have emerged. GRC is a concept that brings together three disparate activities under one banner:
• Governance—The oversight, direction and high-level monitoring and control of an enterprise to ensure the achievement of defined and approved objectives
• Risk—The combination of the probability of an event and its consequence
• Compliance—The processes to achieve legislative and regulatory requirements and meet enterprise policies and procedures

GRC tools have been developed by vendors such as SAP to include continuous compliance monitoring solutions as well as tools that help the enterprise manage much broader business risks. The tools assist with assuring stakeholders that the business is reliable, compliant and sustainable.[16] The following section discusses the SAP GRC toolset, SAP BusinessObjects GRC, as an example of the key features as well as security and audit considerations associated with the SAP GRC tool.

---

[14] Rasmussen, M.; P. Hamerman; *Segregation Of Duties: A Building Block for Enterprise IT Controls*, Forrester, USA, March 2007
[15] Proctor, Paul E.; Jay Heiser; Neil MacDonald; *MarketScope for Segregation of Duties Controls Within ERP*, Gartner, USA, February 2007
[16] *www.su53.com/sap-security-and-grc/what-is-sap-grc*

# SAP BusinessObjects GRC

Companies spent at least US $27 billion on addressing tactical compliance issues in 2006,[17] yet they remain vulnerable to risks and burdened with high costs. SAP BusinessObjects GRC (Governance, Risk and Compliance) provides tools for managing business risks. SAP acquired SAP BusinessObjects GRC from Virsa Systems in 2006. SAP BusinessObjects GRC solutions help enterprises streamline their approach to governance by ensuring that compliance initiatives are linked to the business strategy across the enterprise. SAP GRC tools help enterprises gain corporate accountability by demonstrating to stakeholders that an enterprise is reliable, compliant and sustainable. These solutions enable risk management and support regulatory and policy compliance across processes supported by both SAP and non-SAP software.[18] As discussed in chapter 14, the SAP BusinessObjects GRC toolset may help organizations attain compliance with financial reporting requirements such as the US Sarbanes-Oxley Act of 2002 (SOX), Japanese-SOX or the Basic Standard for Enterprises' Internal Control (equivalent of SOX in China).

As described by SAP, the GRC solution includes the following components:
• SAP BusinessObjects Access Control—Prevents fraud and minimizes the cost of continuous compliance and control by preventing access and authorization risks in cross-enterprise IT systems
• SAP BusinessObjects Process Control—Centrally monitors key controls over cross-enterprise systems to ensure compliance and enable business process control management
• SAP BusinessObjects Risk Management—Maximizes business outcomes and reduces market penalties from high-impact events by balancing business opportunities with financial, legal and operational risks
• SAP BusinessObjects Global Trade Services—Ensures trade compliance, expedited cross-border transactions, and optimum utilization of trade agreements by managing all foreign trade processes with a comprehensive platform
• SAP EHS (Environment, Health and Safety Compliance Management)—Helps to ensure proactive compliance by aligning business processes with environmental, occupational, and product safety regulations and organizational policies
• Data privacy composite application by SAP and Cisco—Proactively enforces global and local data privacy policies across the extended enterprise

This chapter further describes the SAP BusinessObjects Access Control and Process Control components' ability to provide continuous control monitoring features. This section provides a high-level understanding of the key features of Access Control and Process Control and highlights important factors to consider when auditing them.

---

[17] Business Trends Quarterly, *www.btquarterly.com/?mc=segregations-duties&page=grc-viewarticle*
[18] *www.sap.com/solutions/sapbusinessobjects/large/governance-risk-compliance/index.epx*

## SAP BusinessObjects Access Control

SAP BusinessObjects Access Control (GRC Access Control) has a centralized web-based architecture that leverages the SAP NetWeaver Web Application Server. (While SAP NetWeaver has been addressed at a high level in this book, it will be covered at a more granular level in a future ISACA publication.) The GRC Access Control product allows enterprises to continuously identify, monitor and prevent risks related to logical access controls, i.e., the assignment of unauthorized privileges. Also, it provides information that may be used by IT auditors in assessing the following controls activities:

- Appropriate SoD is enforced within SAP.
- Access (IT and business functionality) to SAP ERP is restricted to only authorized individuals and limited based on job functions, including privilege access.
- Critical system activities are logged and monitored.
- User access review is performed periodically.

The GRC Access Control component comprises the following four main product capabilities that enable the control activities mentioned above:
1. Risk Analysis and Remediation (RAR)
2. Superuser Privilege Management (SPM)
3. Compliant User Provisioning (CUP)
4. Enterprise Role Management (ERM)

**Figure 13.1** summarizes how the GRC Access Control features can facilitate end-to-end access control compliance within an enterprise.

Prior to version 5.X, GRC Access Control existed in an ABAP version only for Compliance Calibrator and Firefighter (the former names for Risk Analysis and Compliance and Superuser Privilege Management). Compliance Calibrator was created by Virsa Systems, later acquired by SAP. The ABAP version meant that users were accessing the tools directly via the SAP back end system as opposed to the web-based version that uses system connectors to link to the SAP back end or non-SAP back end systems. While some users are still running the ABAP version, this chapter focuses on the web-based version 5.3 (released in 2008), since this is the latest version that is currently used for new implementations and for upgrades.

Each of the four capabilities is also described in more detail in the following section.

# Risk Analysis and Remediation (RAR)

The previous version name for the RAR application was Compliance Calibrator. It was originally available only in the SAP ABAP version.

| Figure 13.1—Establishing End-to-end Compliance Via the SAP GRC Access Control Application | | | | |
|---|---|---|---|---|
| Minimal Time to Compliance | Continuous Access Management | | | Effective Management Oversight and Audit |
| **Get Clean** | **Stay Clean** | | | **Stay in Control** |
| **Risk Analysis and Remediation** Ensure rapid, cost-effective, and comprehensive initial cleanup | **Enterprise Role Management** Enforce SoD compliance at design time | **Compliant User Provisioning** Prevent SoD violations at runtime | **Superuser Privilege Management** Close #1 audit issue with temporary emergency access | **Periodic Access Review and Audit** Focus on remaining challenges during recurring audits |
| **Risk analysis, remediation, and prevention services** | | | | |
| **Cross-enterprise library of best-practice SoD rules** | | | | |

The key features of RAR include:
- Risk identification—A customizable framework for defining SoD rules as well as critical transactions/roles/profiles, used as a basis to perform analysis for monitoring SoD conflicts and critical access
- Remediation—A documentation feature that supports the design of mitigating controls and the remediation of identified risks
- Reporting—Provides reports on analysis performed by each of the other features and includes an alert framework for escalation of conflicts and mitigating controls to management
- Prevention—Used to perform "what if" simulations of access change risks; can help prevent specific access or conflicts from being assigned

RAR is supported by a centralized web architecture with the following benefits:
- The ability to operate across multiple SAP instances or other ERP systems, e.g., Oracle, JDE
- No impact to the production server, although the data used for analysis are extracted from the live system
- Provides role-based access (views) using the SAP User Management Engine (UME), part of NetWeaver. This functionality permits use of the tool by key users (e.g., auditors or managers) without needing to grant those users direct access to the back end SAP system. Refer to chapter 14 for further details.

As shown in **figure 13.2**, the main functions within RAR are known as:
- Informer
- Rule Architect
- Mitigation
- Alert Monitor

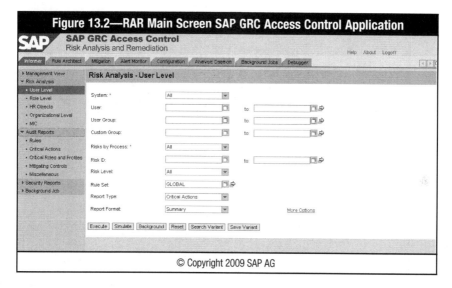

Figure 13.2—RAR Main Screen SAP GRC Access Control Application

© Copyright 2009 SAP AG

## Informer

The informer function provides:
- Risk analysis—Reports that illustrate users and their privileges, e.g., users, user groups, roles, profiles, HR Objects and organizational levels
- Simulation—Performs "what if" analysis of adding or removing privileges, e.g,. roles, profiles

## Rule Architect

The Rule Architect provides:
- Customizable SoD framework—SoD rule building, used for defining risks related to user access
- Customizable critical access framework—For defining critical actions, roles and profiles as well as the organizational rules that the enterprise wants to monitor:
  - Actions—Transactions and associated authorizations
  - Functions—Group of actions based on common tasks or job roles
  - Risks—Association of two or more conflicting functions
  - Business processes—Logical group of functions and risks
  - Systems—The SAP instance for which the Rule Architect has been configured
  - Rules—A combination of conflicting actions and associated permissions. Rules are automatically created when the risks and functions have been created or updated.

The SoD Rule Architect uses the structure defined in **figure 13.3**.

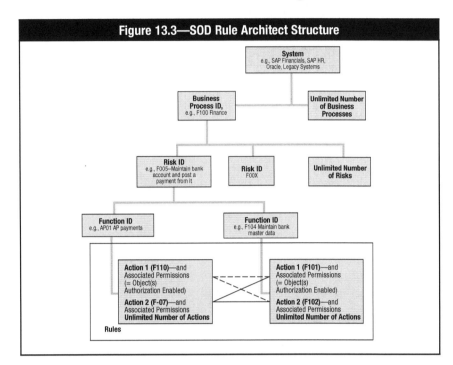

Figure 13.3—SOD Rule Architect Structure

## Mitigation

The mitigating controls feature facilitates the documentation of mitigating controls where it is not possible to remove conflicting access, e.g., due to the size of business or team involved. The following mandatory information is recorded:

- Description of the mitigating controls design—For example, an SAP report of changes to vendor bank details reviewed by the accounts payable manager on a daily basis and compared to source documentation to confirm that only authorized changes have been made
- Identification of control approvers—Those who validate that the mitigating control is described accurately and is effectively designed
- Identification of control monitors—Those who perform the mitigating control related to the SoD conflict. In the previous example, the control monitor is the accounts payable manager.
- Identification of the business unit—To which the mitigating control applies, ensuring that the controls are made specifically for each business unit

## Alert Monitor

The Alert Monitor is used to inform an administrator when:

- Conflicting actions have been executed
- Critical actions have been executed
- Mitigating controls have not been performed within the specified timeframe

For example, the Alert Monitor may be used to allow:
- The identification of potential SoD issues when an enterprise does not have sufficient staff to adequately segregate the functions within the organization, e.g., an employee is in the vendor master data management team but is also required to approve payments when the approver is not available. An administrator will be alerted when conflicting transactions are executed by this employee and will be able to review the actions performed for appropriateness.
- An administrator to be alerted when an employee has executed the critical transaction SCC4 and ensure that the changes performed in SAP have been authorized

## RAR Reports

Various reports are available within RAR, providing different levels of information, including:
- Summary Report—Shows the users or roles and their corresponding risk and action conflicts
- Executive Summary Report—Provides risk descriptions and counts of rules with conflicts
- Detail Report—Provides details on the roles, related actions and permissions that are causing the conflicts. This report is used to understand the access and permission conflicts and risks created and may be used to determine required remediation (e.g., what roles or action/permission should be removed from the users or role).

# Superuser Privilege Management (SPM)

SPM, previously known as Firefighter, is unlike the three other GRC tools (RAR, ERM and CUP). Although SPM is configured and used as part of the back end SAP application, SPM reports can still be executed through the web front end.

SPM provides the ability to extend selected users' capabilities within the back end system (i.e., SAP ECC). The assignment of wide-ranging (SAP standard) profiles is one of the most common issues encountered when auditing SAP. SPM provides a solution to control the assignment of privileged access to users through Firefighter IDs. The Firefighter IDs are configured to provide predefined authorizations for specific periods. Typically, they would be used when users are required to perform emergency activities that require authorization over and above their normal job roles. SPM is used to control the assignment and monitor the activities of the superuser access. SPM provides an audit log of the activities performed using these Firefighter IDs that should then be independently reviewed for appropriateness.

SPM version 5.3 (released in 2008) provides for the assignment of SAP roles for Firefighter purposes, in a similar manner to the assignment of Firefighter accounts.

## SPM Main Features

SPM controls emergency access by:

- Assigning predefined authorizations to specific privileged accounts for a defined period using valid "from" and "to" dates
- Forcing a separate logon to SAP via the proxy user (Firefighter ID)
- Ensuring that the reason for using the privileged access is documented within SPM
- Allowing only one Firefighter account to be used by one person at a time, ensuring accountability
- Providing auditable reporting where:
  - Activities are logged without requiring additional system logging (e.g., SM20)
  - Reports are created to review the activities performed while using the privileged Firefighter accounts

## Implementing SPM

To use SPM, the following key steps need to be performed:

1. Assign one of the following four predefined SPM roles to the relevant user:
   - Administrator—Performs application configuration and assigns IDs to owners and controllers
   - ID owner—Assigns ID to firefighters and monitors the critical activities performed by these accounts
   - Controller—Views reports and receives notification e-mail messages to assist the owners in reviewing firefighter activities
   - Firefighter—Accesses and uses the emergency roles via the Firefighter ID
2. Create Firefighter IDs with roles for performing critical activities.
3. Establish ownership by assigning an owner to each Firefighter ID.
4. Determine procedures and documentation requirements (justification, reason, activity, etc.) for using a Firefighter ID.
5. Schedule the background job for archiving audit log reports, and create a process to review the audit logs on a regular basis.

SoD is enforced within SPM:

- Administrators cannot assign themselves as Firefighter ID owners.
- Only owners can assign firefighters to their Firefighter IDs.
- Owners cannot assign themselves as firefighters, once appropriate configuration has been implemented.

As illustrated in **Figure 13.4**, the firefighter can log onto either the ID FIREFIGHT01 or FIREFIGHT02 to perform Basis activities. When firefighters log onto an ID, they are required to provide a reason code and details of the actions they expect to perform. All activities performed by the firefighter are logged.

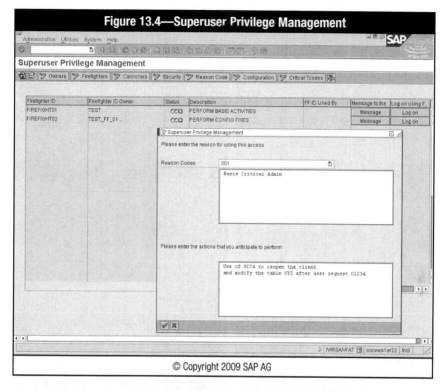

Figure 13.4—Superuser Privilege Management

© Copyright 2009 SAP AG

The log report, as shown in **Figure 13.5**, records the activities performed by the FIRETEST01 user using the FIREFIGHT01 account. These reports can be reviewed via the web front end or through the back end SAP application.

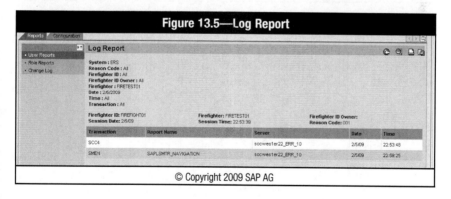

Figure 13.5—Log Report

© Copyright 2009 SAP AG

# Compliant User Provisioning (CUP)

CUP, as shown in **figure 13.6**, provides workflow-driven automated provisioning for SAP and legacy systems, provides "what if" SoD risk simulation and manages workflow approvals. Semi-automated user access reviews may be enforced, reducing IT involvement. Workflow capabilities provided by SPM, RAR and ERM are performed in the background by CUP. CUP is available only as a web front-end tool.

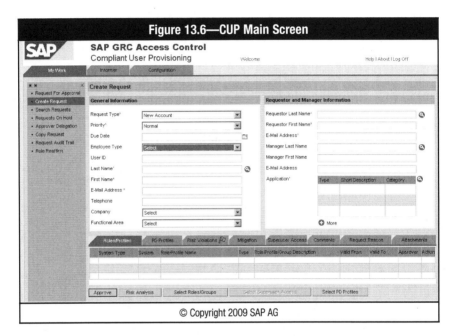

**Figure 13.6—CUP Main Screen**

© Copyright 2009 SAP AG

## CUP Main Features

CUP manages end-user requests for the following activities:
- Creating new accounts and assigning roles
- Maintaining existing user accounts (change, delete and lock/unlock)
- Obtaining status of requests
- Providing an automatic trigger (when connected to an HR system) for user provisioning activities on HR events (new hires, terminations, transfers, etc.)

CUP can source existing identity management data from SAP, e.g., SAP HR, UME or non-SAP systems, e.g., Lightweight Directory Access Protocol (LDAP), Oracle, PeopleSoft, JD Edwards. These data can be interfaced to CUP on a one-off basis or as required.

Existing controls can be automated by CUP to meet the organization's needs around user provisioning. This may include the following automated controls:
- Mandatory approval for user maintenance (typically by a user's manager)
- Mandatory approval for role assignment, validity dates or removal (typically by the role owner)
- Audit trail of user change request status and approval workflow, risk changes, mitigation controls maintenance and assignment, and role maintenance
- Mandatory risk analysis to prevent assignment of roles to users that create SoD conflicts or that give critical access
- Documentation and assignment of mitigating controls when a user has been assigned conflicting roles or critical actions
- Regular user access or SoD review

## Enterprise Role Management (ERM)

ERM allows enterprises to better manage user access roles through centralization and standardization of role maintenance. ERM was previously known as Role Expert and is available only as a web-based tool.

### ERM Main Features

ERM main features, as shown in **figure 13.7**, include:
- Role documentation, including the capability to compare roles existing in the SAP back end with the roles defined in ERM. This may be useful if changes have been made directly in the SAP back end system instead of via the standard ERM update method.
- Risk analysis that is enforceable after any new roles or changes to the roles
- An approval workflow to ensure that the changes are authorized before the role is automatically generated in SAP (new, modified or deleted roles)
- Availability of audit reports to track role modifications
- Interfaces of ERM with CUP to facilitate user provisioning by automatically importing new and modified roles to be assigned to the user

## SAP BusinessObjects Process Control

SAP BusinessObjects Process Control (Process Control) is a solution for internal controls management that enables members of audit and internal controls teams to gain better visibility of key business processes and ensure a high level of reliability in financial statement reporting.[19]

Process Control uses a controls-based approach to managing risks associated with business processes. It provides the necessary capabilities to:
- Document the existing business control objectives and activities (manual and automated)

---

[19] *www.sdn.sap.com/irj/bpx/bpx-grc?rid=/webcontent/uuid/604abd64-cc72-2b10-8d9b-f5053afca153*

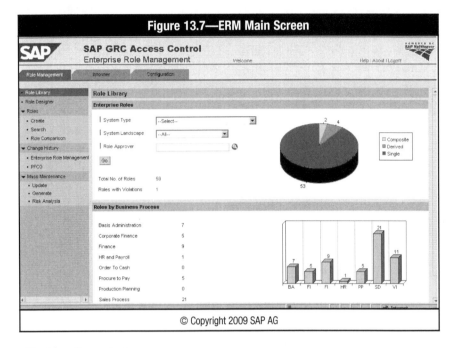

Figure 13.7—ERM Main Screen

© Copyright 2009 SAP AG

- Evaluate the controls
- Certify the state of the controls
- Report and analyze control information

Compliance managers, business process owners and auditors can use Process Control to complete and review control descriptions, record testing documentation, and evaluate the design and operating effectiveness of the control environment. An audit trail lists the key activities and changes in the internal control framework (e.g., control updates, testing and certification). In addition, controls may be configured to trigger automatic notification of changes to control configurations.

## BusinessObjects Process Control Main Features

The four major capabilities[20] of BusinessObjects Process Control are:
- Control documentation—Process Control provides the enterprise with a flexible data structure to create the framework needed for documenting its control environment. Using categories, the user can create specific controls at various levels in the enterprise:
  - Local controls, to be maintained locally
  - Central control, to be maintain at the corporate level
- Control evaluation—Process Control has four predefined evaluation processes. Assessment provides for user self-assessment of assigned control design. Evaluation testing allows users to test controls manually using a documented test plan or automatically using the system programs and rules. The three main types of controls are:

[20] *http://help.sap.com/saphelp_grcpc25/helpdata/en/b9/407fdacae445c3b321c29ce3cb820e/frameset.htm*

- Configuration (e.g., using three-way match tolerances for purchase orders, goods receipts and invoices)
- Reporting (e.g., reviewing vendor bank detail change exception reports for appropriateness)
- User access (e.g., evaluating the appropriateness of user access to create new employee master data)

Process Control also provides monitoring of noncompliant business events as defined in the configured rules (e.g., duplicate payments). Evaluation can be scheduled including timeframe, organization, personnel and evaluation type.

SAP provides predefined controls within Process Control to perform continuous monitoring. For example, the following controls can be configured:[21]
- Control to identify duplicate vendor invoices on the basis of system reference number—Although SAP ERP has configuration controls that can prevent vendor overpayments, the potential to override these controls exists. These monitoring events can detect those incidents. Enterprises are likely to gain the most benefit by taking a comprehensive approach to monitoring all payment transactions and then reducing monitoring activity under a threshold if exception volumes are too large.
- Control to identify sales to a one-time customer exceeding a pre-established order value threshold—Large transaction sales to one-time customers are not typical and may be a result of processing errors. Monitoring for unexpected sales to one-time customers provides management an effective technique to efficiently detect order entry errors and positively impact customer satisfaction.

• Certification—To support the regulatory environment (e.g., SOX 404), Process Control provides a documented sign-off process that can be used by auditors as evidence that the controls have been adequately documented and designed and are operating effectively.
• Reporting and analysis—Process Control provides various reports and audit trails to monitor control status, including providing evidence that controls have been reviewed by internal or external auditors.

**Figure 13.8** illustrates Process Control key features and shows how Process Control supports end-to-end compliance management.

## Key Auditing Considerations
When using tools to assist in testing SAP, auditors first need to confirm that the tool is appropriately configured and the process for managing the tool is appropriately defined to ensure completeness and accuracy of data.

Some audit procedures should be performed each year, whereas others may be configured as part of the initial installation of the tool.

---

[21] *http://help.sap.com/saphelp_grcpc25/helpdata/en/b9/407fdacae445c3b321c29ce3cb820e/frameset.htm*

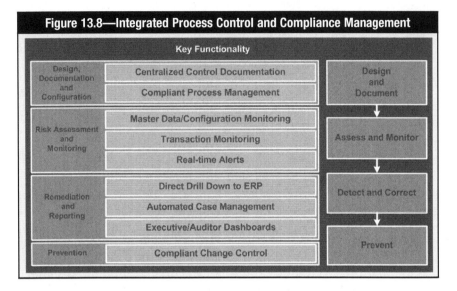

Figure 13.8—Integrated Process Control and Compliance Management

**Figure 13.9** describes specific auditing considerations for each component of SAP BusinessObjects GRC Access Control and also SAP BusinessObjects GRC Process Control. These audit considerations may also guide an IT auditor in reviewing any BusinessObjects GRC tools as well as other non-SAP continuous auditing tools.

| Figure 13.9—SAP CRC Component Audit Considerations | |
|---|---|
| **SAP GRC Component** | **Audit Considerations** |
| **All modules and components**<br><br>**Note:** the considerations outlined in this section should be assessed for all components each year. | **Security:**<br>• Review logical access controls for each SAP Business Objects tool used to confirm that user access, in particular administrator privileges, are restricted to appropriate personnel.<br>• Ensure that formal procedures exist for granting and removing access to the tool.<br>• Verify that password controls for the SAP web front end (UME) and back end reduce the risk of unauthorized access.<br>• Ensure that appropriate security audit logging is configured.<br>• Verify that adequate SoD exists between the administrators who configure the tool and the end users. Further, end-user privileges should be assessed to ensure that conflicting functionality is not assigned (e.g., administrators should not have the opportunity to take advantage of the tool that would breach internal audit controls).<br>• Review who has access to maintain the tables relating to the SAP GRC solution and ensure appropriateness. These users may be different from those nominated as administrators of the tools. |

| Figure 13.9—SAP CRC Component Audit Considerations *(cont.)* ||
| SAP GRC Component | Audit Considerations |
| --- | --- |
| **All modules and components** *(cont.)* | **Change Management:**<br>• Ensure that a formal change management process (including approval for change initiation and testing procedures) is implemented.<br>• Where configuration change history is available from the toolsets, e.g., RAR, CUP and SPM, extract a list of changes for the financial period and use this to assess the configuration changes made to the tool.<br>• The default tables being used by the GRC components should be made active for logging in the SAP Data Dictionary. This will ensure that even if standard change history is not enabled/available in the tools, the changes made to these tables can still be reviewed for appropriateness. |
| | **Operations:**<br>• Confirm that the processes for administering and using the tool are documented and up to date and have been communicated to affected parties.<br>• Verify that all functionalities of the GRC components required to be used by the enterprise have been appropriately tested and are operating as expected.<br>• Confirm that the outputs of the GRC solution meet the needs of key stakeholders and key stakeholders understand the information being presented to them.<br>• Check that users of the GRC solution have received appropriate training.<br>• Understand and assess the configuration of key batch jobs and interfaces related to the communication between the SAP back end and the different modules of the SAP Business Objects system.<br>• Confirm that access to perform batch and interface administration is restricted to appropriate personnel.<br>• Verify that adequate monitoring procedures are in place to ensure that batch or interface processing errors would be detected in a timely manner. |
| **SAP BusinessObjects Access Control** ||
| **Risk Analysis and Remediation** | • Ensure that the appropriate business representatives and the IT functions have been identified. This should include a documented definition of ownership over the rules established, responsibility for the resolution of issues and the involvement of the right people with appropriate knowledge to interpret the outcomes of the analysis reports.<br>• Confirm that SoD conflicts and sensitive access are correctly designed according to business requirements and good practice. The design should reflect the content, the business processes and control framework with which it is associated. |

| Figure 13.9—SAP CRC Component Audit Considerations *(cont.)* | |
|---|---|
| **SAP GRC Component** | **Audit Considerations** |
| **SAP BusinessObjects Access Control** *(cont.)* | |
| **Risk Analysis and Remediation** *(cont.)* | • Assess whether SoD conflicts and sensitive access are correctly designed and implemented within RAR, i.e., the SAP transactions codes applicable for the functions defined in RAR are complete and accurate. Also, ensure appropriate governance of the authorization objects and that applicable activity values have been updated using transaction SU24, since these are the base for the SAP authorization configured in the rules. Refer to chapter 4 for further details around SU24 functionality.<br>• Identify customized SAP transaction codes and confirm that these are included in the SoD rule set.<br>• Ensure that performance optimization has not been tuned to a point where the reports are not relevant (objects authorization removed from the SoD rules to obtain better performance).<br>• Confirm that the roles and profiles excluded from the analysis are correctly defined and are reviewed in addition to the SoD analysis.<br>• Validate that the variants used for the risk analysis reports are correctly defined, i.e. all relevant risks, users or user groups and mitigated risks have been included in the analysis report to be reviewed.<br>• Confirm whether user group assignments are complete and accurate within the SAP user master data records, if RAR reports are executed and reviewed based on user groups.<br>• Confirm that customized reports are adequately tested by simulating the query results using the SAP back end functionality or an independent toolset.<br>• Validate whether RAR reports are being generated and reviewed in a timely manner.<br>• Assess the rationale for standard rules that have been disabled through configuration.<br>• Verify that mitigating controls are adequately documented and assigned to the risks identified, i.e., the controls are completely mitigating the identified risks and are enabled for a limited time to enforce regular review of the controls' appropriateness.<br>• Verify that the appropriate monitor and approver have been assigned to each mitigating control to establish responsibility and accountability for the operational effectiveness of the control.<br>• Validate that monitors and approvers are aware of their responsibilities and understand their roles and that each control is operating effectively. |
| **Superuser Privilege Management** | • Confirm that all critical access has been appropriately included and assigned to the relevant SPM users.<br>• Confirm that accesses that are to be assigned via SPM are clearly documented. The activities that should be done through normal user accounts should not be available in SPM. |

| Figure 13.9—SAP CRC Component Audit Considerations *(cont.)* | |
|---|---|
| **SAP GRC Component** | **Audit Considerations** |
| **Superuser Privilege Management** *(cont.)* | • Check that SPM users are not granted privileged access within their normal user roles that would allow them to bypass the SPM tool. In addition, check that there are no SoD conflicts that may arise as a result of a user having SPM access combined with normal user roles. While the SPM access is logged, the normal user access is not logged in the same manner. In addition, users have the ability to log on with multiple Firefighter IDs at one time if they are assigned more than one Firefighter ID by owners; this may cause SoD violations.<br>• Ensure that no Firefighter ID has been assigned SAP standard profiles (e.g., SAP_ALL). This would mean that some of the controls configured within SPM could be bypassed. For example, it may be possible to delete or change the SAP STAT files, which are the basis for Firefighter users' activity logs.<br>• Ensure that Firefighter ID owners and controllers are appropriate and their roles and responsibilities are documented and communicated to affected parties.<br>• Ensure that the tools have been configured so that Firefighter ID owners or administrators cannot assign a Firefighter ID to themselves. This will help to avoid potential SoD conflicts.<br>• Confirm that the logs of the critical activities are reviewed appropriately and on a timely basis by a suitably qualified independent party. These logs should then be retained for audit purposes. Ensure that a process is in place to identify and follow up exceptions when the Firefighter role-based assignment has not been configured and opted.<br>• Confirm that Firefighter ID has not been set up as a dialog, but as a service user.<br>• Confirm that users cannot log on directly into SAP ECC using Firefighter IDs since this may allow users to bypass SPM controls (refer to SAP Note 99220).<br><br>While the IT auditor is assessing the tool implementation, he/she should also be aware of the following to adapt the scope of the review as required:<br>• Because SPM works only on the SAP back end, the critical activities performed within Enterprise Portal or other non-ABAP-based systems (e.g., Master Data Management) cannot be configured and logged within the tool. |
| **Compliance User Provisioning** | • Understand and assess the design of the user provisioning process (e.g., approvers and workflow paths are appropriately defined).<br>• Ensure that the user provisioning process defined during the implementation of the tool is correctly implemented (e.g., only authorized approvers are granted authorization privileges within CUP). |

| Figure 13.9—SAP CRC Component Audit Considerations *(cont.)* | |
|---|---|
| **SAP GRC Component** | **Audit Considerations** |
| **Compliance User Provisioning** *(cont.)* | • In particular, check that:<br>  - Every role has an approver. Otherwise, it will be automatically provisioned.<br>  - Administrator access is appropriate to ensure that there are no unauthorized changes to user access<br>  - Roles/profiles that are not intended to be provisioned are not loaded into CUP (e.g., SAP_ALL, SAP_NEW)<br>  - If Manager is an approval step, the source from which CUP draws the manager information is correct but may be manually entered or overridden.<br>  - The configuration enforces that users are not provisioned if unmitigated SoD conflicts exist.<br>• Ensure that maintenance of new users and role assignments is not allowed in the SAP back end (e.g., using the transaction code SU01) since this would allow users to bypass the approval workflow conditions that have been established in CUP.<br><br>While the IT auditor is assessing the tool implementation, he/she should also be aware of the following to adapt the scope of the review as required:<br>• When integrated with RAR, CUP will use only the default ruleset to check for SoD violations.<br>• When integrated with RAR, any approver may have the ability to assign mitigating controls to a user without approval.<br>• When integrated with SPM, users may have the ability to request SPM IDs through CUP.<br>• Requests can be deleted directly from the database, thus removing the audit trail of the workflows. As such, consider how such occurrences could be identified and monitored.<br>• By default, the user validity date is set to 12/31/9999. |
| **Enterprise Role Management** | • Understand and assess the design of the role maintenance process (e.g., approvers are appropriately defined and role approvers [affecting the user provisioning process in CUP] are appropriately assigned)<br>• Ensure that the role maintenance process defined during the implementation of the tool is correctly implemented (e.g., only authorized approvers are granted authorization privileges within ERM).<br>• Ensure that maintenance of roles is not allowed in the SAP back end (e.g., using the transaction code PFCG, SU02 or SU03), since this would allow users to bypass the approval workflow conditions that have been established in ERM.<br>• Confirm that the USOBT_C table (transaction code SU24), which provides authorization object data, is maintained since ERM pulls the authorization object data from this table.<br>• Check whether all the roles are still created in the development/QA environment and transported into production after ERM implementation. Role modification and creation still need to be tested prior to being used in the production environment.<br>• Ensure that, in addition to SoD checks that are performed before roles are generated, manual SoD checks are performed at the composite role or user level impacted by the creation or changes. |

| Figure 13.9—SAP CRC Component Audit Considerations *(cont.)* | |
|---|---|
| **SAP GRC Component** | **Audit Considerations** |
| **SAP BusinessObjects Process Control** | |
| **Process Control** | • Confirm that master data, i.e., control framework, and testing documentation have been effectively designed as part of the implementation of the tool. This might include the scoping of the business processes and classes of transactions for inclusion in the framework as well as the sampling strategy for testing.<br>• Perform a gap analysis of the processes and controls against good practices (e.g., CobiT) to ensure appropriateness of the risks and control objectives as well as the associated manual and automated controls designed.<br>• Confirm that regulatory requirements have been met.<br>• Assess whether the master data design is accurately implemented within Process Control.<br>• Confirm that the roles and responsibilities have been adequately assigned to controls owners and testers.<br>• Ensure that a defined process and adequate monitoring are in place to remediate and update controls when deficiencies from the automated control or manual tests are identified.<br>• Ensure that control activities for automatically checking configurations within SAP are correctly linked to embedded SAP controls.<br>• Ensure that issues identified as potential exceptions are being resolved in a timely manner.<br>• Ensure that root cause analysis is being performed for recurring issues identified, and the root cause is being addressed in a timely manner.<br>• Review a sample of issues that have been resolved and verify that the resolution was appropriate.<br>• Ensure that users are not monitoring their own exceptions.<br>• Assess the adequacy of tolerance levels configured within rule sets that monitor transactional activity (e.g., >1 percent or US $1,000 might be appropriate for one business area but not another).<br>• Review changes to rule sets and tolerance levels to ensure that the change was authorized and appropriate (e.g., not an effort to exclude an individual or his/her activities from a report).<br>• Review the adequacy of rules and tolerance levels in light of the business environment (e.g., tolerances that may have been applicable before the financial meltdown may be too broad today) or ensure that a process exists to periodically evaluate the relevance of rule sets and adjust accordingly. |

# Summary

This chapter provided an overall understanding of the SAP BusinessObjects GRC Access Control and Process Control solutions in an SAP ERP environment. The chapter summarized key features of the tools, including key audit considerations when relying on information produced through these tools.

# 14. Trends and Discussions Around SAP ERP and ERP Audit

This chapter focuses on the trends with SAP products and provides information related to ERP audit discussions that continue to evolve, namely:
• The implications of the changing compliance landscape for ERP control over financial reporting
• An extension to the traditional ERP control framework to encompass the integrated ERP environment

Available tools to assist with corporate governance are discussed and a sample control framework for the integrated ERP environment is provided.

## SAP Product and Technology Changes

SAP ERP is the SAP new generation of ERP, succeeding the SAP R/3 series. Over the past few years, SAP transitioned its clients to SAP ERP 6.0, which is reflected by SAP's end of maintenance schedules for the SAP R/3 ERP series. Official maintenance for SAP R/3 4.6C ended in 2006, and SAP® R/3 Enterprise® (4.7) ended in March 2009, although it may be possible for individual contract arrangements to be extended through negotiation with SAP to 2009 and 2010, respectively. However, with the new SAP maintenance model, Enterprise Support, customers will receive an additional year of extended maintenance which will ensure that customers receive maintenance until 2010 for SAP R/3 4.6C and 2013 for SAP® R/3 Enterprise®.[22] Research by Forrester[23] suggests that the main reason for a customer to upgrade to SAP ERP 6.0 is the end of standard and extended maintenance.

This publication addresses security, audit and control features for SAP ERP 6.0 (also known as SAP ERP Central Component, ECC 6.0), the core ERP solution, supported by the SAP NetWeaver® platform. As the customer take-up of additional SAP NetWeaver® components (e.g., Enterprise Portal [EP] or Master Data Management [MDM]) accelerates, the real implications for auditors will become clearer. It is likely that ERP audit frameworks and audit techniques will have to be reconsidered.

One of the most important aspects of the SAP ERP products is the enablement of business integration. SAP R/3 was originally designed with an enterprisecentric point of view, enabling integration and enhancement of business processes within an enterprise. As SAP R/3 has evolved, enhancements have enabled limited

---

[22] Wang. R.; Sharyn Leaver; Meghan Donnelly; "Coping With SAP's Pricey Maintenance Hike," Forrester, USA, 10 October 2008
[23] Wang, R.; "Enhancement Packages Improve SAP Upgrade Value," Forrester, USA, 29 May 2008

business process integration beyond the organizational boundaries. In contrast, the inherent design of SAP ERP, combined with additions to the SAP product suite, enables extended and collaborative business process integration with suppliers, business partners, customers and internal organizations. This integration is made possible through the SAP NetWeaver® platform architecture and its associated functions, including integration components and development tools. This is discussed further in chapter 2.

The SAP NetWeaver platform has been designed around a service-oriented architecture (SOA) principle that acts as a blueprint for enabling the technology integration required to achieve business process integration. This concept goes beyond the traditional *ad hoc* nature of application-to-application integration to create an open architecture that uses technology standards, such as Web Services and Java, or proprietary standards, such as Microsoft.Net.[24]

If enterprises use Java applications via the SAP NetWeaver platform, the audit approach will need to include an overall understanding of user access management, including a review of the User Management Engine (UME). The UME provides centralized user management for all Java applications and can be configured to work with user management data from multiple data sources. It is seamlessly integrated into the SAP NetWeaver Application Server (AS) Java as its default user store and can be managed using the administration tools of the AS Java.[25]

In addition, as the implementation of these SAP NetWeaver components increases within an enterprise's IT environment, the IT auditor will need to consider the impact on the audit approach. As such, the following SAP NetWeaver components may be of particular interest:
- SAP Solution Manager (SolMan)—SAP systems are becoming increasingly distributed across geographies, and business processes are covering more than one system, as was the case in the past. SAP SolMan provides assistance with the implementation and management of system landscapes in such complex environments. As part of the solution, SAP delivers best practices through the following features:[26]
  – Implementing and upgrading SAP solutions
  – Solution monitoring
  – System and support
  – Change management
  – Service desk

---

[24] *http://www.microsoft.com/en/us/default.aspx*
[25] *http://help.sap.com/saphelp_erp60_sp/helpdata/EN/81/0e0f61b566dc44bbb4055b3ccd25be/frameset.htm*
[26] *http://help.sap.com/saphelp_sm40/helpdata/en/45/51fbdbd4941803e10000000a1553f7/frameset.htm*

• SAP NetWeaver Master Data Management—Due to limited implementation of the previous Master Data Management (MDM) solution, SAP altered its approach by acquiring a solution from A2i. The new product is a component of SAP NetWeaver and allows a unique source of information for vendors, customers, employees, products or any object master data in an enterprise.
• SAP NetWeaver Identity Management—With the acquisition of MaXware in 2007, SAP released its own identity management solution. As the use of SOA environments will increase in enterprises, the need for more secure and effective user access management across multiple applications in real-time will lead to an increasing use of identity management solutions.

With the acquisition of Business Object in 2007, SAP has integrated or repackaged the following products:
• SAP BusinessObject XI allows better business intelligence (BI) by providing immediate access to information discovery and delivery, information management, and query, reporting, and analysis, providing a range of solutions for all enterprises.
• SAP BusinessObjects EPM solutions allows enterprise performance management (e.g., strategy management).
• SAP BusinessObject GRC solutions (discussed in chapter 13)

The SAP Business Suite 7 was launched in February 2009 and offers:
• SAP Product Lifecycle Management (PLM)
• SAP Supplier Relationship Management (SRM)
• SAP Supply Chain Management (SCM)
• SAP Customer Relationship Management (CRM)
• SAP ERP
• Industry applications

As mentioned by Forrester in March 2009, although the functionality detailed above existed previously, these have been repackaged in the new release of SAP (ECC 7.0). SAP has also introduced key technical evolutions,[27] including:
• The new synchronized release strategy, which applies to all the components in the SAP Business Suite. This means that enterprises can upgrade only the enhancement packages they need rather than the complete set of modules.
• Predefined roles and business processes (value scenarios), which are provided with the new release to facilitate customization of the SAP product to the organizational context
• The user interface, improved with the new SAP NetWeaver Business Client, which replaces the previous SAP GUI and offers better integration of the SAP BusinessObject Portfolio

---

[27] Hamerman, P.D.; R. Wang; "SAP Harmonizes Portfolio With Business Suite 7," Forrester, USA, 17 March 2009

# The Changing Compliance Landscape

Increased pressures from government regulations, financial markets and shareholders, combined with corporate collapses and acts of management fraud in recent years, have resulted in a continuing focus on corporate governance and risk management. The result has been a landslide of corporate regulations around the world with significant implications for financial and nonfinancial reporting, such as:

- US Sarbanes-Oxley Act of 2002—One of the most far-reaching pieces of legislation to impact financial reporting, Sarbanes-Oxley compliance efforts have focused on sections 302 and 404 of the Act.[28] Other regulations, such as JSOX, the Japanese equivalent to Sarbanes-Oxley; the French Financial Security Law, *Loi sur la Securite Financiere* (LSF); or the Basic Standard for Enterprises' Internal Control, the Chinese equivalent of Sarbanes-Oxley, had similar impacts on enterprises.
- At the same time that the Sarbanes-Oxley Act was introduced, the US Securities and Exchange Commission (SEC) introduced a requirement that progressively shortened the "grace period" between the end of the financial year and the due date for the lodging of financial statements with the SEC. This accelerated the reporting schedule, and subsequently introduced changes such as the automation of significant aspects of the financial reporting process. ERPs, and SAP in particular, have had an important role in this regard.
- New Basel Capital Accord (Basel II)—Basel II requires banks to maintain minimum levels of capital with the objective of better aligning regulatory capital measures with the inherent risk profile of a bank, considering credit risk, market risk, operational risk and other risks. If the bank can demonstrate a risk management and control regime that reduces its risk profile, the accord allows for a reduction in the level of capital held.
- International Financial Reporting Standards (IFRS)—Many of the standards existing in the IFRS were known as the International Audit Standard (IAS) prior to 2001. Although not a recent regulation, the focus has now shifted toward the global implementation of the IFRS standards. IFRS promotes the adoption of a single set of global accounting standards requiring high-quality, transparent and comparable information in an organization's financial statements. The European Commission (EC) adopted the consolidated text of IFRS in the European Union (EU) in 2008 (for detailed information about IAS/IFRS, refer to *www.iasplus.com*). Based on continuing convergence, the SEC has announced that US companies will be allowed to report under these new standards as early as 2009, and compliance for all US companies may be required by 2014, assuming certain project milestones are met. This means that enterprises may be required to make changes to the way in which account balances are presented in their financial statements (e.g., elimination of internally generated goodwill) and provision of additional disclosures in the notes to their annual report, where appropriate.

---

[28] Anand, S.; *Essentials of Sarbanes-Oxley*, John Wiley & Sons, Inc., USA, 2007

• Sustainability and Corporate Responsibility—Enterprises worldwide are under increasing pressure by stakeholders to conduct themselves in a more socially responsible manner. This includes environmental regulations such as ISO 14064, the Kyoto protocol enforced in a number of countries though local regulations, such as the *National Greenhouse and Energy Reporting Act 2007* in Australia. The energy sector is particularly impacted and will need to monitor and report accurate information about greenhouse gases and other emissions, as well as ensuring the information reported is audited.

• Data Privacy—There is a global spotlight on privacy with more countries adopting data privacy regulations. Data privacy is important to business integrity and trust, and is also becoming a priority for a number of enterprises to ensure that information, particularly sensitive personal information (e.g., credit card numbers, health records), is handled with due regard to data privacy and security.

To support corporate governance reforms, such as Sarbanes-Oxley, many enterprises around the world have adopted an internal controls framework such as COSO, COCO or Turnbull. The COSO framework (discussed in chapter 3) is commonly used by enterprises to define an internal control framework and methodology and could be adapted to manage the financial reporting risks associated with an ERP environment. The framework covers five interrelated components:

1. Control environment (the tone at the top)
2. Risk assessment (risk identification and analysis)
3. Control activities (process-level controls in support of significant accounts in the financial statements, e.g., review of the control system and segregation of duties)
4. Information and communication (identification, capture and reporting of financial and operating information that is useful to control the organization's activities)
5. Monitoring (assessment of the robustness and relevance of the internal control activities)

An internal control system is judged to be effective if the five components are present and functioning effectively for operations, financial reporting and compliance.

As enterprises have scrambled their way toward compliance with a plethora of regulations, the role of IT in meeting the requirements of these regulations has been highlighted. **Figure 14.1** illustrates how IT controls are embedded within each element of an enterprise's business. The role of ERPs is particularly important at the IT application control level, as data from numerous business processes are integrated and are input directly into the financial statements. As such, the ERP is at the heart of the control requirements of corporate governance and risk management regulations that affect the financial reporting process.

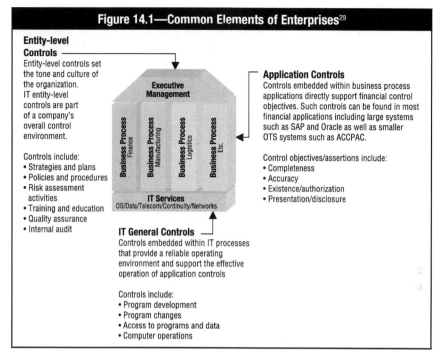

**Figure 14.1—Common Elements of Enterprises[29]**

**Entity-level Controls**

Entity-level controls set the tone and culture of the organization. IT entity-level controls are part of a company's overall control environment.

Controls include:
- Strategies and plans
- Policies and procedures
- Risk assessment activities
- Training and education
- Quality assurance
- Internal audit

**Executive Management**

Business Process Finance

Business Process Manufacturing

Business Process Logistics

Business Process Etc.

**IT Services**
OS/Data/Telecom/Continuity/Networks

**Application Controls**

Controls embedded within business process applications directly support financial control objectives. Such controls can be found in most financial applications including large systems such as SAP and Oracle as well as smaller OTS systems such as ACCPAC.

Control objectives/assertions include:
- Completeness
- Accuracy
- Existence/authorization
- Presentation/disclosure

**IT General Controls**

Controls embedded within IT processes that provide a reliable operating environment and support the effective operation of application controls

Controls include:
- Program development
- Program changes
- Access to programs and data
- Computer operations

When designing internal controls using the COSO framework, enterprises should consider enabling certain functionalities in their ERP systems or implementing new technologies to achieve the following objectives:
- Effectiveness and efficiency of operations[30]
- Reliability of financial reporting
- Compliance with the applicable laws and regulations

The key areas that should be considered by enterprises to ensure compliance with financial reporting regulations include:
- Data capturing capability—The ability of the ERP system to capture sufficient information to meet the requirements of corporate governance regulations, such as IFRS. A risk management system designed to identify, assess, monitor and manage risk, and inform investors of material changes to the company's risk profile[31] should be implemented.
- Reporting functionality—The ability of the ERP system to extract meaningful information for internal and external reporting purposes

[29] *Op. Cit., IT Control Objectives for Sarbanes-Oxley, 2nd Edition*
[30] *Op. Cit., Enterprise Risk Management—Integrated Framework*
[31] Group of 100 : A Guide to Compliance With ASX Principle 7: Recognise and Manage Risk, Australia, August 2008, *www.group100.com.au/publications/g100_deloitte_ASX_p7Guide_200808.pdf*

• Accountability—The ability of the ERP system to provide adequate and sufficient evidence of automated controls, such as digital sign-offs and automated reconciliations, and logs of changes to key data. This assists with providing greater visibility over segregation of duties in the underlying business processes that support the significant accounts in the financial statements.

The potential for control automation is the largest benefit of using ERP systems to support corporate governance and financial reporting. When enterprises design any form of internal controls, they must first consider the potential for automating the required controls through the ERP. Control automation can reduce the impact on worker productivity by eliminating additional effort associated with manual controls. The effectiveness of controls can be enhanced by automatically enforcing security restrictions and ensuring that a complete record of the controls history is maintained for auditing requirements.

In addition to the benefits associated with automated controls, ERP vendors such as SAP have begun to introduce specific functionality and tools to address increasingly complex corporate governance requirements.

## Using SAP Tools to Support Corporate Governance

SAP and various third parties have responded to regulatory requirements with audit tools that integrate with SAP ERP to assist individual corporations to step up to the challenges of complying with new legislation. SAP BusinessObject GRC solutions, including Access Control and Process Control, combined with SAP® Strategic Enterprise Management (SAP® SEM®), can assist with meeting Sarbanes-Oxley compliance with SAP ERP.[32]

SAP BusinessObject GRC Access Control and Process Control are an important component of SAP's Sarbanes-Oxley toolset. They can assist with the monitoring of internal controls management, including user access management and segregation of duties violations, in support of compliance with Sarbanes-Oxley sections 404 and 409. It is included as part of SAP BusinessObject GRC solutions and discussed in more detailed in chapter 13.

In addition to SAP GRC Access Control and Process Control, SEM may assist with its integration across all areas of the enterprise. It is possible to drill down from the management cockpit to the detail level, allowing management to assess events potentially requiring disclosure. SEM's Stakeholder Relationship Management module can be used to communicate the business strategy, changes and any impacts to stakeholders through push or pull services, thus ensuring that stakeholders are kept updated of any changes and meeting disclosure requirements.[33]

---

[32] SAP AG, *Enterprise Governance and Sarbanes-Oxley Compliance With mySAP ERP Financials*, Germany, 2005
[33] Hindupur, S.; IT Toolbox SAP Knowledge Base, "Sarbanes-Oxley Act: How Using SEM Can Help," Deloitte Consulting, 2004, *http://hosteddocs.ittoolbox.com/SH111204.pdf*

In support of Sarbanes-Oxley section 301, the SAP NetWeaver Portal offers an anonymous "whistle-blowing" feature. Enterprises can configure an online form to meet their own internal policies or relevant corporate governance requirements, using portal technology to deploy the feature.

SAP's comprehensive banking compliance solution is through SAP Bank Analyzer, which can be used with SAP ERP installations. In combination with the SAP Accounting for Financial Instruments application, SAP Bank Analyzer can assist with IFRS compliance for IAS 32 and IAS 39, which dictates how financial instruments should be classified, recognized and measured for inclusion in financial statements. For assistance with other regulatory requirements for financial statements, SAP ERP Financials provides extensive functionality for parallel accounting that supports IFRS and local regulations around the world to support adherence with complex accounting standards, achievement of capital market requirements, and reliability and transparency of financial reporting. It addresses specific issues such as financial instruments, business combinations and share base payments.[34]

SAP Bank Analyzer can also be used for SAP ERP Basel II compliance through SAP Basel II. It creates standard reports covering all requirements under pillar three of the Accord and is built to enable compliance with future risk regulations. The SAP solution for Basel II builds on existing risk management capabilities of SAP for Banking solution portfolio and captures credit, operational and market risk for analysis and reporting purposes. Based on an enterprise's financial database, it facilitates exposure calculation, credit portfolio modeling, limit management, and processing of data for the requisite regulatory reporting.[35]

The SAP BusinessObject portfolio offers solutions to help manage compliance with data privacy, sustainability and corporate responsibility regulations (as discussed in chapter 13). In 2008, SAP and Cisco released a composite application to enforce real-time, global and local data privacy policies across the enterprise's business applications and network. SAP Environment, Health and Safety (EHS) Management can be used to manage the enterprise's compliance with various regulations by monitoring operational risks related to the environment (e.g., gas emission, carbon footprint), health and safety (e.g., product safety, worldwide recycling legislation) or corporate sustainability initiatives (e.g., actively manage EHS risks to protect people).

These SAP ERP solutions and tools enable enterprises to utilize SAP products to assist with corporate governance compliance. While additional functionality may exist within other SAP solutions that provide additional assistance with corporate governance compliance, enterprises with current SAP ERP installations are well supported.

---

[34] SAP AG, *Achieving IFRS Compliance: Succeed With SAP® Software, Consulting, and Training*, Germany, 2008
[35] *Ibid.*

Regardless of the technology solution that an enterprise utilizes to assist with its compliance programs (whether it is an ERP system, or functionality built into systems spread across the enterprise), merely having the technology or employing consultants to configure the technology does not suggest that an enterprise is compliant with specific regulations. With regard to Sarbanes-Oxley compliance, the entire process of identifying risks, defining control objectives, designing controls, implementing controls (possibly as part of an ERP system), and regularly reviewing and testing these controls is more important than the technology itself.

## Integrated ERP Audit

In the first edition of this book, this section was titled "E-enabled ERP Audit." However e-commerce is no longer a new direction for an enterprise's business; rather, it is increasingly becoming part of an enterprise's business-as-usual activities. Technology has enabled an enterprise's customers and suppliers to be integrated throughout the value chain using Internet technologies such as electronic data interchange, e-commerce and open data standards such as XML. Although the integrated business model has matured, many of the risks and controls originally identified during the e-commerce boom remain pertinent. With business integration, the auditor must be aware of the implications for security controls, the tools released by SAP that enable this integration, and the impact on Sarbanes-Oxley compliance.

The focus in the past, from a business perspective, was on achieving efficiencies within the enterprise through implementation of enterprise applications. However, with the advent of business integration, the focus has shifted to integrated ERP applications. The integrated economy can be grouped into five key elements as follows:
- Sell side—Customer solutions and services focusing on the sales, marketing and service processes and leveraging various customer relationship management (CRM), web-based and call center technologies to achieve an effective total customer experience. These technologies improve multichannel transactions and relationships with customers, expand marketing and sales reach, and empower customers to serve themselves.
- Buy side—Supply chain solutions and services that focus on supply chain processes, including procurement, and leverage supply chain optimization, e-procurement and other Internet technologies to enhance transactions and relationships with suppliers. They automate and optimize processes across the enterprise and drive efficiencies across the entire value chain.
- Inside—Transformation solutions and services within an enterprise that focus on the management, financial and human resource processes. They leverage core ERP, Internet and other technologies to enhance and build intellectual capital, process transactions, develop employees and improve decision making and productivity.

- Exchanges—Marketplace solutions and services that focus on digital trading exchanges. They leverage Internet technologies to create virtual business communities that facilitate commerce and collaboration, reduce costs and link fragmented networks of buyers and sellers.
- Outside—Solutions and services that extend to sell-side, inside and buy-side solutions by enabling businesses to focus on core strengths and transfer technology and/or business processes to an external service provider. This offering extends across areas such as outsourcing and business acceleration services.

**Figure 14.2** shows an example of what the integrated ERP enterprise may look like. SAP has developed the SAP Enterprise Portal to enable such integration natively through an SOA on the NetWeaver platform. The SAP Enterprise Portal enables employees, customers, partners and suppliers to access all of the content and applications they need from a single point.

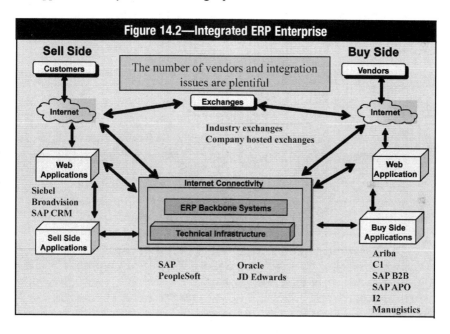

Figure 14.2—Integrated ERP Enterprise

**Figure 14.3** shows an example of a network overview for an ERP and the Internet. The current version of SAP ERP includes a number of components that facilitate Internet connectivity.

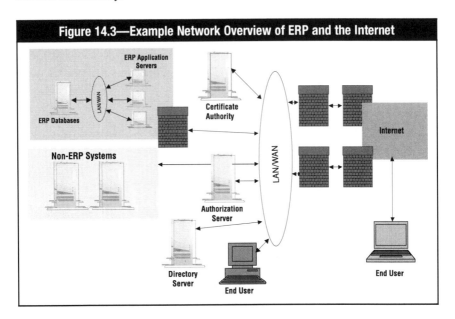

Figure 14.3—Example Network Overview of ERP and the Internet

Enterprises face increased risk associated with integrated business and must develop control solutions to effectively manage those risks. Risks associated with integration include:

- Security risk—The Internet can be used to gain unauthorized access to an enterprise's internal systems or to the systems of business partners. By enabling customers and third parties to access data and/or functionality in an ERP, the potential for security breaches is greatly increased.
- Legal risk—Part of the Internet service may break local or foreign laws. This includes the supply of incorrect information to the customer or unauthorized use of credit card details or other personal details. There are also questions regarding the transfer of personal information across borders that must be investigated.
- Image risk—Hackers can vandalize web sites, making unauthorized changes to the site content that can affect an enterprise's reputation. The enterprise's image can be harmed by media coverage of a hacking attempt. In the state of California (USA), if there has been a known security violation that could expose customers' personal information, this must be publicly disclosed.
- Repudiation of transaction risk—The Internet does not guarantee successful transmission of packets, therefore transactions that are lost or rejected may not be retransmitted to the system for processing, resulting in incomplete transactions.
- Denial of service (disruption risk)—Disruptions to technology could shut down online business processes. This includes system shutdowns due to natural disasters, fire, terrorism, etc.

## Integrated ERP Control Framework

In response to the integration-enabled ERP environment, an enterprise needs to extend its traditional ERP control framework to include the following areas, as depicted in **figure 14.4**, to address the risks arising from integration:

- Identity management—Are we dealing with whom we think we are? Appropriate management of participant identities enables building a trusted exchange community. Single sign-on facilities can facilitate identity management and greatly reduce security administration costs. However, they may also increase the risk as a user may inadvertently be assigned access to several systems, and hackers can gain access to numerous enterprise systems by violating just one authentication system.
- Content quality—Is the information that is being used internally and provided to customers and vendors accurate, timely, pertinent and current? When making enterprise information available to external parties, the importance of providing timely and correct information increases dramatically.
- Privacy/confidentiality—Is information restricted to only authorized organizations and individuals? Are customers' personal details (e.g., credit card numbers, spending habits and contact details) appropriately safeguarded?
- Collaborative commerce—Do the extended electronic business processes incorporating customers and suppliers have the appropriate integrity and security controls built in (e.g., how a credit limit will be checked when purchasing goods via the web)?
- Integration integrity—Are all elements of transactions fully and completely processed throughout the extended value chain (e.g., appropriate control totals, data editing criteria and security between program interfaces)?

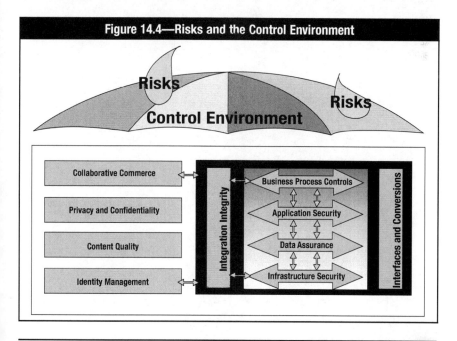

Figure 14.4—Risks and the Control Environment

Sarbanes-Oxley financial reporting compliance (as discussed earlier in this chapter) aims to tighten internal controls throughout an enterprise. With the integrated enterprise, auditors must consider extending the scope of their Sarbanes-Oxley control environment to that of partners, suppliers and, potentially, customers. The risks previously mentioned can span across all of these third parties and cannot be mitigated without consideration for the control environments of these third parties. When considering third-party controls, auditors should focus on controls embedded within contracts and the security control environment of the third parties.

## Conclusion

The advent of ERPs has necessitated a change in the audit approach (i.e., toward a business process focus, greater emphasis on application security, configurable controls and continuous assurance). The audit approach is continuing to change, with ERP at the heart of the controls required to meet the changing compliance landscape. The rigor of internal controls required by Sarbanes-Oxley, IFRS and Basel II, etc., combined with the advent of collaborative business and integrated ERPs, requires a change in the enterprises's concept of its audit universe. The existing focus and paradigms may need further development to audit in the integrated ERP environment. As SAP clients begin to transition from SAP core enterprise resource planning to the use of SAP products powered by the SOA NetWeaver platform, auditors have an excellent opportunity to build in the internal controls required for the future and assist their enterprises to maximize the very real and tangible business benefits that can be achieved with enterprise applications.

# Appendix A—Frequently Asked Questions

1.  Should the SAP ERP administrator have access to functional modules under the SAP ERP software?

    No. The SAP ERP administrator's role should be restricted to administration of the system and maintaining user access as requested by the data owners. SAP_ALL access should not be required by an SAP ERP administrator for carrying out his or her responsibilities (refer to chapters 4 and 12 for more details on this topic).

2.  Should the authorization to develop queries be given freely to all users?

    No. Incorrectly structured queries can adversely affect system performance. Further, in an SAP ERP environment the query requirements of users may be able to be predetermined. Therefore, queries should be developed on the development client and fully tested on the integration client. Users should have access only to run the queries on the production system, as opposed to develop them.

3.  Is evaluating the SAP ERP software performance the responsibility of IT auditors?

    In an ERP environment the IT auditor should be able to look beyond security and controls and suggest options for system performance improvement as well. The SAP ERP software does have quite a few system performance monitoring tools and an auditor should point out the need for appropriate procedures for review of these measures by the system administrator.

    A few tips to ensure performance efficiency may include:
    – Scheduling high-volume processes (e.g., generation of the trial balance report, stock valuation, purchase orders clearing) during nonpeak periods
    – Restricting S_Query access
    – Restricting the number of concurrent sessions a user can initiate (In a production environment, do users really need more than two sessions?)

4.  Why "park" an incomplete document rather than "hold" it?

    The SAP ERP software has two options to store incomplete documents that will be completed and posted later. While the Hold Document option enables a user to temporarily store an incomplete document, the problem with this option is that only the user who has held the document can complete and post it into the system. No one else can access the held document. On the other hand, a list of documents generated by the Park option can be viewed by anyone with access to run the Compact Journal report. Thus, parking a document helps in the follow-up of incomplete documents by a person other than the creator. With appropriate access rights, one can even retrieve the document by clicking on the line entry in the report, completing it and posting it into the system. Good control practices dictate that parked documents should be reviewed as part of the period-end closing procedures to ensure that all transactions are posted completely under the relevant posting period.

5. Can special periods (defined 13 through 16) be used to post documents relating to the closed posting periods?

Any number of posting periods can be defined in the SAP ERP system. The usual practice is to define 12 general posting periods corresponding to the 12 months in a year. Posting periods can be mapped to calendar months or to months under a financial year. For instance, posting period 1 can be mapped to January (first month of calendar year) or July (first month in a financial year). If 12 general posting periods are defined, one can define an additional four special posting periods, 13 through 16, to post supplementaries. While an enterprise can define how it would like to align posting periods with its fiscal practice, the posting periods need to be open before a transaction can be posted. Special posting periods are configured to allow adjustment postings associated to year-end closing. Only when the last period in the general posting period is open (i.e., if you are on a 12-period fiscal year, period 12 must be open), is posting allowed to special periods 13 to 16. Any postings to special periods 13 to 16 will be reflected and associated with period 12. If period 12 is closed, even if special periods 13 to 16 are open, no transaction may be posted.

6. What is the significance of the update termination report?

Due to the complexity of a client-server environment that comprises multiple systems, the points of failure between the time a document is posted and the actual update taking place at the database level may not be easily determined in a real-time mode. A fraction of a second failure may result in a document not updating the database. This failure may not be immediately identified. The update termination report (transaction code SM13) lists documents that did not update the database due to technical reasons (not incompletion) and the reasons the update failed. Good control practices dictate that formal procedures for periodic generation and review of the update termination report be in place. It must be noted, however, that the entries in an updated termination report get cleared on a first-in, first-out (FIFO) basis. Hence, it is prudent to generate this report at least once every week for review.

7. Is it possible to directly update a table in the underlying database (Oracle/Informix) using the SQL prompt?

   The SAP ERP software appears to the database management system (DBMS), e.g., Oracle, as a single user. Theoretically, it is possible to update the underlying table structures in Oracle if a user has permission, although the complexity of the table structures makes this difficult and requires some expertise. However, for this reason, access at the DBMS level should be controlled tightly and restricted to the database administration personnel only.

8. If, as with any other RDBMS-based application, it is possible to update a table directly through the RDBMS SQL, will the SAP ERP software detect such external updates automatically or is there any transaction that will detect and report such updates/deletes?

   The SAP ERP software may not detect such external updates. For this reason, it is necessary to have appropriate controls in place at the DBMS level and, for that matter, at the operating system level as well.

9. If the SAP ERP software records all transactions with the user ID of the person who performed the transaction, is there an easily accessible report or query to list transactions—financial or nonfinancial—implemented by a particular user or user ID for a given period?

   Transaction STAD may be used to give an overview of the transactions accessed by a user ID for a particular period of time; however, it does not show the detailed transactions themselves. The period of time that can be reported on may be limited by the size of the redo logs for statistical records. A major challenge with a single comprehensive report of all entries made by a user over a given period is the large number of tables in which transactions are stored and the varying formats of the data in each table. This makes the compilation of a single comprehensive report by user prohibitive. Transaction STAT may provide a starting point, however, and by following the transactions through and identifying the tables accessed (refer to techniques on navigation provided in chapter 2), custom reports or queries may be written to access the required information. This is a specialized task and should be undertaken by persons with the appropriate skills. As most business transactions in the SAP ERP system end up as financial documents eventually, another report that may be useful is RFBABL00. It displays all changed financial documents. If there is a suspicion of unauthorized activity, another alternative may be to use table logging to monitor user activity against key tables.

10. Will problems be encountered when upgrading the SAP ERP software in the future if many modifications are made to the organization's original application?

    Customizing the SAP ERP software may build in additional costs when upgrading since user-developed reports and modifications will need to be retested in the upgraded software system. The purpose of testing is to uncover any problems associated with user modifications and to resolve these problems before going live with the new software release. Therefore, it is important to consider the total cost of ownership when purchasing the software and making modifications. Inevitably, trade-off decisions need to be made between the business benefits of any change and the long-term cost of maintaining it.

11. When conducting a financial audit and substantive testing of account balances, do reconciliations of general ledger account balances need to be reperformed?

    Generally, general ledger control accounts (e.g., accounts receivable, accounts payable, inventory and fixed assets) are "system only," and are set up in the SAP ERP software as reconciliation accounts or automatic postings only. This means that postings may be performed to the general ledger through the subsidiary ledger (e.g., asset register) by the system only, and no journal entries will be allowed. The reconciliation process from a financial audit perspective should then be straightforward (i.e., display the account balance and compare it to the trial balance—there should not be any reconciling items). A list of general ledger reconciliation accounts can be displayed through the table browser (transaction code SE16) and by entering table name SKB1, selecting the appropriate company codes, placing an X in the automatic postings only field and executing the report.

    Reperformance of such reconciliations is necessary. Errors in account determination logic may point some transactions to the wrong reconciliation account. Differences can occur when users reset the automatic postings only field for reconciliation accounts.

12. What makes the audit of the SAP ERP system different from the audit of legacy systems?

    The essential difference between SAP and older legacy application systems is that most processing is performed online in real time, where SAP's integrated modules allow for a single business event initiated in a functional area to be completed through to its final financial application, the GL update, at the time of the initial event.

The impact of this difference on auditing the integrity of data produced by the SAP ERP system is the need to place a high degree of reliance on the controls over the authorization and input of transactions and on the general computer controls supporting the SAP ERP system. A key element in this control structure is the SAP ERP Basis and module configuration of SAP ERP, including the control options that are selected (by turning on switches in tables) and the control over how individual users are authorized to access the system.

Another key difference is the extensive use of tables in the SAP ERP system to determine system functionality and to define which controls are to be used and who has access to what. Controls can be tested by examining these table entries. Obviously, control over changes to these tables and who has access to them becomes very important in an SAP ERP environment. If properly implemented, the SAP ERP Basis module also provides many of the types of general computer controls that would ordinarily be provided by other means in a traditional system.

Because of the high degree of integration and the maintenance of all transactions in a common database, SAP ERP presents significant opportunities for using computer-aided audit techniques (CAATs), such as file interrogation or SAP ERP standard or organization-customized ABAP/4 reports.

13. What is the difference between SAP R/3, SAP R/3 Enterprise, SAP ECC, SAP ERP and mySAP ERP?

SAP R/3 was launched in 1992 by SAP AG with the advent of distributed client-server computing. SAP R/3 allowed real-time data processing on multiple platforms and operating systems. SAP R/3, up to version 4.6C, was based on the SAP Basis platform. SAP R/3 Enterprise was launched in 2003 and was the first step toward e-business, with its Web Application Server (Web AS) platform. The Web AS platform was composed of SAP Basis and other web-enabled components. SAP ERP is the successor of SAP R/3 Enterprise and was originally part of what was known as the mySAP ERP group of e-business integration tools, now named SAP Business Suite. SAP ERP is also known as SAP ECC, Enterprise Central Component. SAP NetWeaver forms the platform for the SAP ERP application. SAP NetWeaver is a stack of integrated components, which includes both new components and components and tools that were previously provided (i.e., SAP Web AS, which includes SAP Basis) as individual separate services and are now integrated to form the SAP NetWeaver platform. With the SAP NetWeaver platform, SAP ERP is able to provide open architecture and web-based services. Refer to chapter 11 for more information about SAP ERP and the SAP NetWeaver platform.

14. Do I need to review SAP NetWeaver as part of an SAP audit?

Before performing an audit of an enterprise's SAP system, it is critical to obtain an understanding of the client's SAP implementation, how the client is using SAP, and whether SAP NetWeaver is being used to support the SAP system. If NetWeaver is being used, the next step is to determine which of its components are being used. It is recommended that the security of the SAP Basis component be included in the audit. It is also important to consider the possibility that user authentication for the SAP system may be managed through Java (User Management Engine, UME). If this is the case, then additional testing over this and testing of the SAP Basis component would be required. Other components of SAP NetWeaver should be assessed to determine whether they have a significant impact on the enterprise's financial statements; if so, they should also be included in the audit.

15. What is the difference between a role and a profile?

Role and profile go hand in hand. Role is used as a template, where one can add T-codes, reports, etc. Profile gives the user authorization. When a role is created, a profile is automatically created. SAP provides several predefined profiles, which contain extensive authorizations. Hence, one should be very careful when assigning these predefined profiles to users.

16. What is the different between a single role and a composite role?

A role is a container that collects the transaction and generates the associated profile. A composite role is a container that can collect several different roles.

17. Why it is not recommended to have multiple clients in one SAP production instance?

Multiple clients in one production instance are not recommended for the following reasons:
• Problems affecting one client immediately affect all other clients.
• A system problem (system crash) immediately affects all clients.
• Poorly written ABAPs will cause a bad response throughout the SAP system, affecting all clients.
• Programs/tables are client-independent. Individual customers cannot make changes to common programs/clients without affecting the others.
• Efficient management of changes would be difficult.

18. What is the difference between a workbench request and a customizing request?

The Transport Organizer maintains change requests. These requests record the changes made to the repository and customizing objects. Based on the objects changed they are:
- Workbench request—Involves changes to cross-client customizing and repository objects. The objects are independent of the client. Hence, the requests are used for transferring and transporting changed repository objects and changed system settings from cross-client tables.
- Customizing request—Involves changes recorded to client-specific customizing objects. These client-specific requests are used for copying and transporting changed system settings from client-specific tables.

19. What are the testing tools available in SAP?

There are tools such as:
- CATT—The Test Workbench contains the Computer-aided Test Tool (CATT) to create automatic test cases. Automatic test cases are performed by the SAP system without user dialog and are most useful for function tests. The result of an automatic test case is a detailed log that documents the test. The use of automatic tests can considerably reduce the test effort.
- Extended Computer-aided Test Tool (eCATT)—This is a built-in testing tool to test SAP systems. By using this testing tool the entire business process can be tested. The tool can also be used with a third-party testing tool. Execution of every test script ends with a log, which explains the results of the test script.

# Appendix B—Recommended Reading

Adam, Frederic; David Sammon; *The Enterprise Resource Planning Decade: Lessons Learned and Issues for the Future*, Idea Group Publishing, USA, 2004

Australian National Audit Office, *Security and Control Update for SAP R/3*, Australia, 2004

Broady, D.V.; H. A. Roland; *SAP GRC for Dummies*, Wiley Publishing Co., USA, 2008

Campbell, S.; V. Mohun; *Mastering Enterprise SOA with SAP NetWeaver and mySAP ERP*, Wiley Publishing Co., USA, 2006

Davenport, T.; "Putting the Enterprise into the Enterprise System," *Harvard Business Review*, July-August 1998, p. 121-130

Hagerty, J.; D. Gaughan; *The Governance, Risk Management, and Compliance (GRC) Landscape, Part 1: A Segmented Marketplace With Distinct Buyers*, AMR Research, USA, June 2008

Hagerty, J.; K. Verma; D. Gaughan; *The Governance, Risk Management, and Compliance (GRC) Landscape, Part 2: Software's Integral Role in GRC Automation*, AMR Research, USA, June 2008

Hurwitz, J. et al., *Service Oriented Architecture for Dummies, 2ⁿᵈ Edition*, Wiley Publishing Co., USA, 2007

ISACA Online Glossary of Terms, *www.isaca.org/glossary*

IT Governance Institute, CobiT 4.1, ISACA, USA, 2007, *www.isaca.org/cobit*

IT Governance Institute, *IT Control Objectives for Sarbanes-Oxley, The Role of IT in the Design and Implementation of Internal Control Over Financial Reporting, 2ⁿᵈ Edition*, ISACA, USA, 2006, *www.isaca.org*

Jay, R.; *SAP NetWeaver Portal Technology: The Complete Reference*, McGraw-Hill, USA, 2008

Lau, K. Linda; *Managing Business With SAP: Planning, Implementation, and Evaluation*, Idea Group Publishing, USA, 2005

Linkies, M.; F. Off; *SAP Security and Authorizations*, SAP Press, USA, 2006

Rasmussen, M.; *A Tale of Two GRC Strategies: Analysis and Comparison of Oracle's and SAP's GRC Strategies*, Forrester, USA, June 2007

Rugillies, Erica; L. Nate Root; Randy Heffner; Erin Kinikin; Colin Teubner; *SAP's Direction: Contextual Collaboration*, Forrester, USA, 2004

SAP, *www.sap.com*, January 2009

SAP Help Portal, *http://help.sap.com*, January 2009

SAP Library—Glossary, *http://help.sap.com/saphelp_46c/helpdata/En/35/2cd77b d7705394e10000009b387c12/frameset.htm, 2001*

SAP Professional Journal, *www.sappro.com*, January 2009

Taiariol, R.; "Segregated Duties in Fashion," *The Internal Auditor*, USA, February 2009

Vogel, A.; I. Kimbell; *mySAP ERP for Dummies*, Wiley Publishing Co., USA, 2005

Woods, D.; J. Word; *SAP NetWeaver for Dummies*, Wiley Publishing Co., USA, 2004

Yusufali, F. Musaji; *Integrated Auditing of ERP Systems*, Wiley Publishing Co., USA, 2003

# Appendix C—Suggested SAP ERP Tables to Log and Review

This suggested list is in no way exclusive. A risk assessment should be performed based on the control framework of each enterprise to determine which tables should be made active for logging.

Consideration should be given to enabling logging on all tables that have been identified as system-critical. Where logs are produced, these should be reviewed on a regular basis using transaction SCU3 or reports RSVTPROT (evaluation of change logs) and RSTBHIST (list of logged tables and table change analysis).

Procedures are required for handling exception situations, such as unauthorized changes to critical tables. All such situations must be addressed and corrective measures taken.

Activating table logging impacts system performance since it entails twice as many database updates as would otherwise be the case and the database storage load is increased substantially (recorded data are compressed without buffering). As such, only in exceptional circumstances is it appropriate to use the ALL setting. Transactional tables should never be logged.

## Basis/Administration Tables

| | | |
|---|---|---|
| AGR series | - | Group profile activity |
| AGR_1016/B | - | Name of the activity group profile |
| AGR_1250/1251 | - | Authorization data for the activity group |
| AGR_1252 | - | Organizational elements for authorizations |
| AGR_AGRS | - | Roles in composite roles |
| AGR_DEFINE | - | Role definition |
| AGR_HIER2 | - | Menu structure information—Customer version |
| AGR_HIERT | - | Role menu texts |
| AGR_OBJ | - | Assignment of menu nodes to role |
| AGR_PROF | - | Profile name for role |
| AGR_TCDTXT | - | Assignment of roles to T-codes |
| AGR_TEXTS | - | File structure for hierarchical menu—Customer |
| AGR_TIME | - | Time stamp for role:  Including profile |
| AGR_USERS | - | Assignment of roles to users |
| DD02 series | - | List of tables and descriptions |
| DD09L | - | Log of all table changes |
| PAT03 | - | Patch directory |
| SDBAC | - | DBA action table |
| SREPOATH | - | ABAP program and authorization groups |

| | | |
|---|---|---|
| T000 series | - | Clients, basic settings, customizing settings |
| T000ATP | - | Basic settings for availability check |
| T000C | - | Table for installing FI-SL customizing |
| T000CM | - | Client-specific FI-AR-CR settings |
| T000F | - | Cross-client FI settings |
| T000GL | - | Flexible general ledger: Customizing check and activation |
| T000K | - | Group |
| T000MD | - | MRP at MRP area level |
| T001 series | - | Company codes |
| T001_CONV | - | Company codes affected by currency conversions |
| T001A | - | Additional local currencies control for company code |
| T001C | - | Valid posting periods for global companies |
| T001CM | - | Permitted credit control areas by company code |
| T001D | - | Validation of accounting documents |
| T001E | - | Company code—Dependent address data |
| T001G | - | Company code—Dependent standard texts |
| T001I | - | Company code—Parameter types |
| T001J | - | Company code—Parameter type names |
| T001K | - | Valuation area |
| T001L | - | Storage locations |
| T001N | - | Company code—EC tax numbers/notifications |
| T001O | - | Cross-system company codes |
| T001Q | - | Substitution in accounting documents |
| T001R | - | Rounding rules for company code and currency |
| T001RWT | - | Rounding rules for company code, withhold.tax type and curr. |
| T001S | - | Accounting clerks |
| T001U | - | Clearing between company codes |
| T001W | - | Plants/branches |
| T001W_EXT | - | Plants (company's own and external) |
| T001WT | - | Company code-specific information per withholding tax type |
| T001X | - | Configuration of external receiving comp.codes |
| T001Y | - | Valuation levels for LIFO inventory valuation |
| T001Z | - | Additional specifications for company code |
| T001B series | - | Fiscal periods for company codes |
| T001B_PS | - | Account assignment objects in general ledger |
| T001B_PS_PER | - | Permitted posting periods for account assignment objects |
| T003 series | - | Document and transaction types |
| T003A | - | Document types for posting with clearing |
| T003B | - | Object types for early entry in financial accounting |
| T003L | - | Transaction type for material ledger |
| T003O, 3P | - | Order types, order type descriptions |
| T004 series | - | Directory of charts of accounts |
| T004F, 4G | - | Field status definition groups, group texts |
| T004M, 4R | - | Rules and rules index for sample accounts |

| | | |
|---|---|---|
| T005 series | - | Countries, county, city including tax information, alternate reporting, etc. |
| T007 series | - | Tax keys, codes, selections for transactions, deferred tax rules, etc. |
| T008, T008T | - | Blocking reasons and names for automatic payment transactions |
| T009 series | - | Fiscal year variants, periods, names, etc. |
| T010O, 10P | - | Posting period variants and names |
| T012 series | - | Banks, allocation methods, transaction types, terms, etc. |
| T014, 14T | - | Credit control areas and names |
| T020, T021 series | - | FI/AM transaction control, line and document layout, fast entry, etc. |
| T022, T022T | - | FI-SL activity: Fixed data and text |
| T023 series | - | Material groups, interest penalties, invoice handling rules, etc. |
| T024 series | - | Staff groups: Purchasing, planning, credit management, MRP, schedulers, etc. |
| T028B, D and E | - | Transaction type of sender bank, electronic banking and text |
| T028R series | - | Repetitive funds transfer types and transactions |
| T030 series | - | Standard accounts tables |
| T033 series | - | FI depreciation tables |
| T038 series | - | Cash management tables |
| T042 series | - | Payment transaction tables |
| T043 series | - | Tolerances: Accounting clerks, customers, vendors, etc. |
| T044A | - | Methods of foreign currency valuation |
| T044Z | - | Changed reconciliation accounts |
| T074 | - | Special general ledger accounts |
| T077 series | - | Account groups |
| T078 series | - | Screen selection, transaction-dependent |
| T079 series | - | Screen selection, entry-dependent |
| T169 series | - | Tolerances for account audits |
| TACT | - | Activities that can be protected |
| TACTT | - | Activities that can be protected, with descriptions |
| TACTZ | - | Authorization objects and valid activities |
| TADIR | - | Development objects and transport attributes |
| TBAER | - | Rules for changing documents |
| TBRG | - | Authorization objects and authorization groups |
| TBRGT | - | Authorization objects and authorization groups, with descriptions |
| TCURR | - | Foreign currency exchange rates |
| TDDAT | - | Table authorization groups |
| TMC4 | - | Global control elements: LIS information structure/control table |
| TOBC | - | Authorization object class |
| TOBCT | - | Authorization object class, with description |
| TOBJ | - | Authorization objects |
| TOBJT | - | Authorization objects and descriptions |

| TPGP | - ABAP program authorization groups |
|---|---|
| TRDIR | - ABAP program and authorization group |
| TSTC | - Transaction listing |
| TSTCA | - Values for transaction code authorizations |
| TSTCT | - Transactions with description |
| TCESYST, TASYS, TSYST, TDEVC | - Correction and transport system configuration tables |
| USOBT series | - Relation transaction to authorization object objects |
| USOBT | - Relation transaction to authorization object (SAP) |
| USOBT_C | - Relation transaction to auth.object (customer) |
| USOBX series | - Relation transaction to authorization object objects |
| USOBX | - Check table for table USOBT |
| USOBXFLAGS | - Temporary table for storing USOBX/T* change |
| USOBX_C | - Check table for table USOBT_C |
| USR01 | - User master records |
| USR02 | - User ID and passwords |
| USR03 | - User address data |
| USR04 | - User master authorizations |
| USR05 | - User master parameter ID |
| USR06 | - Additional data per user |
| USR07 | - Objects/values of last failed authority check |
| USR08 | - Table for user menu entries |
| USR09 | - Entries for user menus (work areas) |
| USR10, UST10C | - User master authorization profiles and composite profiles |
| USR11 | - User master profiles and descriptions (for USR10) |
| USR12 | - User master authorization values |
| USR13 | - Authorization descriptions |
| USR30 | - Additional information for user menu |
| USR40 | - Impermissible passwords |
| USGRP, USGRPT | - User groups and user group text |
| USH02 | - Change history for logon data |
| USH04 | - Change history for authorizations |
| USH10 | - Change history for authorization profiles |
| USH12 | - Change history for authorization values |
| USOBT, USOBX | - Transaction codes and authorization object, with value fields |

## Functional Module Tables

| BNKA | - Bank master |
|---|---|
| KNA1 | - Customer master |
| KNB1 | - Customer/company |
| KNBK | - Customer bank |

| LFA1 | - Vendor master (header) |
| LFB1 | - Vendor/company |
| LFBK | - Vendor bank |
| LFM1 | - Vendor purchasing organization |
| PA0001 | - HR organization assignment |
| PA0002 | - HR personal data |
| PA0006 | - HR people address |
| PA0008 | - HR pay data |
| SKA1 | - Account master |

# Appendix D—SAP ERP Revenue, Expenditure, Inventory, Basis Audit/Assurance Programs

## Revenue Business Cycle

### 1. Introduction

*Overview*

ISACA developed *ITAF™: A Professional Practices Framework for IT Assurance* as a comprehensive and good-practice-setting model. ITAF provides standards that are designed to be mandatory and are the guiding principles under which the IT audit and assurance profession operates. The guidelines provide information and direction for the practice of IT audit and assurance. The tools and techniques provide methodologies, tools and templates to provide direction in the application of IT audit and assurance processes.

*Purpose*

The audit/assurance program is a tool and template to be used as a road map for the completion of a specific assurance process. This audit/assurance program is intended to be utilized by IT audit and assurance professionals with the requisite knowledge of the subject matter under review, as described in ITAF, section 2200—General Standards. The audit/assurance programs are part of ITAF, section 4000—IT Assurance Tools and Techniques.

*Control Framework*

The audit/assurance programs have been developed in alignment with the CoBiT framework—specifically CoBiT 4.1—using generally applicable and accepted good practices. They reflect ITAF, sections 3400—IT Management Processes, 3600—IT Audit and Assurance Processes, and 3800—IT Audit and Assurance Management.

Many enterprises have embraced several frameworks at an enterprise level, including the Committee of Sponsoring Organizations of the Treadway Commission (COSO) Internal Control Framework. The importance of the control framework has been enhanced due to regulatory requirements by the US Securities and Exchange Commission (SEC) as directed by the US Sarbanes-Oxley Act of 2002 and similar legislation in other countries. They seek to integrate control framework elements used by the general audit/assurance team into the IT audit and assurance framework. Since COSO is widely used, it has been selected for inclusion in this audit/assurance program. The reviewer may delete or rename columns in the audit program to align with the enterprise's control framework.

### IT Governance, Risk and Control

IT governance, risk and control are critical in the performance of any assurance management process. Governance of the process under review will be evaluated as part of the policies and management oversight controls. Risk plays an important role in evaluating what to audit and how management approaches and manages risk. Both issues will be evaluated as steps in the audit/assurance program. Controls are the primary evaluation point in the process. The audit/assurance program will identify the control objectives with steps to determine control design and effectiveness.

### Responsibilities of IT Audit and Assurance Professionals

IT audit and assurance professionals are expected to customize this document to the environment in which they are performing an assurance process. This document is to be used as a review tool and starting point. It may be modified by the IT audit and assurance professional; it is not intended to be a checklist or questionnaire. It is assumed that the IT audit and assurance professional holds the Certified Information Systems Auditor (CISA) designation, or has the necessary subject matter expertise required to conduct the work and is supervised by a professional with the CISA designation and necessary subject matter expertise to adequately review the work performed.

## II. Using This Document

This audit/assurance program was developed to assist the audit and assurance professional in designing and executing a review. Details regarding the format and use of the document follow.

### Work Program Steps

The first column of the program describes the steps to be performed. The numbering scheme used provides built-in work paper numbering for ease of cross-reference to the specific work paper for that section. IT audit and assurance professionals are encouraged to make modifications to this document to reflect the specific environment under review.

### CobiT Cross-reference

The CobiT cross-reference provides the audit and assurance professional with the ability to refer to the specific CobiT control objective that supports the audit/assurance step. The CobiT control objective should be identified for each audit/assurance step in the section. Multiple cross-references are not uncommon. Processes at lower levels in the work program are too granular to be cross-referenced to CobiT. The audit/assurance program is organized in a manner to facilitate an evaluation through a structure parallel to the development process. CobiT provides in-depth control objectives and suggested control practices at each level. As the professional reviews each control, he/she should refer to CobiT 4.1 or the *IT Assurance Guide: Using CobiT* for good-practice control guidance.

*COSO Components*

As noted in the introduction, COSO and similar frameworks have become increasingly popular among audit and assurance professionals. This ties the assurance work to the enterprise's control framework. While the IT audit/assurance function has CobiT as a framework, operational audit and assurance professionals use the framework established by the enterprise. Since COSO is the most prevalent internal control framework, it has been included in this document and is a bridge to align IT audit/assurance with the rest of the audit/assurance function. Many audit/assurance organizations include the COSO control components within their report and summarize assurance activities to the audit committee of the board of directors.

For each control, the audit and assurance professional should indicate the COSO component(s) addressed. It is possible, but generally not necessary, to extend this analysis to the specific audit step level.

The original COSO internal control framework contained five components. In 2004, COSO was revised as the *Enterprise Risk Management (ERM) Integrated Framework* and extended to eight components. The primary difference between the two frameworks is the additional focus on ERM and integration into the business decision model. ERM is in the process of being adopted by large enterprises. The two frameworks are compared in **figure AD1**.

| Figure AD1—Comparison of COSO Internal Control and ERM Integrated Frameworks | |
|---|---|
| **Internal Control Framework** | **ERM Integrated Framework** |
| **Control Environment:** The control environment sets the tone of an organization, influencing the control consciousness of its people. It is the foundation for all other components of internal control, providing discipline and structure. Control environment factors include the integrity, ethical values, management's operating style, delegation of authority systems, as well as the processes for managing and developing people in the organization. | **Internal Environment:** The internal environment encompasses the tone of an organization, and sets the basis for how risk is viewed and addressed by an enterprise's people, including risk management philosophy and risk appetite, integrity and ethical values, and the environment in which they operate. |
| | **Objective Setting:** Objectives must exist before management can identify potential events affecting their achievement. Enterprise risk management ensures that management has in place a process to set objectives and that the chosen objectives support and align with the enterprise's mission and are consistent with its risk appetite. |
| | **Event Identification:** Internal and external events affecting achievement of an enterprise's objectives must be identified, distinguishing between risks and opportunities. Opportunities are channeled back to management's strategy or objective-setting processes. |

| Figure AD1—Comparison of COSO Internal Control and ERM Integrated Frameworks *(cont.)* | |
| --- | --- |
| **Internal Control Framework** | **ERM Integrated Framework** |
| **Risk Assessment:** Every enterprise faces a variety of risks from external and internal sources that must be assessed. A precondition to risk assessment is establishment of objectives, and thus risk assessment is the identification and analysis of relevant risks to achievement of assigned objectives. Risk assessment is a prerequisite for determining how the risks should be managed. | **Risk Assessment:** Risks are analyzed, considering the likelihood and impact, as a basis for determining how they could be managed. Risk areas are assessed on an inherent and residual basis. |
| | **Risk Response:** Management selects risk responses—avoiding, accepting, reducing, or sharing risk—developing a set of actions to align risks with the enterprise's risk tolerances and risk appetite. |
| **Control Activities:** Control activities are the policies and procedures that help ensure that management directives are carried out. They help ensure that necessary actions are taken to address risks to achievement of the enterprise's objectives. Control activities occur throughout the organization, at all levels and in all functions. They include a range of activities as diverse as approvals, authorizations, verifications, reconciliations, reviews of operating performance, security of assets and segregation of duties. | **Control Activities:** Policies and procedures are established and implemented to help ensure the risk responses are effectively carried out. |
| **Information and Communication:** Information systems play a key role in internal control systems as they produce reports, including operational, financial and compliance-related information that make it possible to run and control the business. In a broader sense, effective communication must ensure information flows down, across and up the organization. Effective communication should also be ensured with external parties, such as customers, suppliers, regulators and shareholders. | **Information and Communication:** Relevant information is identified, captured, and communicated in a form and timeframe that enable people to carry out their responsibilities. Effective communication also occurs in a broader sense, flowing down, across, and up the enterprise. |
| **Monitoring:** Internal control systems need to be monitored—a process that assesses the quality of the system's performance over time. This is accomplished through ongoing monitoring activities or separate evaluations. Internal control deficiencies detected through these monitoring activities should be reported upstream and corrective actions should be taken to ensure continuous improvement of the system. | **Monitoring:** The entirety of enterprise risk management is monitored and modifications made as necessary. Monitoring is accomplished through ongoing management activities, separate evaluations, or both. |
| Information for **figure AD1** was obtained from the COSO web site *www.coso.org/aboutus.htm*. | |

The original COSO internal control framework addresses the needs of the IT audit and assurance professional: control environment, risk assessment, control activities, information and communication, and monitoring. As such, ISACA has elected to utilize the five-component model for these audit/assurance programs. As more enterprises implement the ERM model, the additional three columns can be added, if relevant. When completing the COSO component columns, consider the definitions of the components as described in **figure AD1**.

### Reference/Hyperlink
Good practices require the audit and assurance professional to create a work paper for each line item, which describes the work performed, issues identified and conclusions. The reference/hyperlink is to be used to cross-reference the audit/assurance step to the work paper that supports it. The numbering system of this document provides a ready numbering scheme for the work papers. If desired, a link to the work paper can be pasted into this column.

### Issue Cross-reference
This column can be used to flag a finding/issue that the IT audit and assurance professional wants to further investigate or establish as a potential finding. The potential findings should be documented in a work paper that indicates the disposition of the findings (formally reported, reported as a memo or verbal finding, or waived).

### Comments
The comments column can be used to indicate the waiving of a step or other notations. It is not to be used in place of a work paper describing the work performed.

## III. Controls Maturity Analysis
One of the consistent requests of stakeholders who have undergone IT audit/assurance reviews is a desire to understand how their performance compares to good practices. Audit and assurance professionals must provide an objective basis for the review conclusions. Maturity modeling for management and control over IT processes is based on a method of evaluating the organization, so it can be rated from a maturity level of nonexistent (0) to optimized (5). This approach is derived from the maturity model that the Software Engineering Institute (SEI) of Carnegie Mellon University defined for the maturity of software development.

The *IT Assurance Guide: Using CobiT*, appendix VII—Maturity Model for Internal Control, in **figure AD2**, provides a generic maturity model showing the status of the internal control environment and the establishment of internal controls in an enterprise. It shows how the management of internal control, and an awareness of the need to establish better internal controls, typically develops from an *ad hoc* to an optimized level. The model provides a high-level guide to help CobiT users appreciate what is required for effective internal controls in IT and to help position their enterprise on the maturity scale.

| | Figure AD2—Maturity Model for Internal Control | |
|---|---|---|
| Maturity Level | Status of the Internal Control Environment | Establishment of Internal Controls |
| 0 Nonexistent | There is no recognition of the need for internal control. Control is not part of the organization's culture or mission. There is a high risk of control deficiencies and incidents. | There is no intent to assess the need for internal control. Incidents are dealt with as they arise. |
| 1 Initial/ad hoc | There is some recognition of the need for internal control. The approach to risk and control requirements is ad hoc and disorganized, without communication or monitoring. Deficiencies are not identified. Employees are not aware of their responsibilities. | There is no awareness of the need for assessment of what is needed in terms of IT controls. When performed, it is only on an ad hoc basis, at a high level and in reaction to significant incidents. Assessment addresses only the actual incident. |
| 2 Repeatable but intuitive | Controls are in place but are not documented. Their operation is dependent on the knowledge and motivation of individuals. Effectiveness is not adequately evaluated. Many control weaknesses exist and are not adequately addressed; the impact can be severe. Management actions to resolve control issues are not prioritized or consistent. Employees may not be aware of their responsibilities. | Assessment of control needs occurs only when needed for selected IT processes to determine the current level of control maturity, the target level that should be reached and the gaps that exist. An informal workshop approach, involving IT managers and the team involved in the process, is used to define an adequate approach to controls for the process and to motivate an agreed-upon action plan. |
| 3 Defined | Controls are in place and adequately documented. Operating effectiveness is evaluated on a periodic basis and there is an average number of issues. However, the evaluation process is not documented. While management is able to deal predictably with most control issues, some control weaknesses persist and impacts could still be severe. Employees are aware of their responsibilities for control. | Critical IT processes are identified based on value and risk drivers. A detailed analysis is performed to identify control requirements and the root cause of gaps and to develop improvement opportunities. In addition to facilitated workshops, tools are used and interviews are performed to support the analysis and ensure that an IT process owner owns and drives the assessment and improvement process. |

| Figure AD2—Maturity Model for Internal Control *(cont.)* | | |
|---|---|---|
| **Maturity Level** | **Status of the Internal Control Environment** | **Establishment of Internal Controls** |
| 4 Managed and measurable | There is an effective internal control and risk management environment. A formal, documented evaluation of controls occurs frequently. Many controls are automated and regularly reviewed. Management is likely to detect most control issues, but not all issues are routinely identified. There is consistent follow-up to address identified control weaknesses. A limited, tactical use of technology is applied to automate controls. | IT process criticality is regularly defined with full support and agreement from the relevant business process owners. Assessment of control requirements is based on policy and the actual maturity of these processes, following a thorough and measured analysis involving key stakeholders. Accountability for these assessments is clear and enforced. Improvement strategies are supported by business cases. Performance in achieving the desired outcomes is consistently monitored. External control reviews are organized occasionally. |
| 5 Optimized | An enterprisewide risk and control program provides continuous and effective control and risk issues resolution. Internal control and risk management are integrated with enterprise practices, supported with automated real-time monitoring with full accountability for control monitoring, risk management and compliance enforcement. Control evaluation is continuous, based on self-assessments and gap and root cause analyses. Employees are proactively involved in control improvements. | Business changes consider the criticality of IT processes and cover any need to reassess process control capability. IT process owners regularly perform self-assessments to confirm that controls are at the right level of maturity to meet business needs and they consider maturity attributes to find ways to make controls more efficient and effective. The organization benchmarks to external best practices and seeks external advice on internal control effectiveness. For critical processes, independent reviews take place to provide assurance that the controls are at the desired level of maturity and working as planned. |

The maturity model evaluation is one of the final steps in the evaluation process. The IT audit and assurance professional can address the key controls within the scope of the work program and formulate an objective assessment of the maturity levels of the control practices. The maturity assessment can be a part of the audit/assurance report, and used as a metric from year to year to document progression in the enhancement of controls. However, it must be noted that the perception of the maturity level may vary between the process/IT asset owner and the auditor. Therefore, an auditor should obtain the concerned stakeholder's concurrence before submitting the final report to management.

At the conclusion of the review, once all findings and recommendations are completed, the professional assesses the current state of the CobiT control framework

and assigns it a maturity level using the six-level scale. Some practitioners utilize decimals (x.25, x.5, x.75) to indicate gradations in the maturity model. As a further reference, CoBiT provides a definition of the maturity designations by control objective. While this approach is not mandatory, the process is provided as a separate section at the end of the audit/assurance program for those enterprises that wish to implement it. It is suggested that a maturity assessment be made at the CoBiT control level. To provide further value to the client/customer, the professional can also obtain maturity targets from the client/customer. Using the assessed and target maturity levels, the professional can create an effective graphic presentation that describes the achievement or gaps between the actual and targeted maturity goals.

## IV. Assurance and Control Framework
### ISACA IT Assurance Framework and Standards
ISACA has long recognized the specialized nature of IT assurance and strives to advance globally applicable standards. Guidelines and procedures provide detailed guidance on how to follow those standards. IT Audit/Assurance Standard S15 IT Controls, and IT Audit and Assurance Guideline G38 Access Controls are relevant to this audit/assurance program.

### ISACA Controls Framework
CoBiT is an IT governance framework and supporting tool set that allows managers to bridge the gap among control requirements, technical issues and business risks. CoBiT enables clear policy development and good practice for IT control throughout enterprises.

Utilizing CoBiT as the control framework on which IT audit/assurance activities are based aligns IT audit/assurance with good practices as developed by the enterprise.

Refer to ISACA's *CoBiT Control Practices:  Guidance to Achieve Control Objectives for Successful IT Governance, 2nd Edition*, published in 2007, for the related control practice value and risk drivers.

## V. Executive Summary of Audit/Assurance Focus
### SAP ERP Security
The review of SAP helps management ensure that it is secure. Since launching its first product offering almost 30 years ago, SAP has grown globally. It has approximately 12 million users and 96,400 installations in more than 120 countries and is the third-largest independent software company in the world. The company name, SAP, is a German acronym that loosely translates in English to Systems, Applications and Products in data processing.

Before SAP ERP, SAP had two main products:  the mainframe system SAP® R/2® and the client/server-based system SAP R/3. Both R/2 and R/3 are targeted to business application solutions and feature complexity, business and organizational experience, and integration. The R/2 and R/3 terminology is sometimes taken to mean release 2 and release 3, respectively; however, this is not the case. The R in R/2 and R/3 means "real time." Release levels are annotated separately to the R/2 or R/3 descriptors. For example, in SAP R/3 4.6B, the 4 is the major release number, the 6 is the minor release number following a major release, and the B is the version within a release.

R/3 was introduced in 1992 with a three-tier architecture paradigm. In recent years, SAP has introduced Service Oriented Architecture (SOA) as part of SAP ERP. This combines ERP with an open technology platform that can integrate SAP and non-SAP systems on the SAP NetWeaver® platform. The current core ERP solution offered by SAP is called SAP Enterprise Central Component (ECC 6.0), referred to here as SAP ERP.

### Business Impact and Risk
SAP is widely used in many enterprises. Improper configuration of SAP could result in an inability for the enterprise to execute its critical processes.

Risks resulting from ineffective or incorrect configurations or use of SAP could result in some of the following:
• Disclosure of privileged information
• Single points of failure
• Low data quality
• Loss of physical assets
• Loss of intellectual property
• Loss of competitive advantage
• Loss of customer confidence
• Violation of regulatory requirements

### Objective and Scope
**Objective**—The objective of the SAP ERP audit/assurance review is to provide management with an independent assessment relating to the effectiveness of configuration and security of the enterprise's SAP ERP architecture.

**Scope**—The review will focus on configuration of the relevant SAP ERP components and modules within the enterprise. The selection of the specific components and modules will be based upon the risks introduced to the enterprise by these components and modules.

### Minimum Audit Skills
This review is considered highly technical. The IT audit and assurance professional must have an understanding of SAP best practice processes and requirements, and be highly conversant in SAP tools, exposures and functionality. It should not be assumed that an audit and assurance professional holding the CISA designation has the requisite skills to perform this review.

## VI. Revenue Business Cycle—Audit/Assurance Program

| Audit/Assurance Program Step | CobiT Cross-reference | COSO | | | | | Reference Hyperlink | Issue Cross-reference | Comments |
|---|---|---|---|---|---|---|---|---|---|
| | | Control Environment | Risk Assessment | Control Activities | Information and Communication | Monitoring | | | |
| **A. Prior Audit/Examination Report Follow-up** | | | | | | | | | |
| 1. Review prior report, if one exists, verify completion of any agreed-upon corrections and note remaining deficiencies. | ME1 | | | | | | | | |
| 1.1 Determine whether:<br>• Senior management has assigned responsibilities for information, its processing and its use<br>• User management is responsible for providing information that supports the entity's objectives and policies<br>• Information systems management is responsible for providing the capabilities necessary for achievement of the defined information systems objectives and policies of the entity<br>• Senior management approves plans for development and acquisition of information systems<br>• There are procedures to ensure that the information system being developed or acquired meets user requirements<br>• There are procedures to ensure that information systems, programs and configuration changes are tested adequately prior to implementation<br>• All personnel involved in the system acquisition and configuration activities receive adequate training and supervision | ME1 | | | | | | | | |

## VI. Revenue Business Cycle—Audit/Assurance Program (cont.)

| Audit/Assurance Program Step | CobiT Cross-reference | COSO | | | | | Reference Hyperlink | Issue Cross-reference | Comments |
|---|---|---|---|---|---|---|---|---|---|
| | | Control Environment | Risk Assessment | Control Activities | Information and Communication | Monitoring | | | |
| **A. Prior Audit/Examination Report Follow-up (cont.)** | | | | | | | | | |
| 1.1 *(cont.)* <br> • There are procedures to ensure that information systems are implemented/configured/upgraded in accordance with the established standards <br> • User management participates in the conversion of data from the existing system to the new system <br> • Final approval is obtained from user management prior to going live with a new information/upgraded system <br> • There are procedures to document and schedule all changes to information systems (including key ABAP programs) <br> • There are procedures to ensure that only authorized changes are initiated <br> • There are procedures for the approval, monitoring and control of the acquisition and upgrade of hardware and systems software <br> • There are procedures to allow for and control emergency changes <br> • There are procedures to ensure that only authorized, tested and documented changes to information systems are accepted into the production client <br> • There is a process for monitoring the volume of named and concurrent SAP ERP users to ensure that the license agreement is not being violated | | | | | | | | | |

## VI. Revenue Business Cycle—Audit/Assurance Program (cont.)

| Audit/Assurance Program Step | CobiT Cross-reference | COSO | | | | | Reference Hyperlink | Issue Cross-reference | Comments |
| --- | --- | --- | --- | --- | --- | --- | --- | --- | --- |
| | | Control Environment | Risk Assessment | Control Activities | Information and Communication | Monitoring | | | |
| **A. Prior Audit/Examination Report Follow-up** *(cont.)* | | | | | | | | | |
| 1.1 *(cont.)*<br>• The organization structure, established by senior management, provides for an appropriate segregation of incompatible functions<br>• The database, application and presentation servers are located in a physically separate and protected environment (i.e., a data center)<br>• Emergency, backup and recovery plans are documented and tested on a regular basis to ensure that they remain current and operational<br>• Backup and recovery plans allow users of information systems to resume operations in the event of an interruption<br>• Application controls are designed with regard to any weaknesses in segregation, security, development and processing controls that may affect the information system<br>• Access to the Implementation Guide (IMG) during production has been restricted<br>• The production client settings have been flagged to not allow changes to programs and configuration | | | | | | | | | |

## VI. Revenue Business Cycle—Audit/Assurance Program (cont.)

| Audit/Assurance Program Step | CoBiT Cross-reference | COSO | | | | | | Reference Hyperlink | Issue Cross-reference | Comments |
| --- | --- | --- | --- | --- | --- | --- | --- | --- | --- | --- |
| | | Control Environment | Risk Assessment | Control Activities | Information and Communication | Monitoring | | | | |
| **B. Preliminary Audit Steps** | | | | | | | | | | |
| 1. Gain an understanding of the SAP ERP environment. | | | | | | | | | | |
| 1.1 The same background information obtained for the SAP ERP Basis Security audit plan is required for and relevant to the business cycles. In particular, the following information is important:<br>• Version and release of SAP ERP implemented<br>• Total number of named users (for comparison with logical access security testing results)<br>• Number of SAP instances and clients<br>• Accounting period, company codes and chart of accounts<br>• Identification of the components being used (Human Capital Management, Financials, Operations, Corporate Services)<br>• Whether the organization has created any locally developed ABAP programs or reports<br>• Details of the risk assessment approach taken in the organization to identify and prioritize risks<br>• Copies of the organization's key security policies and standards | PO2<br>PO3<br>PO4<br>PO6<br>PO9<br>DS2<br>DS5<br>AI2<br>AI6<br>ME1<br>ME2 | | | | | | | | | |

## VI. Revenue Business Cycle—Audit/Assurance Program (cont.)

| Audit/Assurance Program Step | CobiT Cross-reference | COSO | | | | | Reference Hyperlink | Issue Cross-reference | Comments |
| --- | --- | --- | --- | --- | --- | --- | --- | --- | --- |
| | | Control Environment | Risk Assessment | Control Activities | Information and Communication | Monitoring | | | |
| **B. Preliminary Audit Steps (cont.)** | | | | | | | | | |
| 1.2 Obtain details of the following:<br>• Organizational Management Model as it relates to sales/revenue activity, i.e., sales organization unit structure in SAP ERP and company sales organization chart (required when evaluating the results of access security control testing)<br>• An interview of the systems implementation team, if possible, and process design documentation for sales and distribution | AI1<br>DS5<br>DS6 | | | | | | | | |
| 2. Identify the significant risks and determine the key controls. | | | | | | | | | |
| 2.1 Develop a high-level process flow diagram and overall understanding of the Revenue processing cycle, including the following subprocesses:<br>• Maintain pricing/customer master data<br>• Sales order processing<br>• Invoice processing<br>• Payment receipt | PO9<br>AI1<br>DS13 | | | | | | | | |
| 2.2 Assess the key risks, determine key controls or control weaknesses, and test controls (refer to sample testing program below and chapter 4 for techniques for testing configurable controls and logical access security) regarding the following factors:<br>• The controls culture of the organization (e.g., a just-enough control philosophy) | PO9<br>DS5<br>DS9<br>ME2 | | | | | | | | |

## VI. Revenue Business Cycle—Audit/Assurance Program (cont.)

| Audit/Assurance Program Step | CobiT Cross-reference | COSO | | | | | Reference Hyperlink | Issue Cross-reference | Comments |
|---|---|---|---|---|---|---|---|---|---|
| | | Control Environment | Risk Assessment | Control Activities | Information and Communication | Monitoring | | | |
| **B. Preliminary Audit Steps (cont.)** | | | | | | | | | |
| 2.2 (cont.)<br>• The need to exercise judgment to determine the key controls in the process and whether the controls structure is adequate (Any weaknesses in the control structure should be reported to executive management and resolved.) | | | | | | | | | |
| **C. Detailed Audit Steps** | | | | | | | | | |
| **1. Maintain customer/pricing master data.** | | | | | | | | | |
| **1.1 Changes made to master data are valid, complete, accurate and timely.** | | | | | | | | | |
| 1.1.1 Determine whether the following reports of changes to master data have been compared to authorized source documents and/or a manual log of requested changes to ensure they were input accurately and on a timely basis:<br>• For customer master data, use transaction code OV51 (also accessible using transaction code SA38 and program RFDABL00) to generate a list denoting the date and time of change, old and new values for fields, and details of the user who input the change. | AI2<br>AI6<br>DS6<br>DS11 | | | X | | | | | |

## VI. Revenue Business Cycle—Audit/Assurance Program (cont.)

| Audit/Assurance Program Step | CobiT Cross-reference | COSO | | | | | Reference Hyperlink | Issue Cross-reference | Comments |
|---|---|---|---|---|---|---|---|---|---|
| | | Control Environment | Risk Assessment | Control Activities | Information and Communication | Monitoring | | | |
| **C. Detailed Audit Steps (cont.)** | | | | | | | | | |
| 1.1.1 (cont.) <br>• Use transaction code S_ALR_87009993 (also accessible using transaction code SA38 and program RFDKLIAB) to display changes to credit management and credit information change details for comparison to authorized source documents. <br>• Use transaction MM04 to display master data changes for individual materials. <br>• Generate a list of pricing changes using transaction VK12 and subsequently selecting the following path from menu options: Environment ▶ Changes ▶ Change Report. Check the accuracy of changes made to the pricing master records and also the time at which these changes have been applied (which is essential to the effective processing of pricing changes) against authorized source documentation. | | | | | | | | | |

## VI. Revenue Business Cycle—Audit/Assurance Program (cont.)

| Audit/Assurance Program Step | CobiT Cross-reference | COSO | | | | | Reference Hyperlink | Issue Cross-reference | Comments |
|---|---|---|---|---|---|---|---|---|---|
| | | Control Environment | Risk Assessment | Control Activities | Information and Communication | Monitoring | | | |
| **C. Detailed Audit Steps *(cont.)*** | | | | | | | | | |
| 1.1.2 Review organization policy and process design specifications regarding access to maintain master data. Test user access to create and maintain customer, material and pricing master data as follows:<br>• Customer master data—Transaction codes FD01/FD02/FD05/FD06 (Finance), VD01/VD02/VD05/VD06 (Sales), XD01/XD02/XD05/XD06/XD07/XD99 (Central)<br>• Material master data—Transaction codes MM01 (Create), MM02 (Change), MM06 (Delete)<br>• Pricing master data—Transaction codes VK11 and VK12 | AI2<br>AI6<br>DS5<br>DS11 | | | X | | | | | |
| 1.1.3 Determine whether the configurable control settings address the risks pertaining to the validity, completeness and accuracy of master data and whether they have been set in accordance with management intentions. View the settings online using the IMG as follows:<br>• Customer Account Groups: Transaction SPRO Menu Path—Financial Accounting ▲ Accounts Receivable and Accounts Payable ▲ Customer Accounts ▶ Master Data ▲ Preparation for Creating Customer Master Data ▲ Define Account Group With Screen Layout (Customers) | P09<br>DS9<br>DS11<br>DS12 | | | X | | | | | |

## VI. Revenue Business Cycle—Audit/Assurance Program (cont.)

| Audit/Assurance Program Step | CobiT Cross-reference | COSO | | | | | Reference Hyperlink | Issue Cross-reference | Comments |
|---|---|---|---|---|---|---|---|---|---|
| | | Control Environment | Risk Assessment | Control Activities | Information and Communication | Monitoring | | | |
| **C. Detailed Audit Steps (cont.)** | | | | | | | | | |
| 1.1.3 (cont.) <br> • Material Types: Transaction SPRO Menu Path—Logistics—General ▶ Material Master ▶ Basic Settings ▶ Material Types ▶ Define Attributes of Material Types <br> • Industry Sector: Transaction SPRO Path—Logistics—General ▶ Material Master ▶ Field Selection ▶ Define industry sectors and industry-sector specific field selection <br> • Understand the organization's pricing policy and its configuration in SAP ERP (e.g., hard-coded, manual override possible, user enters price). Pricing condition types and records can be reviewed against the organization's pricing policy using the following menu path and transaction codes: Transaction SPRO Menu Path—Sales and Distribution ▶ Basic Functions ▶ Pricing: <br> – V-44 for material price condition record <br> – V-48 for price list type condition records <br> – V-52 for customer-specific condition type | | | | | | | | | |

## VI. Revenue Business Cycle—Audit/Assurance Program (cont.)

| Audit/Assurance Program Step | C₀ʙᵢT Cross-reference | Control Environment | Risk Assessment | Control Activities | Information and Communication | Monitoring | Reference Hyperlink | Issue Cross-reference | Comments |
|---|---|---|---|---|---|---|---|---|---|
| **C. Detailed Audit Steps (cont.)** | | | | | | | | | |
| **1.2 Master data remain current and pertinent.** | | | | | | | | | |
| 1.2.1 Determine whether management runs the following reports, or equivalent, by master data type and confirm evidence of management's review of the data for currency and ongoing pertinence:<br>• Customer master data—Run transaction code F.20<br>• Material master data—Run transaction code MMS3<br>• Pricing master data—Run transaction code VK13<br><br>Transaction F.32 provides an overview of customers for which no credit limit has been entered. Check the output from transaction F.32 to confirm a credit limit has been set for customers in the range requiring a limit. | PO8<br>DS3<br>DS11<br>ME1 | | | X | | | | | |

279

## VI. Revenue Business Cycle—Audit/Assurance Program (cont.)

| Audit/Assurance Program Step | CobiT Cross-reference | Control Environment | Risk Assessment | Control Activities | Information and Communication | Monitoring | Reference Hyperlink | Issue Cross-reference | Comments |
|---|---|---|---|---|---|---|---|---|---|
| | | | | COSO | | | | | |
| **C. Detailed Audit Steps** *(cont.)* | | | | | | | | | |
| **2. Sales Order Purchasing** | | | | | | | | | |
| **2.1 Sales orders are processed with valid prices and terms and processing is complete, accurate and timely.** | | | | | | | | | |
| 2.1.1 Determine whether the ability to create, change or delete sales orders, contracts, and delivery schedules is restricted to authorized personnel by testing access to the following transactions:<br>• Create (VA01)/Change (VA02) Sales Order<br>• Create (VA31)/Change (VA32) Delivery Schedules<br>• Create (VA41)/Change (VA42) Contracts | | | | | | | | | |
| 2.1.2 Refer to master data integrity point 1.1.2. | | | | | | | | | |
| 2.1.3 Refer to master data integrity point 1.1.3. | | | | | | | | | |
| 2.1.4 Understand the policies and procedures regarding reconciliation of sales orders. Review operations activity at selected times and check for evidence that reconciliations are being performed. | | | | | | | | | |

## VI. Revenue Business Cycle—Audit/Assurance Program (cont.)

| Audit/Assurance Program Step | COBIT Cross-reference | COSO | | | | | | Reference Hyperlink | Issue Cross-reference | Comments |
|---|---|---|---|---|---|---|---|---|---|---|
| | | Control Environment | Risk Assessment | Control Activities | Information and Communication | Monitoring | | | | |
| **C. Detailed Audit Steps** *(cont.)* | | | | | | | | | | |
| **2.2. Orders are processed within approved customer credit limits.** | | | | | | | | | | |
| 2.2.1 Determine whether the configurable control settings address the risks pertaining to the processing of orders outside customer credit limits and whether they have been set in accordance with management intentions. View the settings online using the IMG as follows: <br>• Transaction SPRO Menu Path—Financial Accounting ▶ Accounts Receivable and Accounts Payable ▶ Credit Management ▶ Credit Control Account <br>• Execute transaction OVAK to show the type of credit check performed for the corresponding transaction types in order processing. <br>• Execute transaction OVA7 to determine whether a credit check is performed for appropriate document types being used. <br>• Execute transaction OVAD to show the credit groups that have been assigned to the delivery types being used. <br>• Execute transaction OVA8 to show an overview of defined credit checks for credit control areas. | | | | | | | | | | |

## VI. Revenue Business Cycle—Audit/Assurance Program (cont.)

| Audit/Assurance Program Step | CoBiT Cross-reference | COSO Control Environment | COSO Risk Assessment | COSO Control Activities | COSO Information and Communication | COSO Monitoring | Reference Hyperlink | Issue Cross-reference | Comments |
|---|---|---|---|---|---|---|---|---|---|
| **C. Detailed Audit Steps (cont.)** | | | | | | | | | |
| **2.3 Order entry data are completely and accurately transferred to the shipping and invoicing activities.** | | | | | | | | | |
| 2.3.1 Obtain a full list of incomplete sales documents from the system using transaction V.00 (also accessible using transaction code SA38 and program RVAUFERR). Review items on the list with the appropriate operational management, and ascertain whether there are legitimate reasons for the sales documents that remain incomplete. | | | | | | | | | |
| **3. Invoice Processing** | | | | | | | | | |
| **3.1 Controls are in place to prevent duplicate shipments or delay in the shipping of goods to customers.** | | | | | | | | | |
| 3.1.1 Generate the list of current system configuration settings relating to copy control between sales and shipping documents using transaction VTLA— Display Copying Control: Sales Document to Delivery Document. Select each combination of delivery type and sales document type, and click the Item button. | | | | | | | | | |

## VI. Revenue Business Cycle—Audit/Assurance Program (cont.)

| Audit/Assurance Program Step | CobiT Cross-reference | COSO | | | | | Reference Hyperlink | Issue Cross-reference | Comments |
| --- | --- | --- | --- | --- | --- | --- | --- | --- | --- |
| | | Control Environment | Risk Assessment | Control Activities | Information and Communication | Monitoring | | | |
| **C. Detailed Audit Steps** *(cont.)* | | | | | | | | | |
| 3.1.1 *(cont.)* Double-click on each item category, and verify that the entry for the indicator quantity/value pos/neg has been set to + (automatic update occurs between documents as deliveries are made for line items specified in the sales document). Depending on the volume of shipping and sales input manually it may also be necessary to verify a sample of shipping and sales input for accuracy. | | | | | | | | | |
| 3.1.2 Determine whether the following shipping reports are used to assist in controlling the shipping process:<br>• Backlog—V.15<br>• Process Delivery Due List—VL04<br>• Outbound Deliveries for Picking—VL06<br>• Outbound Deliveries for Confirmation —VL06C<br>• Outbound Deliveries to be Loaded —VL06L | | | | | | | | | |

## VI. Revenue Business Cycle—Audit/Assurance Program (cont.)

| Audit/Assurance Program Step | CobiT Cross-reference | COSO | | | | | Reference Hyperlink | Issue Cross-reference | Comments |
|---|---|---|---|---|---|---|---|---|---|
| | | Control Environment | Risk Assessment | Control Activities | Information and Communication | Monitoring | | | |
| **C. Detailed Audit Steps (cont.)** | | | | | | | | | |
| **3.2 Invoices are generated using authorized terms and prices and are accurately calculated and recorded.** | | | | | | | | | |
| 3.2.1 Display current system settings relating to invoice preparation online using the IMG: Transaction SPRO Menu Path—Sales and Distribution ▶ Billing ▶ Billing Documents. | | | | | | | | | |
| Determine whether the connection between source and target documents supports the accurate flow of billing details through the sales process and supports the accurate calculation and posting of invoice data. | | | | | | | | | |
| **3.3. All goods shipped are invoiced, in a timely manner.** | | | | | | | | | |
| 3.3.1 Execute transaction VF04—Process Billing Due List. All goods/services that have not been invoiced, or that have been only partially invoiced, will appear on the list, sorted by invoice due date. Review the aging of items in the list. For items outstanding for more than one billing period, seek an explanation from management as to why the items have not been billed. | | | | | | | | | |

## VI. Revenue Business Cycle—Audit/Assurance Program (cont.)

| Audit/Assurance Program Step | CobiT Cross-reference | COSO | | | | | Reference Hyperlink | Issue Cross-reference | Comments |
|---|---|---|---|---|---|---|---|---|---|
| | | Control Environment | Risk Assessment | Control Activities | Information and Communication | Monitoring | | | |
| **C. Detailed Audit Steps (cont.)** | | | | | | | | | |
| 3.3.2 Assess user access to picking lists, delivery notes and goods issues by testing access to the following transactions:<br>• Create Single Delivery—VL01<br>• Process Delivery Due List—VL04<br>• Change Outbound Deliveries—VL02 | | | | | | | | | |
| 3.3.3 Execute transaction VF03 Display Invoice and click on the expansion button next to the billing document field and select Billing Documents Still to be Passed Onto Accounting. Obtain explanation for any invoices that appear in this list. Test user access to transactions to enter invoices and confirm this is consistent with staff job roles and management's intentions.<br>• Sales Accounts Receivable Entry—VF01 and VF04<br>• Finance Entry—FB70 | | | | | | | | | |
| **3.4 Credit notes and adjustments to accounts receivable are accurately calculated and recorded.** | | | | | | | | | |
| 3.4.1 Assess user access to sales order return and credit notes transactions as follows:<br>• Sales entry:  Create Sales Document—VA01<br>• Sales entry:  Change Sales Document—VA02<br>• Finance Entry—FB75 | | | | | | | | | |

## VI. Revenue Business Cycle—Audit/Assurance Program (cont.)

| Audit/Assurance Program Step | CobiT Cross-reference | COSO | | | | | Reference Hyperlink | Issue Cross-reference | Comments |
|---|---|---|---|---|---|---|---|---|---|
| | | Control Environment | Risk Assessment | Control Activities | Information and Communication | Monitoring | | | |
| **C. Detailed Audit Steps** *(cont.)* | | | | | | | | | |
| **3.5 Credit notes for all goods returned and adjustments to accounts receivable are issued in accordance with organization policy and in a timely manner.** | | | | | | | | | |
| 3.5.1 View the sales document types configured by using transaction VOV8. Look for the entire sales document types that relate to sales order returns and credit requests. Double-click on one of these document types. In the General Control section of the screen, there is a reference mandatory field. Verify that the setting has been set to M. Repeat this for all of the other relevant document types. Discuss the reference field settings in place for the selected document types with management. Determine whether the configuration in place is set as management intended. | | | | | | | | | |
| 3.5.2 Review the configuration settings for delivery and billing blocks online using the IMG as follows:<br>• Shipping: Transaction SPRO Menu Path—Logistics Execution ▲ Shipping ▲ Deliveries ▲ Define Reasons for Blocking in Shipping | | | | | | | | | |

## VI. Revenue Business Cycle—Audit/Assurance Program (cont.)

| Audit/Assurance Program Step | CobiT Cross-reference | COSO | | | | | Reference Hyperlink | Issue Cross-reference | Comments |
|---|---|---|---|---|---|---|---|---|---|
| | | Control Environment | Risk Assessment | Control Activities | Information and Communication | Monitoring | | | |
| **C. Detailed Audit Steps (cont.)** | | | | | | | | | |
| 3.5.2 (cont.) | | | | | | | | | |
| • Billing: Transaction SPRO Manu Path—Sales and Distribution ▷ Billing-Billing Documents ▷ Define Blocking ▷ Reason for Billing | | | | | | | | | |
| Determine whether the settings support the processing of credits in line with the organization's credit management policy and are consistent with management's intention. | | | | | | | | | |
| **4. Payment Receipt** | | | | | | | | | |
| **4.1 Cash receipts are entered accurately, completely and in a timely manner.** | | | | | | | | | |
| 4.1.1 Take a sample of bank reconciliations and test for adequate clearance of reconciling items and approval by finance management. | | | | | | | | | |
| 4.1.2 Determine whether the system has been configured to not allow processing of cash receipts outside of approved bank accounts. Execute transaction FI12 and ascertain to which bank accounts a cash receipt can be posted. Determine whether this is consistent with management's intentions. | | | | | | | | | |

## VI. Revenue Business Cycle—Audit/Assurance Program (cont.)

| Audit/Assurance Program Step | CobiT Cross-reference | COSO Control Environment | Risk Assessment | Control Activities | Information and Communication | Monitoring | Reference Hyperlink | Issue Cross-reference | Comments |
|---|---|---|---|---|---|---|---|---|---|
| **C. Detailed Audit Steps (cont.)** | | | | | | | | | |
| 4.1.3 Use the transaction code F.21—Customer Open Items (also accessible using transaction code SA38 and program RFDEPL00) to review customer open items. The report lists each item and the amount owed. At the end of the listing, the total amount still to be collected is calculated. Transaction code S_ALR_87009956 - Customer Open. | | | | | | | | | |
| **4.2 Cash receipts are valid and are not duplicated.** | | | | | | | | | |
| 4.2.1 Review the accounts receivable reconciliation and determine whether there are any amounts unallocated or any reconciling items. Determine the aging of these items and inquire of management as to the reasons for these items remaining unallocated or unreconciled. | | | | | | | | | |
| **4.3 Cash discounts are calculated and recorded accurately.** | | | | | | | | | |
| 4.3.1 Review the settings in place for tolerance levels for allowable cash discounts and cash payment differences by the following transactions:<br>• OBA4, to determine the tolerance groups that have been set up for users and the tolerance limits that have been set for those groups | | | | | | | | | |

## VI. Revenue Business Cycle—Audit/Assurance Program (cont.)

| Audit/Assurance Program Step | CobiT Cross-reference | COSO | | | | | Reference Hyperlink | Issue Cross-reference | Comments |
| --- | --- | --- | --- | --- | --- | --- | --- | --- | --- |
| | | Control Environment | Risk Assessment | Control Activities | Information and Communication | Monitoring | | | |
| **C. Detailed Audit Steps (cont.)** | | | | | | | | | |
| 4.3.1 (cont.)<br>• OB57, to determine the users who have been allocated to the groups identified earlier<br><br>Discuss with management the settings that are in place for tolerance levels for allowable cash discounts and cash payment differences. Determine whether the configuration in place agrees with management's intentions. | | | | | | | | | |
| **4.4 Timely collection of cash receipts is monitored.** | | | | | | | | | |
| 4.4.1 As for 4.1.3, determine whether accounts receivable aging reports are reviewed regularly to ensure that the collection of payments is being performed in a timely manner. | | | | | | | | | |

## VII. Revenue Business Cycle—Maturity Assessment

The maturity assessment is an opportunity for the reviewer to assess the maturity of the processes reviewed. Based on the results of audit/assurance review, and the reviewer's observations, assign a maturity level to each of the following CobiT control practices.

| CobiT Control Practice | Assessed Maturity | Target Maturity | Reference Hyperlink | Comments |
|---|---|---|---|---|
| **AI6.1 Change Standards and Procedures**<br>1. Develop, document and promulgate a change management framework that specifies the policies and processes, including:<br>• Roles and responsibilities<br>• Classification and prioritization of all changes based on business risk<br>• Assessment of impact<br>• Authorization and approval of all changes by the business process owners and IT<br>• Tracking and status of changes<br>• Impact on data integrity (e.g., all changes to data files being made under system and application control rather than by direct user intervention)<br>2. Establish and maintain version control over all changes.<br>3. Implement roles and responsibilities that involve business process owners and appropriate technical IT functions. Ensure appropriate segregation of duties.<br>4. Establish appropriate record management practices and audit trails to record key steps in the change management process. Ensure timely closure of changes. Elevate and report to management changes that are not closed in a timely fashion.<br>5. Consider the impact of contracted services providers (e.g., of infrastructure, application development and shared services) on the change management process. Consider integration of organizational change management processes with change management processes of service providers. Consider the impact of the organizational change management process on contractual terms and SLAs. | | | | |

## VII. Revenue Business Cycle—Maturity Assessment (cont.)

| CobiT Control Practice | Assessed Maturity | Target Maturity | Reference Hyperlink | Comments |
|---|---|---|---|---|
| **AI6.2 Impact Assessment, Prioritization and Authorization**<br>1. Develop a process to allow business process owners and IT to request changes to infrastructure, systems or applications. Develop controls to ensure that all such changes arise only through the change request management process.<br>2. Categorize all requested changes (e.g., infrastructure, operating systems, networks, application systems, purchased/packaged application software).<br>3. Prioritize all requested changes. Ensure that the change management process identifies both the business and technical needs for the change. Consider legal, regulatory and contractual reasons for the requested change.<br>4. Assess all requests in a structured fashion. Ensure that the assessment process addresses impact analysis on infrastructure, systems and applications. Consider security, legal, contractual and compliance implications of the requested change. Consider also interdependencies amongst changes. Involve business process owners in the assessment process, as appropriate.<br>5. Ensure that each change is formally approved by business process owners and IT technical stakeholders, as appropriate. | | | | |
| **AI6.4 Change Status Tracking and Reporting**<br>1. Ensure that a documented process exists within the overall change management process to declare, assess, authorize and record an emergency change.<br>2. Ensure that emergency changes are processed in accordance with the emergency change element of the formal change management process.<br>3. Ensure that all emergency access arrangements for changes are appropriately authorized, documented and revoked after the change has been applied.<br>4. Conduct a postimplementation review of all emergency changes, involving all concerned parties. The review should consider implications for aspects such as further application system maintenance, impact on development and test environments, application software development quality, documentation and manuals, and data integrity. | | | | |

## VII. Revenue Business Cycle—Maturity Assessment (cont.)

| CobiT Control Practice | Assessed Maturity | Target Maturity | Reference Hyperlink | Comments |
|---|---|---|---|---|
| **DS5.3 Identity Management**<br>1. Establish and communicate policies and procedures to uniquely identify, authenticate and authorize access mechanisms and access rights for all users on a need-to-know/need-to-have basis, based on predetermined and preapproved roles. Clearly state accountability of any user for any action on any of the systems and/or applications involved.<br>2. Ensure that roles and access authorization criteria for assigning user access rights take into account:<br>• Sensitivity of information and applications involved (data classification)<br>• Policies for information protection and dissemination (legal, regulatory, internal policies and contractual requirements)<br>• Roles and responsibilities as defined within the enterprise<br>• The need-to-have access rights associated with the function<br>• Standard but individual user access profiles for common job roles in the organization<br>• Requirements to guarantee appropriate segregation of duties<br>3. Establish a method for authenticating and authorizing users to establish responsibility and enforce access rights in line with sensitivity of information and functional application requirements and infrastructure components, and in compliance with applicable laws, regulations, internal policies and contractual agreements.<br>4. Define and implement a procedure for identifying new users and recording, approving and maintaining access rights. This needs to be requested by user management, approved by the system owner and implemented by the responsible security person.<br>5. Ensure that a timely information flow is in place that reports changes in jobs (i.e., people in, people out, people change). Grant, revoke and adapt user access rights in co-ordination with human resources and user departments for users who are new, who have left the organization, or who have changed roles or jobs. | | | | |

## VII. Revenue Business Cycle—Maturity Assessment (cont.)

| CoʙɪT Control Practice | Assessed Maturity | Target Maturity | Reference Hyperlink | Comments |
|---|---|---|---|---|
| **DS5.4 User Account Management**<br>1. Ensure that access control procedures include but are not limited to:<br>• Using unique user IDs to enable users to be linked to and held accountable for their actions<br>• Awareness that the use of group IDs results in the loss of individual accountability and are permitted only when justified for business or operational reasons and compensated by mitigating controls. Group IDs must be approved and documented.<br>• Checking that the user has authorization from the system owner for the use of the information system or service, and the level of access granted is appropriate to the business purpose and consistent with the organizational security policy<br>• A procedure to require users to understand and acknowledge their access rights and the conditions of such access<br>• Ensuring that internal and external service providers do not provide access until authorization procedures have been completed<br>• Maintaining a formal record, including access levels, of all persons registered to use the service<br>• A timely and regular review of user IDs and access rights<br>2. Ensure that management reviews or reallocates user access rights at regular intervals using a formal process. User access rights should be reviewed or reallocated after any job changes, such as transfer, promotion, demotion or termination of employment. Authorizations for special privileged access rights should be reviewed independently at more frequent intervals. | | | | |

## VII. Revenue Business Cycle—Maturity Assessment (cont.)

| CobiT Control Practice | Assessed Maturity | Target Maturity | Reference Hyperlink | Comments |
|---|---|---|---|---|
| **DS9.1 Configuration Repository and Baseline**<br>1. Implement a configuration repository to capture and maintain configuration management items. The repository should include hardware; application software; middleware; parameters; documentation; procedures; and tools for operating, accessing and using the systems, services, version numbers and licensing details.<br>2. Implement a tool to enable the effective logging of configuration management information within a repository.<br>3. Provide a unique identifier to a configuration item so the item can be easily tracked and related to physical asset tags and financial records.<br>4. Define and document configuration baselines for components across development, test and production environments, to enable identification of system configuration at specific points in time (past, present and planned).<br>5. Establish a process to revert to the baseline configuration in the event of problems, if determined appropriate after initial investigation.<br>6. Install mechanisms to monitor changes against the defined repository and baseline. Provide management reports for exceptions, reconciliation and decision making. | | | | |
| **DS9.2 Identification and Maintenance of Configuration Items**<br>1. Define and implement a policy requiring all configuration items and their attributes and versions to be identified and maintained.<br>2. Tag physical assets according to a defined policy. Consider using an automated mechanism, such as barcodes.<br>3. Define a policy that integrates incident, change and problem management procedures with the maintenance of the configuration repository.<br>4. Define a process to record new, modified and deleted configuration items and their relative attributes and versions. Identify and maintain the relationships between configuration items in the configuration repository.<br>5. Establish a process to maintain an audit trail for all changes to configuration items.<br>6. Define a process to identify critical configuration items in relationship to business functions (component failure impact analysis).<br>7. Record all assets—including new hardware and software, procured or internally developed—within the configuration management data repository.<br>8. Define and implement a process to ensure that valid licenses are in place to prevent the inclusion of unauthorized software. | | | | |

## VII. Revenue Business Cycle—Maturity Assessment (cont.)

| CobiT Control Practice | Assessed Maturity | Target Maturity | Reference Hyperlink | Comments |
|---|---|---|---|---|
| **DS9.3 Configuration Integrity Review**<br>1. To validate the integrity of configuration data, implement a process to ensure that configuration items are monitored. Compare recorded data against actual physical existence, and ensure that errors and deviations are reported and corrected.<br>2. Using automated discovery tools where appropriate, reconcile actual installed software and hardware periodically against the configuration database, license records and physical tags.<br>3. Periodically review against the policy for software usage the existence of any software in violation or in excess of current policies and license agreements. Report deviations for correction. | | | | |

# Expenditure Business Cycle

## *I. Introduction*

### *Overview*

ISACA developed *ITAF™: A Professional Practices Framework for IT Assurance* as a comprehensive and good-practice-setting model. ITAF provides standards that are designed to be mandatory and are the guiding principles under which the IT audit and assurance profession operates. The guidelines provide information and direction for the practice of IT audit and assurance. The tools and techniques provide methodologies, tools and templates to provide direction in the application of IT audit and assurance processes.

### *Purpose*

The audit/assurance program is a tool and template to be used as a road map for the completion of a specific assurance process. This audit/assurance program is intended to be utilized by IT audit and assurance professionals with the requisite knowledge of the subject matter under review, as described in ITAF, section 2200—General Standards. The audit/assurance programs are part of ITAF, section 4000—IT Assurance Tools and Techniques.

### *Control Framework*

The audit/assurance programs have been developed in alignment with the CoBiT framework—specifically CoBiT 4.1—using generally applicable and accepted good practices. They reflect ITAF, sections 3400—IT Management Processes, 3600—IT Audit and Assurance Processes, and 3800—IT Audit and Assurance Management.

Many enterprises have embraced several frameworks at an enterprise level, including the Committee of Sponsoring Organizations of the Treadway Commission (COSO) Internal Control Framework. The importance of the control framework has been enhanced due to regulatory requirements by the US Securities and Exchange Commission (SEC) as directed by the US Sarbanes-Oxley Act of 2002 and similar legislation in other countries. They seek to integrate control framework elements used by the general audit/assurance team into the IT audit and assurance framework. Since COSO is widely used, it has been selected for inclusion in this audit/assurance program. The reviewer may delete or rename columns in the audit program to align with the enterprise's control framework.

### *IT Governance, Risk and Control*

IT governance, risk and control are critical in the performance of any assurance management process. Governance of the process under review will be evaluated as part of the policies and management oversight controls. Risk plays an important role in evaluating what to audit and how management approaches and manages risk. Both issues will be evaluated as steps in the audit/assurance program. Controls are the primary evaluation point in the process. The audit/assurance program will identify the control objectives with steps to determine control design and effectiveness.

*Responsibilities of IT Audit and Assurance Professionals*
IT audit and assurance professionals are expected to customize this document
to the environment in which they are performing an assurance process. This
document is to be used as a review tool and starting point. It may be modified
by the IT audit and assurance professional; it is not intended to be a checklist or
questionnaire. It is assumed that the IT audit and assurance professional holds the
Certified Information Systems Auditor (CISA) designation, or has the necessary
subject matter expertise required to conduct the work and is supervised by a
professional with the CISA designation and necessary subject matter expertise to
adequately review the work performed.

## II. Using This Document
This audit/assurance program was developed to assist the audit and assurance
professional in designing and executing a review. Details regarding the format and
use of the document follow.

### Work Program Steps
The first column of the program describes the steps to be performed. The
numbering scheme used provides built-in work paper numbering for ease of
cross-reference to the specific work paper for that section. IT audit and assurance
professionals are encouraged to make modifications to this document to reflect the
specific environment under review.

### COBIT Cross-reference
The COBIT cross-reference provides the audit and assurance professional with
the ability to refer to the specific COBIT control objective that supports the
audit/assurance step. The COBIT control objective should be identified for
each audit/assurance step in the section. Multiple cross-references are not
uncommon. Processes at lower levels in the work program are too granular to be
cross-referenced to COBIT. The audit/assurance program is organized in a manner
to facilitate an evaluation through a structure parallel to the development process.
COBIT provides in-depth control objectives and suggested control practices at each
level. As the professional reviews each control, he/she should refer to COBIT 4.1 or
the *IT Assurance Guide: Using COBIT* for good-practice control guidance.

### COSO Components
As noted in the introduction, COSO and similar frameworks have become
increasingly popular among audit and assurance professionals. This ties the
assurance work to the enterprise's control framework. While the IT
audit/assurance function has COBIT as a framework, operational audit and
assurance professionals use the framework established by the enterprise. Since
COSO is the most prevalent internal control framework, it has been included in
this document and is a bridge to align IT audit/assurance with the rest of the
audit/assurance function. Many audit/assurance organizations include the COSO
control components within their report and summarize assurance activities to the
audit committee of the board of directors.

For each control, the audit and assurance professional should indicate the COSO component(s) addressed. It is possible, but generally not necessary, to extend this analysis to the specific audit step level.

The original COSO internal control framework contained five components. In 2004, COSO was revised as the *Enterprise Risk Management (ERM) Integrated Framework* and extended to eight components. The primary difference between the two frameworks is the additional focus on ERM and integration into the business decision model. ERM is in the process of being adopted by large enterprises. The two frameworks are compared in **figure AD1**.

| Figure AD1—Comparison of COSO Internal Control and ERM Integrated Frameworks | |
|---|---|
| **Internal Control Framework** | **ERM Integrated Framework** |
| **Control Environment:** The control environment sets the tone of an organization, influencing the control consciousness of its people. It is the foundation for all other components of internal control, providing discipline and structure. Control environment factors include the integrity, ethical values, management's operating style, delegation of authority systems, as well as the processes for managing and developing people in the organization. | **Internal Environment:** The internal environment encompasses the tone of an organization, and sets the basis for how risk is viewed and addressed by an enterprise's people, including risk management philosophy and risk appetite, integrity and ethical values, and the environment in which they operate. |
| | **Objective Setting:** Objectives must exist before management can identify potential events affecting their achievement. Enterprise risk management ensures that management has in place a process to set objectives and that the chosen objectives support and align with the enterprise's mission and are consistent with its risk appetite. |
| | **Event Identification:** Internal and external events affecting achievement of an enterprise's objectives must be identified, distinguishing between risks and opportunities. Opportunities are channeled back to management's strategy or objective-setting processes. |
| **Risk Assessment:** Every enterprise faces a variety of risks from external and internal sources that must be assessed. A precondition to risk assessment is establishment of objectives, and thus risk assessment is the identification and analysis of relevant risks to achievement of assigned objectives. Risk assessment is a prerequisite for determining how the risks should be managed. | **Risk Assessment:** Risks are analyzed, considering the likelihood and impact, as a basis for determining how they could be managed. Risk areas are assessed on an inherent and residual basis. |
| | **Risk Response:** Management selects risk responses—avoiding, accepting, reducing, or sharing risk—developing a set of actions to align risks with the enterprise's risk tolerances and risk appetite. |

| Figure AD1—Comparison of COSO Internal Control and ERM Integrated Frameworks *(cont.)* | |
|---|---|
| **Internal Control Framework** | **ERM Integrated Framework** |
| **Control Activities:** Control activities are the policies and procedures that help ensure that management directives are carried out. They help ensure that necessary actions are taken to address risks to achievement of the enterprise's objectives. Control activities occur throughout the organization, at all levels and in all functions. They include a range of activities as diverse as approvals, authorizations, verifications, reconciliations, reviews of operating performance, security of assets and segregation of duties. | **Control Activities:** Policies and procedures are established and implemented to help ensure the risk responses are effectively carried out. |
| **Information and Communication:** Information systems play a key role in internal control systems as they produce reports, including operational, financial and compliance-related information that make it possible to run and control the business. In a broader sense, effective communication must ensure information flows down, across and up the organization. Effective communication should also be ensured with external parties, such as customers, suppliers, regulators and shareholders. | **Information and Communication:** Relevant information is identified, captured, and communicated in a form and timeframe that enable people to carry out their responsibilities. Effective communication also occurs in a broader sense, flowing down, across, and up the enterprise. |
| **Monitoring:** Internal control systems need to be monitored—a process that assesses the quality of the system's performance over time. This is accomplished through ongoing monitoring activities or separate evaluations. Internal control deficiencies detected through these monitoring activities should be reported upstream and corrective actions should be taken to ensure continuous improvement of the system. | **Monitoring:** The entirety of enterprise risk management is monitored and modifications made as necessary. Monitoring is accomplished through ongoing management activities, separate evaluations, or both. |
| Information for **figure AD1** was obtained from the COSO web site *www.coso.org/aboutus.htm.* | |

The original COSO internal control framework addresses the needs of the IT audit and assurance professional: control environment, risk assessment, control activities, information and communication, and monitoring. As such, ISACA has elected to utilize the five-component model for these audit/assurance programs. As more enterprises implement the ERM model, the additional three columns can be added, if relevant. When completing the COSO component columns, consider the definitions of the components as described in **figure AD1**.

### *Reference/Hyperlink*
Good practices require the audit and assurance professional to create a work paper for each line item, which describes the work performed, issues identified and conclusions. The reference/hyperlink is to be used to cross-reference the audit/assurance step to the work paper that supports it. The numbering system of this document provides a ready numbering scheme for the work papers. If desired, a link to the work paper can be pasted into this column.

### *Issue Cross-reference*
This column can be used to flag a finding/issue that the IT audit and assurance professional wants to further investigate or establish as a potential finding. The potential findings should be documented in a work paper that indicates the disposition of the findings (formally reported, reported as a memo or verbal finding, or waived).

### *Comments*
The comments column can be used to indicate the waiving of a step or other notations. It is not to be used in place of a work paper describing the work performed.

## *III. Controls Maturity Analysis*
One of the consistent requests of stakeholders who have undergone IT audit/assurance reviews is a desire to understand how their performance compares to good practices. Audit and assurance professionals must provide an objective basis for the review conclusions. Maturity modeling for management and control over IT processes is based on a method of evaluating the organization, so it can be rated from a maturity level of nonexistent (0) to optimized (5). This approach is derived from the maturity model that the Software Engineering Institute (SEI) of Carnegie Mellon University defined for the maturity of software development.

The *IT Assurance Guide: Using CobiT*, appendix VII—Maturity Model for Internal Control, in **figure AD2**, provides a generic maturity model showing the status of the internal control environment and the establishment of internal controls in an enterprise. It shows how the management of internal control, and an awareness of the need to establish better internal controls, typically develops from an *ad hoc* to an optimized level. The model provides a high-level guide to help CobiT users appreciate what is required for effective internal controls in IT and to help position their enterprise on the maturity scale.

| Figure AD2—Maturity Model for Internal Control | | |
|---|---|---|
| **Maturity Level** | **Status of the Internal Control Environment** | **Establishment of Internal Controls** |
| 0 Nonexistent | There is no recognition of the need for internal control. Control is not part of the organization's culture or mission. There is a high risk of control deficiencies and incidents. | There is no intent to assess the need for internal control. Incidents are dealt with as they arise. |
| 1 Initial/*ad hoc* | There is some recognition of the need for internal control. The approach to risk and control requirements is *ad hoc* and disorganized, without communication or monitoring. Deficiencies are not identified. Employees are not aware of their responsibilities. | There is no awareness of the need for assessment of what is needed in terms of IT controls. When performed, it is only on an *ad hoc* basis, at a high level and in reaction to significant incidents. Assessment addresses only the actual incident. |
| 2 Repeatable but intuitive | Controls are in place but are not documented. Their operation is dependent on the knowledge and motivation of individuals. Effectiveness is not adequately evaluated. Many control weaknesses exist and are not adequately addressed; the impact can be severe. Management actions to resolve control issues are not prioritized or consistent. Employees may not be aware of their responsibilities. | Assessment of control needs occurs only when needed for selected IT processes to determine the current level of control maturity, the target level that should be reached and the gaps that exist. An informal workshop approach, involving IT managers and the team involved in the process, is used to define an adequate approach to controls for the process and to motivate an agreed-upon action plan. |
| 3 Defined | Controls are in place and adequately documented. Operating effectiveness is evaluated on a periodic basis and there is an average number of issues. However, the evaluation process is not documented. While management is able to deal predictably with most control issues, some control weaknesses persist and impacts could still be severe. Employees are aware of their responsibilities for control. | Critical IT processes are identified based on value and risk drivers. A detailed analysis is performed to identify control requirements and the root cause of gaps and to develop improvement opportunities. In addition to facilitated workshops, tools are used and interviews are performed to support the analysis and ensure that an IT process owner owns and drives the assessment and improvement process. |

| | Figure AD2—Maturity Model for Internal Control *(cont.)* | |
|---|---|---|
| **Maturity Level** | **Status of the Internal Control Environment** | **Establishment of Internal Controls** |
| 4 Managed and measurable | There is an effective internal control and risk management environment. A formal, documented evaluation of controls occurs frequently. Many controls are automated and regularly reviewed. Management is likely to detect most control issues, but not all issues are routinely identified. There is consistent follow-up to address identified control weaknesses. A limited, tactical use of technology is applied to automate controls. | IT process criticality is regularly defined with full support and agreement from the relevant business process owners. Assessment of control requirements is based on policy and the actual maturity of these processes, following a thorough and measured analysis involving key stakeholders. Accountability for these assessments is clear and enforced. Improvement strategies are supported by business cases. Performance in achieving the desired outcomes is consistently monitored. External control reviews are organized occasionally. |
| 5 Optimized | An enterprisewide risk and control program provides continuous and effective control and risk issues resolution. Internal control and risk management are integrated with enterprise practices, supported with automated real-time monitoring with full accountability for control monitoring, risk management and compliance enforcement. Control evaluation is continuous, based on self-assessments and gap and root cause analyses. Employees are proactively involved in control improvements. | Business changes consider the criticality of IT processes and cover any need to reassess process control capability. IT process owners regularly perform self-assessments to confirm that controls are at the right level of maturity to meet business needs and they consider maturity attributes to find ways to make controls more efficient and effective. The organization benchmarks to external best practices and seeks external advice on internal control effectiveness. For critical processes, independent reviews take place to provide assurance that the controls are at the desired level of maturity and working as planned. |

The maturity model evaluation is one of the final steps in the evaluation process. The IT audit and assurance professional can address the key controls within the scope of the work program and formulate an objective assessment of the maturity levels of the control practices. The maturity assessment can be a part of the audit/assurance report, and used as a metric from year to year to document progression in the enhancement of controls. However, it must be noted that the perception of the maturity level may vary between the process/IT asset owner and the auditor. Therefore, an auditor should obtain the concerned stakeholder's concurrence before submitting the final report to management.

At the conclusion of the review, once all findings and recommendations are completed, the professional assesses the current state of the COBIT control framework

and assigns it a maturity level using the six-level scale. Some practitioners utilize decimals (x.25, x.5, x.75) to indicate gradations in the maturity model. As a further reference, CobiT provides a definition of the maturity designations by control objective. While this approach is not mandatory, the process is provided as a separate section at the end of the audit/assurance program for those enterprises that wish to implement it. It is suggested that a maturity assessment be made at the CobiT control level. To provide further value to the client/customer, the professional can also obtain maturity targets from the client/customer. Using the assessed and target maturity levels, the professional can create an effective graphic presentation that describes the achievement or gaps between the actual and targeted maturity goals.

## IV. Assurance and Control Framework
### ISACA IT Assurance Framework and Standards
ISACA has long recognized the specialized nature of IT assurance and strives to advance globally applicable standards. Guidelines and procedures provide detailed guidance on how to follow those standards. IT Audit/Assurance Standard S15 IT Controls, and IT Audit/Assurance Guideline G38 Access Controls are relevant to this audit/assurance program.

### ISACA Controls Framework
CobiT is an IT governance framework and supporting tool set that allows managers to bridge the gap among control requirements, technical issues and business risks. CobiT enables clear policy development and good practice for IT control throughout enterprises.

Utilizing CobiT as the control framework on which IT audit/assurance activities are based aligns IT audit/assurance with good practices as developed by the enterprise.

Refer to ISACA's *CobiT Control Practices: Guidance to Achieve Control Objectives for Successful IT Governance, 2nd Edition*, published in 2007, for the related control practice value and risk drivers.

## V. Executive Summary of Audit/Assurance Focus
### SAP ERP Security
The review of SAP helps management ensure that it is secure. Since launching its first product offering almost 30 years ago, SAP has grown globally. It has approximately 12 million users and 96,400 installations in more than 120 countries and is the third-largest independent software company in the world. The company name, SAP, is a German acronym that loosely translates in English to Systems, Applications and Products in data processing.

Before SAP ERP, SAP had two main products: the mainframe system SAP® R/2® and the client/server-based system SAP R/3. Both R/2 and R/3 are targeted to business application solutions and feature complexity, business and organizational experience, and integration. The R/2 and R/3 terminology is sometimes taken to mean release 2 and release 3, respectively; however, this is not the case. The R in R/2 and R/3 means "real time." Release levels are annotated separately to the R/2 or R/3 descriptors. For example, in SAP R/3 4.6B, the 4 is the major release number, the 6 is the minor release number following a major release, and the B is the version within a release.

R/3 was introduced in 1992 with a three-tier architecture paradigm. In recent years, SAP has introduced Service Oriented Architecture (SOA) as part of SAP ERP. This combines ERP with an open technology platform that can integrate SAP and non-SAP systems on the SAP NetWeaver® platform. The current core ERP solution offered by SAP is called SAP Enterprise Central Component (ECC 6.0), referred to here as SAP ERP.

### Business Impact and Risk
SAP is widely used in many enterprises. Improper configuration of SAP could result in an inability for the enterprise to execute its critical processes.

Risks resulting from ineffective or incorrect configurations or use of SAP could result in some of the following:
• Disclosure of privileged information
• Single points of failure
• Low data quality
• Loss of physical assets
• Loss of intellectual property
• Loss of competitive advantage
• Loss of customer confidence
• Violation of regulatory requirements

### Objective and Scope
**Objective**—The objective of the SAP ERP audit/assurance review is to provide management with an independent assessment relating to the effectiveness of configuration and security of the enterprise's SAP ERP architecture.

**Scope**—The review will focus on configuration of the relevant SAP ERP components and modules within the enterprise. The selection of the specific components and modules will be based upon the risks introduced to the enterprise by these components and modules.

### Minimum Audit Skills
This review is considered highly technical. The IT audit and assurance professional must have an understanding of SAP best practice processes and requirements, and be highly conversant in SAP tools, exposures and functionality. It should not be assumed that an audit and assurance professional holding the CISA designation has the requisite skills to perform this review.

## VI. Expenditure Business Cycle—Audit/Assurance Program

| Audit/Assurance Program Step | CobiT Cross-reference | COSO Control Environment | Risk Assessment | Control Activities | Information and Communication | Monitoring | Reference Hyperlink | Issue Cross-reference | Comments |
|---|---|---|---|---|---|---|---|---|---|
| **A. Prior Audit/Examination Report Follow-up** | | | | | | | | | |
| 1. Review prior report, if one exists, verify completion of any agreed-upon corrections and note remaining deficiencies. | ME1 | | | | | | | | |
| 1.1 Review prior report, if one exists, verify completion of any agreed-upon corrections and note remaining deficiencies. | ME1 | | | | | | | | |
| 1.2 Determine whether:<br>• Senior management has assigned responsibilities for information, its processing and its use<br>• User management is responsible for providing information that supports the entity's objectives and policies<br>• Information systems management is responsible for providing the capabilities necessary for achievement of the defined information systems objectives and policies of the entity<br>• Senior management approves plans for development and acquisition of information systems<br>• There are procedures to ensure that the information system being developed or acquired meets user requirements<br>• There are procedures to ensure that information systems, programs and configuration changes are tested adequately prior to implementation | ME1 | | | | | | | | |

## VI. Expenditure Business Cycle—Audit/Assurance Program (cont.)

| Audit/Assurance Program Step | CoBiT Cross-reference | COSO | | | | | | Reference Hyperlink | Issue Cross-reference | Comments |
| --- | --- | --- | --- | --- | --- | --- | --- | --- | --- | --- |
| | | Control Environment | Risk Assessment | Control Activities | Information and Communication | Monitoring | | | | |
| **A. Prior Audit/Examination Report Follow-Up** *(cont.)* | | | | | | | | | | |
| 1.2 *(cont.)* | | | | | | | | | | |
| • All personnel involved in the system acquisition and configuration activities receive adequate training and supervision | | | | | | | | | | |
| • There are procedures to ensure that information systems are implemented/configured/upgraded in accordance with the established standards | | | | | | | | | | |
| • User management participates in the conversion of data from the existing system to the new system | | | | | | | | | | |
| • Final approval is obtained from user management prior to going live with a new information/upgraded system | | | | | | | | | | |
| • There are procedures to document and schedule all changes to information systems (including key ABAP programs) | | | | | | | | | | |
| • There are procedures to ensure that only authorized changes are initiated | | | | | | | | | | |
| • There are procedures to ensure that only authorized, tested and documented changes to information systems are accepted into the production client | | | | | | | | | | |
| • There are procedures to allow for and control emergency changes | | | | | | | | | | |
| • There are procedures for the approval, monitoring and control of the acquisition and upgrade of hardware and systems software | | | | | | | | | | |

## VI. Expenditure Business Cycle—Audit/Assurance Program (cont.)

| Audit/Assurance Program Step | CobiT Cross-reference | Control Environment | Risk Assessment | Control Activities | Information and Communication | Monitoring | Reference Hyperlink | Issue Cross-reference | Comments |
|---|---|---|---|---|---|---|---|---|---|
| **A. Prior Audit/Examination Report Follow-up** *(cont.)* | | | | | | | | | |
| 1.2 *(cont.)*<br>• There is a process for monitoring the volume of named and concurrent SAP ERP users to ensure that the license agreement is not being violated<br>• The organization structure, established by senior management, provides for an appropriate segregation of incompatible functions<br>• The database, application and presentation servers are located in a physically separate and protected environment (i.e., a data center)<br>• Emergency, backup and recovery plans are documented and tested on a regular basis to ensure that they remain current and operational<br>• Backup and recovery plans allow users of information systems to resume operations in the event of an interruption<br>• Application controls are designed with regard to any weaknesses in segregation, security, development and processing controls that may affect the information system<br>• Access to the Implementation Guide (IMG) during production has been restricted<br>• The production client settings have been flagged to not allow changes to programs and configuration | | | | | | | | | |

## VI. Expenditure Business Cycle—Audit/Assurance Program (cont.)

| Audit/Assurance Program Step | CobiT Cross-reference | COSO | | | | | Reference Hyperlink | Issue Cross-reference | Comments |
|---|---|---|---|---|---|---|---|---|---|
| | | Control Environment | Risk Assessment | Control Activities | Information and Communication | Monitoring | | | |
| **B. Preliminary Audit Steps** | | | | | | | | | |
| 1. Gain an understanding of the SAP ERP environment. | | | | | | | | | |
| 1.1 The same background information obtained for the SAP ERP Basis Security audit plan is required for and relevant to the business cycles. In particular, the following information is important:<br>• Version and release of SAP ERP implemented<br>• Total number of named users (for comparison with logical access security testing results)<br>• Number of SAP instances and clients<br>• Accounting period, company codes and chart of accounts<br>• Identification of the components being used (Human Capital Management, Financials, Operations, Corporate Services)<br>• Whether the organization has created any locally developed ABAP programs or reports<br>• Details of the risk assessment approach taken in the organization to identify and prioritize risks<br>• Copies of the organization's key security policies and standards | PO2<br>PO3<br>PO4<br>PO6<br>PO9<br>DS2<br>DS5<br>AI2<br>AI6<br>ME2 | | | | | | | | |
| 1.2 Obtain details of the following:<br>• Organizational Management Model as it relates to expenditure activity, i.e., purchasing organization unit structure in SAP ERP and purchasing/accounts payable organization chart (required when evaluating the results of access security control testing) | AI1<br>DS5<br>DS6 | | | | | | | | |

## VI. Expenditure Business Cycle—Audit/Assurance Program (cont.)

| Audit/Assurance Program Step | CobiT Cross-reference | COSO | | | | | Reference Hyperlink | Issue Cross-reference | Comments |
|---|---|---|---|---|---|---|---|---|---|
| | | Control Environment | Risk Assessment | Control Activities | Information and Communication | Monitoring | | | |
| **B. Preliminary Audit Steps (cont.)** | | | | | | | | | |
| 1.2 (cont.)<br>• An interview of the systems implementation team, if possible, and process design documentation for materials management | | | | | | | | | |
| 2. Identify the significant risks and determine the key controls. | | | | | | | | | |
| 2.1 Develop a high-level process flow diagram and overall understanding of the Expenditure processing cycle, including the following subprocesses:<br>• Master data maintenance<br>• Purchasing<br>• Invoice processing<br>• Processing disbursements | P09<br>AI1<br>DS11 | | | | | | | | |
| 2.2 Assess the key risks, determine key controls or control weaknesses, and test controls (refer to sample testing program below and chapter IV for techniques for testing configurable controls and logical access security) regarding the following factors:<br>• The controls culture of the organization (e.g., a just-enough control philosophy)<br>• The need to exercise judgment to determine the key controls in the process and whether the controls structure is adequate (Any weaknesses in the control structure should be reported to executive management and resolved.) | P09<br>DS5<br>DS9<br>ME2 | | | | | | | | |

# VI. Expenditure Business Cycle—Audit/Assurance Program (cont.)

| Audit/Assurance Program Step | CobiT Cross-reference | COSO | | | | | Reference Hyperlink | Issue Cross-reference | Comments |
| --- | --- | --- | --- | --- | --- | --- | --- | --- | --- |
| | | Control Environment | Risk Assessment | Control Activities | Information and Communication | Monitoring | | | |
| **C. Detailed Audit Steps** | | | | | | | | | |
| **1. Master Data Maintenance** | | | | | | | | | |
| **1.1 Changes made to master data are valid, complete, accurate and timely.** | | | | | | | | | |
| 1.1.1 Determine whether the changes made to the master data are complete, accurate and timely. Using the specified transaction code or SA38, determine whether the following report of changes to master data are compared to authorized source documents and/or a manual log of requested changes to ensure that they were input accurately and on a timely basis: <br>• For vendor master data, use transaction code S_ALR_87010039 (also accessible through transaction code SA38 and program RFKABL00) to produce a list of master data changes. | AI6 DS11 | | | X | | | | | |
| 1.1.2 Determine whether access to create and change vendor pricing master data is restricted to a dedicated area and to authorized individuals. Review organization policy and process design specifications regarding access to maintain master data. Test user access by using transaction code SUIM ▶ Users ▶ Users by Complex Selection Criteria (also accessible using transaction code SA38 and program | | | | | | | | | |

## VI. Expenditure Business Cycle—Audit/Assurance Program (cont.)

| Audit/Assurance Program Step | CobiT Cross-reference | COSO | | | | | Reference Hyperlink | Issue Cross-reference | Comments |
| --- | --- | --- | --- | --- | --- | --- | --- | --- | --- |
| | | Control Environment | Risk Assessment | Control Activities | Information and Communication | Monitoring | | | |
| **C. Detailed Audit Steps *(cont.)*** | | | | | | | | | |
| 1.1.2 *(cont.)*<br>RSUSR002; refer to chapter 4 on how to test user access) to create and maintain vendor master data as follows:<br>• Finance entry—Transaction codes FK01 (Create), FK02 (Change), FK05 (Block/Unblock), FK06 (Delete)<br>• Purchasing entry—Transaction codes MK01 (Create), MK02 (Change), MK05 (Block/Unblock), MK06 (Delete)<br>• Centralized entry—Transaction codes XK01 (Create), XK02 (Change), XK05 (Block/Unblock), XK06 (Delete)<br><br>Test user access to transactions to maintain vendor pricing information<br>• Create info record—ME11<br>• Change info record—ME12<br>• Delete info record—ME15<br>• Create condition—MEK1<br>• Change condition—MEK2<br>• Create condition with reference—MEK4 | | | | | | | | | |

## VI. Expenditure Business Cycle—Audit/Assurance Program (cont.)

| Audit/Assurance Program Step | CobiT Cross-reference | Control Environment | Risk Assessment | Control Activities | Information and Communication | Monitoring | Reference Hyperlink | Issue Cross-reference | Comments |
|---|---|---|---|---|---|---|---|---|---|
| **C. Detailed Audit Steps** *(cont.)* | | | | | | | | | |
| 1.1.3 Determine whether the configurable control settings address the risks pertaining to the validity, completeness and accuracy of master data and whether they have been set in accordance with management intentions. View the settings online using transaction code OBD3 and ascertain whether account groups have been set up covering one-time vendor or other vendor accounts. For high-risk account groups such as one-time vendors, check whether authorization has been marked as a required field. | DS9 DS11 DS12 | | | X | | | | | |
| 1.1.4 Determine whether a naming convention should be used for vendor names (e.g., as per letterhead) to minimize the risk of establishing duplicated vendor master records. Extract a list of vendor account names from table LFA1 (fields: NAME 1 = name, LIFNR = vendor number). Review a sample for compliance with the organization's naming convention. View or search the list (using scan search software tools, if available) for potential duplicates. | P09 DS11 | | | X | | | | | |

## VI. Expenditure Business Cycle—Audit/Assurance Program (cont.)

| Audit/Assurance Program Step | CobiT Cross-reference | COSO | | | | | | Reference Hyperlink | Issue Cross-reference | Comments |
| | | Control Environment | Risk Assessment | Control Activities | Information and Communication | Monitoring | | | |
|---|---|---|---|---|---|---|---|---|---|
| **C. Detailed Audit Steps (cont.)** | | | | | | | | | |
| **1.2 Inventory master data remain current and pertinent.** | | | | | | | | | |
| 1.2.1 Determine whether management periodically reviews master data to check their currency and ongoing pertinence, and whether the appropriate management displays or produces a list of vendors using report RFKVZ00 or equivalent. Confirm evidence of management's review of the data on a rotating basis for currency and ongoing pertinence. | DS11 ME1 | | | X | | | | | |
| **2. Purchasing** | | | | | | | | | |
| **2.1 Purchase order entry and changes are valid, complete, accurate and timely.** | | | | | | | | | |
| 2.1.1 Determine whether purchase orders are handled with a valid process and terms and if processing is complete, accurate and timely. Determine whether the ability to create, change or cancel purchase requisitions, purchase orders and outline agreements (standing purchase orders) is restricted to authorized personnel by testing access to the following transactions:<br>• Create Purchase Requisition—ME51/ME51N<br>• Change Purchase Requisition—ME52/ME52N | DS5 DS11 | | | X | | | | | |

## VI. Expenditure Business Cycle—Audit/Assurance Program (cont.)

| Audit/Assurance Program Step | CobiT Cross-reference | COSO | | | | | Reference Hyperlink | Issue Cross-reference | Comments |
|---|---|---|---|---|---|---|---|---|---|
| | | Control Environment | Risk Assessment | Control Activities | Information and Communication | Monitoring | | | |
| **C. Detailed Audit Steps** *(cont.)* | | | | | | | | | |
| 2.1.1 *(cont.)* <br> • Release Purchase Requisition—ME54/ME54N <br> • Collective Release of Purchase Requisition—ME55 <br> • Create Purchase Order, Vendor Known—ME21/ME21N <br> • Change Purchase Order—ME22/ME22N | | | | | | | | | |
| 2.1.2 Determine whether the SAP ERP source list functionality allows specified materials to be purchased only from vendors included in the source list for the specified material. Through discussions with management, determine (types of) materials for which source lists should be available in the system. Also, determine (types of) materials for which a source list should not be present. Examine a selection of materials and view the corresponding source list using the following reports to corroborate the performance of the control activity in the appropriate accounting period: <br> • ME06 reports on all material items and whether they belong to a source list or not. | DS11 | | | X | | | | | |

## VI. Expenditure Business Cycle—Audit/Assurance Program (cont.)

| Audit/Assurance Program Step | CoBiT Cross-reference | Control Environment | Risk Assessment | Control Activities | Information and Communication | Monitoring | Reference Hyperlink | Issue Cross-reference | Comments |
|---|---|---|---|---|---|---|---|---|---|
| **C. Detailed Audit Steps *(cont.)*** | | | | | | | | | |
| 2.1.2 *(cont.)* <br>• MEOM shows all material items and any associated vendors (including historic data). To run MEOM, specify a material or a range of materials. Use the match code, click on the Search Help option and choose option J—material by material group— to get a list of materials. <br>• Select the previously mentioned sample of orders and check against source list reports to determine whether specific materials have been procured with unlisted vendors. | | | | | | | | | |
| 2.1.3 Determine whether the SAP ERP release strategy is used to authorize purchase orders, outline agreements (standing purchase orders) and unusual purchases (e.g., capital outlays). Obtain sufficient understanding of the system configuration to assess the adequacy of the release strategy as defined and implemented by the organization, as well as the function and effectiveness of established policies, procedures, standards and guidance. Execute the following transactions to obtain an understanding of the way the system has been configured: | DS5 <br>DS9 <br>DS13 <br>ME1 | | | X | | | | | |

## VI. Expenditure Business Cycle—Audit/Assurance Program (cont.)

### C. Detailed Audit Steps (cont.)

| Audit/Assurance Program Step | CobiT Cross-reference | COSO | | | | | Reference Hyperlink | Issue Cross-reference | Comments |
|---|---|---|---|---|---|---|---|---|---|
| | | Control Environment | Risk Assessment | Control Activities | Information and Communication | Monitoring | | | |
| **2.1.3** *(cont.)* | | | | | | | | | |
| • Release procedure: Purchase Orders— Transaction SPRO menu path: Materials Management ▲ Purchasing ▲ Purchase Order ▲ Release Procedure for Purchase Orders ▲ Define Release Procedure for Purchase Orders | | | | | | | | | |
| • Requisitions (with classification)— Transaction SPRO menu path: Material Management ▲ Purchasing ▲ Purchase Requisitions ▲ Release Procedure ▲ Procedure with Classification ▲ Set Up Procedure with Classification | | | | | | | | | |
| – Click on Release Strategy. Select the strategies one by one, by double-clicking on the strategy. Note the release codes that are shown and check authorization (authorization objects M_BANF_FRG and M_EINK_FRG) for these release codes. | | | | | | | | | |
| – Click on Classification. This will show the conditions under which the purchase document will be blocked. Ascertain whether these conditions comply with management's intentions. | | | | | | | | | |

## VI. Expenditure Business Cycle—Audit/Assurance Program (cont.)

| Audit/Assurance Program Step | CoBiT Cross-reference | COSO | | | | | | Reference Hyperlink | Issue Cross-reference | Comments |
| --- | --- | --- | --- | --- | --- | --- | --- | --- | --- | --- |
| | | Control Environment | Risk Assessment | Control Activities | Information and Communication | Monitoring | | | | |
| **C. Detailed Audit Steps** *(cont.)* | | | | | | | | | | |
| 2.1.3 *(cont.)* | | | | | | | | | | |
| • Release procedure: Purchase Requisitions (without classification)— Transaction SPRO menu path: Material Management ▶ Purchasing ▶ Purchase Requisitions ▶ Release Procedure ▶ Set Up Procedure Without Classification | | | | | | | | | | |
| – Click on Release Prerequisites. Note the release codes that are shown and check authorization for these release codes. | | | | | | | | | | |
| – Re-execute the above SPRO menu path and click on Determination of Release Strategy. This will show the conditions under which the purchase document will be blocked. Ascertain whether these conditions comply with management's intentions. | | | | | | | | | | |
| • Test user access to transactions for release strategies: | | | | | | | | | | |
| – Release Purchase Order—ME28 | | | | | | | | | | |
| – Release Outline Agreement—ME35 | | | | | | | | | | |
| – Release Purchase Requisition—ME54 | | | | | | | | | | |
| – Collective Release of Purchase Requisitions—ME55 | | | | | | | | | | |

## VI. Expenditure Business Cycle—Audit/Assurance Program (cont.)

| Audit/Assurance Program Step | CobiT Cross-reference | COSO | | | | | Reference Hyperlink | Issue Cross-reference | Comments |
|---|---|---|---|---|---|---|---|---|---|
| | | Control Environment | Risk Assessment | Control Activities | Information and Communication | Monitoring | | | |
| **C. Detailed Audit Steps (cont.)** | | | | | | | | | |
| **2.2 Goods are received only for valid purchase orders and goods receipts are recorded completely, accurately and in a timely manner.** | | | | | | | | | |
| 2.2.1 Determine whether goods (or materials or equipment) are received only when there are valid purchase orders, or if goods receipts are always recorded completely, accurately and in a timely manner. | DS5 DS9 | | | X | | | | | |
| Determine whether an investigation takes place when receipts have no purchase order or exceed the purchase order quantity by more than an established amount. Does management review exception reports of goods not received on time for recorded purchases? Run transaction code VL10B (also accessible using transaction code SA38 and program RM06EM00) to produce a listing of outstanding purchase orders. | | | | | | | | | |
| Ascertain from management whether there are any reasons for any long-outstanding items on the report. | | | | | | | | | |

## VI. Expenditure Business Cycle—Audit/Assurance Program (cont.)

| Audit/Assurance Program Step | CobiT Cross-reference | Control Environment | Risk Assessment | Control Activities | Information and Communication | Monitoring | Reference Hyperlink | Issue Cross-reference | Comments |
|---|---|---|---|---|---|---|---|---|---|
| **C. Detailed Audit Steps (cont.)** | | | | | | | | | |
| 2.2.2 Determine whether order entry data are transferred completely and accurately to the shipping and invoicing activities, and if the ability to input, change or cancel goods received transactions is restricted to authorized inbound logistics/raw materials personnel. Test user access to transactions for goods receipt as follows:<br>• Goods Receipt for Purchase Order—MB01<br>• Goods Receipts, Purchase Order<br>• Unknown—MB0A<br>• Goods Receipt for Production Order—MB31<br>• Other Goods Receipts—MB1C<br>• Cancel/Reverse Material Document—MBST<br><br>Test user access to high-risk movement types transaction code MB1C, authorization object M_MSEG_BWA and fields ACTV and movement types BWART 561 through 566. These special movement types reflect the initial stock entry in the SAP ERP system at the time of conversion to the SAP ERP system. | AI2<br>DS5<br>DS11 | | | X | | | | | |

## VI. Expenditure Business Cycle—Audit/Assurance Program (cont.)

**C. Detailed Audit Steps (cont.)**

| Audit/Assurance Program Step | CobiT Cross-reference | Control Environment | Risk Assessment | Control Activities | Information and Communication | Monitoring | Reference Hyperlink | Issue Cross-reference | Comments |
|---|---|---|---|---|---|---|---|---|---|
| **2.3 Defective goods are returned to suppliers in a timely manner.** | | | | | | | | | |
| 2.3.1 Determine whether defective goods (or materials or equipment) are returned in a timely manner to suppliers, are adequately segregated from other goods in a quality assurance bonding area, and are regularly monitored (assigned a specific movement type, e.g., 122) to ensure timely return to suppliers, and whether credit is received in a timely manner. Ascertain from management the movement type used to block processing and for returning rejected goods to suppliers (e.g., movement type 122). Execute transaction MB51 with the appropriate movement type. Determine whether there are any long-outstanding materials pending return to suppliers or receipt of appropriate credits. | DS2 DS11 | | | X | | | | | |

## VI. Expenditure Business Cycle—Audit/Assurance Program (cont.)

| Audit/Assurance Program Step | CobiT Cross-reference | COSO | | | | | Reference Hyperlink | Issue Cross-reference | Comments |
|---|---|---|---|---|---|---|---|---|---|
| | | Control Environment | Risk Assessment | Control Activities | Information and Communication | Monitoring | | | |
| **C. Detailed Audit Steps *(cont.)*** | | | | | | | | | |
| **3. Invoice Processing** | | | | | | | | | |
| **3.1 Amounts posted to accounts payable represent goods or services received.** | | | | | | | | | |
| 3.1.1 Determine whether amounts posted to accounts payable represent goods or services received; the ability to input, change, cancel or release vendor invoices for payment is restricted to authorized personnel; and the ability to input vendor invoices that do not have a purchase order and/or goods receipt is restricted to authorized personnel. Test user access to transactions for invoice processing:<br>• Enter Invoice—MRHR, MIRO, MR01<br>• Change Invoice—FB02<br>• Process Blocked Invoice—MR02<br>• Cancel Invoice—MR08<br>• Enter Credit Memo—MRHG | AI6<br>DS6<br>DS9 | | | X | | | | | |
| **3.2 Accounts payable amounts are calculated completely and accurately and recorded in a timely manner.** | | | | | | | | | |
| 3.2.1 Determine whether the SAP ERP software is configured to perform a three-way match. Transaction SPRO menu path: Materials Management ▷ Purchasing ▷ Purchase Order ▷ Define Screen Layout at Document Level | DS5<br>DS9 | | | X | | | | | |

## VI. Expenditure Business Cycle—Audit/Assurance Program (cont.)

| Audit/Assurance Program Step | CobiT Cross-reference | COSO | | | | | Reference Hyperlink | Issue Cross-reference | Comments |
|---|---|---|---|---|---|---|---|---|---|
| | | Control Environment | Risk Assessment | Control Activities | Information and Communication | Monitoring | | | |
| **C. Detailed Audit Steps (cont.)** | | | | | | | | | |
| 3.2.1 (cont.)<br>(Change View field selection at document level: Overview) by selecting ME21—Create Purchase Order and then selecting GR/IR Control. Determine whether GR/IR Control has been set globally to required entry. If the GR/IR Control indicator has not been set globally for all vendors, determine whether it has been set for particular vendors by displaying table LFM1, field name WEBRE, using transaction SE16. Where GR/IR Control has not been set, ascertain from management whether there are any reasons. | | | | | | | | | |
| 3.2.2 Determine whether the SAP ERP software is configured with quantity and price tolerance limits. Check tolerance limits for price variances and message settings for invoice verification (online matching) as follows:<br>• Variance settings: Execute transaction OMR6. The system will show an overview of the defined tolerance limits. Double-click on the entries that relate to the organization being audited. Check two entries: one for tolerance key PE (price) and one for tolerance key SE (discount). | DS9<br>DS10 | | | X | | | | | |

## VI. Expenditure Business Cycle—Audit/Assurance Program (cont.)

| Audit/Assurance Program Step | CobiT Cross-reference | COSO | | | | | Reference Hyperlink | Issue Cross-reference | Comments |
|---|---|---|---|---|---|---|---|---|---|
| | | Control Environment | Risk Assessment | Control Activities | Information and Communication | Monitoring | | | |
| **C. Detailed Audit Steps (cont.)** | | | | | | | | | |
| 3.2.2 (cont.) Note the values shown. Both a lower and upper limit may be specified as a percentage value. (PE also allows setting of an absolute value.) • Message settings: – Transaction SPRO menu path: Materials Management ▶ Purchasing ▶ Environment Data ▶ Define Attributes of System Messages – Click on the Position button. Enter values 00, 06 and 207 (message for price variance) and press Enter. Note the value in the cat field. Possible values are W for warning and E for error. Ascertain whether the values noted comply with management intentions. | | | | | | | | | |
| 3.2.3 Determine if GR/IR account balances using transaction code S_P6B_12000135 (also accessible using transaction code SA38 and program RM07MSAL) are executed and reviewed periodically. Check that there are appropriate procedures in place to investigate unmatched purchase orders. In particular, long-outstanding items should be followed up and cleared. | AI6 | | | X | | | | | |

## VI. Expenditure Business Cycle—Audit/Assurance Program (cont.)

| Audit/Assurance Program Step | CobiT Cross-reference | COSO | | | | | Reference Hyperlink | Issue Cross-reference | Comments |
|---|---|---|---|---|---|---|---|---|---|
| | | Control Environment | Risk Assessment | Control Activities | Information and Communication | Monitoring | | | |
| **C. Detailed Audit Steps (cont.)** | | | | | | | | | |
| 3.2.4 Determine whether reports of outstanding purchase orders are reviewed regularly. Run the transaction code SA38 and program RM06EM00 to produce a listing of purchase orders outstanding and review long-outstanding items with management. | PO11 | | | X | | | | | |
| 3.2.5 Determine whether the SAP ERP software restricts the ability to modify the exchange rate table to authorized personnel, management approves values in the centrally maintained exchange rate table and the SAP ERP software automatically calculates foreign currency translations based on values in the centrally maintained exchange rate table. Determine whether management reviews a sample of changes to exchange rates above a certain percentage with regard to the volume and value of foreign currency transactions for the organization. Test user access to the exchange rates and the related authorization objects:<br>• Exchange rate via standard transaction—First, execute transaction SUCU. Click on Position. Enter value V_TCURR and press Enter. Note the value in the authorization group field. Then test user access to transaction code OB08, authorization object: | AI6<br>DS5 | | | X | | | | | |

## VI. Expenditure Business Cycle—Audit/Assurance Program (cont.)

| Audit/Assurance Program Step | CobiT Cross-reference | COSO | | | | | Reference Hyperlink | Issue Cross-reference | Comments |
|---|---|---|---|---|---|---|---|---|---|
| | | Control Environment | Risk Assessment | Control Activities | Information and Communication | Monitoring | | | |
| **C. Detailed Audit Steps *(cont.)*** | | | | | | | | | |
| 3.2.5 *(cont.)*<br>field activity: value 02 and field authorization group: value noted with transaction SUCU.<br>• Exchange rate via view maintenance—First, execute transaction SUCU. Click on Position. Enter table name value V_T001R, click on Choose. Note the value in the authorization group field.<br><br>Do the same for table V_TCURF. Then test user access to transaction codes as follows with authorization object: S_TABU_DIS (Class Basis: Administration), field activity: 02 and field authorization group: value noted with transaction SUCU:<br>– Maintain Table Rounding Units—OB90<br>– Maintain Table Foreign Currency Ratios—OBBS<br>– Table View Maintenance—SM30 | | | | | | | | | |
| **3.3 Credit notes and other adjustments are calculated completely and accurately and recorded in a timely manner.** | | | | | | | | | |
| 3.3.1 Determine whether the ability to input, change, cancel or release credit notes is restricted to authorized personnel. Test user access to post invoices directly to vendor accounts:<br>• Enter Credit Note—MRHG<br>• Enter Invoice—MRHR, MIRO, MR01 | P02<br>DS5 | | | X | | | | | |

## VI. Expenditure Business Cycle—Audit/Assurance Program (cont.)

| Audit/Assurance Program Step | CobiT Cross-reference | COSO | | | | | Reference Hyperlink | Issue Cross-reference | Comments |
|---|---|---|---|---|---|---|---|---|---|
| | | Control Environment | Risk Assessment | Control Activities | Information and Communication | Monitoring | | | |
| **C. Detailed Audit Steps (cont.)** | | | | | | | | | |
| **4. Processing Disbursements** | | | | | | | | | |
| **4.1 Disbursements are made only for goods and services received, and are calculated accurately, recorded and distributed to the appropriate suppliers in a timely manner.** | | | | | | | | | |
| 4.1.1 Determine whether disbursements are made only for goods and services received, and are calculated accurately, recorded and distributed to the appropriate suppliers in a timely manner. Determine whether management approves the SAP ERP payment run parameter specification. Test user access to transactions to process disbursements:<br>• Automatic Payment Transactions—F110S<br>• Parameters for Payment—F110<br>• Payment With Printout—F-58 | DS5 P06 | | | X | | | | | |
| 4.1.2 Test user access to blocked invoices :<br>• Change Document—FB02<br>• Change Line Items—FB09<br>• Block/Unblock Vendor (Centrally)—XK05<br>• Block/Unblock Vendor—FK05 | | | | | | | | | |

## VII. Expenditure Business Cycle—Maturity Assessment

The maturity assessment is an opportunity for the reviewer to assess the maturity of the processes reviewed. Based on the results of audit/assurance review, and the reviewer's observations, assign a maturity level to each of the following CobiT control practices.

| CobiT Control Practice | Assessed Maturity | Target Maturity | Reference Hyperlink | Comments |
|---|---|---|---|---|
| **AI6.1 Change Standards and Procedures**<br>1. Develop, document and promulgate a change management framework that specifies the policies and processes, including:<br>• Roles and responsibilities<br>• Classification and prioritization of all changes based on business risk<br>• Assessment of impact<br>• Authorization and approval of all changes by the business process owners and IT<br>• Tracking and status of changes<br>• Impact on data integrity (e.g., all changes to data files being made under system and application control rather than by direct user intervention)<br>2. Establish and maintain version control over all changes.<br>3. Implement roles and responsibilities that involve business process owners and appropriate technical IT functions. Ensure appropriate segregation of duties.<br>4. Establish appropriate record management practices and audit trails to record key steps in the change management process. Ensure timely closure of changes. Elevate and report to management changes that are not closed in a timely fashion.<br>5. Consider the impact of contracted services providers (e.g., of infrastructure, application development and shared services) on the change management process. Consider integration of organizational change management processes with change management processes of service providers. Consider the impact of the organizational change management process on contractual terms and SLAs. | | | | |

327

## VII. Expenditure Business Cycle—Maturity Assessment (cont.)

| CobiT Control Practice | Assessed Maturity | Target Maturity | Reference Hyperlink | Comments |
|---|---|---|---|---|
| **AI6.2 Impact Assessment, Prioritization and Authorization**<br>1. Develop a process to allow business process owners and IT to request changes to infrastructure, systems or applications. Develop controls to ensure that all such changes arise only through the change request management process.<br>2. Categorize all requested changes (e.g., infrastructure, operating systems, networks, application systems, purchased/packaged application software).<br>3. Prioritize all requested changes. Ensure that the change management process identifies both the business and technical needs for the change. Consider legal, regulatory and contractual reasons for the requested change.<br>4. Assess all requests in a structured fashion. Ensure that the assessment process addresses impact analysis on infrastructure, systems and applications. Consider security, legal, contractual and compliance implications of the requested change. Consider also interdependencies among changes. Involve business process owners in the assessment process, as appropriate.<br>5. Ensure that each change is formally approved by business process owners and IT technical stakeholders, as appropriate. | | | | |
| **AI6.4 Change Status Tracking and Reporting**<br>1. Ensure that a documented process exists within the overall change management process to declare, assess, authorize and record an emergency change.<br>2. Ensure that emergency changes are processed in accordance with the emergency change element of the formal change management process.<br>3. Ensure that all emergency access arrangements for changes are appropriately authorized, documented and revoked after the change has been applied.<br>4. Conduct a postimplementation review of all emergency changes, involving all concerned parties. The review should consider implications for aspects such as further application system maintenance, impact on development and test environments, application software development quality, documentation and manuals, and data integrity. | | | | |

## VII. Expenditure Business Cycle—Maturity Assessment (cont.)

| CobiT Control Practice | Assessed Maturity | Target Maturity | Reference Hyperlink | Comments |
|---|---|---|---|---|
| **DS5.3 Identity Management**<br>1. Establish and communicate policies and procedures to uniquely identify, authenticate and authorize access mechanisms and access rights for all users on a need-to-know/need-to-have basis, based on predetermined and preapproved roles. Clearly state accountability of any user for any action on any of the systems and/or applications involved.<br>2. Ensure that roles and access authorization criteria for assigning user access rights take into account:<br>  • Sensitivity of information and applications involved (data classification)<br>  • Policies for information protection and dissemination (legal, regulatory, internal policies and contractual requirements)<br>  • Roles and responsibilities as defined within the enterprise<br>  • The need-to-have access rights associated with the function<br>  • Standard but individual user access profiles for common job roles in the organization<br>  • Requirements to guarantee appropriate segregation of duties<br>3. Establish a method for authenticating and authorizing users to establish responsibility and enforce access rights in line with sensitivity of information and functional application requirements and infrastructure components, and in compliance with applicable laws, regulations, internal policies and contractual agreements.<br>4. Define and implement a procedure for identifying new users and recording, approving and maintaining access rights. This needs to be requested by user management, approved by the system owner and implemented by the responsible security person.<br>5. Ensure that a timely information flow is in place that reports changes in jobs (i.e., people in, people out, people change). Grant, revoke and adapt user access rights in co-ordination with human resources and user departments for users who are new, who have left the organization, or who have changed roles or jobs. | | | | |

## VII. Expenditure Business Cycle—Maturity Assessment (cont.)

| CobiT Control Practice | Assessed Maturity | Target Maturity | Reference Hyperlink | Comments |
|---|---|---|---|---|
| **DS5.4 User Account Management**<br>1. Ensure that access control procedures include but are not limited to:<br>• Using unique user IDs to enable users to be linked to and held accountable for their actions<br>• Awareness that the use of group IDs results in the loss of individual accountability and are permitted only when justified for business or operational reasons and compensated by mitigating controls. Group IDs must be approved and documented.<br>• Checking that the user has authorization from the system owner for the use of the information system or service, and the level of access granted is appropriate to the business purpose and consistent with the organizational security policy<br>• A procedure to require users to understand and acknowledge their access rights and the conditions of such access<br>• Ensuring that internal and external service providers do not provide access until authorization procedures have been completed<br>• Maintaining a formal record, including access levels, of all persons registered to use the service<br>• A timely and regular review of user IDs and access rights<br>2. Ensure that management reviews or reallocates user access rights at regular intervals using a formal process. User access rights should be reviewed or reallocated after any job changes, such as transfer, promotion, demotion or termination of employment. Authorizations for special privileged access rights should be reviewed independently at more frequent intervals. | | | | |

## VII. Expenditure Business Cycle—Maturity Assessment (cont.)

| CobiT Control Practice | Assessed Maturity | Target Maturity | Reference Hyperlink | Comments |
|---|---|---|---|---|
| **DS9.1 Configuration Repository and Baseline**<br>1. Implement a configuration repository to capture and maintain configuration management items. The repository should include hardware; application software; middleware; parameters; documentation; procedures; and tools for operating, accessing and using the systems, services, version numbers and licensing details.<br>2. Implement a tool to enable the effective logging of configuration management information within a repository.<br>3. Provide a unique identifier to a configuration item so the item can be easily tracked and related to physical asset tags and financial records.<br>4. Define and document configuration baselines for components across development, test and production environments, to enable identification of system configuration at specific points in time (past, present and planned).<br>5. Establish a process to revert to the baseline configuration in the event of problems, if determined appropriate after initial investigation.<br>6. Install mechanisms to monitor changes against the defined repository and baseline. Provide management reports for exceptions, reconciliation and decision making. | | | | |
| **DS9.2 Identification and Maintenance of Configuration Items**<br>1. Define and implement a policy requiring all configuration items and their attributes and versions to be identified and maintained.<br>2. Tag physical assets according to a defined policy. Consider using an automated mechanism, such as barcodes.<br>3. Define a policy that integrates incident, change and problem management procedures with the maintenance of the configuration repository.<br>4. Define a process to record new, modified and deleted configuration items and their relative attributes and versions. Identify and maintain the relationships between configuration items in the configuration repository.<br>5. Establish a process to maintain an audit trail for all changes to configuration items.<br>6. Define a process to identify critical configuration items in relationship to business functions (component failure impact analysis).<br>7. Record all assets—including new hardware and software, procured or internally developed—within the configuration management data repository.<br>8. Define and implement a process to ensure that valid licenses are in place to prevent the inclusion of unauthorized software. | | | | |

## VII. Expenditure Business Cycle—Maturity Assessment (cont.)

| CobiT Control Practice | Assessed Maturity | Target Maturity | Reference Hyperlink | Comments |
|---|---|---|---|---|
| **DS9.3 Configuration Integrity Review**<br>1. To validate the integrity of configuration data, implement a process to ensure that configuration items are monitored. Compare recorded data against actual physical existence, and ensure that errors and deviations are reported and corrected.<br>2. Using automated discovery tools where appropriate, reconcile actual installed software and hardware periodically against the configuration database, license records and physical tags.<br>3. Periodically review against the policy for software usage the existence of any software in violation or in excess of current policies and license agreements. Report deviations for correction. | | | | |

# Inventory Business Cycle

## I. Introduction
### Overview
ISACA developed *ITAF™: A Professional Practices Framework for IT Assurance* as a comprehensive and good-practice-setting model. ITAF provides standards that are designed to be mandatory and are the guiding principles under which the IT audit and assurance profession operates. The guidelines provide information and direction for the practice of IT audit and assurance. The tools and techniques provide methodologies, tools and templates to provide direction in the application of IT audit and assurance processes.

### Purpose
The audit/assurance program is a tool and template to be used as a roadmap for the completion of a specific assurance process. This audit/assurance program is intended to be utilized by IT audit and assurance professionals with the requisite knowledge of the subject matter under review, as described in ITAF, section 2200—General Standards. The audit/assurance programs are part of ITAF, section 4000—IT Assurance Tools and Techniques.

### Control Framework
The audit/assurance programs have been developed in alignment with the CobiT framework—specifically CobiT 4.1—using generally applicable and accepted good practices. They reflect ITAF, sections 3400—IT Management Processes, 3600—IT Audit and Assurance Processes, and 3800—IT Audit and Assurance Management.

Many enterprises have embraced several frameworks at an enterprise level, including the Committee of Sponsoring Organizations of the Treadway Commission (COSO) Internal Control Framework. The importance of the control framework has been enhanced due to regulatory requirements by the US Securities and Exchange Commission (SEC) as directed by the US Sarbanes-Oxley Act of 2002 and similar legislation in other countries. They seek to integrate control framework elements used by the general audit/assurance team into the IT audit and assurance framework. Since COSO is widely used, it has been selected for inclusion in this audit/assurance program. The reviewer may delete or rename columns in the audit program to align with the enterprise's control framework.

### IT Governance, Risk and Control
IT governance, risk and control are critical in the performance of any assurance management process. Governance of the process under review will be evaluated as part of the policies and management oversight controls. Risk plays an important role in evaluating what to audit and how management approaches and manages risk. Both issues will be evaluated as steps in the audit/assurance program. Controls are the primary evaluation point in the process. The audit/assurance program will identify the control objectives with steps to determine control design and effectiveness.

*Responsibilities of IT Audit and Assurance Professionals*

IT audit and assurance professionals are expected to customize this document to the environment in which they are performing an assurance process. This document is to be used as a review tool and starting point. It may be modified by the IT audit and assurance professional; it is not intended to be a checklist or questionnaire. It is assumed that the IT audit and assurance professional holds the Certified Information Systems Auditor (CISA) designation, or has the necessary subject matter expertise required to conduct the work and is supervised by a professional with the CISA designation and necessary subject matter expertise to adequately review the work performed.

## II. Using This Document

This audit/assurance program was developed to assist the audit and assurance professional in designing and executing a review. Details regarding the format and use of the document follow.

### Work Program Steps

The first column of the program describes the steps to be performed. The numbering scheme used provides built-in work paper numbering for ease of cross-reference to the specific work paper for that section. IT audit and assurance professionals are encouraged to make modifications to this document to reflect the specific environment under review.

### CobiT Cross-reference

The CobiT cross-reference provides the audit and assurance professional with the ability to refer to the specific CobiT control objective that supports the audit/assurance step. The CobiT control objective should be identified for each audit/assurance step in the section. Multiple cross-references are not uncommon. Processes at lower levels in the work program are too granular to be cross-referenced to CobiT. The audit/assurance program is organized in a manner to facilitate an evaluation through a structure parallel to the development process. CobiT provides in-depth control objectives and suggested control practices at each level. As the professional reviews each control, he/she should refer to CobiT 4.1 or the *IT Assurance Guide: Using CobiT* for good-practice control guidance.

### COSO Components

As noted in the introduction, COSO and similar frameworks have become increasingly popular among audit and assurance professionals. This ties the assurance work to the enterprise's control framework. While the IT audit/assurance function has CobiT as a framework, operational audit and assurance professionals use the framework established by the enterprise. Since COSO is the most prevalent internal control framework, it has been included in this document and is a bridge to align IT audit/assurance with the rest of the audit/assurance function. Many audit/assurance organizations include the COSO control components within their report and summarize assurance activities to the audit committee of the board of directors.

For each control, the audit and assurance professional should indicate the COSO component(s) addressed. It is possible, but generally not necessary, to extend this analysis to the specific audit step level.

The original COSO internal control framework contained five components. In 2004, COSO was revised as the *Enterprise Risk Management (ERM) Integrated Framework* and extended to eight components. The primary difference between the two frameworks is the additional focus on ERM and integration into the business decision model. ERM is in the process of being adopted by large enterprises. The two frameworks are compared in **figure AD1**.

| Figure AD1—Comparison of COSO Internal Control and ERM Integrated Frameworks | |
|---|---|
| **Internal Control Framework** | **ERM Integrated Framework** |
| **Control Environment:** The control environment sets the tone of an organization, influencing the control consciousness of its people. It is the foundation for all other components of internal control, providing discipline and structure. Control environment factors include the integrity, ethical values, management's operating style, delegation of authority systems, as well as the processes for managing and developing people in the organization. | **Internal Environment:** The internal environment encompasses the tone of an organization, and sets the basis for how risk is viewed and addressed by an enterprise's people, including risk management philosophy and risk appetite, integrity and ethical values, and the environment in which they operate. |
| | **Objective Setting:** Objectives must exist before management can identify potential events affecting their achievement. Enterprise risk management ensures that management has in place a process to set objectives and that the chosen objectives support and align with the enterprise's mission and are consistent with its risk appetite. |
| | **Event Identification:** Internal and external events affecting achievement of an enterprise's objectives must be identified, distinguishing between risks and opportunities. Opportunities are channeled back to management's strategy or objective-setting processes. |
| **Risk Assessment:** Every enterprise faces a variety of risks from external and internal sources that must be assessed. A precondition to risk assessment is establishment of objectives, and thus risk assessment is the identification and analysis of relevant risks to achievement of assigned objectives. Risk assessment is a prerequisite for determining how the risks should be managed. | **Risk Assessment:** Risks are analyzed, considering the likelihood and impact, as a basis for determining how they could be managed. Risk areas are assessed on an inherent and residual basis. |
| | **Risk Response:** Management selects risk responses—avoiding, accepting, reducing, or sharing risk—developing a set of actions to align risks with the enterprise's risk tolerances and risk appetite. |

| Figure AD1—Comparison of COSO Internal Control and ERM Integrated Frameworks *(cont.)* | |
|---|---|
| **Internal Control Framework** | **ERM Integrated Framework** |
| **Control Activities:** Control activities are the policies and procedures that help ensure that management directives are carried out. They help ensure that necessary actions are taken to address risks to achievement of the enterprise's objectives. Control activities occur throughout the organization, at all levels and in all functions. They include a range of activities as diverse as approvals, authorizations, verifications, reconciliations, reviews of operating performance, security of assets and segregation of duties. | **Control Activities:** Policies and procedures are established and implemented to help ensure the risk responses are effectively carried out. |
| **Information and Communication:** Information systems play a key role in internal control systems as they produce reports, including operational, financial and compliance-related information that make it possible to run and control the business. In a broader sense, effective communication must ensure information flows down, across and up the organization. Effective communication should also be ensured with external parties, such as customers, suppliers, regulators and shareholders. | **Information and Communication:** Relevant information is identified, captured, and communicated in a form and timeframe that enable people to carry out their responsibilities. Effective communication also occurs in a broader sense, flowing down, across, and up the enterprise. |
| **Monitoring:** Internal control systems need to be monitored—a process that assesses the quality of the system's performance over time. This is accomplished through ongoing monitoring activities or separate evaluations. Internal control deficiencies detected through these monitoring activities should be reported upstream and corrective actions should be taken to ensure continuous improvement of the system. | **Monitoring:** The entirety of enterprise risk management is monitored and modifications made as necessary. Monitoring is accomplished through ongoing management activities, separate evaluations, or both. |
| Information for **figure AD1** was obtained from the COSO web site *www.coso.org/aboutus.htm.* | |

The original COSO internal control framework addresses the needs of the IT audit and assurance professional: control environment, risk assessment, control activities, information and communication, and monitoring. As such, ISACA has elected to utilize the five-component model for these audit/assurance programs. As more enterprises implement the ERM model, the additional three columns can be added, if relevant. When completing the COSO component columns, consider the definitions of the components as described in **figure AD1**.

*Reference/Hyperlink*
Good practices require the audit and assurance professional to create a work paper for each line item, which describes the work performed, issues identified and conclusions. The reference/hyperlink is to be used to cross-reference the audit/assurance step to the work paper that supports it. The numbering system of this document provides a ready numbering scheme for the work papers. If desired, a link to the work paper can be pasted into this column.

*Issue Cross-reference*
This column can be used to flag a finding/issue that the IT audit and assurance professional wants to further investigate or establish as a potential finding. The potential findings should be documented in a work paper that indicates the disposition of the findings (formally reported, reported as a memo or verbal finding, or waived).

*Comments*
The comments column can be used to indicate the waiving of a step or other notations. It is not to be used in place of a work paper describing the work performed.

## III. Controls Maturity Analysis
One of the consistent requests of stakeholders who have undergone IT audit/assurance reviews is a desire to understand how their performance compares to good practices. Audit and assurance professionals must provide an objective basis for the review conclusions. Maturity modeling for management and control over IT processes is based on a method of evaluating the organization, so it can be rated from a maturity level of nonexistent (0) to optimized (5). This approach is derived from the maturity model that the Software Engineering Institute (SEI) of Carnegie Mellon University defined for the maturity of software development.

*The IT Assurance Guide: Using CobiT*, appendix VII—Maturity Model for Internal Control, in **figure AD2**, provides a generic maturity model showing the status of the internal control environment and the establishment of internal controls in an enterprise. It shows how the management of internal control, and an awareness of the need to establish better internal controls, typically develops from an ad hoc to an optimized level. The model provides a high-level guide to help CobiT users appreciate what is required for effective internal controls in IT and to help position their enterprise on the maturity scale.

| Figure AD2—Maturity Model for Internal Control | | |
|---|---|---|
| Maturity Level | Status of the Internal Control Environment | Establishment of Internal Controls |
| 0 Nonexistent | There is no recognition of the need for internal control. Control is not part of the organization's culture or mission. There is a high risk of control deficiencies and incidents. | There is no intent to assess the need for internal control. Incidents are dealt with as they arise. |
| 1 Initial/ad hoc | There is some recognition of the need for internal control. The approach to risk and control requirements is ad hoc and disorganized, without communication or monitoring. Deficiencies are not identified. Employees are not aware of their responsibilities. | There is no awareness of the need for assessment of what is needed in terms of IT controls. When performed, it is only on an ad hoc basis, at a high level and in reaction to significant incidents. Assessment addresses only the actual incident. |
| 2 Repeatable but intuitive | Controls are in place but are not documented. Their operation is dependent on the knowledge and motivation of individuals. Effectiveness is not adequately evaluated. Many control weaknesses exist and are not adequately addressed; the impact can be severe. Management actions to resolve control issues are not prioritized or consistent. Employees may not be aware of their responsibilities. | Assessment of control needs occurs only when needed for selected IT processes to determine the current level of control maturity, the target level that should be reached and the gaps that exist. An informal workshop approach, involving IT managers and the team involved in the process, is used to define an adequate approach to controls for the process and to motivate an agreed-upon action plan. |
| 3 Defined | Controls are in place and adequately documented. Operating effectiveness is evaluated on a periodic basis and there is an average number of issues. However, the evaluation process is not documented. While management is able to deal predictably with most control issues, some control weaknesses persist and impacts could still be severe. Employees are aware of their responsibilities for control. | Critical IT processes are identified based on value and risk drivers. A detailed analysis is performed to identify control requirements and the root cause of gaps and to develop improvement opportunities. In addition to facilitated workshops, tools are used and interviews are performed to support the analysis and ensure that an IT process owner owns and drives the assessment and improvement process. |

| Maturity Level | Status of the Internal Control Environment | Establishment of Internal Controls |
|---|---|---|
| **Figure AD2—Maturity Model for Internal Control *(cont.)*** | | |
| 4 Managed and measurable | There is an effective internal control and risk management environment. A formal, documented evaluation of controls occurs frequently. Many controls are automated and regularly reviewed. Management is likely to detect most control issues, but not all issues are routinely identified. There is consistent follow-up to address identified control weaknesses. A limited, tactical use of technology is applied to automate controls. | IT process criticality is regularly defined with full support and agreement from the relevant business process owners. Assessment of control requirements is based on policy and the actual maturity of these processes, following a thorough and measured analysis involving key stakeholders. Accountability for these assessments is clear and enforced. Improvement strategies are supported by business cases. Performance in achieving the desired outcomes is consistently monitored. External control reviews are organized occasionally. |
| 5 Optimized | An enterprisewide risk and control program provides continuous and effective control and risk issues resolution. Internal control and risk management are integrated with enterprise practices, supported with automated real-time monitoring with full accountability for control monitoring, risk management and compliance enforcement. Control evaluation is continuous, based on self-assessments and gap and root cause analyses. Employees are proactively involved in control improvements. | Business changes consider the criticality of IT processes and cover any need to reassess process control capability. IT process owners regularly perform self-assessments to confirm that controls are at the right level of maturity to meet business needs and they consider maturity attributes to find ways to make controls more efficient and effective. The organization benchmarks to external best practices and seeks external advice on internal control effectiveness. For critical processes, independent reviews take place to provide assurance that the controls are at the desired level of maturity and working as planned. |

The maturity model evaluation is one of the final steps in the evaluation process. The IT audit and assurance professional can address the key controls within the scope of the work program and formulate an objective assessment of the maturity levels of the control practices. The maturity assessment can be a part of the audit/assurance report, and used as a metric from year to year to document progression in the enhancement of controls. However, it must be noted that the perception of the maturity level may vary between the process/IT asset owner and the auditor. Therefore, an auditor should obtain the concerned stakeholder's concurrence before submitting the final report to management.

At the conclusion of the review, once all findings and recommendations are completed, the professional assesses the current state of the CobiT control framework

and assigns it a maturity level using the six-level scale. Some practitioners utilize decimals (x.25, x.5, x.75) to indicate gradations in the maturity model. As a further reference, CobiT provides a definition of the maturity designations by control objective. While this approach is not mandatory, the process is provided as a separate section at the end of the audit/assurance program for those enterprises that wish to implement it. It is suggested that a maturity assessment be made at the CobiT control level. To provide further value to the client/customer, the professional can also obtain maturity targets from the client/customer. Using the assessed and target maturity levels, the professional can create an effective graphic presentation that describes the achievement or gaps between the actual and targeted maturity goals.

## IV. Assurance and Control Framework
### ISACA IT Assurance Framework and Standards
ISACA has long recognized the specialized nature of IT assurance and strives to advance globally applicable standards. Guidelines and procedures provide detailed guidance on how to follow those standards. IT Audit and Assurance Standard S15 IT Controls, and IT Audit and Assurance Guideline G38 Access Controls are relevant to this audit/assurance program.

### ISACA Controls Framework
CobiT is an IT governance framework and supporting tool set that allows managers to bridge the gap among control requirements, technical issues and business risks. CobiT enables clear policy development and good practice for IT control throughout enterprises.

Utilizing CobiT as the control framework on which IT audit/assurance activities are based aligns IT audit/assurance with good practices as developed by the enterprise.

Refer to ISACA's *CobiT Control Practices: Guidance to Achieve Control Objectives for Successful IT Governance, 2nd Edition*, published in 2007, for the related control practice value and risk drivers.

## V. Executive Summary of Audit/Assurance Focus
### SAP ERP Security
The review of SAP helps management ensure that it is secure. Since launching its first product offering almost 30 years ago, SAP has grown globally. It has approximately 12 million users and 96,400 installations in more than 120 countries and is the third-largest independent software company in the world. The company name, SAP, is a German acronym that loosely translates in English to Systems, Applications and Products in data processing.

Before SAP ERP, SAP had two main products: the mainframe system SAP® R/2® and the client/server-based system SAP R/3. Both R/2 and R/3 are targeted to business application solutions and feature complexity, business and organizational experience, and integration. The R/2 and R/3 terminology is sometimes taken to mean release 2 and release 3, respectively; however, this is not the case. The R in R/2 and R/3 means "real time." Release levels are annotated separately to the R/2 or R/3 descriptors. For example, in SAP R/3 4.6B, the 4 is the major release number, the 6 is the minor release number following a major release, and the B is the version within a release.

R/3 was introduced in 1992 with a three-tier architecture paradigm. In recent years, SAP has introduced Service Oriented Architecture (SOA) as part of SAP ERP. This combines ERP with an open technology platform that can integrate SAP and non-SAP systems on the SAP NetWeaver® platform. The current core ERP solution offered by SAP is called SAP Enterprise Central Component (ECC 6.0), referred here as SAP ERP.

### Business Impact and Risk
SAP is widely used in many enterprises. Improper configuration of SAP could result in an inability for the enterprise to execute its critical processes.

Risks resulting from ineffective or incorrect configurations or use of SAP could result in some of the following:
• Disclosure of privileged information
• Single points of failure
• Low data quality
• Loss of physical assets
• Loss of intellectual property
• Loss of competitive advantage
• Loss of customer confidence
• Violation of regulatory requirements

### Objective and Scope
**Objective**—The objective of the SAP ERP audit/assurance review is to provide management with an independent assessment relating to the effectiveness of configuration and security of the enterprise's SAP ERP architecture.

**Scope**—The review will focus on configuration of the relevant SAP ERP components and modules within the enterprise. The selection of the specific components and modules will be based upon the risks introduced to the enterprise by these components and modules.

### Minimum Audit Skills
This review is considered highly technical. The IT audit and assurance professional must have an understanding of SAP best practice processes and requirements, and be highly conversant in SAP tools, exposures, and functionality. It should not be assumed that an audit and assurance professional holding the CISA designation has the requisite skills to perform this review.

## VI. Inventory Business Cycle—Audit/Assurance Program

| Audit/Assurance Program Step | CobiT Cross-reference | COSO | | | | | Reference Hyperlink | Issue Cross-reference | Comments |
|---|---|---|---|---|---|---|---|---|---|
| | | Control Environment | Risk Assessment | Control Activities | Information and Communication | Monitoring | | | |
| **A. Prior Audit/Examination Report Follow-up** | | | | | | | | | |
| 1. Review prior report, if one exists, verify completion of any agreed-upon corrections and note remaining deficiencies. | ME1 | | | | | | | | |
| 1.1 Determine whether:<br>• Senior management has assigned responsibilities for information, its processing and its use<br>• User management is responsible for providing information that supports the entity's objectives and policies<br>• Information systems management is responsible for providing the capabilities necessary for achievement of the defined information systems objectives and policies of the entity<br>• Senior management approves plans for development and acquisition of information systems<br>• There are procedures to ensure that the information system being developed or acquired meets user requirements<br>• There are procedures to ensure that information systems, programs and configuration changes are tested adequately prior to implementation | ME1 | | | | | | | | |

## VI. Inventory Business Cycle—Audit/Assurance Program (cont.)

| Audit/Assurance Program Step | CobiT Cross-reference | Control Environment | Risk Assessment | Control Activities | Information and Communication | Monitoring | Reference Hyperlink | Issue Cross-reference | Comments |
|---|---|---|---|---|---|---|---|---|---|
| **A. Prior Audit/Examination Report Follow-up (cont.)** | | | | | | | | | |
| **1.1 (cont.)**<br>• All personnel involved in the system acquisition and configuration activities receive adequate training and supervision<br>• There are procedures to ensure that information systems are implemented/configured/upgraded in accordance with the established standards<br>• User management participates in the conversion of data from the existing system to the new system<br>• Final approval is obtained from user management prior to going live with a new information/upgraded system<br>• There are procedures to document and schedule all changes to information systems (including key ABAP programs)<br>• There are procedures to ensure that only authorized changes are initiated<br>• There are procedures to ensure that only authorized, tested and documented changes to information systems are accepted into the production client<br>• There are procedures to allow for and control emergency changes<br>• There are procedures for the approval, monitoring and control of the acquisition and upgrade of hardware and systems software | | | | | | | | | |

343

## VI. Inventory Business Cycle—Audit/Assurance Program (cont.)

| Audit/Assurance Program Step | CobiT Cross-reference | COSO | | | | | Reference Hyperlink | Issue Cross-reference | Comments |
|---|---|---|---|---|---|---|---|---|---|
| | | Control Environment | Risk Assessment | Control Activities | Information and Communication | Monitoring | | | |
| **A. Prior Audit/Examination Report Follow-up (cont.)** | | | | | | | | | |
| 1.1 *(cont.)* <br> • There is a process for monitoring the volume of named and concurrent SAP ERP users to ensure that the license agreement is not being violated <br> • The organization structure, established by senior management, provides for an appropriate segregation of incompatible functions <br> • The database, application and presentation servers are located in a physically separate and protected environment (i.e., a data center) <br> • Emergency, backup and recovery plans are documented and tested on a regular basis to ensure that they remain current and operational <br> • Backup and recovery plans allow users of information systems to resume operations in the event of an interruption <br> • Application controls are designed with regard to any weaknesses in segregation, security, development and processing controls that may affect the information system <br> • Access to the Implementation Guide (IMG) during production has been restricted <br> • The production client settings have been flagged to not allow changes to programs and configuration | | | | | | | | | |

## VI. Inventory Business Cycle—Audit/Assurance Program (cont.)

| Audit/Assurance Program Step | CobiT Cross-reference | COSO | | | | | Reference Hyperlink | Issue Cross-reference | Comments |
|---|---|---|---|---|---|---|---|---|---|
| | | Control Environment | Risk Assessment | Control Activities | Information and Communication | Monitoring | | | |
| **B. Preliminary Audit Steps** | | | | | | | | | |
| 1. Gain an understanding of the SAP ERP environment. | | | | | | | | | |
| 1.1 The same background information obtained for the SAP ERP Basis Security audit plan is required for and relevant to the business cycles. In particular, the following information is important:<br>• Version and release of SAP ERP implemented<br>• Total number of named users (for comparison with logical access security testing results)<br>• Number of SAP instances and clients<br>• Accounting period, company codes and chart of accounts<br>• Identification of the components being used (Human Capital Management, Financials, Operations, Corporate Services)<br>• Whether the organization has created any locally developed ABAP programs or reports<br>• Details of the risk assessment approach taken in the organization to identify and prioritize risks<br>• Copies of the organization's key security policies and standards | PO2<br>PO3<br>PO4<br>PO6<br>PO9<br>DS2<br>DS5<br>AI2<br>AI6<br>ME2 | | | | | | | | |
| 1.2 Obtain the following relevant business cycle details:<br>• The Organizational Model as it relates to inventory activity, i.e., plant organization unit structure in SAP ERP and manufacturing organization chart (required when evaluating the results of access security control testing) | PO4<br>AI4 | | | | | | | | |

## VI. Inventory Business Cycle—Audit/Assurance Program (cont.)

| Audit/Assurance Program Step | CobiT Cross-reference | COSO | | | | | Reference Hyperlink | Issue Cross-reference | Comments |
|---|---|---|---|---|---|---|---|---|---|
| | | Control Environment | Risk Assessment | Control Activities | Information and Communication | Monitoring | | | |
| **B. Preliminary Audit Steps (cont.)** | | | | | | | | | |
| 1.2 (cont.)<br>• An interview of the systems implementation team, if possible, and process design documentation for materials and warehouse management | | | | | | | | | |
| 2. Identify the significant risks and determine the key controls. | | | | | | | | | |
| 2.1 Develop a high-level process flow diagram and overall understanding of the Inventory processing cycle, including the following subprocesses:<br>• Master data maintenance<br>• Raw materials management<br>• Producing and costing inventory<br>• Handling and shipping finished goods | DS6<br>DS11<br>DS12<br>DS13 | | | | | | | | |
| 2.2 Assess the key risks, determine key controls or control weaknesses, and test controls (refer to detailed sample testing program below and chapter 4 for techniques for testing configurable controls and logical access security) regarding the following factors:<br>• The controls culture of the organization (e.g., a just-enough control philosophy)<br>• The need to exercise judgment to determine the key controls in the process and whether the controls structure is adequate (Any weaknesses in the control structure should be reported to | P09<br>ME2 | | | | | | | | |

## VI. Inventory Business Cycle—Audit/Assurance Program (cont.)

| Audit/Assurance Program Step | CobiT Cross-reference | COSO | | | | | Reference Hyperlink | Issue Cross-reference | Comments |
|---|---|---|---|---|---|---|---|---|---|
| | | Control Environment | Risk Assessment | Control Activities | Information and Communication | Monitoring | | | |
| **C. Detailed Audit Steps** | | | | | | | | | |
| **1. Master Data Maintenance** | | | | | | | | | |
| **1.1 Changes made to master data are valid, complete, accurate and timely.** | | | | | | | | | |
| 1.1.1 Take a sample of inventory file updates using transaction MB59, which allows users to perform a search on multiple materials by a particular range of dates and check back to authorized source documentation. Review the process for physical stock-takes to confirm the complete, accurate, valid and timely recording of stock differences. | DS11 DS13 | | | X | | | | | |
| 1.1.2 Review organization policy and process design specifications regarding access to maintain material master data. Test user access to the following transaction codes:<br>• Create Material—MM01<br>• Change Material—MM02<br>• Flag Material for Deletion—MM06 | DS11 DS13 | | | X | | | | | |

347

## VI. Inventory Business Cycle—Audit/Assurance Program (cont.)

| Audit/Assurance Program Step | CobiT Cross-reference | COSO | | | | | Reference Hyperlink | Issue Cross-reference | Comments |
|---|---|---|---|---|---|---|---|---|---|
| | | Control Environment | Risk Assessment | Control Activities | Information and Communication | Monitoring | | | |
| **C. Detailed Audit Steps (cont.)** | | | | | | | | | |
| 1.1.3 Determine whether the configurable control settings address the risks pertaining to the validity, completeness and accuracy of master data and whether they have been set in accordance with management intentions. View the settings online using the IMG as follows:<br>• Material Types: Transaction SPRO Menu Path— Logistics—General ▶ Material Master ▶ Basic Settings ▶ Material Types ▶ Define Attributes of Material Types<br>• Industry Sector: Transaction SPRO Menu Path—Logistics—General ▶ Material Master ▶ Field Selection ▶ Define industry sectors and industry-sector-specific field selection<br>• Default Price Types: Execute transaction OMW1 and determine whether default settings have been set for the price type for material records.<br>• Tolerances for physical inventory differences: Execute transaction OMJ2 and compare defined tolerances to organizational policy and judge for reasonableness. | PO9<br>DS6<br>DS11<br>DS12<br>DS13<br>ME1<br>ME2 | | | X | | | | | |

## VI. Inventory Business Cycle—Audit/Assurance Program (cont.)

| Audit/Assurance Program Step | CᴏʙɪT Cross-reference | COSO | | | | | | Reference Hyperlink | Issue Cross-reference | Comments |
|---|---|---|---|---|---|---|---|---|---|---|
| | | Control Environment | Risk Assessment | Control Activities | Information and Communication | Monitoring | | | | |
| **C. Detailed Audit Steps *(cont.)*** | | | | | | | | | | |
| **1.2 Inventory master data remain current and pertinent.** | | | | | | | | | | |
| 1.2.1 Determine whether the appropriate management runs the materials list transaction code MM60, or equivalent, by material type and confirm evidence of management's review of the data on a rotating basis for currency and ongoing pertinence. | DS11 ME1 ME4 | | | X | | | | | | |
| **1.3 Settings or changes to the bill of materials or process order settlement rules are valid, complete, accurate and timely.** | | | | | | | | | | |
| 1.3.1 Review organization policy and process design specifications regarding access to maintain bill of materials and process order settlement rules. Test user access to the following transaction codes:<br>• Create Material BOM—CS01<br>• Change Material BOM—CS02<br>• Make Mass Changes—CS20<br>• Change Single-layered BOM—CS72<br>• Change Multi-layered BOM—CS75 | DS13 ME1 | | | X | | | | | | |

## VI. Inventory Business Cycle—Audit/Assurance Program (cont.)

| Audit/Assurance Program Step | CobiT Cross-reference | COSO Control Environment | Risk Assessment | Control Activities | Information and Communication | Monitoring | Reference Hyperlink | Issue Cross-reference | Comments |
|---|---|---|---|---|---|---|---|---|---|
| **C. Detailed Audit Steps (cont.)** | | | | | | | | | |
| 1.3.1 (cont.)<br>• Change settlement rules—COR2; Nondisplayable transaction code KOBK (refer to menu path: Logistics ▶ Production Process ▶ Process Order ▶ Process Order ▶ Display. Enter the process order number and press Enter then go to Header ▶ Settlement Rule) | | | | | | | | | |
| 1.3.2 Take a sample of BOM updates using transaction CS80 and check back to authorized source documentation. | DS13 | | | X | | | | | |
| **2. Raw Materials Management** | | | | | | | | | |
| **2.1 Inventory is salable, usable and safeguarded adequately.** | | | | | | | | | |
| 2.1.1 Confirm that the distribution resource planning (DRP) process takes into account stock on hand, forecast requirements, economic order quantities and back orders. Execute transaction code MB5M and ascertain the reason for any old stock being held (shelf-life list). Use transaction MC46 to identify slow-moving items and MC50 for "dead" stock (i.e., stock that has not been used for a certain period of time). Test that managers are reviewing this information on a regular basis. | DS6 DS13 ME1 | | | X | | | | | |

## VI. Inventory Business Cycle—Audit/Assurance Program (cont.)

| Audit/Assurance Program Step | CobiT Cross-reference | COSO Control Environment | Risk Assessment | Control Activities | Information and Communication | Monitoring | Reference Hyperlink | Issue Cross-reference | Comments |
|---|---|---|---|---|---|---|---|---|---|
| **C. Detailed Audit Steps *(cont.)*** | | | | | | | | | |
| **2.2 Raw materials are received and accepted only with valid purchase orders and are recorded accurately and in a timely manner.** | | | | | | | | | |
| 2.2.1 Test that management executes the report of outstanding purchase orders using transaction ME2L (refer to Expenditure cycle 2.2.1) and follow up on any long-outstanding items. | DS13 | | | X | | | | | |
| 2.2.2 Review the reconciliation of the goods received/invoice received account (transaction code MB5S, refer to Expenditure cycle 3.2.3) and confirm that unmatched items have been investigated in a timely manner. | ME1 ME2 | | | X | | | | | |
| 2.2.3 Test user access to transactions for goods receipt (refer to Expenditure cycle 2.2.2) as follows:<br>• Goods Receipt for Purchase Order—MB01<br>• Goods Receipts Purchase Order Unknown—MB0A<br>• Goods Receipt for Order—MB31<br>• Enter Other Goods Receipts—MB1C<br>• Cancel Material Document—MBST<br>• Goods Movement—MIG0 | DS12 DS13 ME1 | | | X | | | | | |
| 2.2.4 Test the controls over inventory stock takes (refer to 1.1.1). | | | | | | | | | |

## VI. Inventory Business Cycle—Audit/Assurance Program (cont.)

| Audit/Assurance Program Step | CobiT Cross-reference | COSO Control Environment | COSO Risk Assessment | COSO Control Activities | COSO Information and Communication | COSO Monitoring | Reference Hyperlink | Issue Cross-reference | Comments |
|---|---|---|---|---|---|---|---|---|---|
| **C. Detailed Audit Steps (cont.)** | | | | | | | | | |
| **2.3 Defective raw materials are returned to suppliers in a timely manner.** | | | | | | | | | |
| 2.3.1 Ascertain from management the movement type used to block processing and for returning rejected goods to suppliers (e.g., movement type 122). Execute transaction MB51 with the appropriate movement type (refer to Expenditure cycle 2.3.1). Determine whether there are any long-outstanding materials pending return to suppliers or receipt of appropriate credits. | DS13 | | | X | | | | | |
| **3. Producing and Costing Inventory** | | | | | | | | | |
| **3.1 Transfers of materials to/from production, production costs and defective products/scrap are valid and recorded accurately, completely and in the appropriate period.** | | | | | | | | | |
| 3.1.1 Review the policy and procedures concerning the transfer of materials and confirm that the above controls are in place and operating. Test that inventory-in-transit accounts are regularly reviewed to ensure that the accounts are cleared and reconciled. Confirm that default price types have been established for all materials (refer to 1.1.3). | DS6 ME2 | | | X | | | | | |

## VI. Inventory Business Cycle—Audit/Assurance Program (cont.)

| Audit/Assurance Program Step | COBIT Cross-reference | Control Environment | Risk Assessment | Control Activities | Information and Communication | Monitoring | Reference Hyperlink | Issue Cross-reference | Comments |
|---|---|---|---|---|---|---|---|---|---|
| **C. Detailed Audit Steps (cont.)** | | | | | | | | | |
| 3.1.2 Test user access to BOMs (refer to 1.3.1). | | | | | | | | | |
| 3.1.3 Test user access to issue goods (transaction code MB1A), post transfers between plants (transaction code MB1B) and move goods (transaction code MIG0). | DS13 ME1 | | | X | | | | | |
| 3.1.4 Test user access to create (transaction code CR01) or change (transaction code CR02) work centers. | DS13 ME1 | | | X | | | | | |
| **4. Handling and Shipping Finished Goods** | | | | | | | | | |
| **4.1 Finished goods received from production are recorded completely and accurately in the appropriate period.** | | | | | | | | | |
| 4.1.1 Test inventory stock-take procedures (refer to 1.1.1). | DS13 ME1 | | | X | | | | | |
| 4.1.2 Test user access to change settlement rules (refer to 1.3.1). | DS13 ME1 | | | X | | | | | |

## VI. Inventory Business Cycle—Audit/Assurance Program (cont.)

| Audit/Assurance Program Step | CobiT Cross-reference | COSO | | | | | Reference Hyperlink | Issue Cross-reference | Comments |
|---|---|---|---|---|---|---|---|---|---|
| | | Control Environment | Risk Assessment | Control Activities | Information and Communication | Monitoring | | | |
| **C. Detailed Audit Steps (cont.)** | | | | | | | | | |
| **4.2 Goods returned by customers are accepted in accordance with the organization's policies** | AI4 ME1 | | | X | | | | | |
| 4.2.1 Review the policies and procedures for receiving inventory back into the warehouse. Review some returns of inventory and ensure that they are supported with adequate documentation from the quality inspector. Ascertain from management the movement type used for goods returned from customers. Execute transaction MB51 with the appropriate movement type. Determine whether there are any long-outstanding materials pending return to inventory or provision of appropriate credits. | AI4 ME1 | | | X | | | | | |
| **4.3 Shipments are recorded accurately, in a timely manner and in the appropriate period.** | | | | | | | | | |
| 4.3.1 Test user access to Transfer Stock Between Plants (transaction code LT04) or Change Outbound Delivery (transaction code VL02N). | DS13 ME1 | | | X | | | | | |
| 4.3.2 Take a sample of the delivery due list and the Owed to Customer report and test for evidence of management action. Review settings, using transaction code OMWB, and confirm that accounts assignments are set to valid COGS accounts. | DS13 ME1 ME4 | | | X | | | | | |

## VII. Inventory Business Cycle—Maturity Assessment

The maturity assessment is an opportunity for the reviewer to assess the maturity of the processes reviewed. Based on the results of audit/assurance review, and the reviewer's observations, assign a maturity level to each of the following CobiT control practices.

| CobiT Control Practice | Assessed Maturity | Target Maturity | Reference Hyperlink | Comments |
|---|---|---|---|---|
| **AI6.1 Change Standards and Procedures**<br>1. Develop, document and promulgate a change management framework that specifies the policies and processes, including:<br>• Roles and responsibilities<br>• Classification and prioritization of all changes based on business risk<br>• Assessment of impact<br>• Authorization and approval of all changes by the business process owners and IT<br>• Tracking and status of changes<br>• Impact on data integrity (e.g., all changes to data files being made under system and application control rather than by direct user intervention)<br>2. Establish and maintain version control over all changes.<br>3. Implement roles and responsibilities that involve business process owners and appropriate technical IT functions. Ensure appropriate segregation of duties.<br>4. Establish appropriate record management practices and audit trails to record key steps in the change management process. Ensure timely closure of changes. Elevate and report to management changes that are not closed in a timely fashion.<br>5. Consider the impact of contracted services providers (e.g., of infrastructure, application development and shared services) on the change management process. Consider integration of organizational change management processes with change management processes of service providers. Consider the impact of the organizational change management process on contractual terms and SLAs. | | | | |

## VII. Inventory Business Cycle—Maturity Assessment (cont.)

| CobiT Control Practice | Assessed Maturity | Target Maturity | Reference Hyperlink | Comments |
|---|---|---|---|---|
| **AI6.2 Impact Assessment, Prioritization and Authorization**<br>1. Develop a process to allow business process owners and IT to request changes to infrastructure, systems or applications. Develop controls to ensure that all such changes arise only through the change request management process.<br>2. Categorize all requested changes (e.g., infrastructure, operating systems, networks, application systems, purchased/packaged application software).<br>3. Prioritize all requested changes. Ensure that the change management process identifies both the business and technical needs for the change. Consider legal, regulatory and contractual reasons for the requested change.<br>4. Assess all requests in a structured fashion. Ensure that the assessment process addresses impact analysis on infrastructure, systems and applications. Consider security, legal, contractual and compliance implications of the requested change. Consider also interdependencies amongst changes. Involve business process owners in the assessment process, as appropriate.<br>5. Ensure that each change is formally approved by business process owners and IT technical stakeholders, as appropriate. | | | | |
| **AI6.4 Change Status Tracking and Reporting**<br>1. Ensure that a documented process exists within the overall change management process to declare, assess, authorize and record an emergency change.<br>2. Ensure that emergency changes are processed in accordance with the emergency change element of the formal change management process.<br>3. Ensure that all emergency access arrangements for changes are appropriately authorized, documented and revoked after the change has been applied.<br>4. Conduct a postimplementation review of all emergency changes, involving all concerned parties. The review should consider implications for aspects such as further application system maintenance, impact on development and test environments, application software development quality, documentation and manuals, and data integrity. | | | | |

## VII. Inventory Business Cycle—Maturity Assessment (cont.)

| CobiT Control Practice | Assessed Maturity | Target Maturity | Reference Hyperlink | Comments |
|---|---|---|---|---|
| **DS5.3 Identity Management**<br>1. Establish and communicate policies and procedures to uniquely identify, authenticate and authorize access mechanisms and access rights for all users on a need-to-know/need-to-have basis, based on predetermined and preapproved roles. Clearly state accountability of any user for any action on any of the systems and/or applications involved.<br>2. Ensure that roles and access authorization criteria for assigning user access rights take into account:<br>    • Sensitivity of information and applications involved (data classification)<br>    • Policies for information protection and dissemination (legal, regulatory, internal policies and contractual requirements)<br>    • Roles and responsibilities as defined within the enterprise<br>    • The need-to-have access rights associated with the function<br>    • Standard but individual user access profiles for common job roles in the organization<br>    • Requirements to guarantee appropriate segregation of duties<br>3. Establish a method for authenticating and authorizing users to establish responsibility and enforce access rights in line with sensitivity of information and functional application requirements and infrastructure components, and in compliance with applicable laws, regulations, internal policies and contractual agreements.<br>4. Define and implement a procedure for identifying new users and recording, approving and maintaining access rights. This needs to be requested by user management, approved by the system owner and implemented by the responsible security person.<br>5. Ensure that a timely information flow is in place that reports changes in jobs (i.e., people in, people out, people change). Grant, revoke and adapt user access rights in co-ordination with human resources and user departments for users who are new, who have left the organization, or who have changed roles or jobs. | | | | |

## VII. Inventory Business Cycle—Maturity Assessment (cont.)

| CobiT Control Practice | Assessed Maturity | Target Maturity | Reference Hyperlink | Comments |
|---|---|---|---|---|
| **DS5.4 User Account Management**<br>1. Ensure that access control procedures include but are not limited to:<br>• Using unique user IDs to enable users to be linked to and held accountable for their actions<br>• Awareness that the use of group IDs results in the loss of individual accountability and are permitted only when justified for business or operational reasons and compensated by mitigating controls. Group IDs must be approved and documented.<br>• Checking that the user has authorization from the system owner for the use of the information system or service, and the level of access granted is appropriate to the business purpose and consistent with the organizational security policy<br>• A procedure to require users to understand and acknowledge their access rights and the conditions of such access<br>• Ensuring that internal and external service providers do not provide access until authorization procedures have been completed<br>• Maintaining a formal record, including access levels, of all persons registered to use the service<br>• A timely and regular review of user IDs and access rights<br>2. Ensure that management reviews or reallocates user access rights at regular intervals using a formal process. User access rights should be reviewed or reallocated after any job changes, such as transfer, promotion, demotion or termination of employment. Authorizations for special privileged access rights should be reviewed independently at more frequent intervals. | | | | |

## VII. Inventory Business Cycle—Maturity Assessment (cont.)

| CobiT Control Practice | Assessed Maturity | Target Maturity | Reference Hyperlink | Comments |
|---|---|---|---|---|
| **DS9.1 Configuration Repository and Baseline** <br> 1. Implement a configuration repository to capture and maintain configuration management items. The repository should include hardware; application software; middleware; parameters; documentation; procedures; and tools for operating, accessing and using the systems, services, version numbers and licensing details. <br> 2. Implement a tool to enable the effective logging of configuration management information within a repository. <br> 3. Provide a unique identifier to a configuration item so the item can be easily tracked and related to physical asset tags and financial records. <br> 4. Define and document configuration baselines for components across development, test and production environments, to enable identification of system configuration at specific points in time (past, present and planned). <br> 5. Establish a process to revert to the baseline configuration in the event of problems, if determined appropriate after initial investigation. <br> 6. Install mechanisms to monitor changes against the defined repository and baseline. Provide management reports for exceptions, reconciliation and decision making. | | | | |
| **DS9.2 Identification and Maintenance of Configuration Items** <br> 1. Define and implement a policy requiring all configuration items and their attributes and versions to be identified and maintained. <br> 2. Tag physical assets according to a defined policy. Consider using an automated mechanism, such as barcodes. <br> 3. Define a policy that integrates incident, change and problem management procedures with the maintenance of the configuration repository. <br> 4. Define a process to record new, modified and deleted configuration items and their relative attributes and versions. Identify and maintain the relationships between configuration items in the configuration repository. <br> 5. Establish a process to maintain an audit trail for all changes to configuration items. <br> 6. Define a process to identify critical configuration items in relationship to business functions (component failure impact analysis). <br> 7. Record all assets—including new hardware and software, procured or internally developed—within the configuration management data repository. <br> 8. Define and implement a process to ensure that valid licenses are in place to prevent the inclusion of unauthorized software. | | | | |

## VII. Inventory Business Cycle—Maturity Assessment (cont.)

| CobiT Control Practice | Assessed Maturity | Target Maturity | Reference Hyperlink | Comments |
|---|---|---|---|---|
| **DS9.3 Configuration Integrity Review**<br>1. To validate the integrity of configuration data, implement a process to ensure that configuration items are monitored. Compare recorded data against actual physical existence, and ensure that errors and deviations are reported and corrected.<br>2. Using automated discovery tools where appropriate, reconcile actual installed software and hardware periodically against the configuration database, license records and physical tags.<br>3. Periodically review against the policy for software usage the existence of any software in violation or in excess of current policies and license agreements. Report deviations for correction. | | | | |

# Basis Cycle

## *I. Introduction*

### Overview

ISACA developed *ITAF™: A Professional Practices Framework for IT Assurance* as a comprehensive and good-practice-setting model. ITAF provides standards that are designed to be mandatory and are the guiding principles under which the IT audit and assurance profession operates. The guidelines provide information and direction for the practice of IT audit and assurance. The tools and techniques provide methodologies, tools and templates to provide direction in the application of IT audit and assurance processes.

### *Purpose*

The audit/assurance program is a tool and template to be used as a road map for the completion of a specific assurance process. This audit/assurance program is intended to be utilized by IT audit and assurance professionals with the requisite knowledge of the subject matter under review, as described in ITAF, section 2200—General Standards. The audit/assurance programs are part of ITAF, section 4000—IT Assurance Tools and Techniques.

### *Control Framework*

The audit/assurance programs have been developed in alignment with the CoBiT framework—specifically CoBiT 4.1—using generally applicable and accepted good practices. They reflect ITAF, sections 3400—IT Management Processes, 3600—IT Audit and Assurance Processes, and 3800—IT Audit and Assurance Management.

Many enterprises have embraced several frameworks at an enterprise level, including the Committee of Sponsoring Organizations of the Treadway Commission (COSO) Internal Control Framework. The importance of the control framework has been enhanced due to regulatory requirements by the US Securities and Exchange Commission (SEC) as directed by the US Sarbanes-Oxley Act of 2002 and similar legislation in other countries. They seek to integrate control framework elements used by the general audit/assurance team into the IT audit and assurance framework. Since COSO is widely used, it has been selected for inclusion in this audit/assurance program. The reviewer may delete or rename the columns in the audit program to align with the enterprise's control framework.

### *IT Governance, Risk and Control*

IT governance, risk and control are critical in the performance of any assurance management process. Governance of the process under review will be evaluated as part of the policies and management oversight controls. Risk plays an important role in evaluating what to audit and how management approaches and manages risk. Both issues will be evaluated as steps in the audit/assurance program. Controls are the primary evaluation point in the process. The audit/assurance program will identify the control objectives with steps to determine control design and effectiveness.

*Responsibilities of IT Audit and Assurance Professionals*
IT audit and assurance professionals are expected to customize this document
to the environment in which they are performing an assurance process. This
document is to be used as a review tool and starting point. It may be modified
by the IT audit and assurance professional; it is not intended to be a checklist or
questionnaire. It is assumed that the IT audit and assurance professional holds the
Certified Information Systems Auditor (CISA) designation, or has the necessary
subject matter expertise required to conduct the work and is supervised by a
professional with the CISA designation and necessary subject matter expertise to
adequately review the work performed.

## II. Using This Document

This audit/assurance program was developed to assist the audit and assurance
professional in designing and executing a review. Details regarding the format and
use of the document follow.

*Work Program Steps*
The first column of the program describes the steps to be performed. The
numbering scheme used provides built-in work paper numbering for ease of
cross-reference to the specific work paper for that section. IT audit and assurance
professionals are encouraged to make modifications to this document to reflect the
specific environment under review.

*CobiT Cross-reference*
The CobiT cross-reference provides the audit and assurance professional with the
ability to refer to the specific CobiT control objective that supports the
audit/assurance step. The CobiT control objective should be identified for
each audit/assurance step in the section. Multiple cross-references are not
uncommon. Processes at lower levels in the work program are too granular to be
cross-referenced to CobiT. The audit/assurance program is organized in a manner
to facilitate an evaluation through a structure parallel to the development process.
CobiT provides in-depth control objectives and suggested control practices at each
level. As the professional reviews each control, he/she should refer to CobiT 4.1 or
the *IT Assurance Guide: Using CobiT* for good-practice control guidance.

*COSO Components*
As noted in the introduction, COSO and similar frameworks have become
increasingly popular among audit and assurance professionals. This ties the
assurance work to the enterprise's control framework. While the IT
audit/assurance function has CobiT as a framework, operational audit and
assurance professionals use the framework established by the enterprise. Since
COSO is the most prevalent internal control framework, it has been included in
this document and is a bridge to align IT audit/assurance with the rest of the
audit/assurance function. Many audit/assurance organizations include the COSO
control components within their report and summarize assurance activities to the
audit committee of the board of directors.

For each control, the audit and assurance professional should indicate the COSO component(s) addressed. It is possible, but generally not necessary, to extend this analysis to the specific audit step level.

The original COSO internal control framework contained five components. In 2004, COSO was revised as the *Enterprise Risk Management (ERM) Integrated Framework* and extended to eight components. The primary difference between the two frameworks is the additional focus on ERM and integration into the business decision model. ERM is in the process of being adopted by large enterprises. The two frameworks are compared in **figure AD1**.

| Figure AD1—Comparison of COSO Internal Control and ERM Integrated Frameworks | |
|---|---|
| **Internal Control Framework** | **ERM Integrated Framework** |
| **Control Environment:** The control environment sets the tone of an organization, influencing the control consciousness of its people. It is the foundation for all other components of internal control, providing discipline and structure. Control environment factors include the integrity, ethical values, management's operating style, delegation of authority systems, as well as the processes for managing and developing people in the organization. | **Internal Environment:** The internal environment encompasses the tone of an organization, and sets the basis for how risk is viewed and addressed by an enterprise's people, including risk management philosophy and risk appetite, integrity and ethical values, and the environment in which they operate. |
| | **Objective Setting:** Objectives must exist before management can identify potential events affecting their achievement. Enterprise risk management ensures that management has in place a process to set objectives and that the chosen objectives support and align with the enterprise's mission and are consistent with its risk appetite. |
| | **Event Identification:** Internal and external events affecting achievement of an enterprise's objectives must be identified, distinguishing between risks and opportunities. Opportunities are channeled back to management's strategy or objective-setting processes. |
| **Risk Assessment:** Every enterprise faces a variety of risks from external and internal sources that must be assessed. A precondition to risk assessment is establishment of objectives, and thus risk assessment is the identification and analysis of relevant risks to achievement of assigned objectives. Risk assessment is a prerequisite for determining how the risks should be managed. | **Risk Assessment:** Risks are analyzed, considering the likelihood and impact, as a basis for determining how they could be managed. Risk areas are assessed on an inherent and residual basis. |
| | **Risk Response:** Management selects risk responses—avoiding, accepting, reducing, or sharing risk—developing a set of actions to align risks with the enterprise's risk tolerances and risk appetite. |

| Figure AD1—Comparison of COSO Internal Control and ERM Integrated Frameworks *(cont.)* | |
| --- | --- |
| **Internal Control Framework** | **ERM Integrated Framework** |
| **Control Activities:** Control activities are the policies and procedures that help ensure that management directives are carried out. They help ensure that necessary actions are taken to address risks to achievement of the enterprise's objectives. Control activities occur throughout the organization, at all levels and in all functions. They include a range of activities as diverse as approvals, authorizations, verifications, reconciliations, reviews of operating performance, security of assets and segregation of duties. | **Control Activities:** Policies and procedures are established and implemented to help ensure the risk responses are effectively carried out. |
| **Information and Communication:** Information systems play a key role in internal control systems as they produce reports, including operational, financial and compliance-related information that make it possible to run and control the business. In a broader sense, effective communication must ensure information flows down, across and up the organization. Effective communication should also be ensured with external parties, such as customers, suppliers, regulators and shareholders. | **Information and Communication:** Relevant information is identified, captured, and communicated in a form and timeframe that enable people to carry out their responsibilities. Effective communication also occurs in a broader sense, flowing down, across, and up the enterprise. |
| **Monitoring:** Internal control systems need to be monitored—a process that assesses the quality of the system's performance over time. This is accomplished through ongoing monitoring activities or separate evaluations. Internal control deficiencies detected through these monitoring activities should be reported upstream and corrective actions should be taken to ensure continuous improvement of the system. | **Monitoring:** The entirety of enterprise risk management is monitored and modifications made as necessary. Monitoring is accomplished through ongoing management activities, separate evaluations, or both. |
| Information for **figure AD1** was obtained from the COSO web site *www.coso.org/aboutus.htm.* | |

The original COSO internal control framework addresses the needs of the IT audit and assurance professional: control environment, risk assessment, control activities, information and communication, and monitoring. As such, ISACA has elected to utilize the five-component model for these audit/assurance programs. As more enterprises implement the ERM model, the additional three columns can be added, if relevant. When completing the COSO component columns, consider the definitions of the components as described in **figure AD1**.

*Reference/Hyperlink*

Good practices require the audit and assurance professional to create a work paper for each line item, which describes the work performed, issues identified and conclusions. The reference/hyperlink is to be used to cross-reference the audit/assurance step to the work paper that supports it. The numbering system of this document provides a ready numbering scheme for the work papers. If desired, a link to the work paper can be pasted into this column.

*Issue Cross-reference*

This column can be used to flag a finding/issue that the IT audit and assurance professional wants to further investigate or establish as a potential finding. The potential findings should be documented in a work paper that indicates the disposition of the findings (formally reported, reported as a memo or verbal finding, or waived).

*Comments*

The comments column can be used to indicate the waiving of a step or other notations. It is not to be used in place of a work paper describing the work performed.

## III. Controls Maturity Analysis

One of the consistent requests of stakeholders who have undergone IT audit/assurance reviews is a desire to understand how their performance compares to good practices. Audit and assurance professionals must provide an objective basis for the review conclusions. Maturity modeling for management and control over IT processes is based on a method of evaluating the organization, so it can be rated from a maturity level of nonexistent (0) to optimized (5). This approach is derived from the maturity model that the Software Engineering Institute (SEI) of Carnegie Mellon University defined for the maturity of software development.

The *IT Assurance Guide: Using CoBIT*, appendix VII—Maturity Model for Internal Control, in figure AD2, provides a generic maturity model showing the status of the internal control environment and the establishment of internal controls in an enterprise. It shows how the management of internal control, and an awareness of the need to establish better internal controls, typically develops from an *ad hoc* to an optimized level. The model provides a high-level guide to help CoBIT users appreciate what is required for effective internal controls in IT and to help position their enterprise on the maturity scale.

| | Figure AD2—Maturity Model for Internal Control | |
|---|---|---|
| **Maturity Level** | **Status of the Internal Control Environment** | **Establishment of Internal Controls** |
| 0 Nonexistent | There is no recognition of the need for internal control. Control is not part of the organization's culture or mission. There is a high risk of control deficiencies and incidents. | There is no intent to assess the need for internal control. Incidents are dealt with as they arise. |
| 1 Initial/*ad hoc* | There is some recognition of the need for internal control. The approach to risk and control requirements is *ad hoc* and disorganized, without communication or monitoring. Deficiencies are not identified. Employees are not aware of their responsibilities. | There is no awareness of the need for assessment of what is needed in terms of IT controls. When performed, it is only on an *ad hoc* basis, at a high level and in reaction to significant incidents. Assessment addresses only the actual incident. |
| 2 Repeatable but intuitive | Controls are in place but are not documented. Their operation is dependent on the knowledge and motivation of individuals. Effectiveness is not adequately evaluated. Many control weaknesses exist and are not adequately addressed; the impact can be severe. Management actions to resolve control issues are not prioritized or consistent. Employees may not be aware of their responsibilities. | Assessment of control needs occurs only when needed for selected IT processes to determine the current level of control maturity, the target level that should be reached and the gaps that exist. An informal workshop approach, involving IT managers and the team involved in the process, is used to define an adequate approach to controls for the process and to motivate an agreed-upon action plan. |
| 3 Defined | Controls are in place and adequately documented. Operating effectiveness is evaluated on a periodic basis and there is an average number of issues. However, the evaluation process is not documented. While management is able to deal predictably with most control issues, some control weaknesses persist and impacts could still be severe. Employees are aware of their responsibilities for control. | Critical IT processes are identified based on value and risk drivers. A detailed analysis is performed to identify control requirements and the root cause of gaps and to develop improvement opportunities. In addition to facilitated workshops, tools are used and interviews are performed to support the analysis and ensure that an IT process owner owns and drives the assessment and improvement process. |

| Maturity Level | Status of the Internal Control Environment | Establishment of Internal Controls |
|---|---|---|
| **Figure AD2—Maturity Model for Internal Control *(cont.)*** | | |
| 4 Managed and measurable | There is an effective internal control and risk management environment. A formal, documented evaluation of controls occurs frequently. Many controls are automated and regularly reviewed. Management is likely to detect most control issues, but not all issues are routinely identified. There is consistent follow-up to address identified control weaknesses. A limited, tactical use of technology is applied to automate controls. | IT process criticality is regularly defined with full support and agreement from the relevant business process owners. Assessment of control requirements is based on policy and the actual maturity of these processes, following a thorough and measured analysis involving key stakeholders. Accountability for these assessments is clear and enforced. Improvement strategies are supported by business cases. Performance in achieving the desired outcomes is consistently monitored. External control reviews are organized occasionally. |
| 5 Optimized | An enterprisewide risk and control program provides continuous and effective control and risk issues resolution. Internal control and risk management are integrated with enterprise practices, supported with automated real-time monitoring with full accountability for control monitoring, risk management and compliance enforcement. Control evaluation is continuous, based on self-assessments and gap and root cause analyses. Employees are proactively involved in control improvements. | Business changes consider the criticality of IT processes and cover any need to reassess process control capability. IT process owners regularly perform self-assessments to confirm that controls are at the right level of maturity to meet business needs and they consider maturity attributes to find ways to make controls more efficient and effective. The organization benchmarks to external best practices and seeks external advice on internal control effectiveness. For critical processes, independent reviews take place to provide assurance that the controls are at the desired level of maturity and working as planned. |

The maturity model evaluation is one of the final steps in the evaluation process. The IT audit and assurance professional can address the key controls within the scope of the work program and formulate an objective assessment of the maturity levels of the control practices. The maturity assessment can be a part of the audit/assurance report, and used as a metric from year to year to document progression in the enhancement of controls. However, it must be noted that the perception of the maturity level may vary between the process/IT asset owner and the auditor. Therefore, an auditor should obtain the concerned stakeholder's concurrence before submitting the final report to management.

At the conclusion of the review, once all findings and recommendations are completed, the professional assesses the current state of the CobiT control framework

and assigns it a maturity level using the six-level scale. Some practitioners utilize decimals (x.25, x.5, x.75) to indicate gradations in the maturity model. As a further reference, CobiT provides a definition of the maturity designations by control objective. While this approach is not mandatory, the process is provided as a separate section at the end of the audit/assurance program for those enterprises that wish to implement it. It is suggested that a maturity assessment be made at the CobiT control level. To provide further value to the client/customer, the professional can also obtain maturity targets from the client/customer. Using the assessed and target maturity levels, the professional can create an effective graphic presentation that describes the achievement or gaps between the actual and targeted maturity goals.

## IV. Assurance and Control Framework
### ISACA IT Assurance Framework and Standards
ISACA has long recognized the specialized nature of IT assurance and strives to advance globally applicable standards. Guidelines and procedures provide detailed guidance on how to follow those standards. IT Audit/Assurance Standard S15 IT Controls, and IT Audit/ Assurance Guideline G38 Access Controls are relevant to this audit/assurance program.

### ISACA Controls Framework
CobiT is an IT governance framework and supporting tool set that allows managers to bridge the gap among control requirements, technical issues and business risks. CobiT enables clear policy development and good practice for IT control throughout enterprises.

Utilizing CobiT as the control framework on which IT audit/assurance activities are based aligns IT audit/assurance with good practices as developed by the enterprise.

Refer to ISACA's *CobiT Control Practices: Guidance to Achieve Control Objectives for Successful IT Governance, 2nd Edition*, published in 2007, for the related control practice value and risk drivers.

## V. Executive Summary of Audit/Assurance Focus
### SAP ERP Security
The review of SAP helps management ensure that it is secure. Since launching its first product offering almost 30 years ago, SAP has grown globally. It has approximately 12 million users and 96,400 installations in more than 120 countries and is the third-largest independent software company in the world. The company name, SAP, is a German acronym that loosely translates in English to Systems, Applications and Products in data processing.

Before SAP ERP, SAP had two main products: the mainframe system SAP® R/2® and the client/server-based system SAP R/3. Both R/2 and R/3 are targeted to business application solutions and feature complexity, business and organizational experience, and integration. The R/2 and R/3 terminology is sometimes taken to mean release 2 and release 3, respectively; however, this is not the case. The R in R/2 and R/3 means "real time." Release levels are annotated separately to the R/2 or R/3 descriptors. For example, in SAP R/3 4.6B, the 4 is the major release number, the 6 is the minor release number following a major release, and the B is the version within a release.

R/3 was introduced in 1992 with a three-tier architecture paradigm. In recent years, SAP has introduced Service Oriented Architecture (SOA) as part of SAP ERP. This combines ERP with an open technology platform that can integrate SAP and non-SAP systems on the SAP NetWeaver® platform. The current core ERP solution offered by SAP is called SAP Enterprise Central Component (ECC 6.0), referred to here as SAP ERP.

### Business Impact and Risk
SAP is widely used in many enterprises. Improper configuration of SAP could result in an inability for the enterprise to execute its critical processes.

Risks resulting from ineffective or incorrect configurations or use of SAP could result in some of the following:
• Disclosure of privileged information
• Single points of failure
• Low data quality
• Loss of physical assets
• Loss of intellectual property
• Loss of competitive advantage
• Loss of customer confidence
• Violation of regulatory requirements

### Objective and Scope
**Objective**—The objective of the SAP ERP audit/assurance review is to provide management with an independent assessment relating to the effectiveness of configuration and security of the enterprise's SAP ERP architecture.

**Scope**—The review will focus on configuration of the relevant SAP ERP components and modules within the enterprise. The selection of the specific components and modules will be based upon the risks introduced to the enterprise by these components and modules.

### Minimum Audit Skills
This review is considered highly technical. The IT audit and assurance professional must have an understanding of SAP best practice processes and requirements, and be highly conversant in SAP tools, exposures and functionality. It should not be assumed that an audit and assurance professional holding the CISA designation has the requisite skills to perform this review.

## VI. Basis Cycle—Audit/Assurance Program

| Audit/Assurance Program Step | CobiT Cross-reference | COSO Control Environment | Risk Assessment | Control Activities | Information and Communication | Monitoring | Reference Hyperlink | Issue Cross-reference | Comments |
|---|---|---|---|---|---|---|---|---|---|
| **A. Prior Audit/Examination Report Follow-up** | | | | | | | | | |
| 1. Review prior report, if one exists, verify completion of any agreed-upon corrections and note remaining deficiencies. | ME1 | | | | | | | | |
| 1.1 Determine whether:<br>• Senior management has assigned responsibilities for information, its processing and its use<br>• User management is responsible for providing information that supports the entity's objectives and policies<br>• Information systems management is responsible for providing the capabilities necessary for achievement of the defined information systems objectives and policies of the entity<br>• Senior management approves plans for development and acquisition of information systems<br>• There are procedures to ensure that the information system being developed or acquired meets user requirements<br>• There are procedures to ensure that information systems, programs and configuration changes are tested adequately prior to implementation | ME1 | | | | | | | | |

## VI. Basis Cycle—Audit/Assurance Program (cont.)

| Audit/Assurance Program Step | COBIT Cross-reference | Control Environment | Risk Assessment | Control Activities | Information and Communication | Monitoring | Reference Hyperlink | Issue Cross-reference | Comments |
|---|---|---|---|---|---|---|---|---|---|
| **A. Prior Audit/Examination Report Follow-up** *(cont.)* | | | | | | | | | |
| 1.1 *(cont.)* | | | | | | | | | |
| • All personnel involved in the system acquisition and configuration activities receive adequate training and supervision | | | | | | | | | |
| • There are procedures to ensure that information systems are implemented/configured/upgraded in accordance with the established standards | | | | | | | | | |
| • User management participates in the conversion of data from the existing system to the new system | | | | | | | | | |
| • Final approval is obtained from user management prior to going live with a new information/upgraded system | | | | | | | | | |
| • There are procedures to document and schedule all changes to information systems (including key ABAP programs) | | | | | | | | | |
| • There are procedures to ensure that only authorized changes are initiated | | | | | | | | | |
| • There are procedures to ensure that only authorized, tested and documented changes to information systems are accepted into the production client | | | | | | | | | |
| • There are procedures to allow for and control emergency changes | | | | | | | | | |

## VI. Basis Cycle—Audit/Assurance Program (cont.)

| Audit/Assurance Program Step | CobiT Cross-reference | COSO | | | | | Reference Hyperlink | Issue Cross-reference | Comments |
|---|---|---|---|---|---|---|---|---|---|
| | | Control Environment | Risk Assessment | Control Activities | Information and Communication | Monitoring | | | |
| **A. Prior Audit/Examination Report Follow-Up (cont.)** | | | | | | | | | |
| 1.1 *(cont.)* | | | | | | | | | |
| • There are procedures for the approval, monitoring and control of the acquisition and upgrade of hardware and systems software | | | | | | | | | |
| • There is a process for monitoring the volume of named and concurrent SAP ERP users to ensure that the license agreement is not being violated | | | | | | | | | |
| • The organization structure, established by senior management, provides for an appropriate segregation of incompatible functions | | | | | | | | | |
| • The database, application and presentation servers are located in a physically separate and protected environment (i.e., a data center) | | | | | | | | | |
| • Emergency, backup and recovery plans are documented and tested on a regular basis to ensure that they remain current and operational | | | | | | | | | |
| • Backup and recovery plans allow users of information systems to resume operations in the event of an interruption | | | | | | | | | |
| • Application controls are designed with regard to any weaknesses in segregation, security, development and processing controls that may affect the information system | | | | | | | | | |
| • Access to the Implementation Guide (IMG) during production has been restricted | | | | | | | | | |
| • The production client settings have been flagged to not allow changes to programs and | | | | | | | | | |

## VI. Basis Cycle—Audit/Assurance Program (cont.)

| Audit/Assurance Program Step | CobiT Cross-reference | Control Environment | Risk Assessment | Control Activities | Information and Communication | Monitoring | Reference Hyperlink | Issue Cross-reference | Comments |
|---|---|---|---|---|---|---|---|---|---|
| **B. Preliminary Audit Steps** | | | | | | | | | |
| 1. Gain an understanding of the SAP ERP environment. | | | | | | | | | |
| 1.1 Determine what version and release of the SAP ERP software has been implemented. If multiple versions, document the various versions. | PO4 | | | | | | | | |
| 1.2 Obtain details of the following:<br>• Operating system(s) and platforms<br>• Total number of named users (for comparison with limits specified in contract)<br>• Number of SAP ERP instances and clients<br>• Accounting period, company codes and chart of accounts<br>• Database management system used to store data for the SAP ERP system<br>• Location of the servers and the related LAN/WAN connections (need to verify security and controls, including environmental, surrounding the hardware and the network security controls surrounding the connectivity) and, if possible, copies of network topology diagrams<br>• List of business partners, related organizations and remote locations that are permitted to connect to the ERP environment<br>• Various means used to connect to the ERP environment (e.g., dial-up, remote access server, Internet transaction server) and the network diagram, if available | PO2<br>PO3<br>DS2<br>DS12 | | | | | | | | |

## VI. Basis Cycle—Audit/Assurance Program (cont.)

| Audit/Assurance Program Step | CobiT Cross-reference | COSO | | | | | Reference Hyperlink | Issue Cross-reference | Comments |
|---|---|---|---|---|---|---|---|---|---|
| | | Control Environment | Risk Assessment | Control Activities | Information and Communication | Monitoring | | | |
| **B. Preliminary Audit Steps (cont.)** | | | | | | | | | |
| 2. In a standard SAP ERP configuration, confirm that separate systems for development, test and production are implemented. | P02 | | | | | | | | |
| 2.1 Determine whether:<br>• This approach was taken<br>• The instances are totally separate systems or are within the same system | | | | | | | | | |
| 2.2 Determine whether the SAP production environment is connected to other SAP or non-SAP systems. If yes, obtain details as to the nature of connectivity, frequency of information transfers, and security and control measures surrounding these transfers (i.e., to ensure accuracy and completeness). | P02<br>DS5 | | | | | | | | |
| 3. Identify the components being used (Human Capital Management, Financials, Operations, Corporate Services). | P02 | | | | | | | | |
| 3.1 Identify whether the organization has implemented any of the following:<br>• Internet transaction server<br>• Any of the New Dimension products (e.g., Supply Chain Management, Customer Relationship Management, Business Intelligence)<br>• Audit Information System. If implemented, determine how it is used (i.e., only for annual audits or on a regular basis to monitor and report | P02<br>P03<br>ME2 | | | | | | | | |

## VI. Basis Cycle—Audit/Assurance Program (cont.)

| Audit/Assurance Program Step | C₀ᵦᵢT Cross-reference | COSO | | | | | | Reference Hyperlink | Issue Cross-reference | Comments |
|---|---|---|---|---|---|---|---|---|---|---|
| | | Control Environment | Risk Assessment | Control Activities | Information and Communication | Monitoring | | | | |
| **B. Preliminary Audit Steps (cont.)** | | | | | | | | | | |
| 3.2 Determine whether the organization makes use of any mySAP functionality. If yes, describe the functionality and purpose. | PO2 | | | | | | | | | |
| 3.3 Determine whether the organization has created any locally developed APAB/4 programs/reports or tables. If yes, determine how these programs/reports are used. Depending on the importance/extent of use, review and document the development and change management process surrounding the creation/modification of these programs/reports or tables. | AI2 AI6 | | | | | | | | | |
| 3.4 Obtain copies of the organization's key security policies and standards. Highlight key areas of concern, including: • Information security policy • Sensitivity classification • Logical and physical access control requirements • Network security requirements, including requirements for encryption, firewalls, etc. • Platform security requirements (e.g., configuration requirements) | PO6 DS5 DS12 | | | | | | | | | |

## VI. Basis Cycle—Audit/Assurance Program (cont.)

| Audit/Assurance Program Step | CobiT Cross-reference | Control Environment | Risk Assessment | Control Activities | Information and Communication | Monitoring | Reference Hyperlink | Issue Cross-reference | Comments |
|---|---|---|---|---|---|---|---|---|---|
| **B. Preliminary Audit Steps** *(cont.)* | | | | | | | | | |
| 3.5 Obtain information regarding any awareness programs that have been delivered to staff on the key security policies and standards. Consider specifically the frequency of delivery and any statistics on the extent of coverage (i.e., what percentage of staff has received the awareness training). | PO6 DS7 | | | | | | | | |
| 3.6 Maintain authorizations and profiles, for example: <br>• Have job roles, including the related transactions, been defined and documented? <br>• Do procedures for maintaining (creating/changing/deleting) roles exist and are they followed? | PO7 AI4 DS5 | | | | | | | | |
| 3.7 Determine whether adequate access administration procedures exist in written form. Do any of the following procedures exist within the organization? If yes, document the process and comment on compliance with the policies and standards, and the adequacy of resulting documentation. <br>• Procedures to add/change/delete user master records <br>• Procedures to handle temporary access requests <br>• Procedures to handle emergency access requests <br>• Procedures to remove users who have never logged into the system | PO7 AI4 DS5 | | | | | | | | |

## VI. Basis Cycle—Audit/Assurance Program (cont.)

| Audit/Assurance Program Step | CobiT Cross-reference | COSO | | | | | Reference Hyperlink | Issue Cross-reference | Comments |
| --- | --- | --- | --- | --- | --- | --- | --- | --- | --- |
| | | Control Environment | Risk Assessment | Control Activities | Information and Communication | Monitoring | | | |
| **B. Preliminary Audit Steps (cont.)** | | | | | | | | | |
| 3.7 (cont.)<br>• Procedures to automatically notify the administration staff when employees holding sensitive or critical positions leave the organization or change positions | | | | | | | | | |
| 3.8 Obtain copies of the organization's change management policies, processes and procedures, and change documentation. Consider specifically:<br>• Transport processes and procedures, including allowed transport paths<br>• Emergency change processes and procedures<br>• Development standards, including naming conventions, testing requirements and move-to-production requirements | AI4<br>AI6 | | | | | | | | |
| 3.9 Determine whether the organization has a defined process for creating and maintaining clients. If yes, obtain copies and documentation related to the creation and maintenance of clients. | PO2<br>AI6 | | | | | | | | |
| 3.10 Determine the organization's approach to SAP Service Marketplace. Verify the extent of access permitted and processes used to request, approve, authenticate, grant, monitor and terminate SAP Service Marketplace access. | DS2<br>DS5 | | | | | | | | |

## VI. Basis Cycle—Audit/Assurance Program (cont.)

| Audit/Assurance Program Step | CobiT Cross-reference | COSO | | | | | Reference Hyperlink | Issue Cross-reference | Comments |
|---|---|---|---|---|---|---|---|---|---|
| | | Control Environment | Risk Assessment | Control Activities | Information and Communication | Monitoring | | | |
| **B. Preliminary Audit Steps (cont.)** | | | | | | | | | |
| 4. Review outstanding audit findings, if any, from previous years. Assess impact on current audit. | ME1 ME2 | | | | | | | | |
| 5. Identify the significant risks and determine the key controls. | | | | | | | | | |
| 5.1 Obtain details of the risk assessment approach taken in the organization to identify and prioritize risks. | P09 | | | | | | | | |
| 5.2 Obtain copies of and review:<br>• Completed risk assessments impacting the SAP ERP environment<br>• Approved requests to deviate from security policies and standards<br>Assess the impact of the above documents on the planning of the SAP ERP audit. | P09 ME1 | | | | | | | | |
| 5.3 In the case of a recent implementation/upgrade, obtain a copy of the security implementation plan. Assess whether the plan took into account the protection of critical objects within the organization and segregation of duties. Determine whether an appropriate naming convention (i.e., for profiles) has been developed to help security maintenance and to comply with required SAP ERP naming conventions. | P03 P07 DS5 | | | | | | | | |

## VI. Basis Cycle—Audit/Assurance Program (cont.)

| Audit/Assurance Program Step | CoBiT Cross-reference | Control Environment | Risk Assessment | Control Activities | Information and Communication | Monitoring | Reference Hyperlink | Issue Cross-reference | Comments |
|---|---|---|---|---|---|---|---|---|---|
| **C. Detailed Audit Steps** | | | | | | | | | |
| **1. Application Installation (Implementation Guide and Organizational Model)** | | | | | | | | | |
| **1.1 Configuration changes are made in the development environment and transported to production.** | | | | | | | | | |
| 1.1.1 Test that access to the transaction code (SPRO) and the authorization object (S_IMG_ACTV) for the IMG have been restricted in the production environment. | | | | | | | | | |
| 1.1.2 Restrict access to transaction code SCC4, which controls the production client settings. Execute this transaction code, and double-click on each client being tested. Review each of the settings for appropriateness, including the "last changed by" and "last changed" date fields. It is important to note that the No Changes setting should be set for cross-client tables. Protection for the Client Copier and Comparison Tool should be set to No Overwriting. Also ensure that eCAAT and CAAT are set to Not Allowed. | | | | | | | | | |

## VI. Basis Cycle—Audit/Assurance Program (cont.)

| Audit/Assurance Program Step | CobiT Cross-reference | COSO | | | | | Reference Hyperlink | Issue Cross-reference | Comments |
|---|---|---|---|---|---|---|---|---|---|
| | | Control Environment | Risk Assessment | Control Activities | Information and Communication | Monitoring | | | |
| **C. Detailed Audit Steps (cont.)** | | | | | | | | | |
| 1.1.2 *(cont)* Identify changes made directly into production by reviewing a log of changes to table T000. Validate that a business need existed for such direct change and an appropriate change management process was followed. | | | | | | | | | |
| 1.1.3 Obtain information from the system on the OMM by reviewing tables or by utilizing the SAP ERP Audit Information System, which depicts the OMM graphically (refer to figure 12.5). Compare it to the real organization structure and interview management in relation to differences or difficulties that may have emerged during or after the implementation. | | | | | | | | | |
| 1.1.4 Test access to the transaction code (SPRO) and the authorization object (S_IMG_ACTV) for the IMG in the production environment. | | | | | | | | | |

## VI. Basis Cycle—Audit/Assurance Program (cont.)

| Audit/Assurance Program Step | CobiT Cross-reference | COSO | | | | | Reference Hyperlink | Issue Cross-reference | Comments |
|---|---|---|---|---|---|---|---|---|---|
| | | Control Environment | Risk Assessment | Control Activities | Information and Communication | Monitoring | | | |
| **C. Detailed Audit Steps** *(cont.)* | | | | | | | | | |
| 1.1.5 Test the following access to validate who can make changes directly to the production client:<br>a)<br>  T-code: SCC4<br>  Authorization Object: S_TABU_DIS<br>  Activity value: 02<br>  Authorization group: SS<br>  Authorization Object: S_TABU_CLI<br>  Indicators for cross client: x<br>b)<br>  T-code: SCC4<br>  Authorization Object: S_ADMI_FCD<br>  Sys Admin function: T000<br>  Authorization Object: S_CTS_ADMI<br>  Admin Task: INIT | | | | | | | | | |
| **1.2 Changes to critical number ranges are controlled.** | | | | | | | | | |
| 1.2.1 Via transaction SUIM, review authorization object S_NUMBER (*) for those users with the following authorization value sets:<br>• Maintain Number Range Intervals—02<br>• Change Number Range Status—11<br>• Initialize Number Levels—13<br>• Maintain Number Range Objects for all Number Range Objects—17 | | | | | | | | | |

## VI. Basis Cycle—Audit/Assurance Program (cont.)

| Audit/Assurance Program Step | CobiT Cross-reference | COSO | | | | | Reference Hyperlink | Issue Cross-reference | Comments |
|---|---|---|---|---|---|---|---|---|---|
| | | Control Environment | Risk Assessment | Control Activities | Information and Communication | Monitoring | | | |
| **C. Detailed Audit Steps (cont.)** | | | | | | | | | |
| 1.2.2 By using transaction code SE16, browse table TDDAT. In the table name field enter Z* and then Y* to identify all of the custom tables. Determine those tables that have &NC& within the authorization group field. Assess whether these settings (&NC&) are appropriate. | | | | | | | | | |
| 1.2.3 Test access to modify critical tables via the objects S_TABU_DIS (value 02) and transaction codes SM31 or SM30. If the table is cross-client, the user master record must contain a third object, S_TABU_CLI (value X). Use transaction code SUIM ▷ Users ▷ Users by Complex Selection Criteria (also accessible using transaction code SA38 and program RSUSR002) to check for these restrictions.<br><br>Test access to update tables with authorization group SS, since no one should have update access to this critical systems table. | | | | | | | | | |
| **2. Application Development (ABAP/4 Workbench and Transport System)** | | | | | | | | | |
| **2.1 Application modifications are planned, tested and implemented in a phased manner.** | | | | | | | | | |

## VI. Basis Cycle—Audit/Assurance Program (cont.)

| Audit/Assurance Program Step | CobiT Cross-reference | COSO | | | | | | Reference Hyperlink | Issue Cross-reference | Comments |
|---|---|---|---|---|---|---|---|---|---|---|
| | | Control Environment | Risk Assessment | Control Activities | Information and Communication | Monitoring | | | | |
| **C. Detailed Audit Steps *(cont.)*** | | | | | | | | | | |
| 2.1.1 Determine the system landscape and client strategy, and review the change control policies and procedures (including documentation) to transport objects between environments. Work with the Basis/Transport Administrator to obtain a random sample of transports and trace back to documentation. Ensure that authorization for the transport was obtained and confirm that the specified transport path was followed. For emergency changes, ensure that the specified emergency process was followed. Confirm that appropriate authorizations were obtained and documentation was subsequently completed.<br><br>Review the System Change option and confirm it has been set to No Changes Allowed (refer to 1.1.2 above). Review segregation of duties with respect to creating and releasing change requests. Test user access to authorization object S_TRANSPRT and ACTVT; expect 03 and any transport type (TTYPE). Assess the appropriateness of such access in comparison with the users' job functions. | AI6 DS5 | | | X | | | | | | |

## VI. Basis Cycle—Audit/Assurance Program (cont.)

| Audit/Assurance Program Step | CobiT Cross-reference | Control Environment | Risk Assessment | Control Activities | Information and Communication | Monitoring | Reference Hyperlink | Issue Cross-reference | Comments |
|---|---|---|---|---|---|---|---|---|---|
| **C. Detailed Audit Steps** *(cont.)* | | | | | | | | | |
| **2.2 Customized ABAP/4 programs are secured appropriately.** | | | | | | | | | |
| 2.2.1 To identify customized programs that have not been assigned to an authorization group, enter transaction code SE16. Browse the table TRDIR and enter the values of Z* and then Y* in the program name field. This will produce a list of all customized programs, assuming that the organization has followed a standard naming convention when customizing programs. Filter this list for programs that do not have a value in the authorization group field (SECU). Concentrate the investigation on users who have SE38, SA38, SE80 and SE37 transaction codes. These users automatically have access to run many of these programs. | | | | | | | | | |
| 2.2.2 From this list, select a representative sample of customized programs and check the source code to see whether an authority-check statement has been included. Use transaction code SA38 and run the ABAP/4 program RSABAPSC with the appropriate program name and authority check in the ABAP/4 language commands selection field to display the authority-check statements for each of the | | | | | | | | | |

## VI. Basis Cycle—Audit/Assurance Program (cont.)

| Audit/Assurance Program Step | CobiT Cross-reference | COSO | | | | | Reference Hyperlink | Issue Cross-reference | Comments |
|---|---|---|---|---|---|---|---|---|---|
| | | Control Environment | Risk Assessment | Control Activities | Information and Communication | Monitoring | | | |
| **C. Detailed Audit Steps (cont.)** | | | | | | | | | |
| 2.2.2 (cont.) sampled programs. Note that the results may include other programs called by the sampled programs with the appropriate authority-check statements. Confirm the results of the test with management. | | | | | | | | | |
| 2.2.3 Review and assess the value for the parameters below (use RSPARAM report): <br>• Auth/no_check_in_some_cases (Can be either Y or N. If set to the recommended value of Y [permit authorization checks], monitor the content of SU24 carefully to make sure that these entries are set appropriately.) <br>• Auth/rfc_authority_check (recommend set to 2 to permit full checking) | DS5 | | | X | | | | | |
| 2.2.4 Use transaction SUIM ▲ Users ▲ Users by Complex Selection Criteria (also accessible using transaction code SA38 and program RSUSR002) to test the number of users who have access to execute all programs independent of the authorization group assigned. Enter the authorization object S_PROGRAM with the activity value of | | | | | | | | | |

## VI. Basis Cycle—Audit/Assurance Program (cont.)

| Audit/Assurance Program Step | CobiT Cross-reference | Control Environment | Risk Assessment | Control Activities | Information and Communication | Monitoring | Reference Hyperlink | Issue Cross-reference | Comments |
|---|---|---|---|---|---|---|---|---|---|
| **C. Detailed Audit Steps** *(cont.)* | | | | | | | | | |
| 2.2.4 *(cont.)* SUBMIT or BTCSUBMIT and the authorization object S_TCODE with a transaction code of SA38, SE37, SE38 or SE80. | | | | | | | | | |
| 2.2.5 Review the policy, procedures and criteria for establishing program authorization groups, assigning the ABAP/4 programs to groups and including authority-check statements in programs. Compare the results from testing to established policies, procedures, standards and guidance (note that organizations may use additional transactions, tables, authorization objects, ABAP/4 programs, and reports to control their systems). | | | | | | | | | |
| **2.3 The creation or modification of programs is performed in the development system and migrated through the test system to production.** | | | | | | | | | |
| 2.3.1 To produce a list of users who have access to develop programs in the production system, execute transaction SUIM ▶ Users ▶ Users by Complex Selection Criteria (also accessible using transaction code SA38 and program RSUSR002) with the authorization object S_DEVELOP, the activity values of 01, 02 or | | | | | | | | | |

## VI. Basis Cycle—Audit/Assurance Program (cont.)

| Audit/Assurance Program Step | CobiT Cross-reference | COSO | | | | | | Reference Hyperlink | Issue Cross-reference | Comments |
|---|---|---|---|---|---|---|---|---|---|---|
| | | Control Environment | Risk Assessment | Control Activities | Information and Communication | Monitoring | | | | |
| **C. Detailed Audit Steps (cont.)** | | | | | | | | | | |
| 2.3.1 *(cont.)* 06. ABAP/4 programs that are not assigned to an authorization group may be changed by any user with authorization for object S_DEVELOP, depending on whether the user has been assigned a developer's key and the correct object keys. | | | | | | | | | | |
| **2.4 Access for making changes to the dictionary is restricted to authorized individuals.** | | | | | | | | | | |
| 2.4.1 Execute transaction SUIM ▸ Users ▸ Users by Complex Selection Criteria (also accessible using transaction code SA38 and program RSUSR002). Review users with the following authorization to determine whether they are appropriate: Data dictionary object: S_DEVELOP with any of the activity values 01, 02, 06, 07 and access to any of the transaction codes SE11, SE12, SE15, SE16, SE37, SE38, SE80 | | | | | | | | | | |

# VI. Basis Cycle—Audit/Assurance Program (cont.)

| Audit/Assurance Program Step | CobiT Cross-reference | COSO | | | | | Reference Hyperlink | Issue Cross-reference | Comments |
|---|---|---|---|---|---|---|---|---|---|
| | | Control Environment | Risk Assessment | Control Activities | Information and Communication | Monitoring | | | |
| **C. Detailed Audit Steps** *(cont.)* | | | | | | | | | |
| **2.5 Access to modify and develop queries is restricted.** | | | | | | | | | |
| 2.5.1 Using transaction SUIM ▶ Users ▶ Users by Complex Selection Criteria (also accessible using transaction code SA38 and program RSUSR002), enter the authorization object S_QUERY with activity value 02 and transaction code: <br>— SQ01 to identify all users who can create and maintain queries. In addition, use the authorization object S_QUERY with activity value 23 and transaction codes <br>— SQ02 or SQ03 to produce a report identifying all users who can maintain functional areas and user groups. Review the lists with management for reasonableness. | | | | | | | | | |
| **2.6 Relevant company codes are set to Productive in the production environment** | | | | | | | | | |
| 2.6.1 Transaction code OBR3 contains a list of company codes and whether they have been set to Productive. This information is also available in table T001 and can | | | | | | | | | |

## VI. Basis Cycle—Audit/Assurance Program (cont.)

| Audit/Assurance Program Step | CobiT Cross-reference | COSO | | | | | | Reference Hyperlink | Issue Cross-reference | Comments |
| --- | --- | --- | --- | --- | --- | --- | --- | --- | --- | --- |
| | | Control Environment | Risk Assessment | Control Activities | Information and Communication | Monitoring | | | | |
| **C. Detailed Audit Steps (cont.)** | | | | | | | | | | |
| 2.6.1 (cont.) be viewed using transaction code SE16. Perform a review of this list. In instances where company codes have not been set to Productive, investigate the reasons with management. | | | | | | | | | | |
| **3. Application Operations (Computing Center Management System)** | | | | | | | | | | |
| **3.1 The Computing Center Management System (CCMS) is configured appropriately** | | | | | | | | | | |
| 3.1.1 To ensure that the CCMS displays meaningful data, determine via inquiry whether transaction RZ04 was used to set up operations modes, instances and timetables. | | | | | | | | | | |
| 3.1.2 Determine how the organization is monitoring its SAP ERP system. Understand the policies, procedures, standards and guidance regarding the execution of SAPSTART and STOPSAP programs or their equivalent in the organization's environment. Check that only authorized personnel may execute these programs. | | | | | | | | | | |

## VI. Basis Cycle—Audit/Assurance Program (cont.)

| Audit/Assurance Program Step | CobiT Cross-reference | COSO | | | | | | Reference Hyperlink | Issue Cross-reference | Comments |
|---|---|---|---|---|---|---|---|---|---|---|
| | | Control Environment | Risk Assessment | Control Activities | Information and Communication | Monitoring | | | | |
| **C. Detailed Audit Steps *(cont.)*** | | | | | | | | | | |
| 3.1.3 Generate a list of users with the ability to access the Alert Monitor by performing online access authorization testing for these authorization objects S_RZL_ADM, activity values 01 (administrator) and 03 (display) and transaction code, value AL01 (if a 3.x system) or RZ20 (if a 4.x system or SAP ECC system). | | | | | | | | | | |
| **3.2 Batch processing operations are secured appropriately.** | | | | | | | | | | |
| 3.2.1 Obtain a list of batch users by executing transaction SUIM ▸ Users ▸ Users by Complex Selection Criteria (also accessible using transaction code SA38 and program RSUSR002) with the following authorizations: <br>• Batch input: transaction code—SM35, authorization object—S_BDC_MONI, field: BDCAKTI, value: DELE, FREE, LOCK, REOG and field: BDCGROUP, value: * <br>• Batch administration: transaction code—SM36/SM37, authorization object—S _BTCH_ADM, field: BTCADMIN, value: Y <br>• Batch scheduling: transaction code—SM36, authorization object—S_BTCH_JOB, field: JOBACTION, value: DELE, RELE, authorization object—S_BTCH_NAM, value: * | | | | | | | | | | |

## VI. Basis Cycle—Audit/Assurance Program (cont.)

| Audit/Assurance Program Step | CobiT Cross-reference | COSO | | | | | Reference Hyperlink | Issue Cross-reference | Comments |
|---|---|---|---|---|---|---|---|---|---|
| | | Control Environment | Risk Assessment | Control Activities | Information and Communication | Monitoring | | | |
| **C. Detailed Audit Steps (cont.)** | | | | | | | | | |
| 3.2.1 *(cont.)*<br>• Batch processing: transaction code—SM37, authorization object—S_BTCH_JOB, field: JOBACTION, value: DELE, RELE, PLAN, authorization object—S_BTCH_NAM, value: *<br>• Event triggering: transaction code—SM64, authorization object—S_BTCH_ADM, field: BTCADMIN, value: Y | | | | | | | | | |
| 3.2.2 Determine by corroborative inquiry that upload programs have been removed from the production environment as appropriate. | | | | | | | | | |
| **3.3 Default system parameter settings are reviewed and configured to suit the organization's environment.** | | | | | | | | | |
| 3.3.1 Obtain a printout of the values of the following key parameters (run report RSPARAM via transaction code SA38 on each instance, as appropriate) and compare to the requirements as set out in the policies and standards in **figure 12.9.**<br>• Confirm that the system profile parameter files and default.pfl are protected from unauthorized access. Confirm that there | | | | | | | | | |

# VI. Basis Cycle—Audit/Assurance Program (cont.)

| Audit/Assurance Program Step | CobiT Cross-reference | COSO | | | | | Reference Hyperlink | Issue Cross-reference | Comments |
| --- | --- | --- | --- | --- | --- | --- | --- | --- | --- |
| | | Control Environment | Risk Assessment | Control Activities | Information and Communication | Monitoring | | | |
| **C. Detailed Audit Steps** *(cont.)* | | | | | | | | | |
| 3.3.1 *(cont.)* is a mechanism/process to ensure that the profiles are regularly checked to ascertain that they have not been changed inappropriately. Obtain any related change documentation and ensure that: <br> – The documentation is authorized. <br> – Related log entries reflect the expected changes. <br> – A current printout of the RSUSR006 report is obtained and reviewed for unusual items or trends. <br> • Determine whether management has a process for frequent monitoring of unsuccessful logon attempts and/or locked users via a review of this report. If yes, obtain details on the following frequency of monitoring. <br> • Review a reasonable sample of previously followed-up reports and assess the appropriateness of the follow-up on unusual findings. Run transaction SUIM ▲ Users ▲ Users by Complex Selection Criteria (also accessible using transaction code SA38 and program RSUSR002). | | | | | | | | | |

## VI. Basis Cycle—Audit/Assurance Program (cont.)

| Audit/Assurance Program Step | COBIT Cross-reference | COSO | | | | | Reference Hyperlink | Issue Cross-reference | Comments |
| --- | --- | --- | --- | --- | --- | --- | --- | --- | --- |
| | | Control Environment | Risk Assessment | Control Activities | Information and Communication | Monitoring | | | |
| **C. Detailed Audit Steps *(cont.)*** | | | | | | | | | |
| 3.3.1 *(cont.)* <br> • Review and follow up on: <br> – Users with original passwords <br> – Users who have not logged in during the last 60 days <br> – Users who have not changed their passwords in the last 60 days (or any duration that is appropriate for the organization) <br> • Obtain a sample of user master records in the production environment and work with the authorization security administrator and the job descriptions to assess segregation of duties (refer to chapter 4 for more guidance) and the appropriateness of the access granted. | | | | | | | | | |
| 3.3.2 Execute transaction SUIM ▶ Users ▶ Users by Complex Selection Criteria (also accessible using transaction code SA38 and program RSUSR002) with the transaction code SM01 to provide a list of all users who have access to lock or unlock transaction codes in the system. Review and confirm this list with management to ensure that only authorized users have access. | | | | | | | | | |

393

## VI. Basis Cycle—Audit/Assurance Program (cont.)

| Audit/Assurance Program Step | CobiT Cross-reference | COSO | | | | | Reference Hyperlink | Issue Cross-reference | Comments |
|---|---|---|---|---|---|---|---|---|---|
| | | Control Environment | Risk Assessment | Control Activities | Information and Communication | Monitoring | | | |
| **C. Detailed Audit Steps (cont.)** | | | | | | | | | |
| 3.3.3 Enter transaction code SM01 to display a list of transaction codes with a check box beside them. A cross in the check box indicates that the transaction code has been locked. Review sensitive transaction codes to ensure that they have been locked from user access. Such transaction codes include, but are not limited to:<br>• SCC5—Client Delete<br>• SCC1—Client Copy (may overwrite the production client)<br>• SM49—Execute Logical Commands (may allow pass-through to operating system)<br>• SM69—Execute Logical Commands (may allow pass-through to operating system) | | | | | | | | | |
| **3.4 Users are prevented from logging in with trivial or easily guessable passwords** | | | | | | | | | |
| 3.4.1 Based on the review of the key security policies, determine whether there are any character combinations (apart from the SAP ERP standards) that the policy has prohibited from use. If yes, obtain a printout of the contents of table USR40 and confirm that the list of "illegal" words is contained therein. | P06 DS5 | | | X | | | | | |

## VI. Basis Cycle—Audit/Assurance Program (cont.)

| Audit/Assurance Program Step | CobiT Cross-reference | COSO | | | | | Reference Hyperlink | Issue Cross-reference | Comments |
|---|---|---|---|---|---|---|---|---|---|
| | | Control Environment | Risk Assessment | Control Activities | Information and Communication | Monitoring | | | |
| **C. Detailed Audit Steps *(cont.)*** | | | | | | | | | |
| **3.5 SAP Router is configured to act as a gateway to secure communications into and out of the SAP ERP environment.** | | | | | | | | | |
| 3.5.1 Discuss with the operating system administrators the procedures surrounding changes to SAP Router and the procedures surrounding restarting SAP Router when it goes down. | AI4 DS5 ME1 ME2 | | | X | | | | | |
| 3.5.2 Obtain a list of individuals with view and/or change access to the SAP Router binary. Review the list with key management and assess the appropriateness of the segregation of duties. | | | | | | | | | |
| 3.5.3 Request an extract of the SAP Router permissions table (for example, execute the UNIX command SAP router –L <path>) from the operating system administrator. Review the permissions table with the operating systems administrator. Compare with the network diagram to assess the appropriateness of the IP addresses and with change control documentation to confirm that management has appropriately authorized changes. | | | | | | | | | |

## VI. Basis Cycle—Audit/Assurance Program (cont.)

| Audit/Assurance Program Step | CobiT Cross-reference | COSO | | | | | | Reference Hyperlink | Issue Cross-reference | Comments |
| | | Control Environment | Risk Assessment | Control Activities | Information and Communication | Monitoring | | | | |
|---|---|---|---|---|---|---|---|---|---|---|
| **C. Detailed Audit Steps** *(cont.)* | | | | | | | | | | |
| 3.5.4 If logging is active, ascertain the frequency with which the logs are reviewed and followed up. | | | | | | | | | | |
| 3.5.5 Obtain a reasonable sample of the logs and review them with the operating systems administrator. | | | | | | | | | | |
| **3.6 Remote access by software vendors is controlled adequately.** | | | | | | | | | | |
| 3.6.1 Determine the organization's approach to SAP Service Marketplace. Verify the extent of access permitted and the processes used to request, approve, authenticate, grant, monitor and terminate SAP Service Marketplace access. Check that changes are subject to normal testing and migration controls. | DS2 DS5 | | | X | | | | | | |
| 3.6.2 Obtain a list of SAP Service Marketplace users on the production client. Enter transaction code OSS1 using the client's administrator ID. Click on the SAPNET icon followed by the Administration icon. Perform an authorization analysis by authorization object view. This will provide a list of all users assigned to the SAP Service Marketplace by authorization object. | | | | | | | | | | |

## VI. Basis Cycle—Audit/Assurance Program (cont.)

| Audit/Assurance Program Step | CobiT Cross-reference | COSO | | | | | Reference Hyperlink | Issue Cross-reference | Comments |
|---|---|---|---|---|---|---|---|---|---|
| | | Control Environment | Risk Assessment | Control Activities | Information and Communication | Monitoring | | | |
| **C. Detailed Audit Steps (cont.)** | | | | | | | | | |
| 3.6.2 *(cont.* In particular, review for reasonableness with management the users who have been assigned to administration authorization and open service connections. | | | | | | | | | |
| **3.7 SAP ERP Remote Function Call (RFC) and Common Programming Interface—Communications (CPI-C) are secured.** | | | | | | | | | |
| 3.7.1 Ascertain whether the logon information (dialog and/or nondialog users) is stored and reviewed. Obtain a representative sample and review to ensure that dialog users are appropriate (i.e., valid employees with authorization) and that nondialog user IDs are appropriate. To do this, execute transaction code SM59. This will display the table RFCDES, which controls the communication between systems. The table lists the RFC destinations, which will include all SAP ERP connections that are on the system. Expand each of the SAP ERP connections and double-click on each connection to verify that no dialog user ID is listed with its password. | PO2 AI4 DS5 ME1 ME2 | | | X | | | | | |
| 3.7.2 Determine whether these systems are protected with the appropriate network measures (e.g., SAP Router/firewall/ routers). | | | | | | | | | |

## VI. Basis Cycle—Audit/Assurance Program (cont.)

| Audit/Assurance Program Step | CoʙɪT Cross-reference | Control Environment | Risk Assessment | Control Activities | Information and Communication | Monitoring | Reference Hyperlink | Issue Cross-reference | Comments |
|---|---|---|---|---|---|---|---|---|---|
| **C. Detailed Audit Steps (cont.)** | | | | | | | | | |
| 3.7.3 Assess the strength/adequacy (i.e., robustness) of password measures to authenticate RFC connections. | | | | | | | | | |
| 3.7.4 Confirm with the SAP ERP security authorization manager that authority checks are included in functional modules called via RFC. | | | | | | | | | |
| 3.7.5 Via transaction SUIM ▶ Users ▶ Users by Complex Selection Criteria (also accessible using transaction code SA38 and program RSUSR002), identify users who have access to transaction code SM59. Assess whether this access is appropriate (work with user access management). | | | | | | | | | |
| 3.7.6 If using release 4.0 or higher, ascertain whether SNC protection has been applied to RFC calls. If yes, cross-reference to SNC documentation and testing performed earlier. | | | | | | | | | |
| **3.8 The technology infrastructure is configured to secure communications and operations in the SAP ERP environment.** | | | | | | | | | |
| 3.8.1 Firewall | | | | | | | | | |

## VI. Basis Cycle—Audit/Assurance Program (cont.)

| Audit/Assurance Program Step | COBIT Cross-reference | COSO | | | | | | | Reference Hyperlink | Issue Cross-reference | Comments |
|---|---|---|---|---|---|---|---|---|---|---|---|
| | | Control Environment | Risk Assessment | Control Activities | Information and Communication | Monitoring | | | | | |
| **C. Detailed Audit Steps (cont.)** | | | | | | | | | | | |
| 3.8.1.1 Discuss with the firewall administrators the procedures surrounding changes to the firewall rules and recovery of firewalls in the event of an outage. | AI4 DS5 ME1 ME2 | | | X | | | | | | | |
| 3.8.1.2 Obtain a list of individuals with view and/or change access to the firewall rules. Review the list with key management and assess the appropriateness of the segregation of duties. | DS5 | | | X | | | | | | | |
| 3.8.1.3 Review the permissions table with the firewall administrator. Compare with network diagram to assess the appropriateness of the IP addresses. | DS13 | | | X | | | | | | | |
| 3.8.1.4 If logging is set to Logging Active, ascertain the frequency with which the logs are reviewed and followed up. | | | | | | | | | | | |
| 3.8.1.5 Obtain a reasonable sample of the logs and review them with the firewalls administrator. | | | | | | | | | | | |

## VI. Basis Cycle—Audit/Assurance Program (cont.)

| Audit/Assurance Program Step | CobiT Cross-reference | COSO | | | | | Reference Hyperlink | Issue Cross-reference | Comments |
|---|---|---|---|---|---|---|---|---|---|
| | | Control Environment | Risk Assessment | Control Activities | Information and Communication | Monitoring | | | |
| **C. Detailed Audit Steps (cont.)** | | | | | | | | | |
| 3.8.2 Secure Network Communications (SNC) | | | | | | | | | |
| 3.8.2.1 Identify the communication paths that have been protected by SNC/external security product. | AI4 DS5 ME1 ME2 | | | X | | | | | |
| 3.8.2.2 Assess whether the level of protection is appropriate for each of the various communication paths. Use the requirements set out in the information security policy and various risk assessments to assist in the assessment. | | | | | | | | | |
| 3.8.2.3 Review the configuration for each path with the network security administrator for appropriateness. | | | | | | | | | |
| 3.8.3 Secure Store and Forward (SSF) Mechanisms and Digital Signatures | | | | | | | | | |
| 3.8.3.1 Determine whether there are any regional laws or regulations with which the organization must comply that govern the use of digital signatures. If yes, confirm that the organization is in compliance. | DS5 ME3 | | | X | | | | | |

## VI. Basis Cycle—Audit/Assurance Program (cont.)

| Audit/Assurance Program Step | CobiT Cross-reference | COSO Control Environment | Risk Assessment | Control Activities | Information and Communication | Monitoring | Reference Hyperlink | Issue Cross-reference | Comments |
|---|---|---|---|---|---|---|---|---|---|
| **C. Detailed Audit Steps (cont.)** | | | | | | | | | |
| 3.8.3.2 Determine whether the organization uses an external product for SSF. If yes:<br>• Ascertain whether the organization uses hardware- or software-based keys.<br>• Describe the controls surrounding issuance and changing of the public and private keys.<br>• Ascertain whether the organization uses self-signed certificates or CA-signed certificates. | PO2<br>DS5<br>DS13 | | | X | | | | | |
| 3.8.3.3 If using release 4.5 or higher, determine whether SAPSECULIB is used as the default SSF provider. If yes, determine whether the file SAPSECU.pse is protected from unauthorized access. | DS5 | | | X | | | | | |
| 3.8.4 Workstation Security | | | | | | | | | |
| 3.8.4.1 Via inspection, ensure that staff utilizes the available security measures surrounding workstations/PCs (e.g., screen savers, power-on passwords, third-party security | DS5 | | | X | | | | | |

## VI. Basis Cycle—Audit/Assurance Program (cont.)

| Audit/Assurance Program Step | CobiT Cross-reference | COSO Control Environment | COSO Risk Assessment | COSO Control Activities | COSO Information and Communication | COSO Monitoring | Reference Hyperlink | Issue Cross-reference | Comments |
|---|---|---|---|---|---|---|---|---|---|
| **C. Detailed Audit Steps (cont.)** | | | | | | | | | |
| 3.8.4.1 (cont.) products, physical controls). Consider specifically whether: <br>• Users are able to bypass screen saver/power-on passwords. <br>• Screen savers activate automatically or are (as a rule) activated by users when they leave their work areas. | | | | | | | | | |
| 3.8.4.2 Regarding virus protection, determine whether: <br>• Virus scanners are used on the network and/or workstations. <br>• Virus signatures are kept up to date. <br>• There is a procedure for disseminating virus education to users. | DS5 DS13 | | | X | | | | | |
| 3.8.4.3 Assess adequacy of physical controls. Consider specifically: <br>• Are the workstations in secure/restricted areas? <br>• How is the area secured (e.g., security cards, keys, combination locks)? <br>• Do individuals circumvent these controls (i.e., piggyback at entrance, prop open the door)? | DS5 DS12 | | | X | | | | | |

## VI. Basis Cycle—Audit/Assurance Program (cont.)

| Audit/Assurance Program Step | CobiT Cross-reference | COSO | | | | | | Reference Hyperlink | Issue Cross-reference | Comments |
| --- | --- | --- | --- | --- | --- | --- | --- | --- | --- | --- |
| | | Control Environment | Risk Assessment | Control Activities | Information and Communication | Monitoring | | | | |
| **C. Detailed Audit Steps (cont.)** | | | | | | | | | | |
| 3.8.5 Operating System and Database Security | | | | | | | | | | |
| 3.8.5.1 Work with the systems and database administrator to confirm that the default passwords on the standard operating system and database user IDs have been changed, appropriate security parameters have been set and appropriate security procedures are in place and operating. | DS5 | | | X | | | | | | |
| **4. Application Security (Profile Generator and Security Administration)** | | | | | | | | | | |
| **4.1 Duties within the security administration environment are adequately segregated.** | | | | | | | | | | |
| 4.1.1 Determine whether the system administrator tasks are segregated into the following administrator functions by generating user lists for the following authorizations using transaction SUIM ▷ Users ▷ Users by Complex Selection Criteria (also accessible using transaction code SA38 and program RSUSR002):<br>• For the Profile Generator: | | | | | | | | | | |

## VI. Basis Cycle—Audit/Assurance Program (cont.)

| Audit/Assurance Program Step | CoвiT Cross-reference | COSO | | | | | Reference Hyperlink | Issue Cross-reference | Comments |
| --- | --- | --- | --- | --- | --- | --- | --- | --- | --- |
| | | Control Environment | Risk Assessment | Control Activities | Information and Communication | Monitoring | | | |
| **C. Detailed Audit Steps (cont.)** | | | | | | | | | |
| 4.1.1 (cont.) | | | | | | | | | |
| – Create and change roles—Used to define and update roles. Use authorization S_USER_AGR with authorization field values of 01 and 02. Test this in conjunction with transaction code PFCG. | | | | | | | | | |
| – Transport roles—Used to transport or activate roles to/in production. Use authorization S_USER_AGR with authorization field value of 21. Test this in conjunction with transaction code PFCG. | | | | | | | | | |
| – Assign roles/profiles to user master records—Used to assign or transfer roles/profiles into the user master records for the relevant users. Use authorization S_USER_AGR with authorization field value of 02 and authorization S_USER_GRP with authorization field value of 22. Test this in conjunction with transaction code PFCG. Also test the manual maintenance of roles/profiles (SU02/SU03) in use prior to PFCG. | | | | | | | | | |

## VI. Basis Cycle—Audit/Assurance Program (cont.)

| Audit/Assurance Program Step | CobiT Cross-reference | COSO | | | | | Reference Hyperlink | Issue Cross-reference | Comments |
|---|---|---|---|---|---|---|---|---|---|
| | | Control Environment | Risk Assessment | Control Activities | Information and Communication | Monitoring | | | |
| **C. Detailed Audit Steps (cont.)** | | | | | | | | | |
| 4.1.1 (cont.)<br><br>Authorization Maintenance: Use authorization S_USER_AUT with authorization field value 01, 02, 07, 22. Test this in conjunction with transaction SU03.<br><br>User Maintenance: Use authorization S_USER_PRO with authorization field value 01, 02, 07, 22. Test this in conjunction with transaction SU02.<br>• For user master maintenance:<br>– Create/change/lock/delete changes: Use authorization object S_USER_GRP with authorization field values of 01, 02, 05, 06. Test this in conjunction with transaction code SU01.<br>– Assign roles/profiles to user master records: Use authorization S_USER_AGR with authorization field value of 02, and authorization S_USER_GRP with authorization field value 22 and 02.<br><br>If full segregation is not possible among the four functions listed above, management should at minimum consider segregating the creation of roles/profiles and assignment of | | | | | | | | | |

## VI. Basis Cycle—Audit/Assurance Program (cont.)

| Audit/Assurance Program Step | CobiT Cross-reference | COSO | | | | | Reference Hyperlink | Issue Cross-reference | Comments |
|---|---|---|---|---|---|---|---|---|---|
| | | Control Environment | Risk Assessment | Control Activities | Information and Communication | Monitoring | | | |
| **C. Detailed Audit Steps *(cont.)*** | | | | | | | | | |
| 4.1.1 *(cont.)* roles/profiles. If the segregation of duties option is practical, assess SUIM ▷ Change Documents ▷ For Users/For Profiles/For Authorizations (also accessible through transaction code SA38 and programs RSUSR100/101/102) for evidence of review and action by management. | | | | | | | | | |
| 4.1.2 Test user access to effect mass changes to user master records authorization objects S_USER_GRP and S_USER_PRO with authorization field values of 01, 02, 05 and 06, and transaction codes SU10 (Delete/Add a Profile for All Users) and SU12 (Delete All Users). | | | | | | | | | |
| **4.2 Adequate security authorization documentation is maintained.** | | | | | | | | | |
| 4.2.1 Select a random sample of authorized change documentation that pertains to changes to user master records. Run SUIM ▷ Change Documents ▷ For Users (also accessible through transaction code SA38 and program RSUSR100) and assess whether the changes made are as documented. | AI6 DS5 ME1 | | | X | | | | | |

## VI. Basis Cycle—Audit/Assurance Program (cont.)

| Audit/Assurance Program Step | CobiT Cross-reference | Control Environment | Risk Assessment | Control Activities | Information and Communication | Monitoring | Reference Hyperlink | Issue Cross-reference | Comments |
|---|---|---|---|---|---|---|---|---|---|
| **C. Detailed Audit Steps (cont.)** | | | | | | | | | |
| 4.2.2 Select a random sample of authorized change documentation that pertains to changes to profiles. Run SUIM ▶ Change Documents ▶ For Profiles (also accessible through transaction code SA38 and program RSUSR101) and assess whether the changes made are as documented. | AI6 DS5 ME1 | | | X | | | | | |
| 4.2.3 Select a random sample of authorized change documentation that pertains to changes to authorizations. Run SUIM ▶ Change Documents ▶ For Authorizations (also accessible through transaction code SA38 and program RSUSR102) and assess whether the changes made are as documented. | AI6 DS5 ME1 | | | X | | | | | |
| **4.3 The superuser SAP\* is properly secured.** | | | | | | | | | |
| 4.3.1 To determine whether the SAP\* user has been locked, execute transaction SA38 (reporting) with transaction SUIM ▶ Users ▶ Users by Complex Selection Criteria (also accessible using transaction code SA38 and program RSUSR002). Enter SAP\* in the user field and press F8. Verify that the SAP\* group field says SUPER. Click twice on the Other View button. The user status field for SAP\* should say locked. | DS5 | | | X | | | | | |

## VI. Basis Cycle—Audit/Assurance Program (cont.)

| Audit/Assurance Program Step | CobiT Cross-reference | COSO | | | | | Reference Hyperlink | Issue Cross-reference | Comments |
|---|---|---|---|---|---|---|---|---|---|
| | | Control Environment | Risk Assessment | Control Activities | Information and Communication | Monitoring | | | |
| **C. Detailed Audit Steps (cont.)** | | | | | | | | | |
| 4.3.2 For SAP*, run transaction code SA38 and program RSUSR003 to confirm that:<br>• The ID has been deactivated in all clients and a new superuser created.<br>• The password has been changed from the default (i.e., not trivial). | | | | | | | | | |
| **4.4 Default users are secured properly.** | | | | | | | | | |
| 4.4.1 To test whether the default password has been changed for DDIC, SAPCPIC and EarlyWatch, execute the SAP ERP report RSUSR003 and determine whether the default passwords have been changed. To determine whether the SAPCPIC and EarlyWatch users have been locked, execute transaction SUIM ▲ Users ▲ Users by Complex Selection Criteria (also accessible using transaction code SA38 and program RSUSR002). Enter the user name in the user field and press F8. Verify that the group field says SUPER. Click twice on the Other View button. The user status field should say locked. | DS5 | | | X | | | | | |

## VI. Basis Cycle—Audit/Assurance Program (cont.)

| Audit/Assurance Program Step | CobiT Cross-reference | COSO | | | | | | Reference Hyperlink | Issue Cross-reference | Comments |
| --- | --- | --- | --- | --- | --- | --- | --- | --- | --- | --- |
| | | Control Environment | Risk Assessment | Control Activities | Information and Communication | Monitoring | | | | |
| **C. Detailed Audit Steps *(cont.)*** | | | | | | | | | | |
| **4.5 Access to powerful profiles is restricted.** | | | | | | | | | | |
| 4.5.1 Review for appropriateness users assigned the privileged profiles of SAP_ALL and SAP_NEW. Users who have been assigned these superuser profiles/roles should be assigned to user group super or equivalent, which should be maintained by a limited number of Basis personnel only.<br><br>To perform this test, execute transaction SUIM ▲ Users ▲ Users by Complex Selection Criteria (also accessible using transaction code SA38 and program RSUSR002).<br><br>In the part noted as Selection Criteria for User enter SAP_ALL into the profile field. Click on the button to the right of the text box. Enter SAP_NEW in the first empty text box. Click on Copy. This report will list all users who have superuser functionality.<br><br>Check other powerful profiles for user: access<br>• S_A.SYSTEM (System administration authorizations) | | | | | | | | | | |

409

## VI. Basis Cycle—Audit/Assurance Program (cont.)

| Audit/Assurance Program Step | CobiT Cross-reference | COSO | | | | | Reference Hyperlink | Issue Cross-reference | Comments |
|---|---|---|---|---|---|---|---|---|---|
| | | Control Environment | Risk Assessment | Control Activities | Information and Communication | Monitoring | | | |
| **C. Detailed Audit Steps *(cont.)*** | | | | | | | | | |
| 4.5.1 *(cont.)* <br> • S_RZL_ADMIN (CCMS administration authorizations) <br> • S_USER_ALL (All user administration authorizations) <br> • S_A.USER and S_A.ADMIN (used to administer user master record authorizations) <br> • Check the user list identified by this test to ascertain whether individuals who have access to the previously mentioned functionality require this access, based on their job responsibilities and established policies, procedures, standards and guidance. | | | | | | | | | |
| **4.6 The authorization group that contains powerful users is restricted.** | | | | | | | | | |
| 4.6.1 Identify the system administrators within the enterprise and determine to which user groups their user IDs belong. Using transaction SUIM ▶ Users ▶ Users by Complex Selection Criteria (also accessible using transaction code SA38 and program RSUSR002), review the system for users with the authorization object S_USER_AGR (Profile Generator environment) with the activity | | | | | | | | | |

## VI. Basis Cycle—Audit/Assurance Program (cont.)

| Audit/Assurance Program Step | CobiT Cross-reference | COSO | | | | | Reference Hyperlink | Issue Cross-reference | Comments |
|---|---|---|---|---|---|---|---|---|---|
| | | Control Environment | Risk Assessment | Control Activities | Information and Communication | Monitoring | | | |
| **C. Detailed Audit Steps (cont.)** | | | | | | | | | |
| 4.6.1 *(cont.)* values 01, 02, 21 and 22, and transaction code PFCG or the authorization object S_USER_GRP (manual maintenance) with the activity values of 01, 02, 05 and 06 and the transaction code SU01. The authorization field user group in user master maintenance should be similar to one of the values identified above. This would usually be the group SUPER or ITO-SYSTEM. | | | | | | | | | |
| **4.7 Changes to Central User Administration (CUA) are authorized and reviewed regularly by management.** | | | | | | | | | |
| 4.7.1 Because all organizations are structured differently and have different requirements, initial discussions with the organization should be conducted to obtain an understanding of the organization's structure and configuration requirements for CUA. To test whether CUA has been configured appropriately, execute the transaction codes SALE, SCUA and SCUM and review the appropriateness of the configured settings for the organization. | DS5 | | | X | | | | | |

## VI. Basis Cycle—Audit/Assurance Program (cont.)

| Audit/Assurance Program Step | CobiT Cross-reference | COSO | | | | | Reference Hyperlink | Issue Cross-reference | Comments |
|---|---|---|---|---|---|---|---|---|---|
| | | Control Environment | Risk Assessment | Control Activities | Information and Communication | Monitoring | | | |
| **C. Detailed Audit Steps *(cont.)*** | | | | | | | | | |
| **4.8 Changes to critical SAP ERP tables are logged by the system and reviewed by management.** | | | | | | | | | |
| 4.8.1 Review security procedures created by management that identify what tables are being logged and how often these logs are reviewed by management. For changes to be logged, the system profile parameter rec/client needs to be activated. Check this by reviewing the report RSPARAM and ensuring that the value for this parameter is set to ALL or to the client numbers that will have table logging enabled. Enter transaction code SE16 and enter table TPROT as the object name along with an X in the PROTFLAG field. This will identify tables that have their changes logged. Run report RSTBPROT (table log) or RSTBHIST (table change analysis), which lists all changes to tables that have log data changes activated in their technical settings for the period specified. Take a representative sample of changes to these tables and compare these to the original supporting information/documentation. Obtain explanations for any changes for which supporting information or documentation is not available. | DS5 | | | X | | | | | |

## VI. Basis Cycle—Audit/Assurance Program (cont.)

| Audit/Assurance Program Step | CobiT Cross-reference | COSO | | | | | Reference Hyperlink | Issue Cross-reference | Comments |
|---|---|---|---|---|---|---|---|---|---|
| | | Control Environment | Risk Assessment | Control Activities | Information and Communication | Monitoring | | | |
| **C. Detailed Audit Steps** *(cont.)* | | | | | | | | | |
| **4.9 Changes made to the data dictionary are authorized and reviewed regularly** | | | | | | | | | |
| 4.9.1 Understand management's policies and procedures regarding the review of data dictionary reports. Assess the adequacy of such policies, procedures, standards and guidance, taking into account the:<br>• Frequency with which the review is performed<br>• Level of detail in the reports<br>• Other independent data to which management compares the reports<br>• Likelihood that the person performing the review will be able to identify exception items<br>• Nature of exception items that they can be expected to identify | | | | | | | | | |
| **4.10 Access to Systems Administrations Functions is restricted.** | | | | | | | | | |
| 4.10.1 S_ADMI_FCD is an extremely powerful security object that grants access to several critical Basis Administration functions, as well as some functional user functions (such as spool). It should be assigned with great care, and with only the discrete values needed by users. | | | | | | | | | |

## VI. Basis Cycle—Audit/Assurance Program (cont.)

| Audit/Assurance Program Step | CobiT Cross-reference | COSO | | | | | Reference Hyperlink | Issue Cross-reference | Comments |
|---|---|---|---|---|---|---|---|---|---|
| | | Control Environment | Risk Assessment | Control Activities | Information and Communication | Monitoring | | | |
| **C. Detailed Audit Steps (cont.)** | | | | | | | | | |
| 4.10.1 *(cont.)* The object defines one authorization field, system administration functions. Test for the following field values. These values should be restricted to Basis group only. <br>• NADM: Network administration (SM54, SM55, SM58, SM59). Only Basis group. <br>• PADM: Process administration (SM50, SM51, SM04); intercept background job (debugging function in background job administration, transaction SM37). Only Basis group. <br>• SM02: Authorization to create, change and delete system messages <br>• UADM: Update administration (SM13) <br>• T000: Create new client (SCC4) <br>• TLCK: Lock/unlock transaction (SM01) <br>• MEMO: Set SAP memory management quota using report RSMEMORY. <br>• COLA: Administration of OLE automation servers and controls <br> – AUDA—Basis audit administration <br> – RSET—Reset/delete data without archiving <br> – SYNC—Reset buffers <br> – UBUF—Reset all user buffers <br> – TCTR—Table control settings throughout the system <br> – Wild card (*), i.e., all values | | | | | | | | | |

## VI. Basis Cycle—Audit/Assurance Program (cont.)

| Audit/Assurance Program Step | Cobit Cross-reference | COSO | | | | | | Reference Hyperlink | Issue Cross-reference | Comments |
| --- | --- | --- | --- | --- | --- | --- | --- | --- | --- | --- |
| | | Control Environment | Risk Assessment | Control Activities | Information and Communication | Monitoring | | | | |
| **C. Detailed Audit Steps (cont.)** | | | | | | | | | | |
| **4.11 Log and trace files are appropriately configured and secured.** | | | | | | | | | | |
| 4.11.1 For Security Audit log, using release 4.0 or higher:<br>• Confirm that the Security Audit log has been activated by running the report RSPARAM and confirming the following parameter values:<br>– Rsau/enable (activates logging on to application server; if the value is 0, it is not active)<br>– Rsau/local/file (specifies the location of the log; confirms that it is appropriately located)<br>– Rsau/max_diskspace/local (specifies the maximum size of the log; confirms that the size is adequate for the organization)<br>• Obtain a listing of events that are logged (can be done via SM20). Review for appropriateness and link to required logging that may be specified in the security policies and standards.<br>• Determine the frequency and thoroughness of the review of the logs.<br>• If possible, obtain a representative sample of the logs and assess the adequacy of the follow-up process and review for unusual items. | DS5<br>ME1 | | | X | | | | | |

## VI. Basis Cycle—Audit/Assurance Program (cont.)

### C. Detailed Audit Steps (cont.)

| Audit/Assurance Program Step | CobiT Cross-reference | Control Environment | Risk Assessment | COSO Control Activities | Information and Communication | Monitoring | Reference Hyperlink | Issue Cross-reference | Comments |
|---|---|---|---|---|---|---|---|---|---|
| 4.11.2 Review the system log:<br>• Run the report RSPARAM and review the following parameter values to obtain the locations of the log files:<br>–Rslg/local/file (specifies the location of the local log on the application server; default: /usr/sap/<SID>/D20/log/SLOG-<SAP_ instance_#>)<br>–Rslg/collect_daemon/host (specifies the application server that maintains the central log; default: <hostname of main instance>)<br>–Rslg/central/file (specifies the location of the active file for the central log on the application server; default: /usr/ sap/<SID>/SYS/global/SLOGJ)<br>–Rslg/central/old_file (specifies the location of the old file for the central log on the application server; default: /usr/ sap/<SID>/SYS/global/SLOGJO)<br>–Rslg/max_diskspace/local (specifies the maximum length of the local log; default: 0.5 MB)<br>–Rslg/max_diskspace/central (specifies the maximum length of the central log; default: 2 MB)<br>–Rstr/file (the absolute pathname of the trace file: the trace filename is | DS5<br>DS10<br>DS11<br>DS13<br>ME1 | | | X | | | | | |

## VI. Basis Cycle—Audit/Assurance Program (cont.)

| Audit/Assurance Program Step | CobiT Cross-reference | Control Environment | Risk Assessment | Control Activities | Information and Communication | Monitoring | Reference Hyperlink | Issue Cross-reference | Comments |
|---|---|---|---|---|---|---|---|---|---|
| **C. Detailed Audit Steps** *(cont.)* | | | | | | | | | |
| 4.11.2 *(cont.)* <br> • Obtain a listing of events that are logged (can be done via SM21). Review for appropriateness (including the size of each local and central log file) and link to required logging, which may be specified in the security policies and standards. <br> • Determine the frequency and thoroughness of the review of the logs. <br> • If possible, obtain a representative sample of the logs and assess the adequacy of "the follow-up process and review for unusual items. <br> • Work with the operating system administrator to determine who has permissions to these files. Ensure that the access is appropriate. | | | | | | | | | |

## VII. Basis Cycle—Maturity Assessment

The maturity assessment is an opportunity for the reviewer to assess the maturity of the processes reviewed. Based on the results of audit/assurance review, and the reviewer's observations, assign a maturity level to each of the following COBIT control practices.

| COBIT Control Practice | Assessed Maturity | Target Maturity | Reference Hyperlink | Comments |
|---|---|---|---|---|
| **AI6.1 Change Standards and Procedures**<br>1. Develop, document and promulgate a change management framework that specifies the policies and processes, including:<br>• Roles and responsibilities<br>• Classification and prioritization of all changes based on business risk<br>• Assessment of impact<br>• Authorization and approval of all changes by the business process owners and IT<br>• Tracking and status of changes<br>• Impact on data integrity (e.g., all changes to data files being made under system and application control rather than by direct user intervention)<br>2. Establish and maintain version control over all changes.<br>3. Implement roles and responsibilities that involve business process owners and appropriate technical IT functions. Ensure appropriate segregation of duties.<br>4. Establish appropriate record management practices and audit trails to record key steps in the change management process. Ensure timely closure of changes. Elevate and report to management changes that are not closed in a timely fashion.<br>5. Consider the impact of contracted services providers (e.g., of infrastructure, application development and shared services) on the change management process. Consider integration of organizational change management processes with change management processes of service providers. Consider the impact of the organizational change management process on contractual terms and SLAs. | | | | |

## VII. Basis Cycle—Maturity Assessment (cont.)

| CobiT Control Practice | Assessed Maturity | Target Maturity | Reference Hyperlink | Comments |
|---|---|---|---|---|
| **AI6.2 Impact Assessment, Prioritization and Authorization**<br>1. Develop a process to allow business process owners and IT to request changes to infrastructure, systems or applications. Develop controls to ensure that all such changes arise only through the change request management process.<br>2. Categorize all requested changes (e.g., infrastructure, operating systems, networks, application systems, purchased/packaged application software).<br>3. Prioritize all requested changes. Ensure that the change management process identifies both the business and technical needs for the change. Consider legal, regulatory and contractual reasons for the requested change.<br>4. Assess all requests in a structured fashion. Ensure that the assessment process addresses impact analysis on infrastructure, systems and applications. Consider security, legal, contractual and compliance implications of the requested change. Consider also interdependencies amongst changes. Involve business process owners in the assessment process, as appropriate.<br>5. Ensure that each change is formally approved by business process owners and IT technical stakeholders, as appropriate. | | | | |
| **AI6.4 Change Status Tracking and Reporting**<br>1. Ensure that a documented process exists within the overall change management process to declare, assess, authorize and record an emergency change.<br>2. Ensure that emergency changes are processed in accordance with the emergency change element of the formal change management process.<br>3. Ensure that all emergency access arrangements for changes are appropriately authorized, documented and revoked after the change has been applied.<br>4. Conduct a postimplementation review of all emergency changes, involving all concerned parties. The review should consider implications for aspects such as further application system maintenance, impact on development and test environments, application software development quality, documentation and manuals, and data integrity. | | | | |

419

## VII. Basis Cycle—Maturity Assessment (cont.)

| CobiT Control Practice | Assessed Maturity | Target Maturity | Reference Hyperlink | Comments |
|---|---|---|---|---|
| **DS5.3 Identity Management**<br>1. Establish and communicate policies and procedures to uniquely identify, authenticate and authorize access mechanisms and access rights for all users on a need-to-know/need-to-have basis, based on predetermined and preapproved roles. Clearly state accountability of any user for any action on any of the systems and/or applications involved.<br>2. Ensure that roles and access authorization criteria for assigning user access rights take into account:<br>• Sensitivity of information and applications involved (data classification)<br>• Policies for information protection and dissemination (legal, regulatory, internal policies and contractual requirements)<br>• Roles and responsibilities as defined within the enterprise<br>• The need-to-have access rights associated with the function<br>• Standard but individual user access profiles for common job roles in the organization<br>• Requirements to guarantee appropriate segregation of duties<br>3. Establish a method for authenticating and authorizing users to establish responsibility and enforce access rights in line with sensitivity of information and functional application requirements and infrastructure components, and in compliance with applicable laws, regulations, internal policies and contractual agreements.<br>4. Define and implement a procedure for identifying new users and recording, approving and maintaining access rights. This needs to be requested by user management, approved by the system owner and implemented by the responsible security person.<br>5. Ensure that a timely information flow is in place that reports changes in jobs (i.e., people in, people out, people change). Grant, revoke and adapt user access rights in co-ordination with human resources and user departments for users who are new, who have left the organization, or who have changed roles or jobs. | | | | |

## VII. Basis Cycle—Maturity Assessment (cont.)

| CobiT Control Practice | Assessed Maturity | Target Maturity | Reference Hyperlink | Comments |
|---|---|---|---|---|
| **DS5.4 User Account Management**<br>1. Ensure that access control procedures include but are not limited to:<br>  • Using unique user IDs to enable users to be linked to and held accountable for their actions<br>  • Awareness that the use of group IDs results in the loss of individual accountability and are permitted only when justified for business or operational reasons and compensated by mitigating controls. Group IDs must be approved and documented.<br>  • Checking that the user has authorization from the system owner for the use of the information system or service, and the level of access granted is appropriate to the business purpose and consistent with the organizational security policy<br>  • A procedure to require users to understand and acknowledge their access rights and the conditions of such access<br>  • Ensuring that internal and external service providers do not provide access until authorization procedures have been completed<br>  • Maintaining a formal record, including access levels, of all persons registered to use the service<br>  • A timely and regular review of user IDs and access rights<br>2. Ensure that management reviews or reallocates user access rights at regular intervals using a formal process. User access rights should be reviewed or reallocated after any job changes, such as transfer, promotion, demotion or termination of employment. Authorizations for special privileged access rights should be reviewed independently at more frequent intervals. | | | | |

## VII. Basis Cycle—Maturity Assessment (cont.)

| CobiT Control Practice | Assessed Maturity | Target Maturity | Reference Hyperlink | Comments |
|---|---|---|---|---|
| **DS9.1 Configuration Repository and Baseline** <br> 1. Implement a configuration repository to capture and maintain configuration management items. The repository should include hardware; application software; middleware; parameters; documentation; procedures; and tools for operating, accessing and using the systems, services, version numbers and licensing details. <br> 2. Implement a tool to enable the effective logging of configuration management information within a repository. <br> 3. Provide a unique identifier to a configuration item so the item can be easily tracked and related to physical asset tags and financial records. <br> 4. Define and document configuration baselines for components across development, test and production environments, to enable identification of system configuration at specific points in time (past, present and planned). <br> 5. Establish a process to revert to the baseline configuration in the event of problems, if determined appropriate after initial investigation. <br> 6. Install mechanisms to monitor changes against the defined repository and baseline. Provide management reports for exceptions, reconciliation and decision making. | | | | |
| **DS9.2 Identification and Maintenance of Configuration Items** <br> 1. Define and implement a policy requiring all configuration items and their attributes and versions to be identified and maintained. <br> 2. Tag physical assets according to a defined policy. Consider using an automated mechanism, such as barcodes. <br> 3. Define a policy that integrates incident, change and problem management procedures with the maintenance of the configuration repository. <br> 4. Define a process to record new, modified and deleted configuration items and their relative attributes and versions. Identify and maintain the relationships between configuration items in the configuration repository. <br> 5. Establish a process to maintain an audit trail for all changes to configuration items. <br> 6. Define a process to identify critical configuration items in relationship to business functions (component failure impact analysis). <br> 7. Record all assets—including new hardware and software, procured or internally developed—within the configuration management data repository. <br> 8. Define and implement a process to ensure that valid licenses are in place to prevent the inclusion of unauthorized software. | | | | |

## VII. Basis Cycle—Maturity Assessment (cont.)

| CobiT Control Practice | Assessed Maturity | Target Maturity | Reference Hyperlink | Comments |
|---|---|---|---|---|
| **DS9.3 Configuration Integrity Review**<br>1. To validate the integrity of configuration data, implement a process to ensure that configuration items are monitored. Compare recorded data against actual physical existence, and ensure that errors and deviations are reported and corrected.<br>2. Using automated discovery tools where appropriate, reconcile actual installed software and hardware periodically against the configuration database, license records and physical tags.<br>3. Periodically review against the policy for software usage the existence of any software in violation or in excess of current policies and license agreements. Report deviations for correction. | | | | |

# Appendix E—SAP ERP Audit ICQs

The following internal control questionnaires (ICQs) provide suggested control objectives/questions to cover for conducting an audit of the three business cycles covered in this book (Revenue, Inventory and Expenditure), and the SAP Basis component. They also provide references to the relevant CoBiT 4.1 control objectives. Refer to the numbering system in chapter 4 on page 79.

## Revenue Business Cycle ICQ

| Control Objectives/Questions | Response | | | Comments | CoBiT References |
|---|---|---|---|---|---|
| | Yes | No | N/A | | |
| **1. Master Data Maintenance** | | | | | |
| **1.1 Changes made to master data are valid, complete, accurate and timely.** | | | | | |
| 1.1.1 Does relevant management, other than the initiators, check online reports of master data additions and changes back to source documentation on a sample basis? | | | | | DS11 |
| 1.1.2 Is access to create and change master data restricted to authorized individuals? | | | | | DS5 |
| 1.1.3 Have configurable controls been designed into the process to maintain the integrity of master data? | | | | | DS9 |
| **1.2 Master data remain current and pertinent.** | | | | | |
| 1.2.1 Does management periodically review master data to check their accuracy? | | | | | DS11 |
| 1.2.2 Have appropriate credit limits been loaded for customers? | | | | | DS2 |
| **2. Sales Order Processing** | | | | | |
| **2.1 Sales orders are processed with valid prices and terms, and processing is complete, accurate and timely.** | | | | | |
| 2.1.1 Is the ability to create, change or delete sales orders, contracts and delivery schedules restricted to authorized personnel? | | | | | AI6 DS5 |

# Revenue Business Cycle ICQ *(cont.)*

| Control Objectives/Questions | Response | | | Comments | CobiT References |
|---|---|---|---|---|---|
| | Yes | No | N/A | | |
| **2. Sales Order Processing *(cont.)*** | | | | | |
| 2.1.2 Has the ability to modify sales pricing information been restricted to authorized personnel (refer to master data integrity 1.1.2)? | | | | | DS5 |
| 2.1.2 Has the system been configured to limit the overwriting of prices compared to the price master data (SAP allows for no changes or a certain tolerance level)? | | | | | |
| 2.1.3 Has the system been configured such that a sales order is blocked for further processing when the customer either gets too low a price or the price the sales person gives is not satisfactory (refer to master data integrity 1.1.3)? | | | | | DS9 |
| 2.1.4 Are fax orders reconciled periodically between the system and fax printouts to reduce the risk of duplicate orders? | | | | | PO8 |
| **2.2 Orders are processed within approved customer credit limits.** | | | | | |
| 2.2.1 Has the SAP ERP software been configured to disallow the processing of sales orders that exceed customer credit limits? | | | | | DS9 |
| **2.3 Order entry data are completely and accurately transferred to the shipping and invoicing activities.** | | | | | |
| 2.3.1 Are reports of open sales documents prepared and monitored to check for timely shipment? | | | | | DS11 ME1 |
| **3. Shipping, Invoicing, Returns and Adjustments** | | | | | |
| **3.1 Controls are in place to prevent duplicate shipments or delay in the shipping of goods to customers.** | | | | | |
| 3.1.1 Does the SAP ERP software match goods shipped to open line items on an open sales order and close each line item as the goods are shipped, thereby preventing further shipments for those line items? | | | | | DS6 |
| 3.1.2 Are available shipping reports used to assist in controlling the shipping process? | | | | | PO11 |

# Revenue Business Cycle ICQ *(cont.)*

| Control Objectives/Questions | Response | | | Comments | CoBiT References |
|---|---|---|---|---|---|
| | Yes | No | N/A | | |
| **3. Shipping, Invoicing, Returns and Adjustments *(cont.)*** | | | | | |
| **3.2 Invoices are generated using authorized terms and prices and are calculated and recorded accurately.** | | | | | |
| 3.2.1 Does the SAP ERP software automatically calculate invoice amounts and post invoices based on configuration data? | | | | | AI5 |
| **3.3 All goods shipped are invoiced in a timely manner.** | | | | | |
| 3.3.1 Are reports of goods shipped but not invoiced and uninvoiced debit and credit note requests prepared and investigated promptly? | | | | | DS5 |
| 3.3.2 Is the ability to create, change or delete picking slips, delivery notes and goods issues restricted to authorized personnel? | | | | | AI7 |
| 3.3.3 Are reports of invoices issued but not posted in FI prepared and investigated promptly? | | | | | AI7 |
| **3.4 Credit notes and adjustments to accounts receivable are accurately calculated and recorded.** | | | | | |
| 3.4.1 Is the ability to create, change or delete sales order return and credit requests and subsequent credit note transactions restricted to authorized personnel? | | | | | DS5 |
| **3.5 Credit notes for all goods returned and adjustments to accounts receivable are issued in accordance with organization policy and in a timely manner.** | | | | | |
| 3.5.1 Are sales order returns and credit request transactions matched to invoices? | | | | | |
| 3.5.2 Have processing controls, including a billing block or a delivery block, been configured to block credit memos or free-of-charge subsequent delivery documents that do not comply with the organization's policy on credits or returns? | | | | | AI2 DS9 |

## Revenue Business Cycle ICQ *(cont.)*

| Control Objectives/Questions | Response | | | Comments | CobiT References |
|---|---|---|---|---|---|
| | Yes | No | N/A | | |
| **4. Collecting and Processing Cash Receipts** | | | | | |
| **4.1 Cash receipts are entered accurately, completely and in a timely manner.** | | | | | |
| 4.1.1 Are bank statements reconciled to the general ledger regularly? | | | | | |
| 4.1.2 Has the system been configured to not allow processing of cash receipts outside of approved bank accounts? | | | | | DS9 |
| 4.1.3 Are customer open items and accounts receivable aging reports prepared and analyzed regularly? | | | | | AI4 |
| **4.2 Cash receipts are valid and are not duplicated.** | | | | | |
| 4.2.1 Are receipts allocated to a customer's account supported by a remittance advice that cross-references to an invoice number? | | | | | PO4 |
| 4.2.1 Is any unallocated cash or amount received that is not cross-referenced to an invoice number immediately followed up with the customer? | | | | | DS11 |
| **4.3 Cash discounts are calculated and recorded accurately.** | | | | | |
| 4.3.1 Have tolerance levels for allowable cash discounts and cash payment differences in the SAP ERP system been defined such that amounts in excess of such levels cannot be entered into the SAP ERP system? | | | | | PO8 PO9 |
| **4.4 Timely collection of cash receipts is monitored.** | | | | | |
| 4.4.1 As for 4.1.3, are customer open items and accounts receivable aging reports prepared and analyzed regularly? | | | | | PO4 AI4 |

# Expenditure Business Cycle ICQ

| Control Objectives/Questions | Response | | | Comments | CobiT References |
|---|---|---|---|---|---|
| | Yes | No | N/A | | |
| **1. Master Data Maintenance** | | | | | |
| **1.1 Changes made to master data are valid, complete, accurate and timely.** | | | | | |
| 1.1.1 Does relevant management, other than the initiators, check online reports of master data additions and changes back to source documentation on a sample basis? | | | | | PO4 DS11 |
| 1.1.2 Is access to create and change master data restricted to authorized individuals? | | | | | DS5 |
| 1.1.2 Are user accounts validated against HR lists and access in alignment with role requirements? | | | | | |
| 1.1.2 Are user accounts reviewed by management in line with organization policy? | | | | | |
| 1.1.3 Have configurable controls been designed into the process to maintain the integrity of master data? | | | | | DS9 |
| 1.1.4 Is a naming convention used for vendor names (e.g., as per letterhead) to minimize the risk of establishing duplicated vendor master records? | | | | | DS2 |
| **1.2 Inventory master data remain current and pertinent.** | | | | | |
| 1.2.1 Does management periodically review master data to check their accuracy? | | | | | DS11 |
| **2. Purchasing** | | | | | |
| **2.1 Purchase order entry and changes are valid, complete, accurate and timely.** | | | | | |
| 2.1.1 Is the ability to create, change or cancel purchase requisitions, purchase orders and outline agreements (standing purchase orders) restricted to authorized personnel? | | | | | AI6 DS5 |

# Expenditure Business Cycle ICQ *(cont.)*

| Control Objectives/Questions | Response | | | Comments | CobiT References |
|---|---|---|---|---|---|
| | Yes | No | N/A | | |
| **2. Purchasing** *(cont.)* | | | | | |
| 2.1.2 Does the SAP ERP source list functionality allow specified materials to be purchased only from vendors included in the source list for the specified material? | | | | | DS2 |
| 2.1.3 Is the SAP ERP release strategy used to authorize purchase requisitions, purchase orders, outline agreements (standing purchase orders) and unusual purchases (e.g., capital outlays)? | | | | | AI6 |
| **2.2 Goods are received only for valid purchase orders and goods receipts are recorded completely, accurately and in a timely manner.** | | | | | |
| 2.2.1 When goods received are matched to open purchase orders, are receipts with no purchase order or those that exceed the purchase order quantity by more than an established amount investigated? | | | | | DS6 |
| 2.2.1 Does management review exception reports of goods not received on time for recorded purchases? | | | | | DS5 |
| 2.2.2 Is the ability to input, change or cancel goods received transactions restricted to authorized inbound logistics/raw materials personnel? | | | | | DS5 |
| **2.3 Defective goods are returned to suppliers in a timely manner.** | | | | | |
| 2.3.1 Are rejected raw materials adequately segregated from other raw materials in a quality assurance bonding area and are they regularly monitored (assigned a movement type of 122) to ensure timely return to suppliers? | | | | | PO4 |

# Expenditure Business Cycle ICQ *(cont.)*

| Control Objectives/Questions | Response | | | Comments | CobiT References |
|---|---|---|---|---|---|
| | Yes | No | N/A | | |
| **3. Invoice Processing** | | | | | |
| **3.1 Amounts posted to accounts payable represent goods or services received.** | | | | | |
| 3.1.1 Is the ability to input, change, cancel or release vendor invoices for payment restricted to authorized personnel? | | | | | DS5 |
| 3.1.1 Is the ability to input vendor invoices that do not have a purchase order and/or goods receipt as support further restricted to authorized personnel? | | | | | DS5 |
| **3.2 Accounts payable amounts are calculated completely and accurately and recorded in a timely manner.** | | | | | |
| 3.2.1 Is the SAP ERP software configured to perform a three-way match? | | | | | DS9 |
| 3.2.2 Is the SAP ERP software configured with quantity and price tolerance limits? | | | | | DS9 |
| 3.2.3 Is the GR/IR account regularly reconciled? | | | | | DS11 |
| 3.2.4 Are reports of outstanding purchase orders regularly reviewed? | | | | | DS11 |
| 3.2.5 Does the SAP ERP software restrict the ability to modify the exchange rate table to authorized personnel? | | | | | DS5 |
| 3.2.5 Does management approve values in the centrally maintained exchange rate table? | | | | | PO6 |
| 3.2.5 Does the SAP ERP software automatically calculate foreign currency translation, based on values in the centrally maintained exchange rate table? | | | | | DS11 |
| **3.3 Credit notes and other adjustments are calculated completely and accurately and recorded in a timely manner.** | | | | | |
| 3.3.1 Is the ability to input, change, cancel or release credit notes restricted to authorized personnel? | | | | | DS5 |

# Expenditure Business Cycle ICQ *(cont.)*

| Control Objectives/Questions | Response Yes | No | N/A | Comments | CobiT References |
|---|---|---|---|---|---|
| **4. Processing Disbursements** | | | | | |
| **4.1 Disbursements are made only for goods and services received and are calculated, recorded and distributed to the appropriate suppliers accurately in a timely manner.** | | | | | |
| 4.1.1 Does management approve the SAP ERP payment run parameter specification? | | | | | PO6 |
| 4.1.2 Does the SAP ERP software restrict to authorized personnel the ability to release invoices that have been blocked for payment, either for an individual invoice or for a specified vendor? | | | | | DS5 |

# Inventory Business Cycle ICQ

| Control Objectives/Questions | Response Yes | No | N/A | Comments | CobiT References |
|---|---|---|---|---|---|
| **1. Master Data Maintenance** | | | | | |
| **1.1 Changes made to master data are valid, complete, accurate and timely.** | | | | | |
| 1.1.1 Does relevant management, other than the initiators, check online reports (using transaction code MM04) of master data additions and changes back to source documentation on a sample basis? | | | | | DS11 |
| 1.1.1 Do persons independent of day-to-day custody or recording of inventory count physical inventory on a continuous inventory basis? | | | | | ME2 |
| 1.1.1 Are monthly stock-takes performed? | | | | | DS13 |
| 1.1.1 Where inventory adjustment forms are used, are they sequentially prenumbered and is the sequence of such forms accounted for? | | | | | DS13 |

# Inventory Business Cycle ICQ *(cont.)*

| Control Objectives/Questions | Response | | | Comments | CoʙiT References |
|---|---|---|---|---|---|
| | Yes | No | N/A | | |
| **1. Master Data Maintenance *(cont.)*** | | | | | |
| 1.1.2 Have the creation and maintenance of master data been assigned and restricted to a dedicated area within the organization that understands how they may affect organizational processes and the importance of timely changes? | | | | | DS11 |
| 1.1.3 Have configurable controls been designed into the process to maintain the integrity of master data? | | | | | DS9 |
| **1.2 Inventory master data remain current and pertinent.** | | | | | |
| 1.2.1 Does management periodically review master data to check their accuracy? | | | | | DS11 |
| **1.3 Settings or changes to the bill of materials or process order settlement rules are valid, complete, accurate and timely.** | | | | | |
| 1.3.1 Is the ability to create, change or delete the bill of materials restricted to authorized personnel? | | | | | AI6 DS5 |
| 1.3.2 Does relevant management, other than the initiators, check online reports of bill of materials or settlement rule additions and changes back to source documentation on a sample basis? | | | | | PO4 |
| **2. Raw Materials Management** | | | | | |
| **2.1 Inventory is salable, usable and adequately safeguarded.** | | | | | |
| 2.1.1 Are raw material requirements planned based on forecast orders and production plans and does the system functionality monitor and maintain inventory levels in accordance with organization policies? | | | | | DS1 DS3 |

# Inventory Business Cycle ICQ *(cont.)*

| Control Objectives/Questions | Response | | | Comments | CobiT References |
| | Yes | No | N/A | | |
|---|---|---|---|---|---|
| **2. Raw Materials Management *(cont.)*** | | | | | |
| 2.1.1 Is the salability of finished goods and usability of raw materials (including shelf life dates) assessed regularly during continuous inventory counts and are any scrapped goods or raw materials appropriately approved? | | | | | DS3 |
| 2.1.1 Does the quality department test a sample of raw materials and are rejected raw materials adequately segregated from other raw materials into a separate quality assurance bonding area and regularly monitored by the quality department personnel to ensure timely return to suppliers? | | | | | DS6 |
| 2.1.1 Does management review reports of slow-turnover inventory to ensure that it is still salable or usable? | | | | | DS11 |
| 2.1.1 Do goods inwards/outwards personnel monitor all incoming and outgoing vehicles and ensure that all goods leaving the premises are accompanied by duly completed documentation (e.g., intercompany stock transfer order, delivery docket or goods returned note)? | | | | | DS3 |
| 2.1.1 Are goods delivered only to designated, physically secure loading bays within the warehouses and are they accepted only by authorized inbound logistic/raw materials personnel? | | | | | DS3 DS12 |
| 2.1.1 Is inventory stored in properly secured (gates locked at night and premises alarmed), environmentally conditioned warehouse locations where access is restricted to authorized personnel? | | | | | DS12 |

# Inventory Business Cycle ICQ *(cont.)*

| Control Objectives/Questions | Response | | | Comments | CobiT References |
|---|---|---|---|---|---|
| | Yes | No | N/A | | |
| **2. Raw Materials Management *(cont.)*** | | | | | |
| **2.2 Raw materials are received and accepted only with valid purchase orders, and are recorded accurately and in a timely manner.** | | | | | |
| 2.2.1 Are goods received matched online with purchase order details and/or invoices? | | | | | DS13 |
| 2.2.1 Are long-outstanding goods receipt notes, purchase orders and/or invoices investigated on a timely basis and accrued as appropriate? | | | | | ME2 |
| 2.2.1 Are documents cancelled once or on payment of the invoice matched to prevent reuse? | | | | | PO8 |
| 2.2.1 Does management review exception reports of goods not received on time for recorded purchases? | | | | | ME1 |
| 2.2.2 When goods received are matched to open purchase orders, are receipts with no purchase order, or those that exceed the purchase order quantity by more than an established amount, investigated? | | | | | PO8 |
| 2.2.3 Is the ability to input, change or cancel goods received transactions restricted to authorized inbound logistics/raw materials personnel? | | | | | DS5 |
| 2.2.4 Do persons independent of day-to-day custody or recording of inventory count physical inventory on a continuous inventory basis? | | | | | PO4 |
| 2.2.4 Are inventory counts reconciled to inventory records and inventory records reconciled to the general ledger? | | | | | PO8 |

# Inventory Business Cycle ICQ *(cont.)*

| Control Objectives/Questions | Response Yes | No | N/A | Comments | CobiT References |
|---|---|---|---|---|---|
| **2. Raw Materials Management *(cont.)*** | | | | | |
| **2.3 Defective raw materials are returned to suppliers in a timely manner.** | | | | | |
| 2.3.1 Are rejected raw materials adequately segregated from other raw materials in a quality assurance bonding area and are they regularly monitored (assigned a movement type of 122) to ensure timely return to suppliers? | | | | | PO4 ME2 |
| 2.3.1 Are defective raw materials received from suppliers logged and recorded in the quality management system and is the log monitored to ensure that the defective goods are returned promptly and credit is received in a timely manner? | | | | | DS2 |
| **3. Producing and Costing Inventory** | | | | | |
| **3.1 Transfers of materials to/from production, production costs and defective products/ scrap are valid and recorded accurately, completely and in the appropriate period.** | | | | | |
| 3.1.1 Are inventories received, including transfers, counted and compared to the pick list (that is used to record movements of inventory in the financial records) by personnel in the area assuming responsibility for the inventory (e.g., production, goods storage), and are they recorded in the appropriate period? | | | | | DS13 |
| 3.1.1 Does management reconcile the inventory-in-transit accounts regularly and do these accounts net off against other plants' outgoing inventory-in-transit accounts? | | | | | PO8 DS3 |
| 3.1.1 Is an appropriate costing method used for raw materials at purchase order price and is the raw materials costing rolled into finished goods on a monthly basis? | | | | | DS13 |

# Inventory Business Cycle ICQ *(cont.)*

| Control Objectives/Questions | Response | | | Comments | CᴏʙɪT References |
| --- | --- | --- | --- | --- | --- |
| | Yes | No | N/A | | |
| **3. Producing and Costing Inventory *(cont.)*** | | | | | |
| 3.1.1 Does the quality department, based on its knowledge of day-to-day activities, review records of scrapped and reworked items and check whether such items have been correctly identified and properly recorded in the appropriate accounting period? | | | | | DS3 |
| 3.1.1 Is the ability to create or change bills of material restricted to authorized personnel? | | | | | AI6 DS5 |
| 3.1.1 Is access to the material transfers and adjustments transactions appropriately restricted to authorized personnel? | | | | | AI6 DS5 |
| 3.1.1 Is the ability to create or change work centers restricted to authorized personnel? | | | | | AI6 DS5 |
| 3.1.2 Is the ability to create or change bills of material restricted to authorized personnel? | | | | | AI6 DS5 |
| 3.1.3 Is access to the material transfers and adjustments transactions appropriately restricted to authorized personnel? | | | | | AI6 DS5 |
| 3.1.4 Is the ability to create or change work centers restricted to authorized personnel? | | | | | AI6 DS5 |
| **4. Handling and Shipping Finished Goods** | | | | | |
| **4.1 Finished goods received from production are recorded completely and accurately in the appropriate period.** | | | | | |
| 4.1.1 Do persons independent of day-to-day custody or recording of inventory count physical inventory on a continuous inventory basis (refer to 1.1.1)? | | | | | PO4 |
| 4.1.2 Is the changing of the settlement rules restricted to authorized users (refer to 1.3.1)? | | | | | |

# Inventory Business Cycle ICQ *(cont.)*

| Control Objectives/Questions | Response | | | Comments | CoBiT References |
|---|---|---|---|---|---|
| | Yes | No | N/A | | |
| **4. Handling and Shipping Finished Goods** *(cont.)* | | | | | |
| **4.2 Goods returned by customers are accepted in accordance with the organization's policies.** | | | | | |
| 4.2.1 Are quality control inspections performed for finished goods returned by customers and/or received from production to assess whether such goods should be returned to inventory, reworked or scrapped? | | | | | PO11 ME1 |
| 4.2.1 Does the quality assurance team inspect the goods before a credit note can be issued? | | | | | |
| **4.3 Shipments are recorded accurately, in a timely manner and in the appropriate period.** | | | | | |
| 4.3.1 Is access restricted to transferring stock between plants or executing the Post Goods Issue that creates the intercompany stock transfer advice and/or generates an electronic (EDI) or manual invoice? | | | | | DS12 |
| 4.3.1 Do outbound logistics/finished goods personnel monitor all incoming and outgoing vehicles and ensure that all goods leaving the premises are accompanied by duly completed documentation (e.g., delivery docket or goods returned note)? | | | | | ME1 |
| 4.3.1 Before goods are shipped, are the details of the approved order compared to actual goods prepared for shipment by an individual independent of the order picking process? | | | | | PO4 |
| 4.3.2 Are the SAP ERP reports (delivery due list and owed-to-customer report) of open sales documents prepared and monitored to ensure timely shipment? | | | | | DS11 |
| 4.3.2 Does the SAP ERP account assignment configuration ensure that amounts for shipped goods are posted to the appropriate COGS account? | | | | | |

# Basis Security Cycle ICQ

| Control Objectives/Questions | Response | | | Comments | CoBiT References |
|---|---|---|---|---|---|
| | Yes | No | N/A | | |
| **SAP ERP Control Environment** | | | | | |
| **A. Establish control over information and information systems.** | | | | | |
| A1 Has senior management established policies and standards governing the information systems of the entity? | | | | | PO6 |
| A2 Has senior management assigned responsibilities for information, its processing and its use? | | | | | PO2 |
| A3 Is user management responsible for providing information that supports the entity's objectives and policies? | | | | | PO4 |
| A4 Is user management responsible for the completeness, accuracy, authorization, security and timeliness of information? | | | | | PO8 DS11 |
| A5 Is information systems management responsible for providing the information systems capabilities necessary for achievement of the defined information systems objectives and policies of the entity? | | | | | PO3 DS1 DS3 |
| A6 Does senior management approve plans for development and acquisition of information systems? | | | | | PO5 |
| A7 Does senior management monitor the extent to which development/configuration, operation and control of information systems complies with established policies and plans? | | | | | ME1 |
| A8 Are there outstanding audit findings from previous years? | | | | | ME1 ME2 |
| **B. Ensure that the information systems selected (whether new implementation or upgrade) meet the needs of the entity.** | | | | | |
| B1 Are there procedures to ensure that decisions to develop or acquire information systems are made in accordance with the objectives and policies of the entity? | | | | | PO5 AI1 |
| B2 Are there procedures to determine costs, savings and benefits before a decision is made to develop or acquire an information system? | | | | | AI1 |

## Basis Security Cycle ICQ *(cont.)*

| Control Objectives/Questions | Response | | | Comments | CobiT References |
|---|---|---|---|---|---|
| | Yes | No | N/A | | |
| **SAP ERP Control Environment** *(cont.)* | | | | | |
| **B. Ensure that the information systems selected (whether new implementation or upgrade) meet the needs of the entity.** *(cont.)* | | | | | |
| B3 Are there procedures to ensure that the information system being developed or acquired meets user requirements? | | | | | AI1 |
| B4 Are there procedures to ensure that information systems, programs and configuration changes are adequately tested prior to implementation? | | | | | AI2 AI3 |
| **C. Ensure that the acquisition and configuration of information systems (whether new implementation or upgrade) are carried out in an efficient and effective manner.** | | | | | |
| C1 Are standards established and enforced to ensure the efficiency and effectiveness of the systems acquisition and configuration process? | | | | | PO10 AI1 AI2 |
| C2 Are there procedures to ensure that all systems are acquired and configured in accordance with the established standards? | | | | | AI2 |
| C3 Is an approved acquisition plan (project plan) used to measure progress? | | | | | PO10 |
| C4 Do all personnel involved in system acquisition and configuration activities receive adequate training and supervision? | | | | | PO7 |
| **D. Ensure the efficient and effective implementation or upgrade of information systems.** | | | | | |
| D1 Has responsibility been assigned for implementation, configuration and upgrade of information systems? | | | | | PO4 |
| D2 Are there procedures to ensure the efficiency and effectiveness of the implementation, configuration and upgrade of information systems? | | | | | AI4 |
| D3 Are there procedures to ensure that information systems are implemented, configured and upgraded in accordance with the established standards? | | | | | AI3 |
| D4 Is an approved implementation plan used to measure progress? | | | | | PO10 |
| D5 Is effective control maintained over the conversion of information and the initial operation of the information system? | | | | | AI7 |

## Basis Security Cycle ICQ *(cont.)*

| Control Objectives/Questions | Response Yes | No | N/A | Comments | CobiT References |
|---|---|---|---|---|---|
| **SAP ERP Control Environment *(cont.)*** | | | | | |
| **D. Ensure the efficient and effective implementation or upgrade of information systems. *(cont.)*** | | | | | |
| D6 Does user management participate in the conversion of data from the existing system to the new system? | | | | | AI7 |
| D7 Is final approval obtained from user management prior to going live with a new implementation and/or upgraded system? | | | | | AI7 |
| **E. Ensure the efficient and effective maintenance of information systems.** | | | | | |
| E1 Are there procedures to document and schedule all planned changes to information systems (including key ABAP programs)? | | | | | AI6 |
| E2 Are there procedures to ensure that only authorized changes are initiated? | | | | | AI6 |
| E3 Are there procedures to ensure and verify that only authorized, tested and documented changes to information systems are accepted into the production client? | | | | | AI6 AI7 |
| E4 Are there procedures to report planned information systems changes to information systems management and to the users affected? | | | | | AI6 DS8 |
| E5 Are there procedures to allow for and control emergency changes? | | | | | AI6 |
| E6 Are controls in place to prevent and identify unauthorized changes to information systems (including key ABAP programs)? | | | | | AI6 DS5 |
| **F. Ensure that present and future requirements of users of information systems processing can be met.** | | | | | |
| F1 Are there written agreements between users and information systems processing, defining the nature and level of services to be provided? | | | | | DS1 |
| F2 Is there appropriate management reporting within information systems processing? | | | | | DS4 ME1 |

# Basis Security Cycle ICQ *(cont.)*

| | | Response | | | CoʙɪT |
|---|---|:---:|:---:|:---:|---|
| **Control Objectives/Questions** | | Yes | No | N/A | Comments | References |
| **SAP ERP Control Environment *(cont.)*** | | | | | | |
| **F.** | **Ensure that present and future requirements of users of information systems processing can be met. *(cont.)*** | | | | | |
| F3 | Does information systems processing management keep senior and user management informed about technical developments that could support the achievement of the objectives and policies of the entity? | | | | | DS3 DS4 |
| F4 | Are there procedures/capacity planning activities to examine the adequacy of information processing resources to meet entity objectives in the future? | | | | | DS3 |
| F5 | Are there periodic planning activities to examine the adequacy of the volume of skilled staff (i.e., operating system, hardware, network, SAP ERP) to support the systems now and in the future? | | | | | PO7 |
| F6 | Are there procedures for the approval, monitoring and control of the acquisition and upgrade of hardware and systems software? | | | | | AI3 DS3 |
| F7 | Is there a process for monitoring the volume of named and concurrent SAP ERP users to ensure that the license agreement is not being violated? | | | | | DS3 ME3 |
| F8 | If the SAP ERP implementation is not at the most current version, is there a planned upgrade approach? | | | | | PO3 AI3 DS3 |
| **G.** | **Ensure the efficient and effective use of resources within information systems processing.** | | | | | |
| G1 | Are budgets for information systems processing activities prepared on a regular basis? | | | | | PO5 |
| G2 | Are standards established and enforced to ensure efficient and effective use of information systems processing? | | | | | PO6 |
| G3 | Is there an incident management process that ensures that information processing problems are detected and corrected on a timely basis? | | | | | DS5 DS10 |

# Basis Security Cycle ICQ *(cont.)*

| Control Objectives/Questions | Response | | | Comments | CoBiT References |
|---|---|---|---|---|---|
| | Yes | No | N/A | | |
| **SAP ERP Control Environment *(cont.)*** | | | | | |
| **G. Ensure the efficient and effective use of resources within information systems processing. *(cont.)*** | | | | | |
| G4 Are users of information systems processing facilities accountable for the resources used by them? | | | | | DS6 |
| **H. Ensure that there is an appropriate segregation of incompatible functions within the entity.** | | | | | |
| H1 Does the organization structure established by senior management provide for an appropriate segregation of incompatible functions: • Basis administration • Transport/import • Develop program change • Develop role change • User security administration • Change monitoring • User testing • Authorize change • Perform change | | | | | PO4 |
| **I. Ensure that all access to information and information systems is authorized.** | | | | | |
| I1 Are there procedures to ensure and verify that information and information systems are accessed in accordance with established policies and procedures? | | | | | DS5 |
| **J. Ensure that information systems processing is protected physically from unauthorized access and from accidental or deliberate loss or damage.** | | | | | |
| J1 Are the database, application and presentation servers located in a physically separate and protected environment (i.e., a data center)? | | | | | DS12 |
| J2 Are there procedures to ensure that environmental conditions (such as temperature and humidity) for hardware facilities are adequately controlled? | | | | | DS12 |
| **K. Ensure that information processing can be recovered and resumed after operations have been interrupted.** | | | | | |
| K1 Are there procedures to allow information processing to resume operations in the event of an interruption? | | | | | DS4 |

# Basis Security Cycle ICQ *(cont.)*

| Control Objectives/Questions | Response | | | Comments | CobiT References |
|---|---|---|---|---|---|
| | Yes | No | N/A | | |
| **SAP ERP Control Environment *(cont.)*** | | | | | |
| **K. Ensure that information processing can be recovered and resumed after operations have been interrupted. *(cont.)*** | | | | | |
| K2 Are emergency, backup and recovery plans documented and tested on a regular basis to ensure that they remain current and operational? | | | | | DS4 |
| K3 Do personnel receive adequate training and supervision in emergency backup and recovery procedures? | | | | | DS4 DS7 |
| **L. Ensure that critical user activities can be maintained and recovered following interruption.** | | | | | |
| L1 Are there backup and recovery plans to allow users of information systems to resume operations in the event of an interruption? | | | | | DS4 |
| L2 Are all information and resources required by users to resume processing backed up regularly? | | | | | DS4 DS11 |
| L3 Do user personnel receive adequate training and supervision in the conduct of the recovery procedures? | | | | | DS4 DS7 |
| L4 Are application controls designed with regard to any weaknesses in segregation, security, development and processing controls that may affect the information system? | | | | | DS4 DS5 |
| L5 Are there procedures to ensure that output is reviewed by users/management for completeness, accuracy and consistency? | | | | | DS4 ME1 |
| L6 Is there some method of ensuring that control procedures relating to completeness, accuracy and authorization are ensured? | | | | | DS4 ME2 |
| L7 Are there established policies and procedures for record retention? | | | | | PO6 DS4 |
| **1. Application Installation (Implementation Guide and Organizational Model)** | | | | | |
| **1.1 Configuration changes are made in the development environment and transported to production.** | | | | | |
| 1.1.1 Has access to the Implementation Guide (IMG) in production been restricted? | | | | | DS5 |

## Basis Security Cycle ICQ *(cont.)*

| Control Objectives/Questions | Response | | | Comments | CoBiT References |
|---|---|---|---|---|---|
| | Yes | No | N/A | | |
| **SAP ERP Control Environment *(cont.)*** | | | | | |
| **1. Application Installation (Implementation Guide and Organizational Model) *(cont.)*** | | | | | |
| 1.1.2 Have the production client settings been established to not allow changes to programs and configuration? | | | | | DS9 |
| **1.2 The Organizational Model has been configured correctly to meet the needs of the organization.** | | | | | |
| 1.2.1 Was the Organizational Model well thought-out and agreed upon early in the implementation and did the relevant organization groups assist with key design decisions? | | | | | PO4 |
| 1.2.2 Has access to the organization configuration functionality been restricted? | | | | | DS5 |
| **1.3 Changes to critical number ranges are controlled.** | | | | | |
| 1.3.1 Has the SAP ERP software security been appropriately configured to restrict the ability to change critical number ranges (i.e., company codes, chart of accounts and accounting period data)? | | | | | DS5 |
| 1.3.1 Has the production environment been set so modifications are not possible? | | | | | AI6 |
| **1.4 Access to system and customizing tables is narrowly restricted.** | | | | | |
| 1.4.1 Have all of the customized SAP ERP tables been assigned to the appropriate authorization group? | | | | | PO4 DS5 |
| 1.4.2 Has the ability to modify critical tables been appropriately restricted in the production system? | | | | | AI6 DS5 |
| **2. Application Development (ABAP/4 Workbench and Transport System)** | | | | | |
| **2.1 Application modifications are planned, tested and implemented in a phased manner.** | | | | | |
| 2.1.1 Are appropriate change controls procedures followed for all transports? | | | | | AI6 |
| 2.1.1 Has the production system change option been set to No Changes Allowed? | | | | | AI6 |

# Basis Security Cycle ICQ *(cont.)*

| Control Objectives/Questions | Response | | | Comments | CobiT References |
|---|---|---|---|---|---|
| | Yes | No | N/A | | |
| **SAP ERP Control Environment *(cont.)*** | | | | | |
| **2. Application Development (ABAP/4 Workbench and Transport System) *(cont.)*** | | | | | |
| 2.1.1 Has the ability to create vs. release change requests been segregated? | | | | | PO4 |
| **2.2 Customized ABAP/4 programs are secured appropriately.** | | | | | |
| 2.2.1 Have customized ABAP/4 programs been assigned to authorization groups? | | | | | PO4 DS5 |
| 2.2.2 Has an authority-check statement been included within customized ABAP/4 programs so the user's authority to access objects is checked at run time? | | | | | AI6 |
| **2.3 The creation or modification of programs is performed in the development system and migrated through the test system to production.** | | | | | |
| 2.3.1 Has access to directly change production source code within the production environment been restricted and monitoring established? | | | | | AI6 |
| **2.4 Access for making changes to the dictionary is restricted to authorized individuals.** | | | | | |
| 2.4.1 Has the ability to make changes to the SAP ERP data dictionary been restricted and access privileges appropriately assigned based on job responsibilities? | | | | | PO4 |
| **2.5 Access to modify and develop queries is restricted.** | | | | | |
| 2.5.1 Have authorization groups for creating and running the ABAP/4 queries been appropriately established in the SAP ERP software so that some end users can maintain and execute queries while others can only execute existing queries? | | | | | PO4 DS5 |
| **2.6 Relevant company codes are set to Productive in the production environment.** | | | | | |
| 2.6.1 Have company codes that are working productively been set to Productive to reduce the risk that deletion programs may reset the company code data by mistake? | | | | | PO4 AI6 |

## Basis Security Cycle ICQ *(cont.)*

| Control Objectives/Questions | Response | | | Comments | CobiT References |
|---|---|---|---|---|---|
| | Yes | No | N/A | | |
| **SAP ERP Control Environment *(cont.)*** | | | | | |
| **3. Application Operations (Computing Center Management System)** | | | | | |
| **3.1 The Computing Center Management System is configured appropriately.** | | | | | |
| 3.1.1 Have operation modes, instances and the CCMS timetable been correctly defined, such that the CCMS display is meaningful? | | | | | AI2 |
| 3.1.1 Is access to the system and start-up profiles tightly controlled? | | | | | AI6 |
| 3.1.1 Are change procedures followed strictly and changes to the profiles well documented? | | | | | AI6 DS11 |
| 3.1.1 Has access to the CCMS Alert Monitor been properly secured? | | | | | AI6 DS10 |
| **3.2 Batch processing operations are secured appropriately.** | | | | | |
| 3.2.1 Have batch input, batch administration and batch processing capabilities been restricted appropriately? | | | | | DS5 DS11 |
| 3.2.1 Have batch upload programs created to load initial master data and take on balances been deleted from the production environment following go-live? | | | | | AI7 |
| **3.3 Default system parameter settings are reviewed and configured to suit the organization's environment.** | | | | | |
| 3.3.1 During implementation, did the organization set the SAP ERP system profile parameters to appropriate values? | | | | | AI4 |
| **3.4 Critical and sensitive transaction codes are locked in production.** | | | | | |
| 3.4.1 Have sensitive transaction codes been locked in the production environment and does the organization have procedures for locking and unlocking these transaction codes? | | | | | DS5 DS11 |

# Basis Security Cycle ICQ *(cont.)*

| Control Objectives/Questions | Response | | | Comments | CoBiT References |
|---|---|---|---|---|---|
| | Yes | No | N/A | | |
| **SAP ERP Control Environment *(cont.)*** | | | | | |
| **3. Application Operations (Computing Center Management System) *(cont.)*** | | | | | |
| **3.5 Users are prevented from logging on with trivial or easily guessable passwords.** | | | | | |
| 3.5.1 Has management set up a list of "illegal" passwords that users are not allowed to use? | | | | | DS5 DS13 |
| **3.6 SAP Router is configured to act as a gateway to secure communications into and out of the SAP ERP environment.** | | | | | |
| 3.6.1 Is the network protected by SAP Router and a firewall? | | | | | DS5 |
| 3.6.1 Are appropriate change management procedures for any modifications to the SAP Router permission table in place and operating? | | | | | AI6 |
| 3.6.1 Is the SAP Router log file used to monitor remote communications activity? | | | | | DS5 |
| 3.6.1 Are Secure Network Communications (SNC) and an external security product used to protect the communication among the components of the SAP ERP system? | | | | | |
| **3.7 Remote access by software vendors is controlled adequately.** | | | | | |
| 3.7.1 Is SAP's or the support provider's access restricted to a test/ development environment, ideally on a separate file server from the production environment, activated only on request, and all activity logged and reviewed by an individual with the ability to understand the actions that have been taken? | | | | | AI6 DS5 |
| 3.7.2 Are changes subject to normal testing and migration controls before being implemented on the production system? | | | | | AI6 |

# Basis Security Cycle ICQ *(cont.)*

| Control Objectives/Questions | Response | | | Comments | CobiT References |
|---|---|---|---|---|---|
| | Yes | No | N/A | | |
| **SAP ERP Control Environment *(cont.)*** | | | | | |
| **3. Application Operations (Computing Center Management System) *(cont.)*** | | | | | |
| **3.8 SAP ERP Remote Function Call (RFC) and Common Programming Interface—Communications (CPI-C) are secured.** | | | | | |
| 3.8.1 Have the SAP ERP RFC and CPI-C communications been secured so that any user who makes use of a connection will be prompted to enter a username and password? | | | | | DS5 |
| **3.9 The technology infrastructure is configured to secure communications and operations in the SAP ERP environment.** | | | | | |
| 3.9.1 Has the technology infrastructure been configured to secure communications and operations in the SAP ERP environment? Consider the following areas: <br> • Firewall <br> • Secure Network Communications (SNC) <br> • Secure Store and Forward (SSF) mechanisms and digital signatures <br> • Workstation security <br> • Operating system and database security | | | | | PO2 DS5 |
| **4. Application Security (Profile Generator and Security Administration)** | | | | | |
| **4.1 Duties within the security administration environment are adequately segregated.** | | | | | |
| 4.1.1 Has the organization allocated the security administration function among different individuals? | | | | | PO4 |
| **4.2 Adequate security authorization documentation is maintained.** | | | | | |
| 4.2.1 Was original documentation of the SAP ERP authorizations and their use developed and signed off by management during the implementation and has it been maintained adequately? | | | | | AI7 DS4 |

# Basis Security Cycle ICQ *(cont.)*

| Control Objectives/Questions | Response | | | Comments | CobiT References |
|---|---|---|---|---|---|
| | Yes | No | N/A | | |
| **SAP ERP Control Environment *(cont.)*** | | | | | |
| **4. Application Security (Profile Generator and Security Administration) *(cont.)*** | | | | | |
| **4.3 The superuser SAP* is properly secured.** | | | | | |
| 4.3.1  Has the SAP* been assigned to the security administrators authorization group to prevent inadvertent deletion, the password changed from the default, all profiles and authorizations deleted and the user locked? | | | | | DS5 |
| 4.3.2 Has the system parameter (login/ no_automatic_user_ sapstar) been set? | | | | | AI6 |
| **4.4 Default users are secured properly.** | | | | | |
| 4.4.1 Have the passwords for the default users DDIC, SAPCPIC and EarlyWatch been changed from the default? | | | | | DS5 |
| **4.5 Access to powerful profiles is restricted.** | | | | | |
| 4.5.1 Has a new superuser account with the SAP_ALL and SAP_NEW profiles been created with a confidential ID and secret password for emergency use and has access to powerful profiles been restricted appropriately? | | | | | AI1 DS5 |
| 4.5.2 Are procedures in place to ensure that use of the SAP_ALL authority is authorized, approved, logged, monitored and reviewed? | | | | | |
| **4.6 The authorization group that contains powerful users is restricted.** | | | | | |
| 4.6.1 Has the authorization group that contains powerful users been restricted to the new superuser and a backup? | | | | | AI3 DS5 |

## Basis Security Cycle ICQ *(cont.)*

| Control Objectives/Questions | Response | | | Comments | CobiT References |
|---|---|---|---|---|---|
| | Yes | No | N/A | | |
| **SAP ERP Control Environment *(cont.)*** | | | | | |
| **4. Application Security (Profile Generator and Security Administration) *(cont.)*** | | | | | |
| **4.7 Changes to critical SAP ERP tables are logged by the system and reviewed by management.** | | | | | |
| 4.7.1 Are all changes to the critical SAP ERP tables logged by the system and does the periodic review of these logs form part of the security procedures for the organization? (Include the list of tables with logging implemented.) | | | | | AI6 DS11 |
| **4.8 Changes made to the data dictionary are authorized and reviewed regularly.** | | | | | |
| 4.8.1 Are details of modifications to the data dictionary maintained and change control procedures followed? | | | | | AI6 DS11 |
| 4.8.2 Are the SAP ERP Data Dictionary Information System reports (DD reports) regularly generated and reviewed by management? | | | | | DS11 ME1 |
| **4.9 Log and trace files are appropriately configured and secured.** | | | | | |
| 4.9.1 Is logging appropriately configured and are log and trace files secured at the operating system level at the location specified within the system profile? | | | | | DS9 |

# Appendix F—CoᴮⁱT Control Objectives

The chart below indicates the CoᴮⁱT 4.1 control objectives used in the reference column of the SAP ERP internal control questionnaire and the SAP ERP basis security audit program.

| Domain | Process Number | Process Name |
|---|---|---|
| Plan and Organize (PO) | PO1 | Define a strategic IT plan. |
| | PO2 | Define the information architecture. |
| | PO3 | Determine technological direction. |
| | PO4 | Define the IT processes, organization and relationships. |
| | PO5 | Manage the IT investment. |
| | PO6 | Communicate management aims and direction. |
| | PO7 | Manage IT human resources. |
| | PO8 | Manage quality. |
| | PO9 | Assess and manage IT risks. |
| | PO10 | Manage projects. |
| Acquire and Implement (AI) | AI1 | Identify automated solutions. |
| | AI2 | Acquire and maintain application software. |
| | AI3 | Acquire and maintain technology infrastructure. |
| | AI4 | Enable operation and use. |
| | AI5 | Procure IT resources. |
| | AI6 | Manage changes. |
| | AI7 | Install and accredit solutions and changes. |
| Deliver and Support (DS) | DS1 | Define and manage service levels. |
| | DS2 | Manage third-party services. |
| | DS3 | Manage performance and capacity. |
| | DS4 | Ensure continuous service. |
| | DS5 | Ensure systems security. |
| | DS6 | Identify and allocate costs. |
| | DS7 | Educate and train users. |
| | DS8 | Manage service desk and incidents. |
| | DS9 | Manage the configuration. |
| | DS10 | Manage problems. |
| | DS11 | Manage data. |
| | DS12 | Manage the physical environment. |
| | DS13 | Manage operations. |
| Monitor and Evaluate (ME) | ME1 | Monitor and evaluate IT performance. |
| | ME2 | Monitor and evaluate internal control. |
| | ME3 | Ensure compliance with external requirements. |
| | ME4 | Provide IT governance. |

# Appendix G—Transactions Recommended to be Locked

The transactions listed in **figure AG1** are recommended[36] to be locked. The business should review these and lock where possible. Additional high-risk transactions may be identified by functional consultants.

The transactions listed as "dangerous" are those that may have an adverse impact on the system stability and/or data integrity if they are not executed properly. The transactions connected to user's authorization into the system are classified as "security transactions." The transactions with impact on system availability/performance are grouped under "performance."

| Figure AG1—Transactions Recommended to be Locked | | | | |
|---|---|---|---|---|
| Transaction | Description | Dangerous | Security | Performance |
| KA10 | Archive Cost Centers (all) | X | | |
| KA12 | Archive Cost Centers (plan) | X | | |
| KA16 | Archive Cost Centers (line items) | X | | |
| KA18 | Archive Admin.: completely cancelled document | X | | |
| OBR1 | Reset Transaction Data (delete transaction data) | X | | |
| OICP | Profiles: Initial Screen | | X | |
| OMDL | Maintain Users: Initial Screen | | X | |
| OMEH | Maintain Users: Initial Screen | | X | |
| OMEI | Profiles: Initial Screen | | X | |
| OMG7 | Maintain Authorizations: Object Classes | | X | |
| OMWF | Maintain Users: Initial Screen | | X | |
| OMWG | Profiles: Initial Screen | | X | |
| OMWK | Maintain Authorizations: Object Classes | | X | |
| OOPR | Profiles: Initial Screen | | X | |
| OOSB | Change View User Authorizations: Overview | | X | |
| OOSP | Change View Authorization Profiles: Overview | | X | |
| OOUS | Maintain Users: Initial Screen | | X | |

---

[36] Adapted from The R/3 Simplification Group at SAP Labs, *R/3 System Administration Made Easy*, USA, 1999

| Figure AG1—Transactions Recommended to be Locked *(cont.)* | | | | |
|---|---|---|---|---|
| Transaction | Description | Dangerous | Security | Performance |
| OP15 | Profiles: Initial Screen | | X | |
| OPE9 | Profiles: Initial Screen | | X | |
| OPF0 | Maintain Users: Initial Screen | | X | |
| OPF1 | Maintain Authorizations: Object Classes | | X | |
| OTZ1 | Maintain Users: Initial Screen | | X | |
| OTZ2 | Profiles: Initial Screen | | X | |
| OTZ3 | Maintain Authorizations: Object Classes | | X | |
| OVZ6 | Profiles: Initial Screen | | X | |
| OY20 | Maintain Authorizations: Object Classes | | X | |
| OY21 | Profiles: Initial Screen | | X | |
| OY27 | Maintain Users: Initial Screen | | X | |
| OY28 | Maintain Users: Initial Screen | | X | |
| OY29 | Maintain Users: Initial Screen | | X | |
| OY30 | Maintain Users: Initial Screen | | X | |
| SARA | Archive Management: Initial Screen | X | | |
| SCC1 | Client Copy—Special Selections | X | | |
| SCC5 | Client Delete | X | | |
| SE01 | Transport Organizer | X | | |
| SE09 | Workbench Organizer | X | | |
| SE10 | Customizing Organizer | X | | |
| SE16 | Table Data Maintenance | | X | |
| SM30 | Table Data Maintenance | | X | |
| SM31 | Table Data Maintenance | | X | |
| SM49 | External OS Commands | X | | |
| SM59 | Maintain RFC Destinations | X | | |
| SM69 | External OS Commands | X | | |
| SU12 | Delete All Users | X | X | |

Locking critical transactions helps secure sensitive changes and prevents unauthorized access to data. Although several transactions on the list in **figure AG1** are recommended to be locked, some of these transactions have functions that may be required by IT users. Transactions can be easily unlocked for use with transaction SM01. In the input box at the bottom of transaction SM01, enter the transaction code to be locked and press Enter. Check the required transaction code box and lock/unlock using the associated Lock/Unlock button. If the transactions listed in **figure AG1** are not locked, they should be controlled in another manner, such as table logging, documented approvals for use or review of changes.

Details of locked transactions should be maintained—details of who locked the transaction and why it was locked. Changes to transactions should be logged. Control procedures should be implemented to ensure that when locked transactions are unlocked, authorization, purpose, user, time period, etc., are fully documented.

**Figure AG2** shows critical transactions that should be restricted to required IT personnel for authorized use: Basis administrators, ABAP developers, security administrators, etc. Additional control precautions should be considered with critical transactions, such as reviews of changes performed using the transaction codes.

| Figure AG2—Transactions Recommended to be Restricted to Required IT Personnel | | | | |
|---|---|---|---|---|
| **Transaction** | **Description** | **Dangerous** | **Security** | **Performance** |
| RZ10 | Edit System Profiles | X | | |
| SA38 | ABAP: Program Execution | X | | |
| SA38PARAMETER | ABAP: Program Execution | X | | |
| EWFM | ABAP: Program Execution | X | | |
| EWFZ | ABAP: Program Execution | X | | |
| SCC4 | Change Control Settings | X | | |
| SE06 | System Change Option | X | | |
| SE11 | Data Dictionary Maintenance | X | X | |
| SE13 | Maintain Storage Parameters for Table | X | X | |
| SE14 | Utilities for Dictionary Tables | | X | |
| SE15 | Data Dictionary Information System | | X | |
| SE17 | General Table Display | | | X |
| SE38 | ABAP Workbench | | X | |
| SE80 | Repository Browser | X | | |
| SM04 | User Overview | | X | |
| SM12 | System Locks | X | | |
| SM13 | Update Terminates | X | | |
| SM36 | Batch Job Scheduling | | X | |
| SM37 | Batch Job Monitoring | | X | |
| SPRO | Customizing—Edit Project | X | | |
| STMS | Transport Management System | X | | |
| ST05 | SQL Trace | | | X |

| Figure AG2—Transactions Recommended to be Restricted to Required IT Personnel *(cont.)* | | | | |
|---|---|---|---|---|
| Transaction | Description | Dangerous | Security | Performance |
| SU01 | User Maintenance | | X | |
| SU02 | Profiles: Initial Screen | | X | |
| SU03 | Maintain Authorizations: Object Classes | | X | |
| SU10 | Add/Delete Profiles for Users | X | | |

# Index

## A

ABAP/4, 10, 11, 51, 59, 70, 75, 155, 156, 160, 170, 172, 179, 180, 181, 182, 183, 184, 186, 204, 205, 209, 251, 382, 384, 386, 387, 444, 445
Application security, 50, 53, 187
Application server parameters, 190
Audit cycles, 57, 58
Audit framework, 51, 56, 57, 59, 78, 81, 92, 171, 234
Audit information system, 61, 78, 171, 172, 175, 374, 380
Audit methodology, 51
Audit programs, 51, 52, 264-417
Authorization concept, 169
Authorization documentation, 198, 201, 406, 448
Authorization objects, 66, 258

## B

Batch administration, 188, 189, 390
Batch processing, 187, 189, 390, 391, 446
Bill of materials, 139, 144, 146, 349, 432
Business cycles, 57, 58, 59, 78, 79, 169, 273, 308, 345, 424
Business processes, 219
Business risks, 38, 79, 214, 215, 216, 268, 303, 340, 368

## C

Case study, 51, 68, 210
Central user administration (CUA), 168, 169, 206, 411
CobiT, 333, 334, 355, 361, 365, 418
Collaborative commerce, 245
Collecting and processing cash receipts, 107, 108
Company code settings, 180
Compliant User Provisioning (CUP), 217, 224
Computing center management, 11, 164, 170, 172, 389, 446, 447, 448
Condition records, 64
Content quality, 245

Continuous assurance, 246
Control framework, 1, 38, 48, 49, 50, 56, 59, 77, 226, 229, 233, 234, 238, 245, 256, 261, 263, 265, 267, 268, 296, 297, 298, 299, 302, 303, 333, 334, 335, 336, 339, 340, 361, 362, 363, 364, 367, 368
Core business cycles, 58, 59, 78, 79
Credit checks, 86
Critical number ranges, 63, 98, 172, 175, 176, 381, 452
Critical tables, 172
Cross-applications, 57
Customer master data, 82, 95, 98, 277, 279

## D

Data conversion, 38, 48, 53, 54
Data dictionary, 180, 198, 387
Data integrity, 54, 83, 280, 290, 291, 327, 328, 355, 356, 418, 419, 425, 452
Data privacy, 216, 238
Default users, 198, 408, 449
Disbursements, 134, 135

## E

E-business, 1, 47, 251
ECC, 1, 5, 11, 15, 22, 172, 221, 231, 234, 251, 269, 304, 341, 369, 390
E-enabled ERP, 242
Enterprise role management (ERM), 217, 225
ERP audit, 1, 81, 92, 234, 269, 304, 341, 369, 378
Evaluated receipt settlement, 37, 120
Expenditure cycle, 6, 57, 58, 77, 82, 111, 123, 136, 137, 148, 351, 352

## G

Governance, risk and compliance (GRC), 215
GR/IR, 118, 119, 131, 133, 322, 323, 430

## H

Handling and shipping finished goods, 150, 151

## I

Identity management, 10, 224, 236, 245, 292, 329, 357, 420
Implementation Guide (IMG), 10, 97, 156, 157, 170, 172, 272, 307, 344, 372, 443
Industry solutions, 6, 8, 57
Inherent controls, 60
Integrity framework, 1
Internet, 186, 242, 243, 244, 373, 374
Inventory business cycle, 142, 143, 153
Invoice processing, 131, 132
ISACA, 5, 10, 55, 217, 254, 261, 265, 268, 296, 299, 303, 333, 336, 340, 361, 364, 368

## L

Locking transaction codes, 187, 192
Log and trace files, 198, 209, 415, 450
Logging off, 33, 34, 35, 47

## M

Maintenance, 33, 82, 93, 94, 95, 96, 111, 120, 123, 124, 134, 138, 143, 144, 145, 174, 198, 205, 294, 310, 325, 331, 347, 359, 405, 422, 424, 428, 431, 432, 453, 454, 455
Manual controls, 49, 60, 77, 78, 240
Master data maintenance, 93, 94, 95, 123, 124, 143, 144, 145
Master data management (MDM), 236
Materials resource planning (MRP), 3, 138, 139, 147, 257, 258
Modifying critical tables, 30, 177
Multiple sessions, 19, 33
mySAP, 240, 251, 254, 255, 375

## N

NetWeaver, 5, 9, 10, 156, 171, 217, 218, 234, 235, 236, 241, 243, 246, 251, 252, 254, 255, 269, 304, 341, 369
Numbering sequence, 51, 79

## O

Online support system, 187

Organization management model, 156, 157
Organizational Model, 59, 63, 175, 176, 345, 379, 443, 444

## P

Postimplementation, 41, 42, 52, 53, 54, 291, 328, 356, 419
Preimplementation, 52, 53
Processing disbursments, 111, 121, 123, 134, 135, 309, 326, 431
Producing and costing inventory, 138, 143, 346
Profile generator (PFCG), 156, 170
Program interfaces, 38, 41, 47, 48, 197, 245
Project manager, 40
Purchase-to-pay, 2, 57
Purchasing, 111, 112, 123, 125, 126, 127, 129, 130, 133, 136, 139, 160, 258, 280, 309, 311, 313, 321, 428, 429

## Q

Queries, 26, 27, 180, 184

## R

Raw materials management, 138, 143, 346
Release, 4, 11, 61, 100, 114, 115, 127, 129, 130, 269, 304, 314, 316, 317, 341, 369
Release procedure, 114, 115, 316, 317
Relevant authorizations, 69, 72
Remote function call, 187
Restricted passwords, 187
Returns and adjustments, 82, 87, 93, 101, 102, 103, 425, 426
Revenue cycle, 57, 58, 82, 93, 108, 111, 139
Risk analysis and remediation (RAR), 72, 212, 217
Risk-based audit approach, 51, 59, 81
Running reports, 25, 26, 64

## S

Sales order processing, 98, 99, 100
SAP*, 64, 168, 193, 198, 202, 203, 204, 205, 407, 408, 449
SAP_ALL, 198, 204, 205, 247, 409, 449

SAP application linked enabling (ALE), 168
SAP BusinessObjects, 215, 216, 217, 225, 228, 229, 230, 233, 236
SAP business suite, 236, 251
SAP customer relationship management (CRM), 236
SAP ERP architecture, 5, 169, 269, 304, 341, 369
SAP ERP Central Component, 1, 5, 234, 251, 269, 304, 341, 369
SAP ERP instance, 155, 159, 203
SAP ERP modules, 8, 9, 10, 57, 215
SAP_NEW, 198, 204, 205, 232, 409, 449
SAP Router, 187, 194, 195, 395, 397, 447
SAP solution manager (SolMan), 235
SAP supplier relationship management (SRM), 236
SAP supply chain management (SCM), 236
Security administration profiles, 198, 199
Security authorization concept, 64, 169
Security parameters, 47, 50, 64, 155, 168, 169, 187, 214, 403

Segregation of duties, 47, 52, 124, 199
Service oriented architecture (SOA), 5, 48, 269, 304, 341, 369
Shipping, invoicing, returns and adjustments, 87, 101, 102, 103, 425, 426
Superuser privilege management (SPM), 217, 221
Superuser SAP*, 198, 202, 203
System (CCMS), 11, 156, 164, 170, 389
System trace, 70, 210

**T**

Table logging, 198
Technical infrastructure, 1, 38, 44, 60, 154, 170
Testing SAP ERP security, 68
Three-way match, 37, 43, 49, 118, 119, 122, 131, 227, 321, 430
Transaction code(s), 95, 259, 277, 307, 311
Transport management system (TMS), 156, 170, 179, 184

**U**

User management engine (UME), 218, 235

# Professional Guidance Publications

Many ISACA publications contain detailed assessment questionnaires and work programs. Please visit *www.isaca.org/bookstore* or e-mail *bookstore@isaca.org* for more information.

**Frameworks:**
- CoBiT® 4.1, 2007
- *Enterprise Value: Governance of IT Investments: The Val IT Framework 2.0*, 2008
- *ITAF™ A Professional Practices Framework for IT Assurance*, 2008
- *The Risk IT Framework*, 2009

**CoBiT-related Publications:**
- *Aligning CoBiT® 4.1, ITIL V3 and ISO/IEC 27002 for Business Benefit*, 2008
- *Building the Business Case for CoBiT® and Val IT™: Executive Briefing*, 2009
- *CoBiT® and Application Controls, 2009*
- *CoBiT® Control Practices, Guidance to Achieve Control Objectives for Successful IT Governance, 2nd Edition, 2007*
- *CoBiT® Mapping: Mapping of CMMI® for Development V1.2 With CoBiT® 4.0, 2007*
- *CoBiT® Mapping: Mapping of ISO/IEC 17799:2000 With CoBiT®, 2nd Edition, 2006*
- *CoBiT® Mapping: Mapping of ISO/IEC 17799:2005 With CoBiT® 4.0, 2006*
- *CoBiT® Mapping: Mapping of ITIL With CoBiT® 4.0, 2007*
- *CoBiT® Mapping: Mapping of ITIL V3 With CoBiT® 4.1, 2008*
- *CoBiT® Mapping: Mapping of NIST SP800-53 With CoBiT® 4.1, 2007*
- *CoBiT® Mapping: Mapping of PMBOK With CoBiT® 4.0, 2006*
- *CoBiT® Mapping: Mapping of PRINCE2 With CoBiT® 4.0, 2007*
- *CoBiT® Mapping: Mapping of SEI's CMM for Software With CoBiT® 4.0, 2006*
- *CoBiT® Mapping: Mapping of TOGAF 8.1 With CoBiT® 4.0, 2007*
- *CoBiT® Mapping: Overview of International IT Guidance, 2nd Edition, 2006*
- *CoBiT® Quickstart™, 2nd Edition, 2007*
- *CoBiT® Security Baseline™, 2nd Edition, 2007*
- *CoBiT® User Guide for Service Managers, 2009*
- *IT Assurance Guide: Using CoBiT®, 2007*
- *IT Governance Implementation Guide: Using CoBiT® and Val IT, 2nd Edition, 2007*

**Risk IT-related Publication:**
- *The Risk IT Practitioner Guide*, 2009

**Val IT-related Publications:**
- *Enterprise Value: Getting Started With Value Management*, 2008
- *Enterprise Value: Governance of IT Investments: The Business Case*, 2005
- *Val IT™ Mapping: Mapping of Val IT™ to MSP™, PRINCE2™, and ITIL V3®*, 2009

**Management and Executive Guidance:**
• *An Executive View of IT Governance, 2008*
• *An Introduction to the Business Model for Information Security, 2009*
• *Board Briefing on IT Governance, 2ⁿᵈ Edition, 2003*
• *Defining Information Security Management Position Requirements: Guidance for Executives and Managers, 2008*
• *Identifying and Aligning Business Goals and IT Goals: Full Research Report, 2008*
• *Information Security Governance: Guidance for Boards of Directors and Executive Management, 2ⁿᵈ Edition, 2006*
• *Information Security Governance: Guidance for Information Security Managers, 2008*
• *Information Security Governance—Top Actions for Security Managers, 2005*
• *ITGI Enables ISO/IEC 38500:2008 Adoption, 2009*
• *IT Governance and Process Maturity, 2008*
• *IT Governance Domain Practices and Competencies:*
  – *Governance of Outsourcing, 2005*
  – *Information Risks: Whose Business Are They?, 2005*
  – *IT Alignment: Who Is in Charge?, 2005*
  – *Measuring and Demonstrating the Value of IT, 2005*
  – *Optimising Value Creation From IT Investments, 2005*
• *IT Governance Roundtables:*
  – *Defining IT Governance, 2008*
  – *IT Governance Frameworks, 2007*
  – *IT Governance Trends, 2007*
  – *IT Staffing Challenges, 2008*
  – *Unlocking Value, 2009*
  – *Value Delivery, 2008*
• *Managing Information Integrity: Security, Control and Audit Issues, 2004*
• *Understanding How Business Goals Drive IT Goals, 2008*
• *Unlocking Value: An Executive Primer on the Critical Role of IT Governance, 2008*

**Practitioner Guidance:**
• *Audit/Assurance Programs:*
  – *Change Management Audit/Assurance Program, 2009*
  – *Generic Application Audit/Assurance Program, 2009*
  – *Identity Management Audit/Assurance Program, 2009*
  – *IT Continuity Planning Audit/Assurance Program, 2009*
  – *Network Perimeter Security Audit/Assurance Program, 2009*
  – *Outsourced IT Environments Audit/Assurance Program, 2009*
  – *Security Incident Management Audit/Assurance Program, 2009*
  – *Systems Development and Project Management Audit/Assurance Program, 2009*
  – *UNIX/LINUX Operating System Security Audit/Assurance Program, 2009*
  – *z/OS Security Audit/Assurance Program, 2009*
• *Cybercrime: Incident Response and Digital Forensics, 2005*
• *Enterprise Identity Management: Managing Secure and Controllable Access in the Extended Enterprise Environment, 2004*

- *Information Security Career Progression Survey Results,* 2008
- *Information Security Harmonisation—Classification of Global Guidance,* 2005
- *IT Control Objectives for Basel II,* 2007
- *IT Control Objectives for Sarbanes-Oxley: The Role of IT in the Design and Implementation of Internal Control Over Financial Reporting, 2nd Edition, 2006*
- *Oracle® Database Security, Audit and Control Features,* 2004
- *OS/390—z/OS: Security, Control and Audit Features,* 2003
- *Peer-to-peer Networking Security and Control,* 2003
- *Risks of Customer Relationship Management: A Security, Control and Audit Approach,* 2003
- *Security, Audit and Control Features Oracle® E-Business Suite: A Technical and Risk Management Reference Guide, 2nd Edition, 2006*
- *Security, Audit and Control Features PeopleSoft®: A Technical and Risk Management Reference Guide, 2nd Edition, 2006*
- *Security Awareness: Best Practices to Serve Your Enterprise,* 2005
- *Security Critical Issues,* 2005
- *Security Provisioning: Managing Access in Extended Enterprises,* 2002
- *Stepping Through the IS Audit, 2nd Edition,* 2004
- *Stepping Through the InfoSec Program,* 2007
- *Top Business/Technology Survey Results,* 2008